2

HEAVEN!!

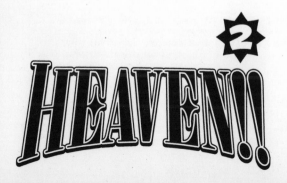

Heaven!! Volume 2
Created by Shizuru Seino

Translation - Haruko Furukawa
English Adaptation - Jay Antani
Copy Editor - Sarah Mercurio
Retouch and Lettering - Star Print Brokers
Production Artist - Courtney Geter
Graphic Designer - Louis Csontos

Editor - Paul Morrissey
Digital Imaging Manager - Chris Buford
Pre-Production Supervisor - Erika Terriquez
Production Manager - Elisabeth Brizzi
Managing Editor - Vy Nguyen
Creative Director - Anne Marie Horne
Editor-in-Chief - Rob Tokar
Publisher - Mike Kiley
President and C.O.O. - John Parker
C.E.O. and Chief Creative Officer - Stuart Levy

A  Manga

TOKYOPOP and 🐸 are trademarks or registered trademarks of TOKYOPOP Inc.

TOKYOPOP Inc.
5900 Wilshire Blvd. Suite 2000
Los Angeles, CA 90036

E-mail: info@TOKYOPOP.com
Come visit us online at www.TOKYOPOP.com

ISBN: 978-1-59816-817-4

First TOKYOPOP printing: December 2007
10 9 8 7 6 5 4 3 2 1
Printed in the USA or Canada

VOLUME 2
BY SHIZURU SEINO

HAMBURG // LONDON // LOS ANGELES // TOKYO

HEAVEN!

CHARACTERS

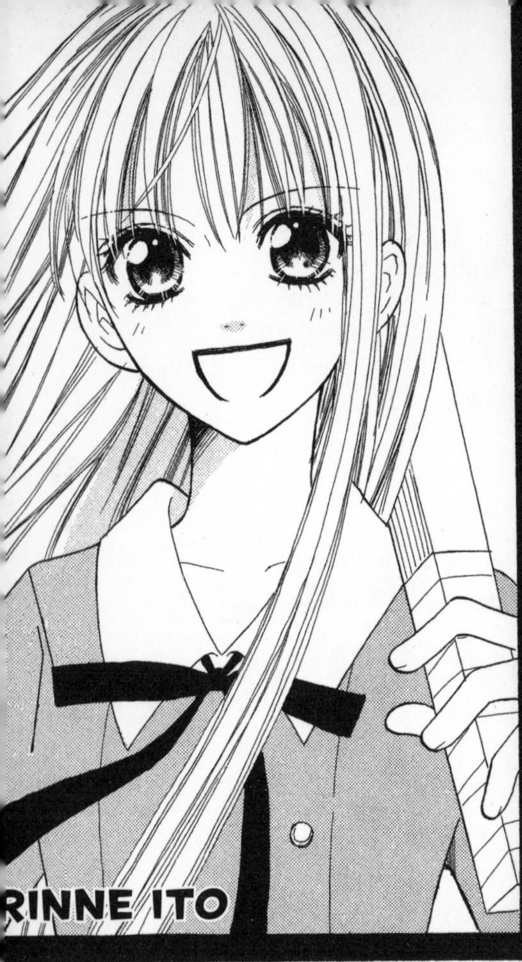
RINNE ITO

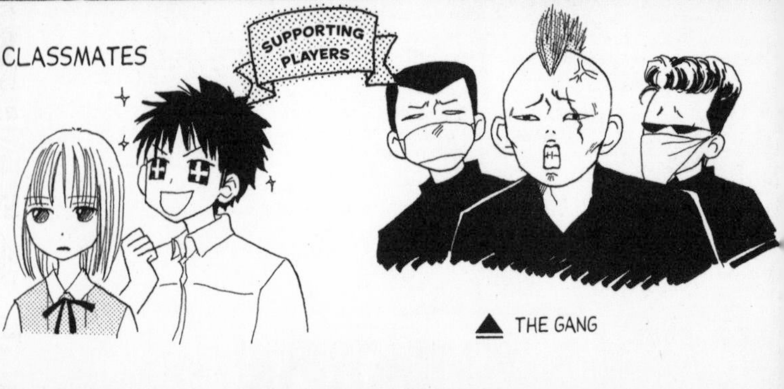
SUPPORTING PLAYERS
▼ CLASSMATES
▲ THE GANG

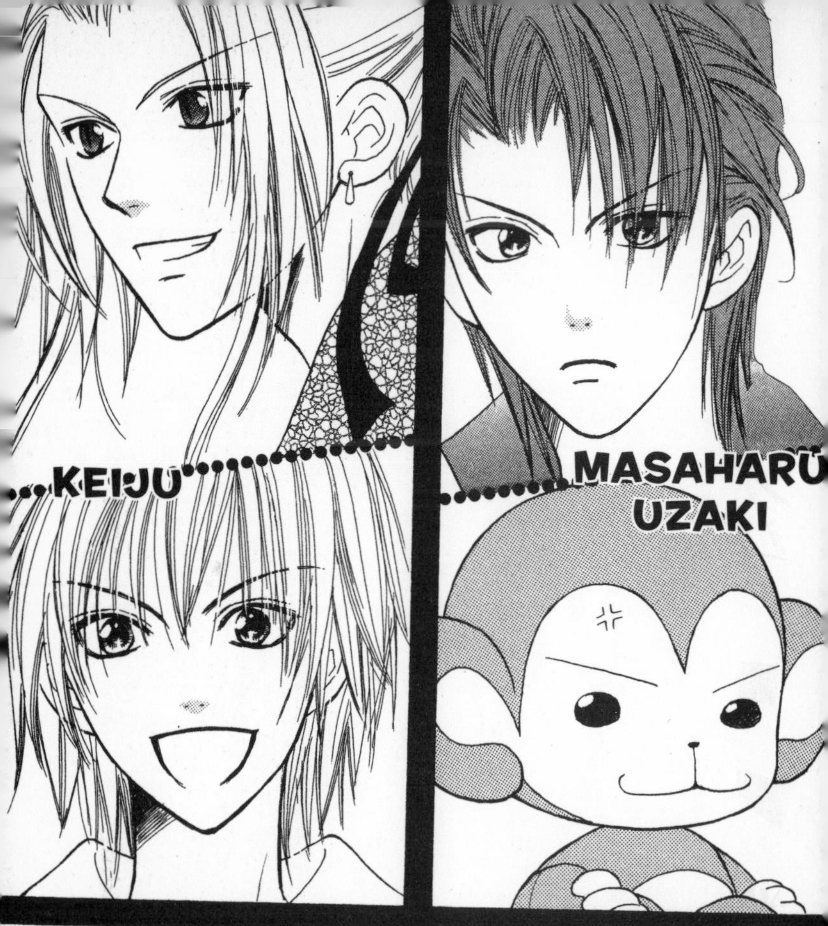
MASAHARU UZAKI
...KEIJU

HEAVEN!!

THE STORY SO FAR...

- RINNE ITO, A MEDIUM, HAPPENS TO BE INVOLVED WITH MASAHARU, THE SCHOOL'S BAD BOY. MASAHARU'S BODY IS POSSESSED BY KEIJU (A SELF-PROCLAIMED GOD), WHILE HIS SPIRIT'S BEEN SHOVED INSIDE THE BODY OF A STUFFED TOY MONKEY!!
- BECAUSE OF RINNE'S HARISEN, MASAHARU'S SPIRIT IS TRANSFERRED BACK INSIDE THE MONKEY, AND KEIJU GETS MASAHARU'S BODY BACK. EVERYTHING'S BACK TO HOW IT WAS BEFORE. COULD THAT BE TRUE?!
- POSSESSING MASAHARU'S BODY, KEIJU TURNS INTO AN UNSTOPPABLE LADIES' MAN, AND DOES WHATEVER HE WANTS IN THE PURSUIT OF PLEASURE. AFTER A MAJOR STRUGGLE, MASAHARU GETS HIS BODY BACK.

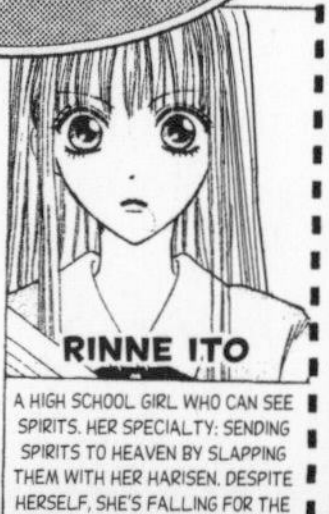

RINNE ITO

A HIGH SCHOOL GIRL WHO CAN SEE SPIRITS. HER SPECIALTY: SENDING SPIRITS TO HEAVEN BY SLAPPING THEM WITH HER HARISEN. DESPITE HERSELF, SHE'S FALLING FOR THE SMOOTH-TALKING PLAYER, KEIJU.

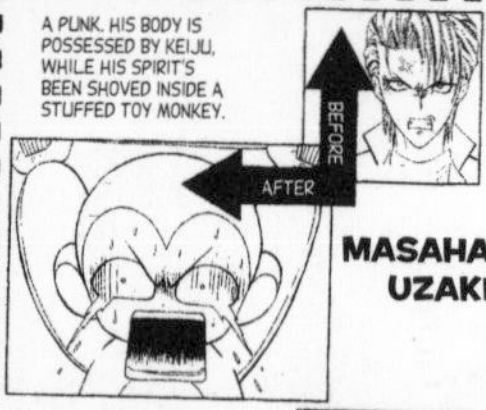
BEFORE
AFTER

MASAHARU UZAKI

A PUNK. HIS BODY IS POSSESSED BY KEIJU, WHILE HIS SPIRIT'S BEEN SHOVED INSIDE A STUFFED TOY MONKEY.

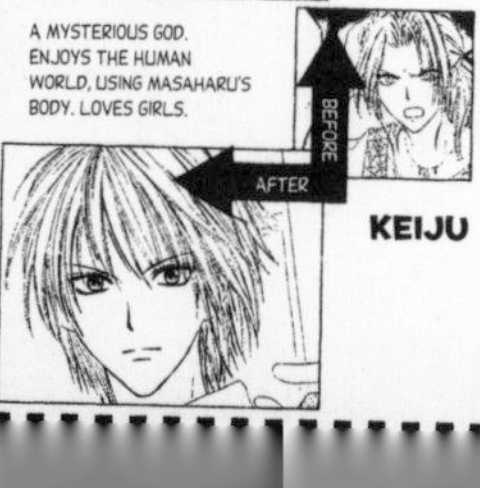
BEFORE
AFTER

KEIJU

A MYSTERIOUS GOD. ENJOYS THE HUMAN WORLD, USING MASAHARU'S BODY. LOVES GIRLS.

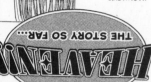

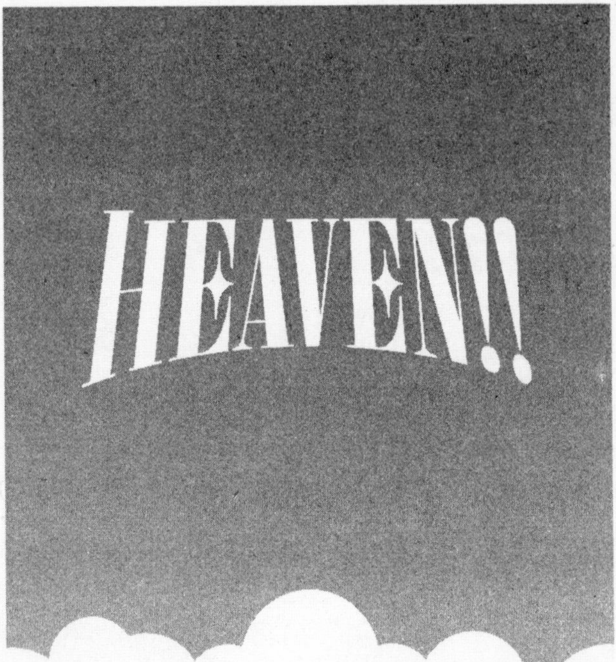
HEAVEN!!

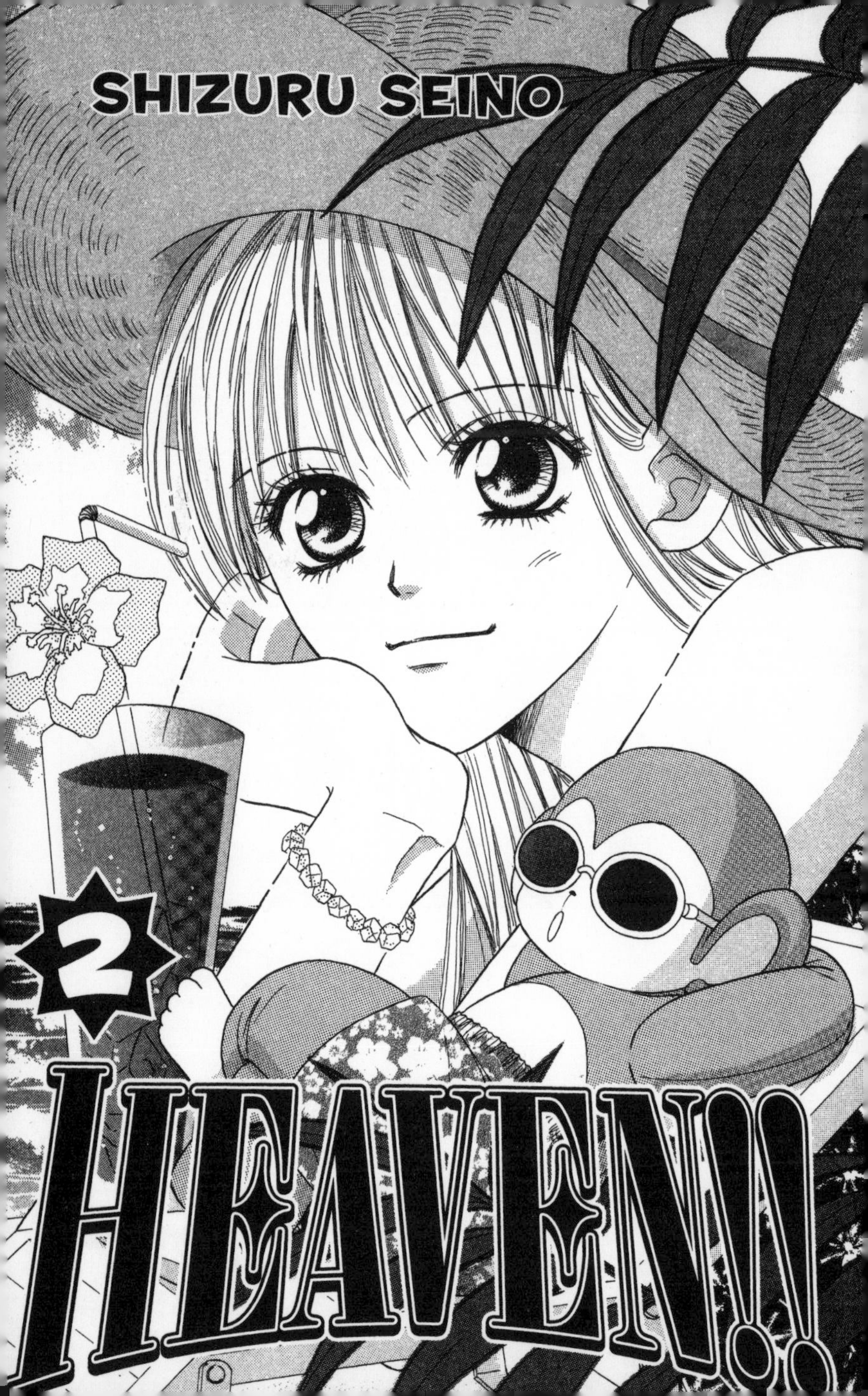
SHIZURU SEINO
2
HEAVEN!!

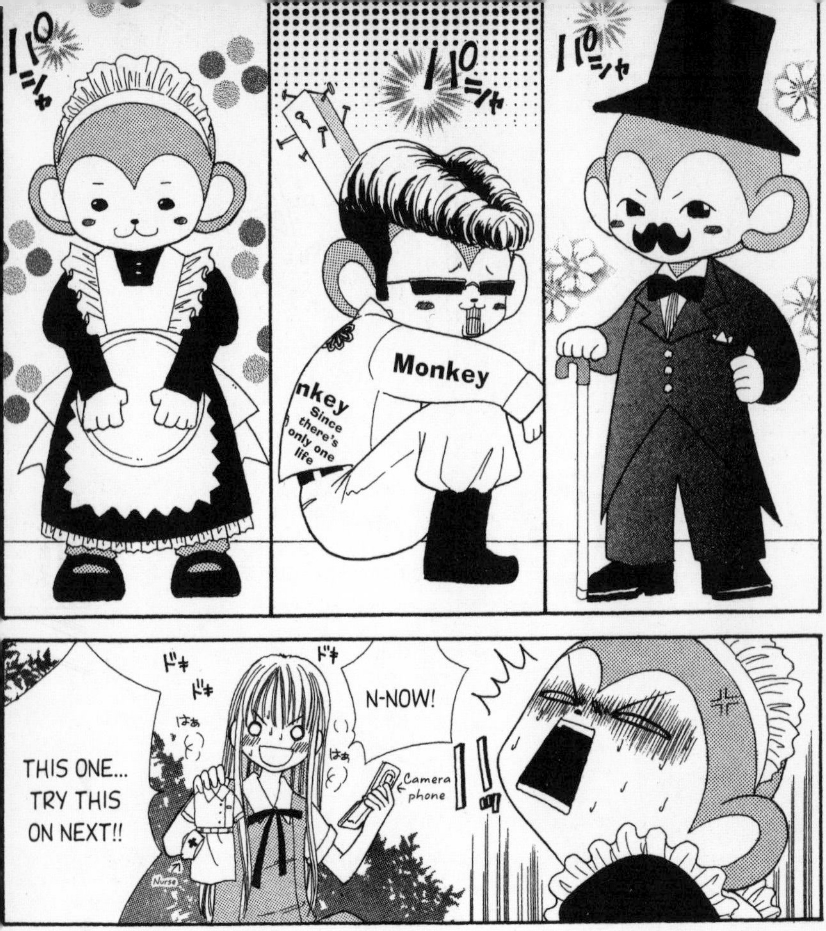
パシャ
パシャ
Monkey
nkey
Since there's only one life
パシャ
!!
N-NOW!
Camera phone
ドキ
ドキ
ドキ
はぁ
はぁ
THIS ONE... TRY THIS ON NEXT!!
Nurse

HEAVEN!!

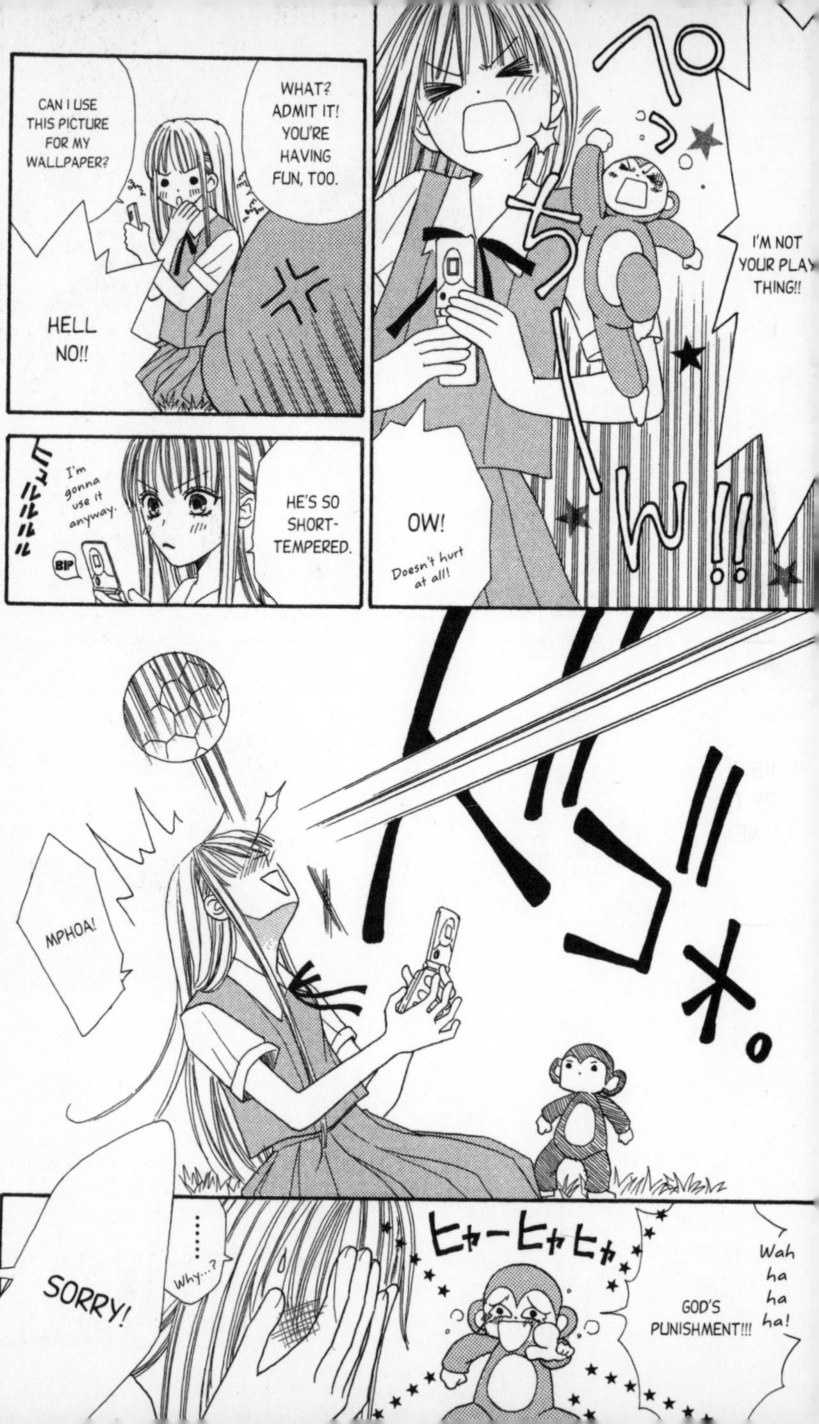
I'M NOT YOUR PLAY THING!!
W!!
OW!
Doesn't hurt at all!
CAN I USE THIS PICTURE FOR MY WALLPAPER?
WHAT? ADMIT IT! YOU'RE HAVING FUN, TOO.
HELL NO!!
HE'S SO SHORT-TEMPERED.
I'm gonna use it anyway.
BIP
MPHOA!
Wah ha ha ha!
GOD'S PUNISHMENT!!!
ヒャーヒャヒャ
......
Why...?
SORRY!

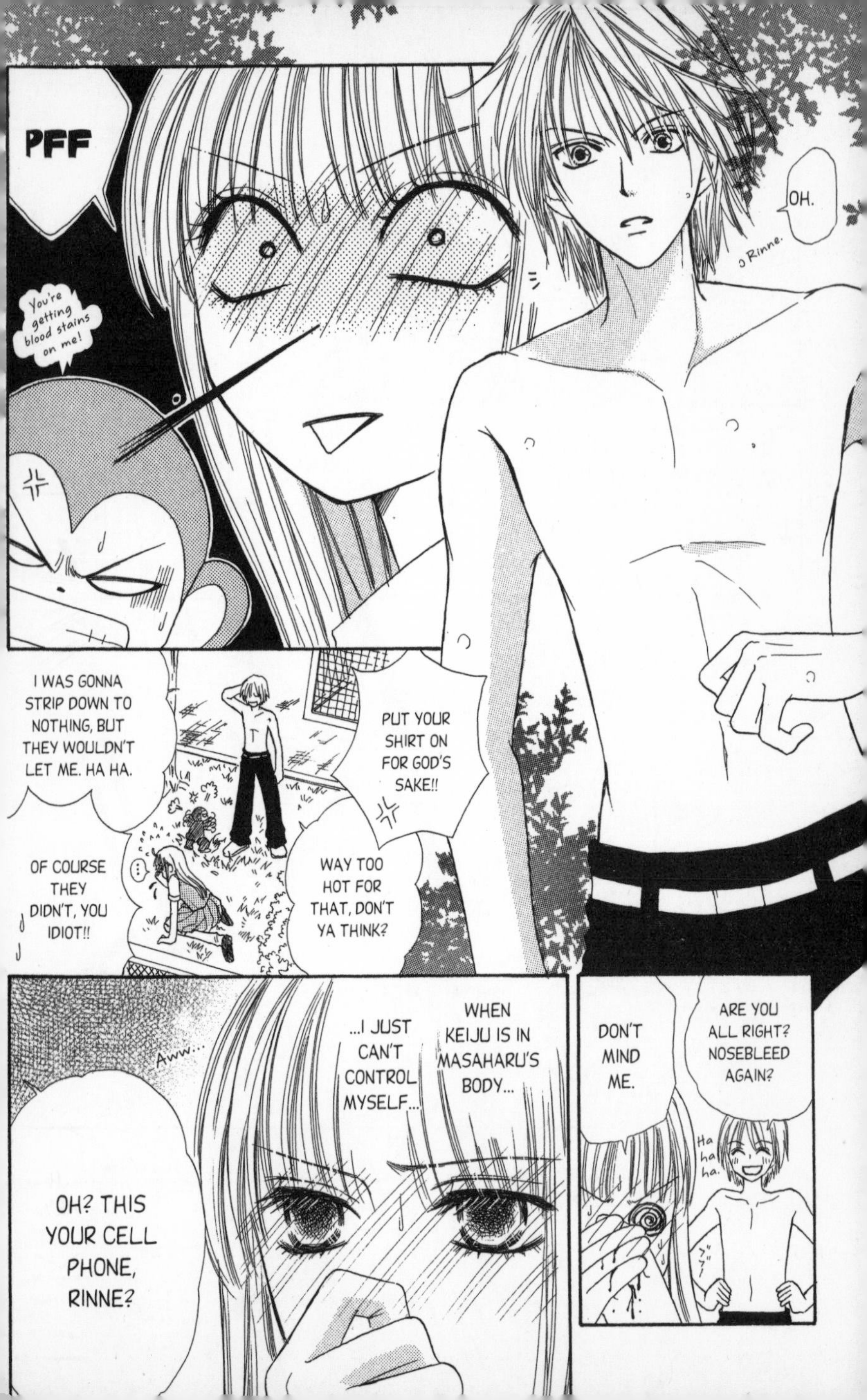

OH.
Rinne.
PFF
You're getting blood stains on me!
I WAS GONNA STRIP DOWN TO NOTHING, BUT THEY WOULDN'T LET ME. HA HA.
PUT YOUR SHIRT ON FOR GOD'S SAKE!!
WAY TOO HOT FOR THAT, DON'T YA THINK?
OF COURSE THEY DIDN'T, YOU IDIOT!!
ARE YOU ALL RIGHT? NOSEBLEED AGAIN?
Ha ha ha.
DON'T MIND ME.
WHEN KEIJU IS IN MASAHARU'S BODY...
...I JUST CAN'T CONTROL MYSELF...
Aww...
OH? THIS YOUR CELL PHONE, RINNE?

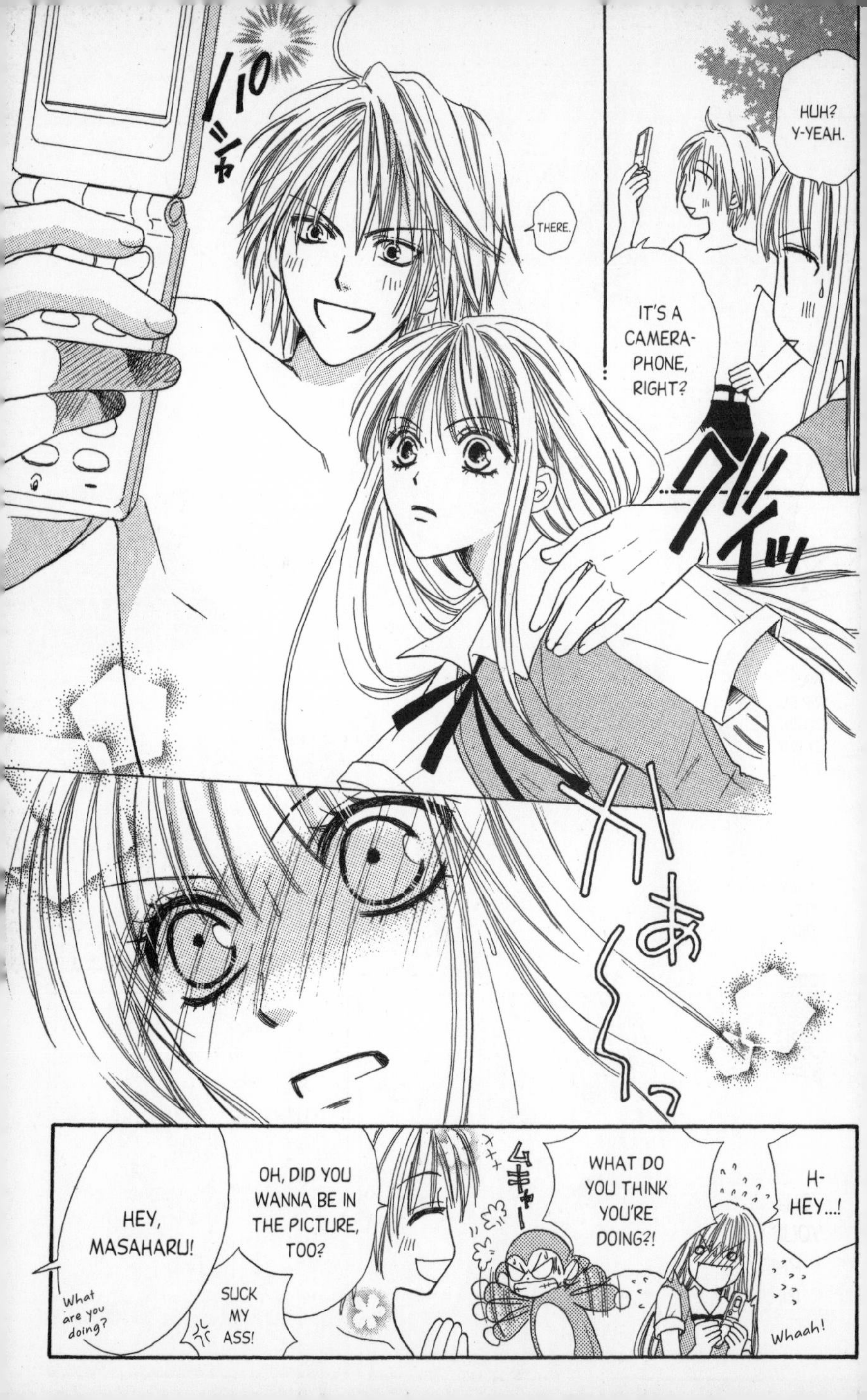
HUH? Y-YEAH.
IT'S A CAMERA-PHONE, RIGHT?
THERE.
H-HEY...!
Whaah!
WHAT DO YOU THINK YOU'RE DOING?!
OH, DID YOU WANNA BE IN THE PICTURE, TOO?
SUCK MY ASS!
HEY, MASAHARU!
What are you doing?

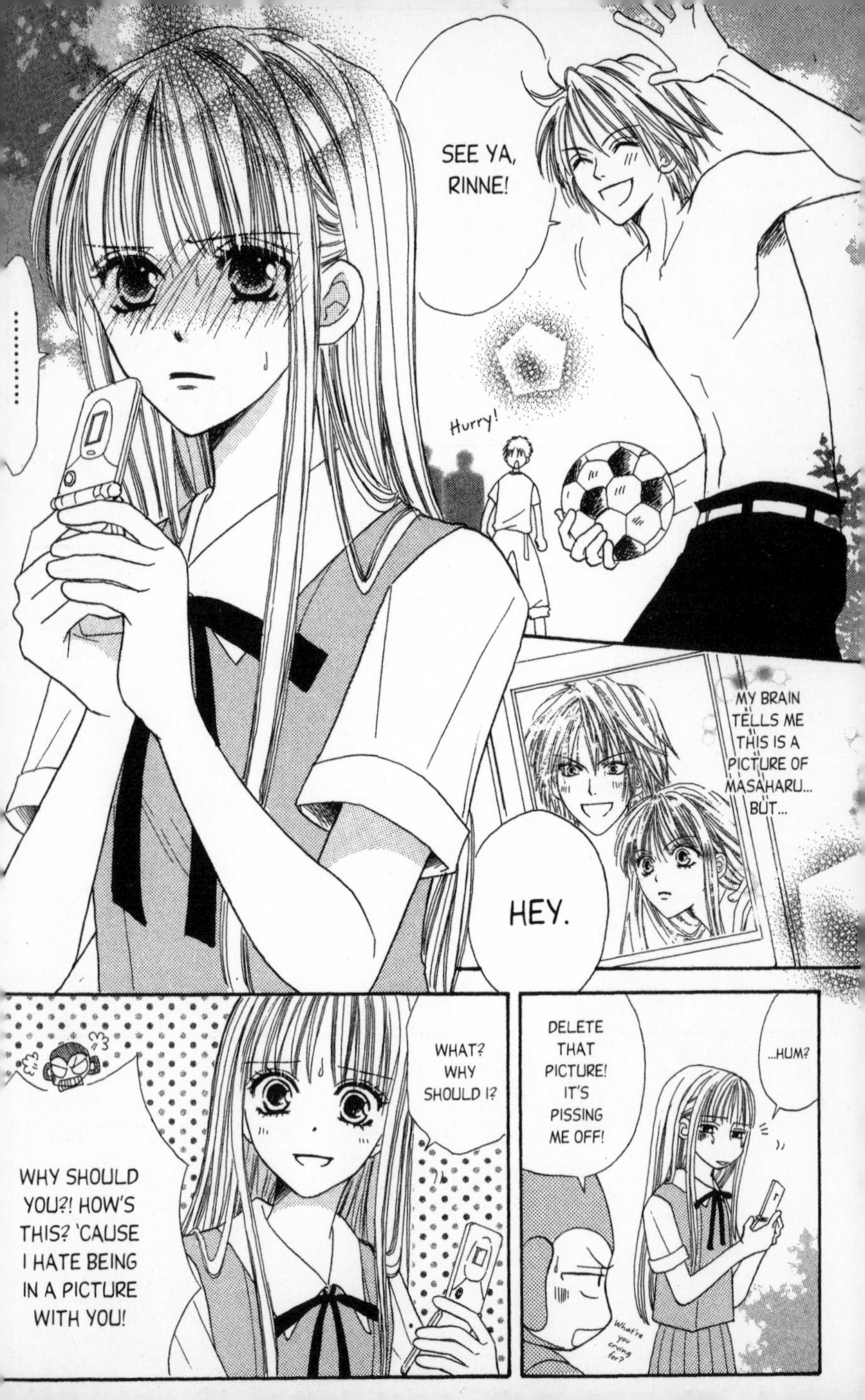
SEE YA, RINNE!
Hurry!
MY BRAIN TELLS ME THIS IS A PICTURE OF MASAHARU... BUT...
HEY.
....
...HUM?
What're you crying for?
DELETE THAT PICTURE! IT'S PISSING ME OFF!
WHAT? WHY SHOULD I?
WHY SHOULD YOU?! HOW'S THIS? 'CAUSE I HATE BEING IN A PICTURE WITH YOU!

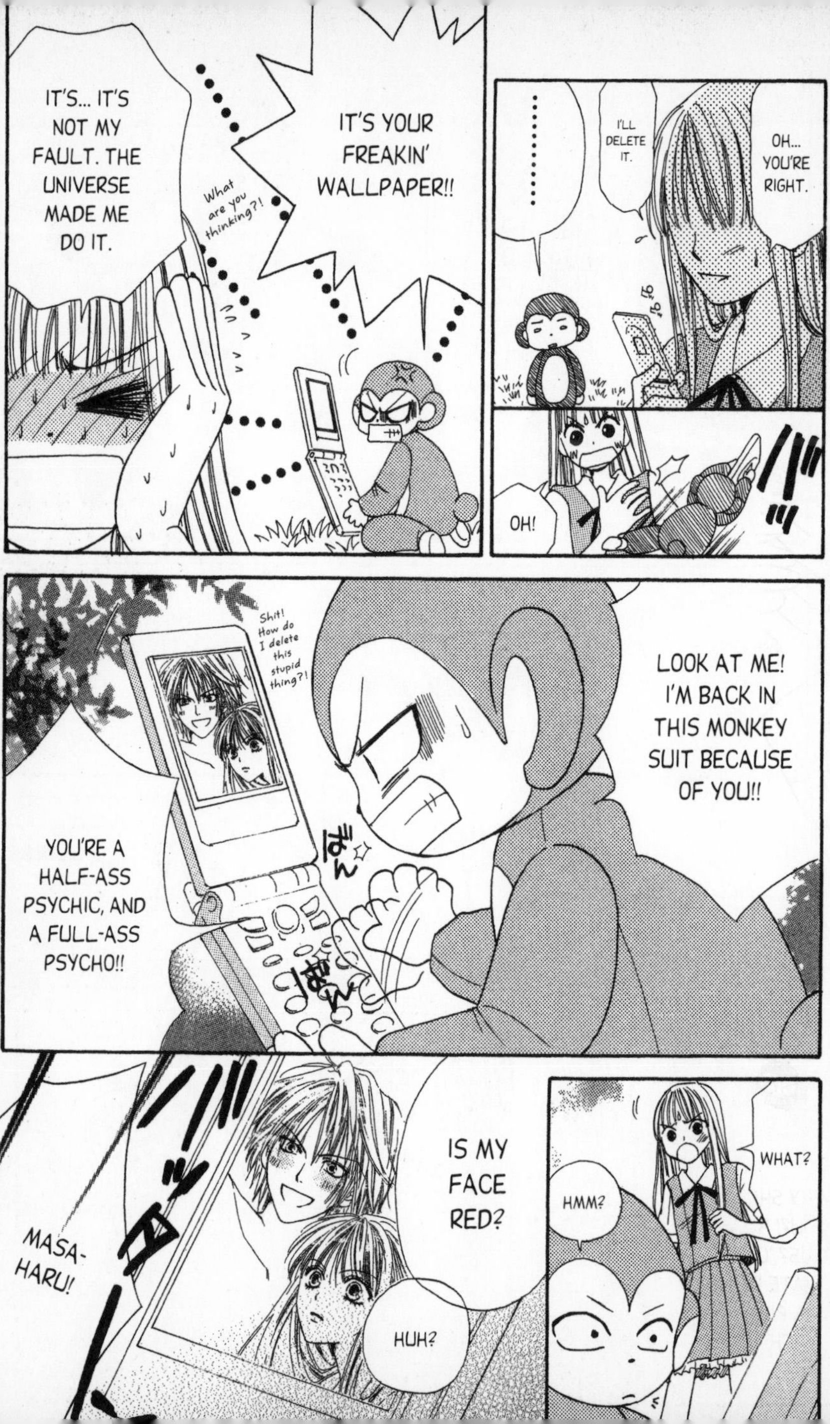
OH... YOU'RE RIGHT.
I'LL DELETE IT.
......
OH!
IT'S YOUR FREAKIN' WALLPAPER!!
What are you thinking?!
IT'S... IT'S NOT MY FAULT. THE UNIVERSE MADE ME DO IT.
LOOK AT ME! I'M BACK IN THIS MONKEY SUIT BECAUSE OF YOU!!
Shit! How do I delete this stupid thing?!
YOU'RE A HALF-ASS PSYCHIC, AND A FULL-ASS PSYCHO!!
WHAT?
HMM?
IS MY FACE RED?
HUH?
MASA-HARU!

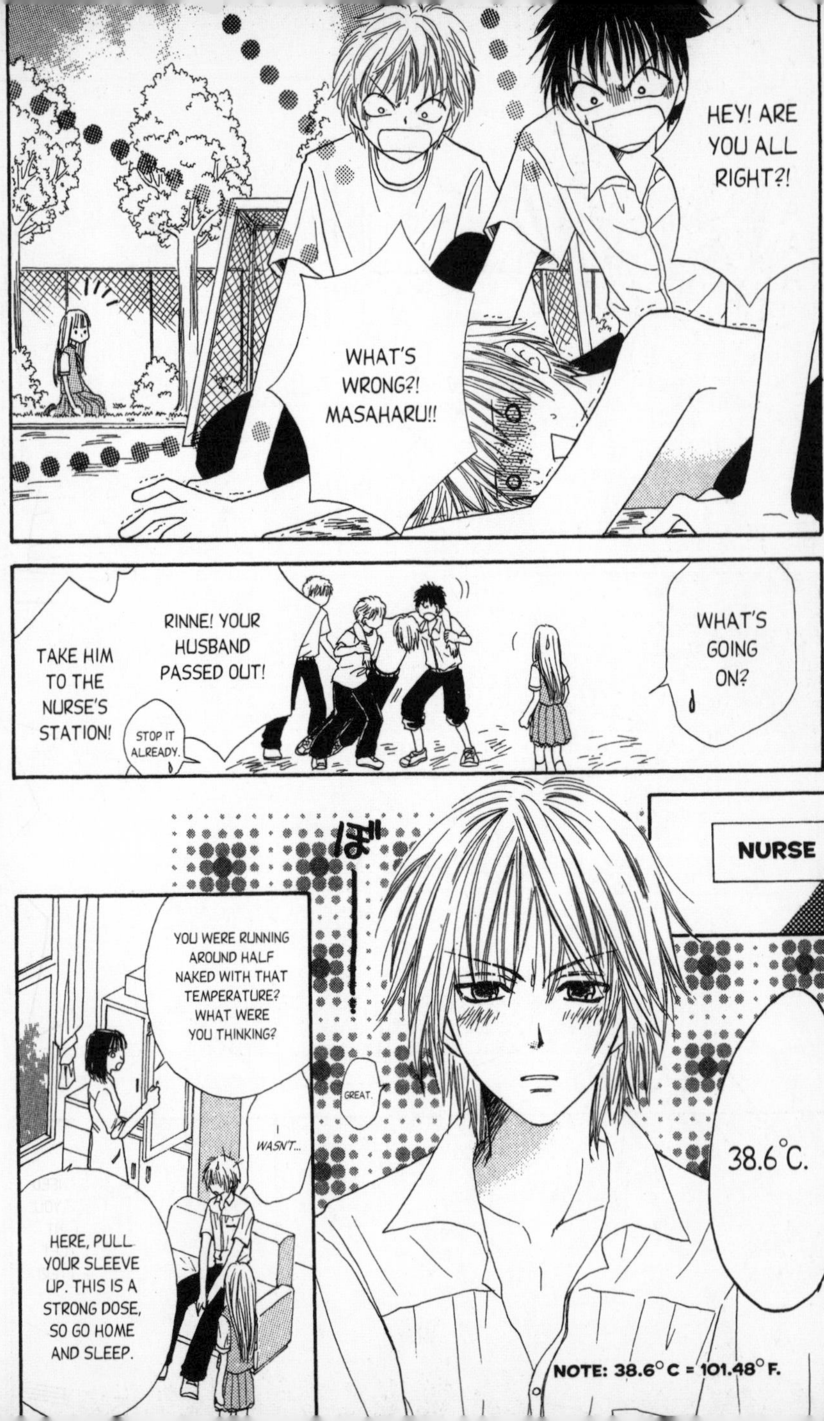
HEY! ARE YOU ALL RIGHT?!
WHAT'S WRONG?! MASAHARU!!
WHAT'S GOING ON?
RINNE! YOUR HUSBAND PASSED OUT!
TAKE HIM TO THE NURSE'S STATION!
STOP IT ALREADY.
NURSE
ぼー
38.6°C.
NOTE: 38.6° C = 101.48° F.
GREAT.
YOU WERE RUNNING AROUND HALF NAKED WITH THAT TEMPERATURE? WHAT WERE YOU THINKING?
I WASN'T...
HERE, PULL YOUR SLEEVE UP. THIS IS A STRONG DOSE, SO GO HOME AND SLEEP.

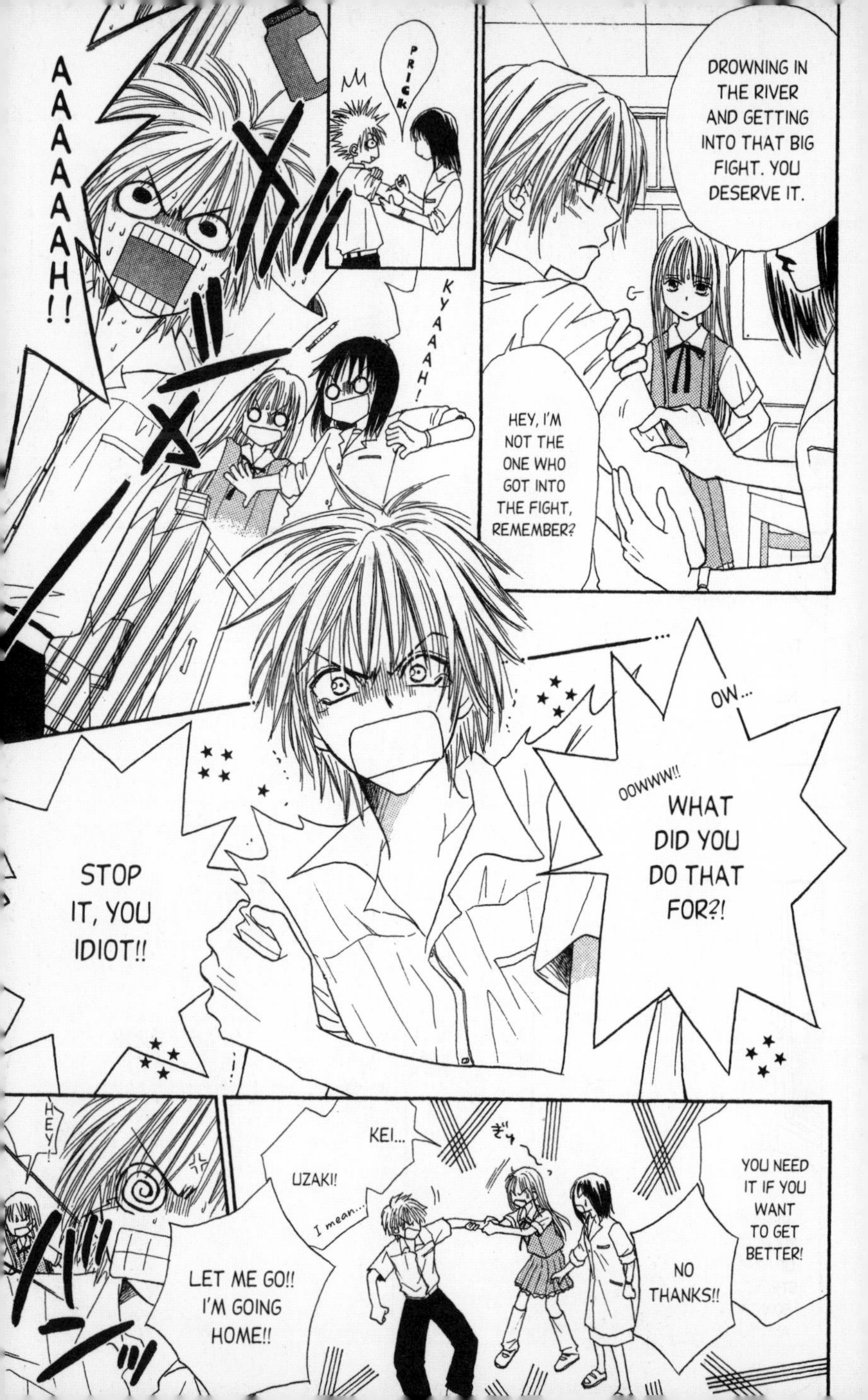
DROWNING IN THE RIVER AND GETTING INTO THAT BIG FIGHT. YOU DESERVE IT.
HEY, I'M NOT THE ONE WHO GOT INTO THE FIGHT, REMEMBER?
PRICK
AAAAAAAH!!
KYAAAAH!
OW...
OOWWW!!
WHAT DID YOU DO THAT FOR?!
STOP IT, YOU IDIOT!!
YOU NEED IT IF YOU WANT TO GET BETTER!
NO THANKS!!
KEI...
UZAKI!
I mean...
LET ME GO!! I'M GOING HOME!!
HEY!

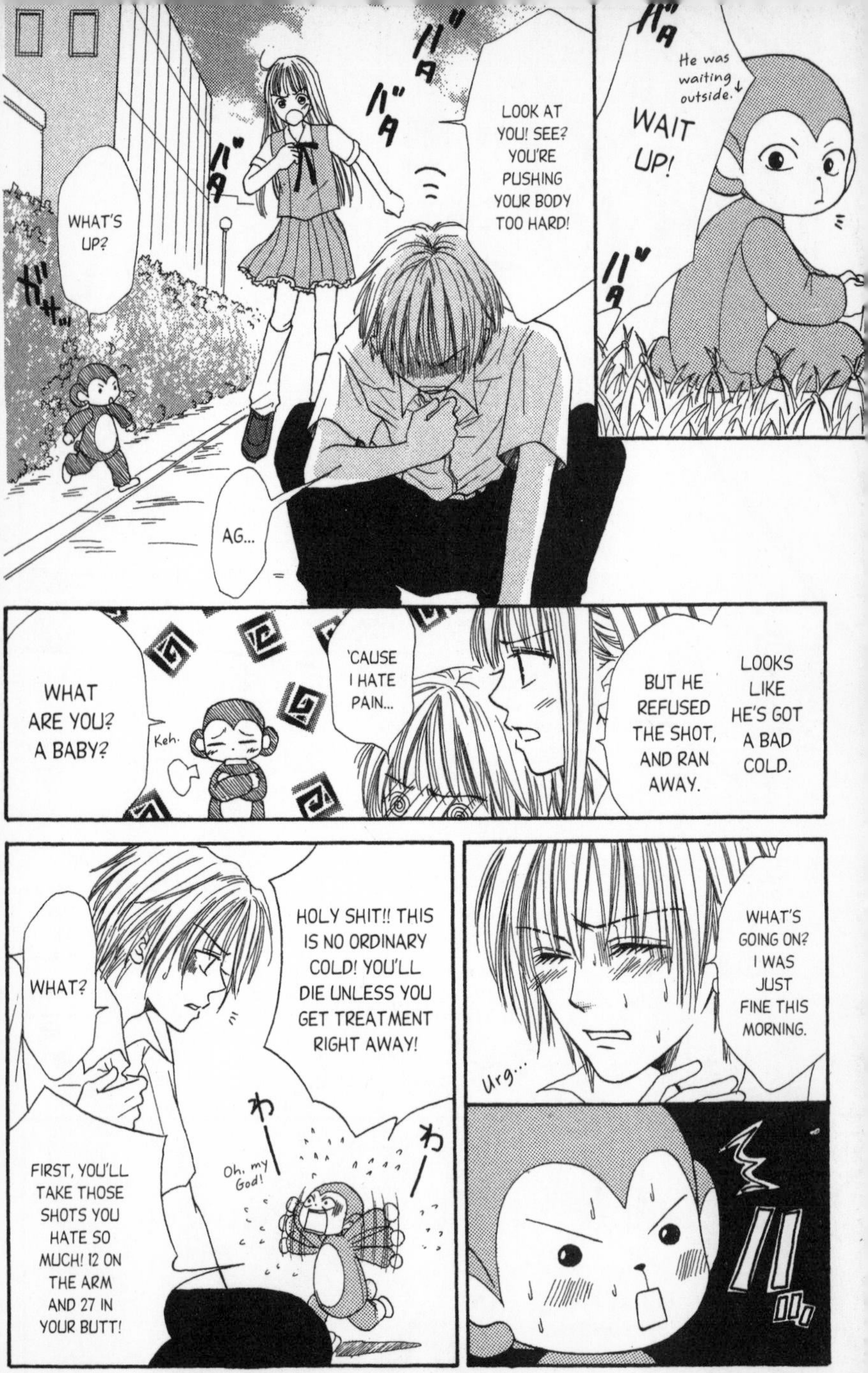
He was waiting outside.
WAIT UP!
LOOK AT YOU! SEE? YOU'RE PUSHING YOUR BODY TOO HARD!
WHAT'S UP?
AG...
LOOKS LIKE HE'S GOT A BAD COLD.
BUT HE REFUSED THE SHOT, AND RAN AWAY.
'CAUSE I HATE PAIN...
Keh.
WHAT ARE YOU? A BABY?
WHAT'S GOING ON? I WAS JUST FINE THIS MORNING.
Urg...
HOLY SHIT!! THIS IS NO ORDINARY COLD! YOU'LL DIE UNLESS YOU GET TREATMENT RIGHT AWAY!
WHAT?
Oh, my God!
FIRST, YOU'LL TAKE THOSE SHOTS YOU HATE SO MUCH! 12 ON THE ARM AND 27 IN YOUR BUTT!

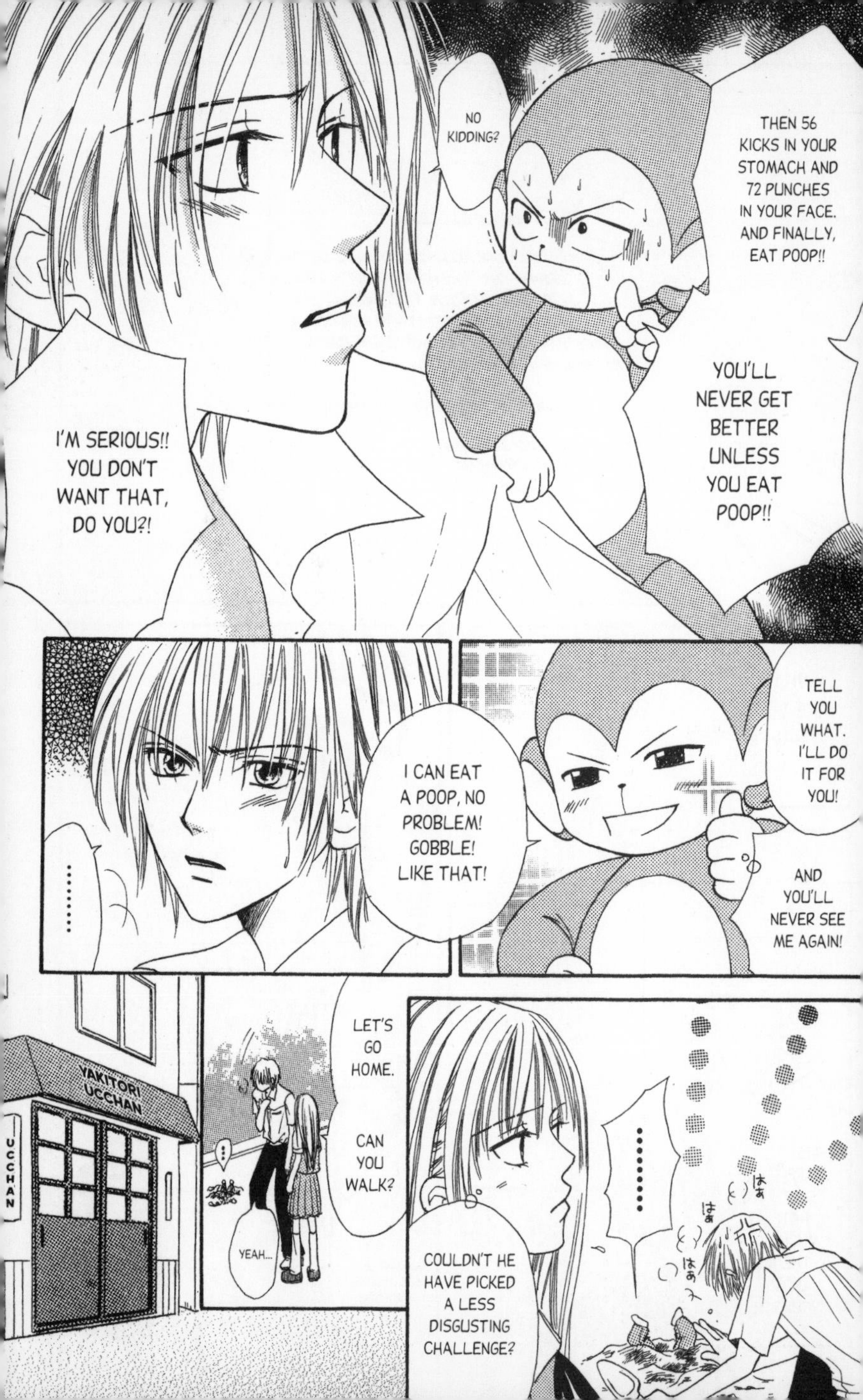
THEN 56 KICKS IN YOUR STOMACH AND 72 PUNCHES IN YOUR FACE. AND FINALLY, EAT POOP!!
NO KIDDING?
YOU'LL NEVER GET BETTER UNLESS YOU EAT POOP!!
I'M SERIOUS!! YOU DON'T WANT THAT, DO YOU?!
TELL YOU WHAT. I'LL DO IT FOR YOU!
AND YOU'LL NEVER SEE ME AGAIN!
I CAN EAT A POOP, NO PROBLEM! GOBBLE! LIKE THAT!
....
....
COULDN'T HE HAVE PICKED A LESS DISGUSTING CHALLENGE?
はあ
はあ
はあ
YAKITORI UCCHAN
UCCHAN
LET'S GO HOME.
CAN YOU WALK?
...
YEAH...

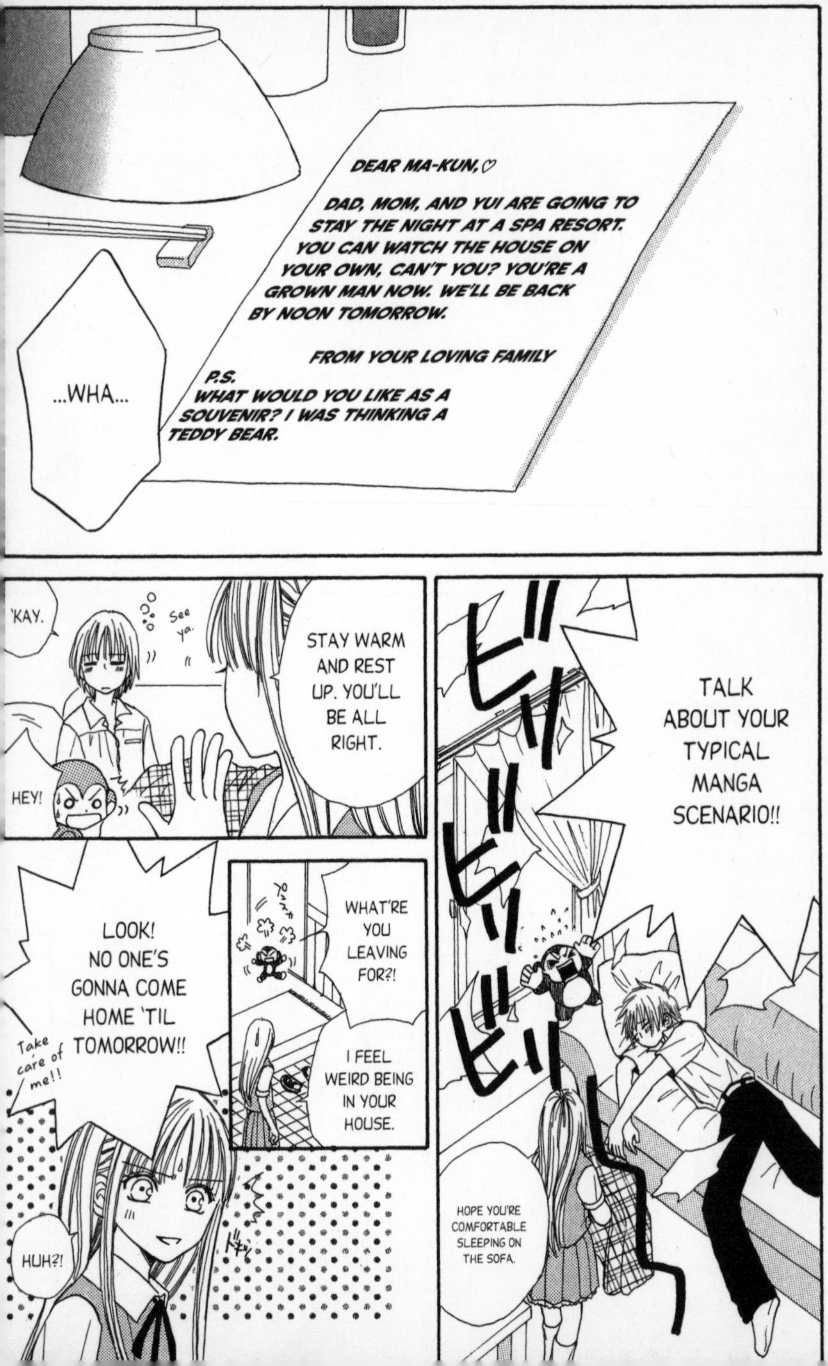
DEAR MA-KUN,♡
DAD, MOM, AND YUI ARE GOING TO STAY THE NIGHT AT A SPA RESORT. YOU CAN WATCH THE HOUSE ON YOUR OWN, CAN'T YOU? YOU'RE A GROWN MAN NOW. WE'LL BE BACK BY NOON TOMORROW.
FROM YOUR LOVING FAMILY
P.S. WHAT WOULD YOU LIKE AS A SOUVENIR? I WAS THINKING A TEDDY BEAR.
...WHA...
TALK ABOUT YOUR TYPICAL MANGA SCENARIO!!
HOPE YOU'RE COMFORTABLE SLEEPING ON THE SOFA.
STAY WARM AND REST UP. YOU'LL BE ALL RIGHT.
See ya.
'KAY.
HEY!
WHAT'RE YOU LEAVING FOR?!
I FEEL WEIRD BEING IN YOUR HOUSE.
LOOK! NO ONE'S GONNA COME HOME 'TIL TOMORROW!!
Take care of me!!
HUH?!

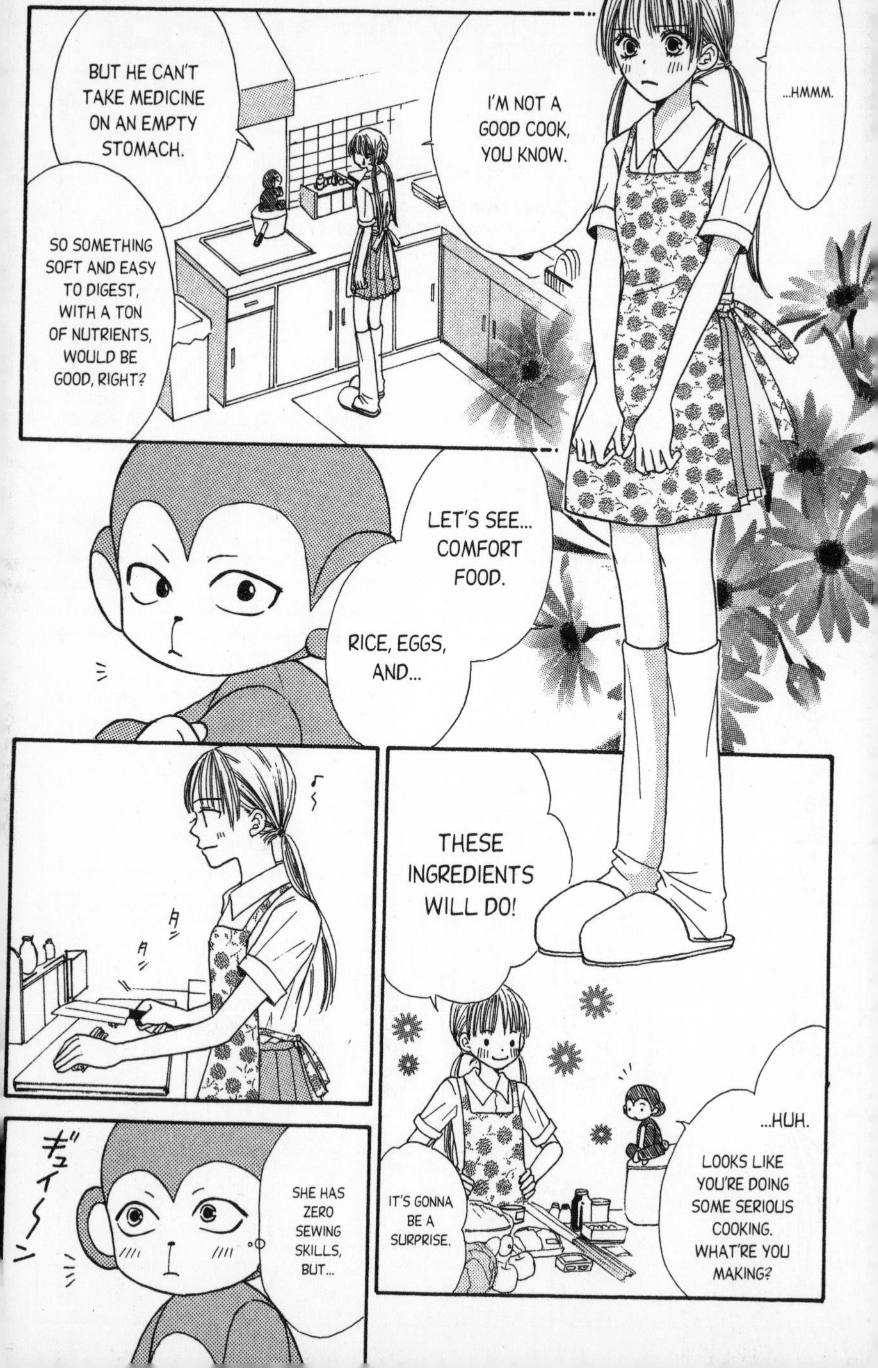
...HMMM.
I'M NOT A GOOD COOK, YOU KNOW.
BUT HE CAN'T TAKE MEDICINE ON AN EMPTY STOMACH.
SO SOMETHING SOFT AND EASY TO DIGEST, WITH A TON OF NUTRIENTS, WOULD BE GOOD, RIGHT?
LET'S SEE... COMFORT FOOD.
RICE, EGGS, AND...
THESE INGREDIENTS WILL DO!
...HUH.
LOOKS LIKE YOU'RE DOING SOME SERIOUS COOKING. WHAT'RE YOU MAKING?
IT'S GONNA BE A SURPRISE.
タ
タ
SHE HAS ZERO SEWING SKILLS, BUT...
ギュイ〜ン

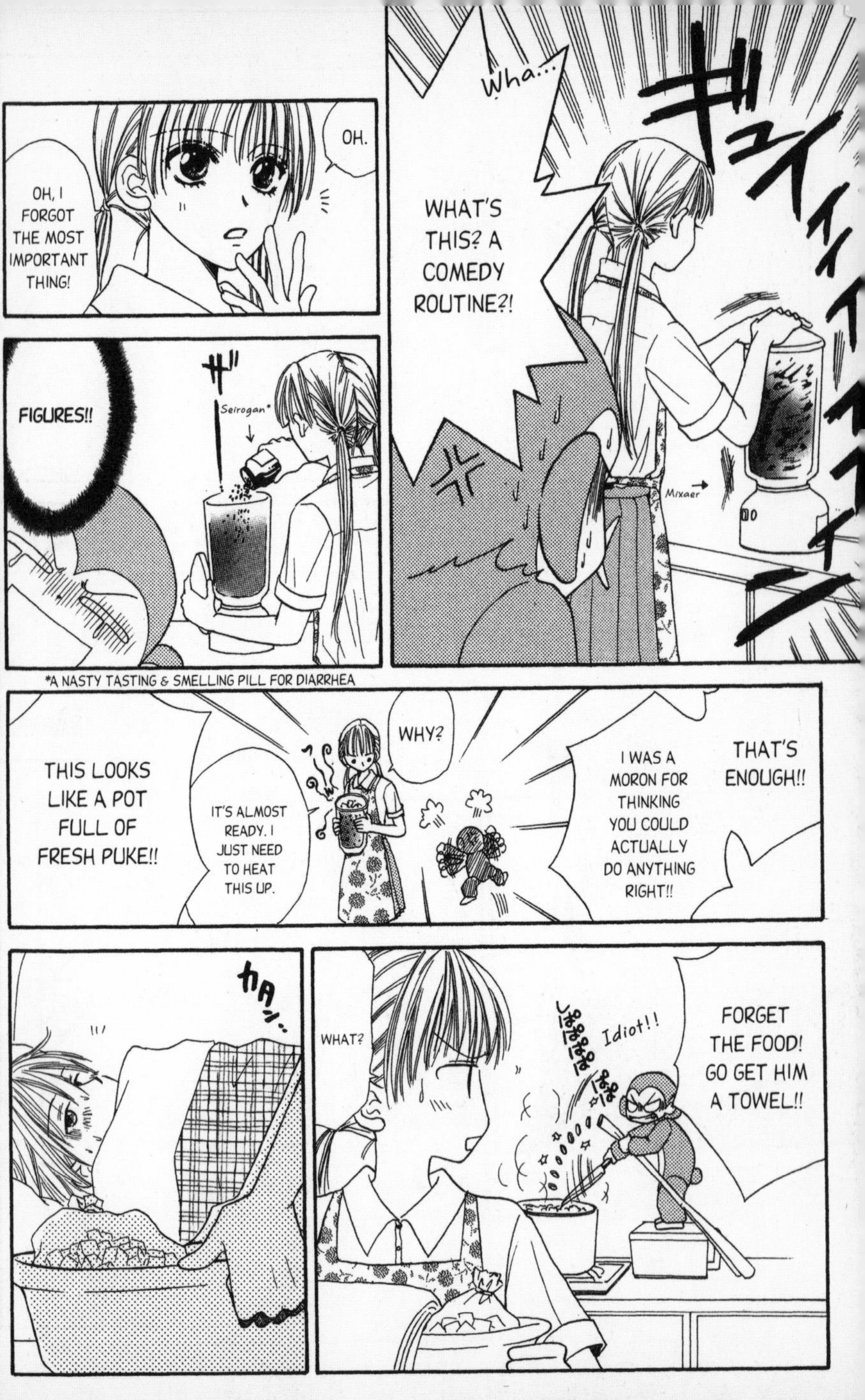
Wha...
WHAT'S THIS? A COMEDY ROUTINE?!
Mixaer
OH.
OH, I FORGOT THE MOST IMPORTANT THING!
FIGURES!!
Seirogan*
THAT'S ENOUGH!!
I WAS A MORON FOR THINKING YOU COULD ACTUALLY DO ANYTHING RIGHT!!
WHY?
IT'S ALMOST READY. I JUST NEED TO HEAT THIS UP.
THIS LOOKS LIKE A POT FULL OF FRESH PUKE!!
FORGET THE FOOD! GO GET HIM A TOWEL!!
Idiot!!
WHAT?

*A NASTY TASTING & SMELLING PILL FOR DIARRHEA

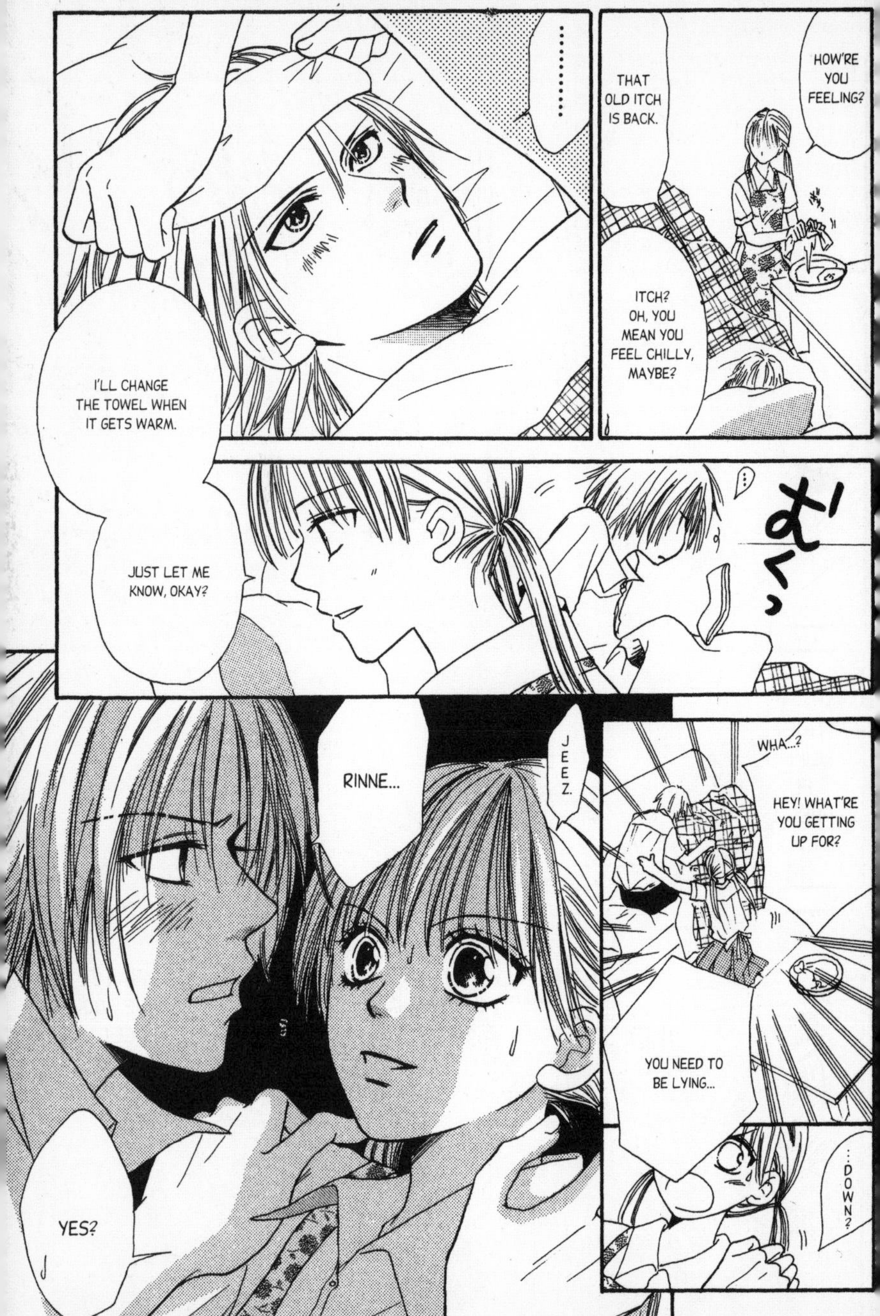
HOW'RE YOU FEELING?
THAT OLD ITCH IS BACK.
ITCH? OH, YOU MEAN YOU FEEL CHILLY, MAYBE?
......
I'LL CHANGE THE TOWEL WHEN IT GETS WARM.
JUST LET ME KNOW, OKAY?
...
むくっ
WHA...?
HEY! WHAT'RE YOU GETTING UP FOR?
YOU NEED TO BE LYING...
...DOWN?
JEEZ.
RINNE...
YES?

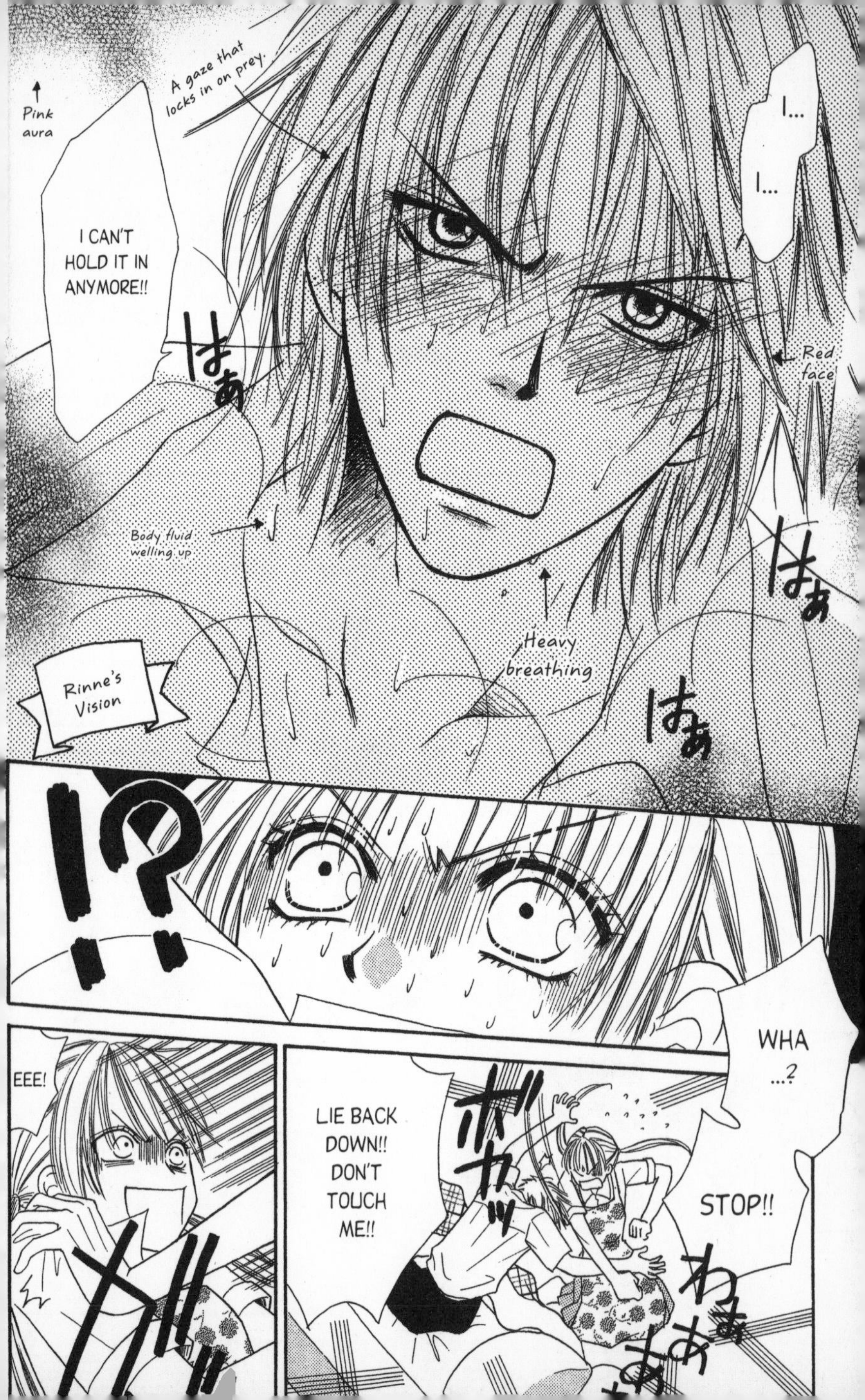
I...
I...
A gaze that locks in on prey.
Pink aura
I CAN'T HOLD IT IN ANYMORE!!
はぁ
Red face
Body fluid welling up
はぁ
Heavy breathing
はぁ
Rinne's Vision
!?
WHA ...?
STOP!!
わあああ
ボカッ
LIE BACK DOWN!! DON'T TOUCH ME!!
EEE!
メメ

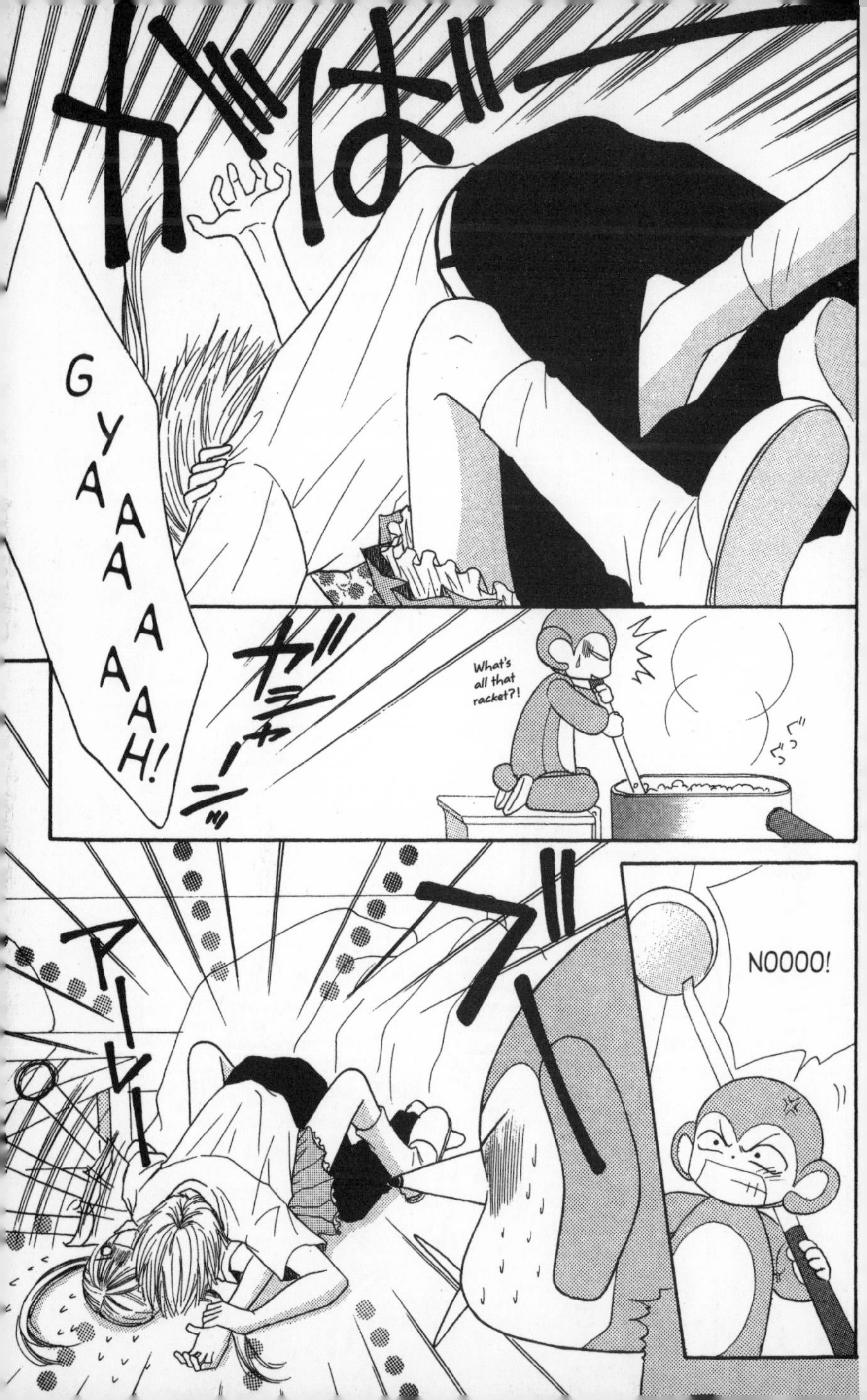
GYAAAAAAH!
What's all that racket?!
NOOOO!

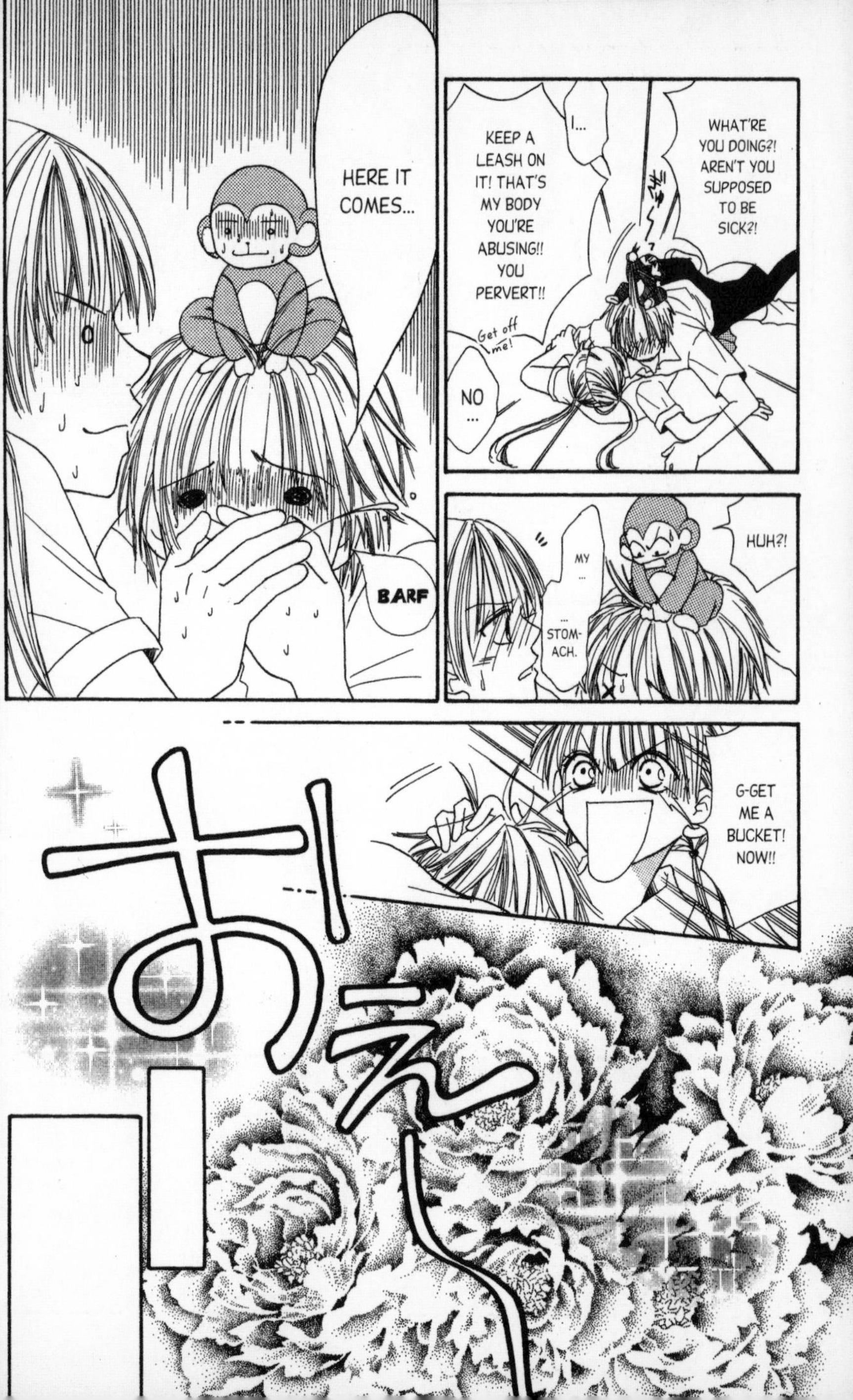
WHAT'RE YOU DOING?! AREN'T YOU SUPPOSED TO BE SICK?!
I...
KEEP A LEASH ON IT! THAT'S MY BODY YOU'RE ABUSING!! YOU PERVERT!!
Get off me!
NO ...
HUH?!
MY ...
... STOM-ACH.
HERE IT COMES...
BARF
G-GET ME A BUCKET! NOW!!
おえ

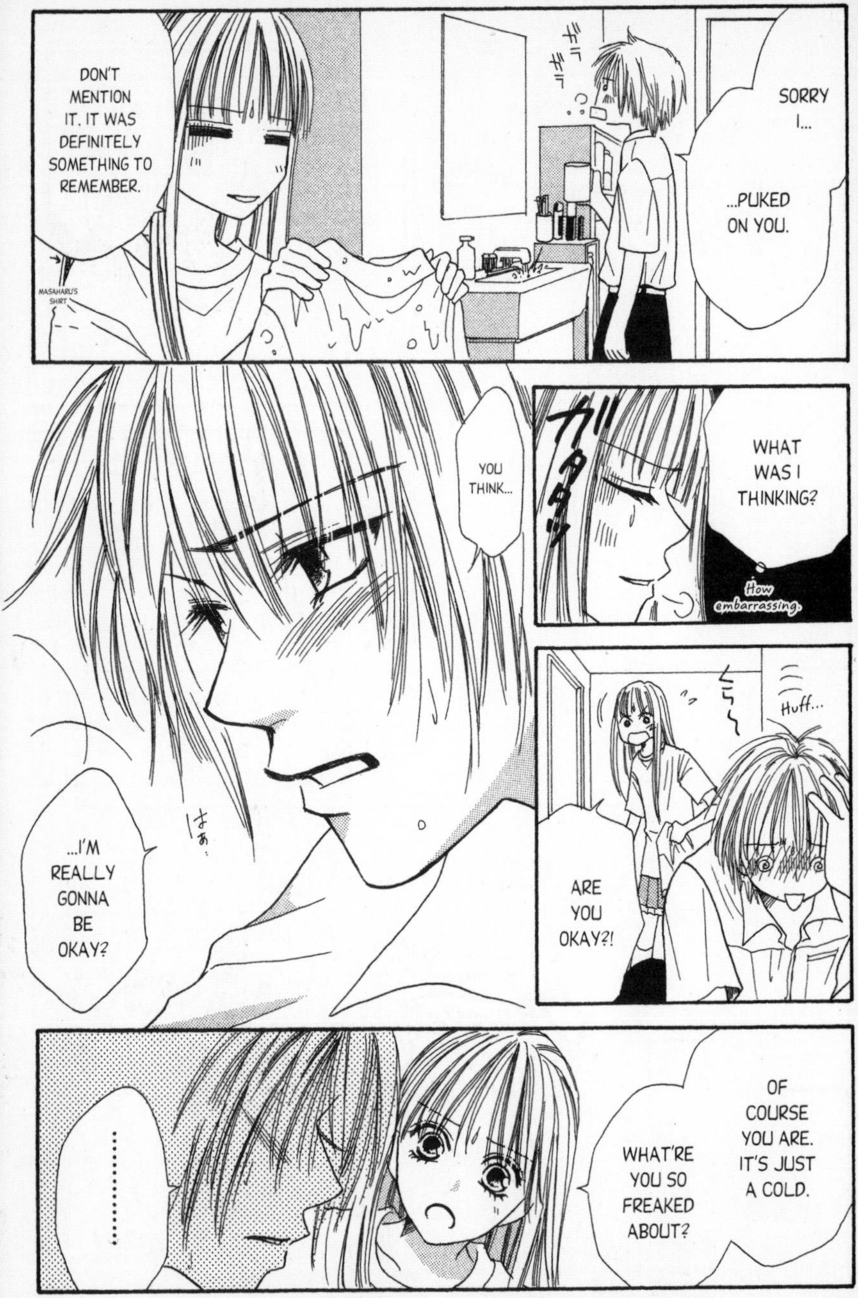
ガラ ガラ
SORRY I...
...PUKED ON YOU.
DON'T MENTION IT. IT WAS DEFINITELY SOMETHING TO REMEMBER.
MASAHARU'S SHIRT
WHAT WAS I THINKING?
How embarrassing.
ガタタッ
YOU THINK...
Huff...
ARE YOU OKAY?!
はぁ
...I'M REALLY GONNA BE OKAY?
OF COURSE YOU ARE. IT'S JUST A COLD.
WHAT'RE YOU SO FREAKED ABOUT?
....

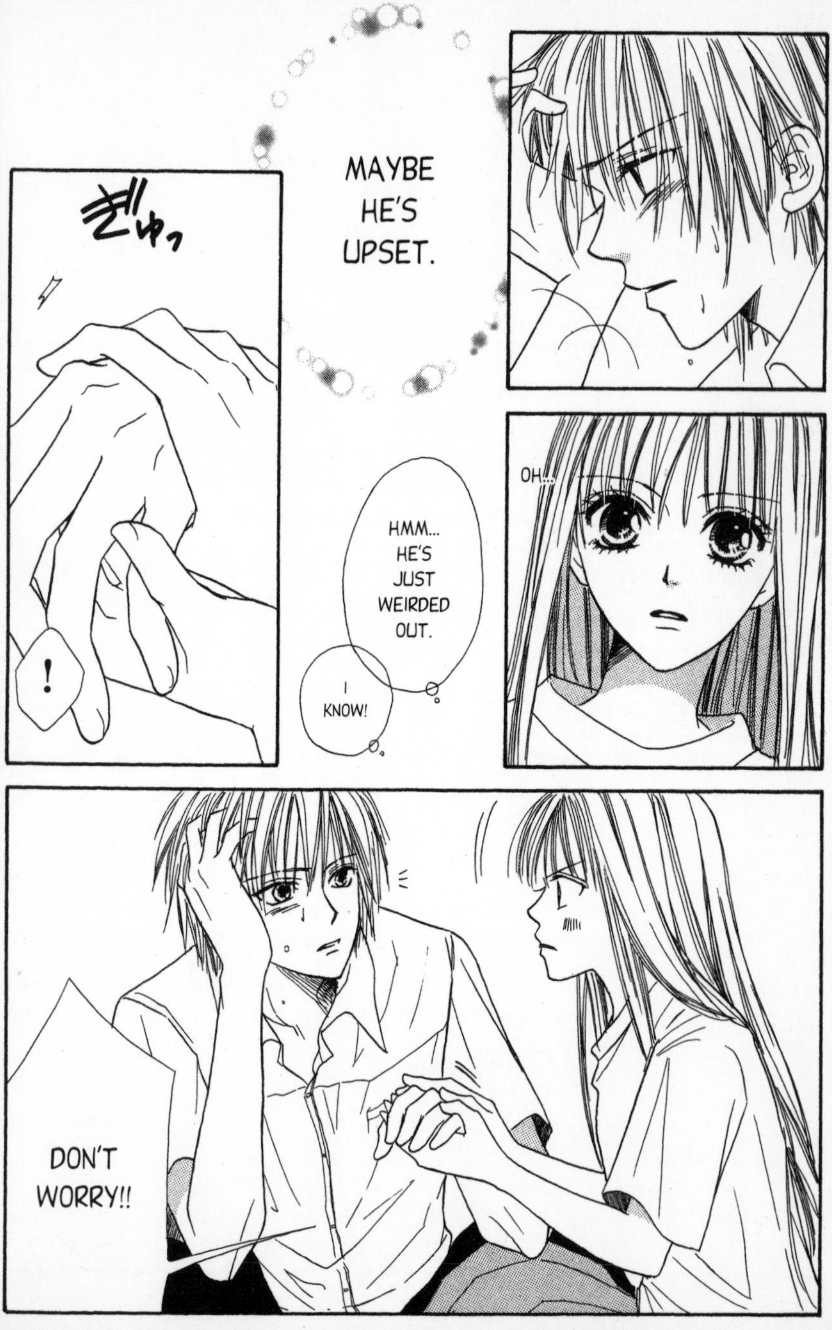
MAYBE HE'S UPSET.
OH...
HMM... HE'S JUST WEIRDED OUT.
I KNOW!
ぎゅっ
!
DON'T WORRY!!

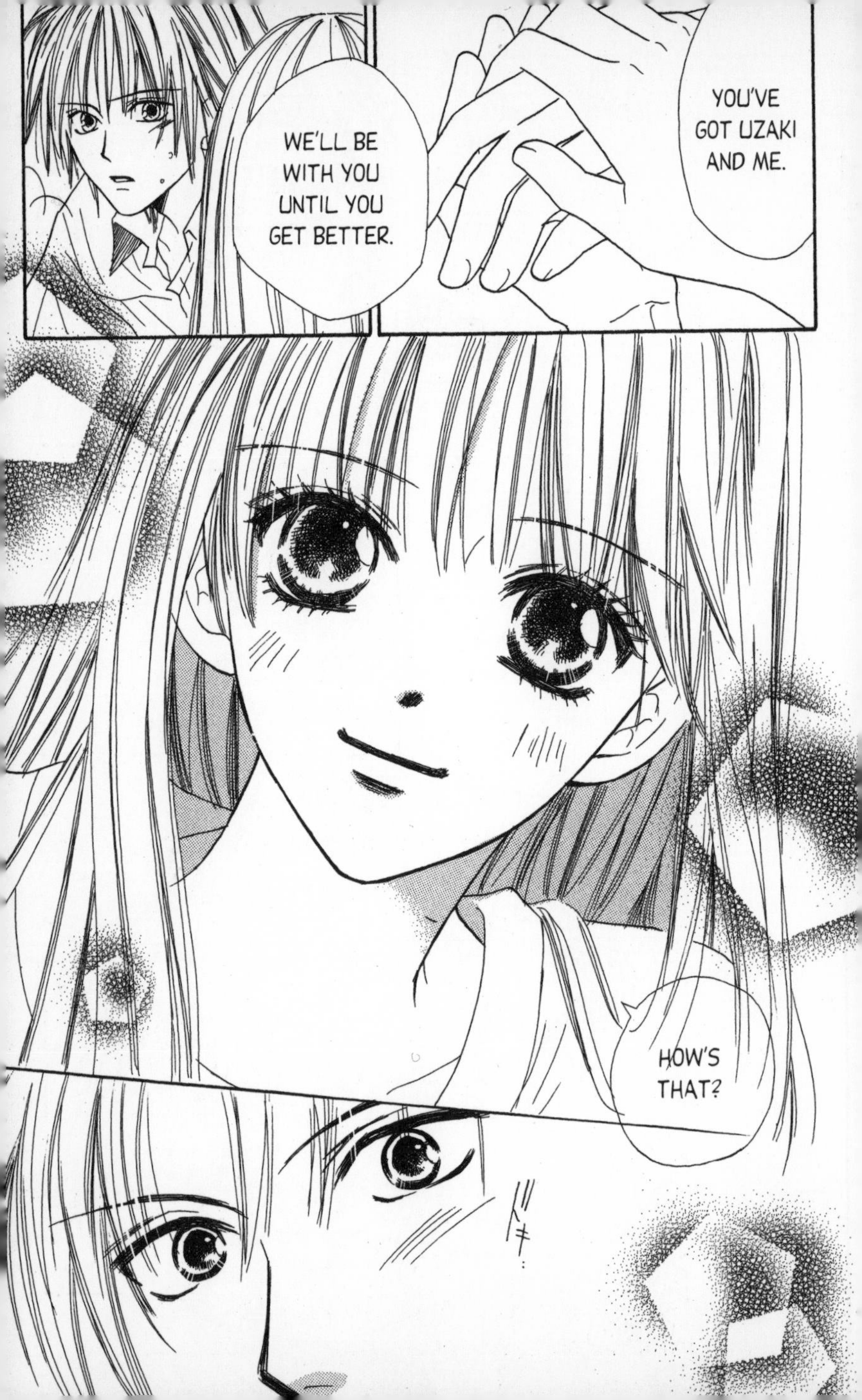
YOU'VE GOT UZAKI AND ME.
WE'LL BE WITH YOU UNTIL YOU GET BETTER.
HOW'S THAT?
ドキ

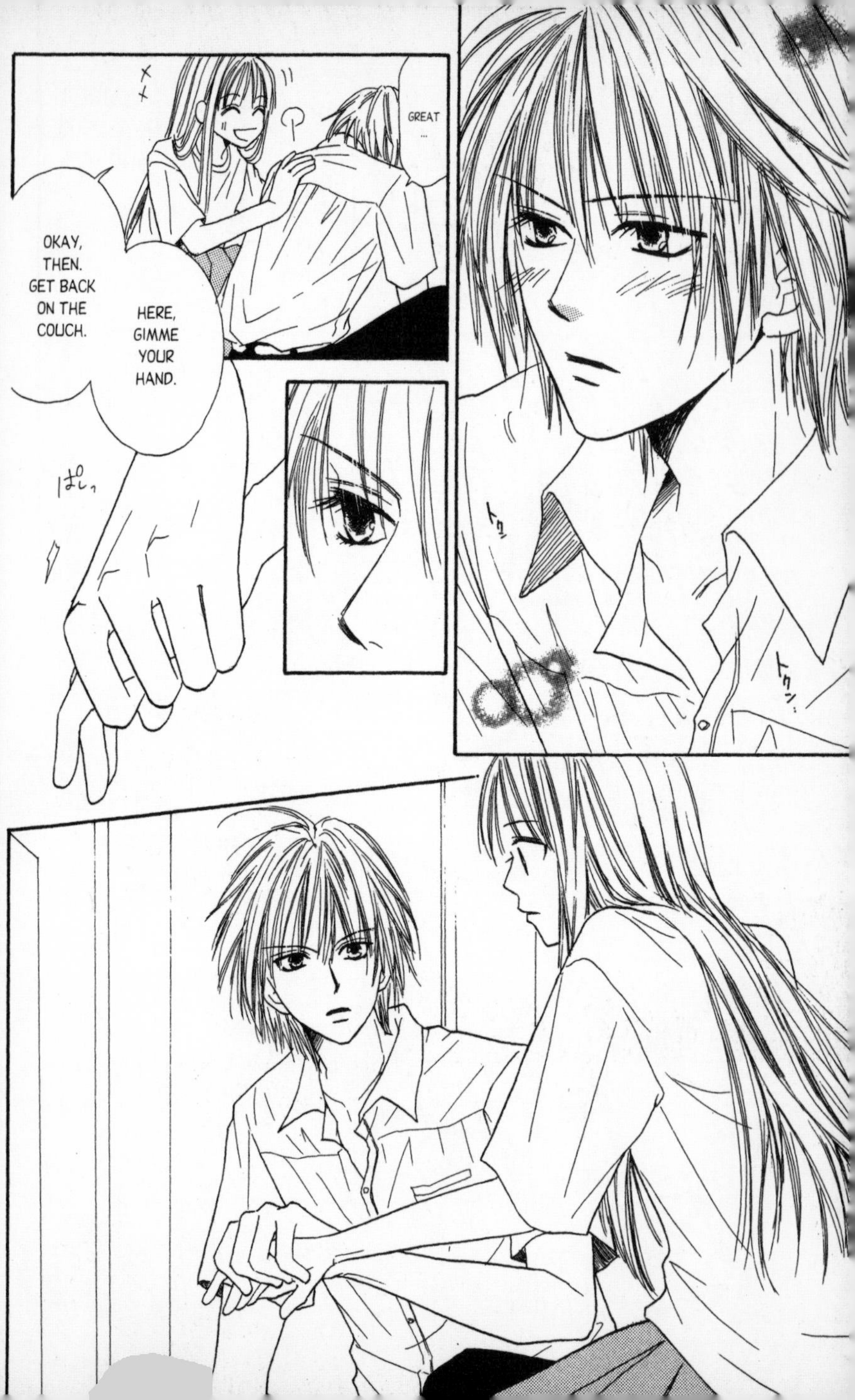
GREAT ...
OKAY, THEN. GET BACK ON THE COUCH.
HERE, GIMME YOUR HAND.
ぱしっ
トク
トクン

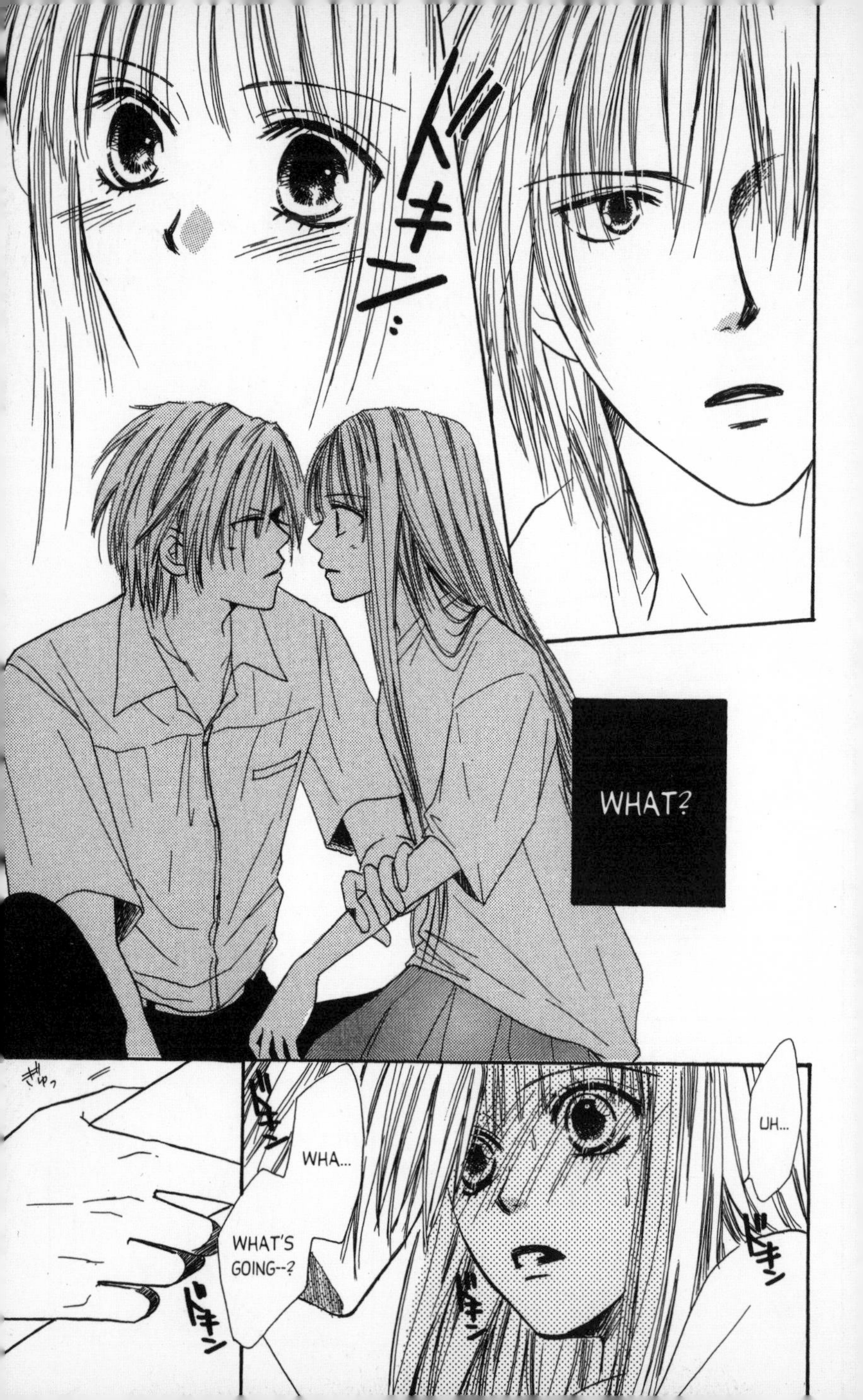
ドキーン
WHAT?
UH...
ドキン
ドキン
WHA...
WHAT'S GOING--?
ドキン
ぎゅっ

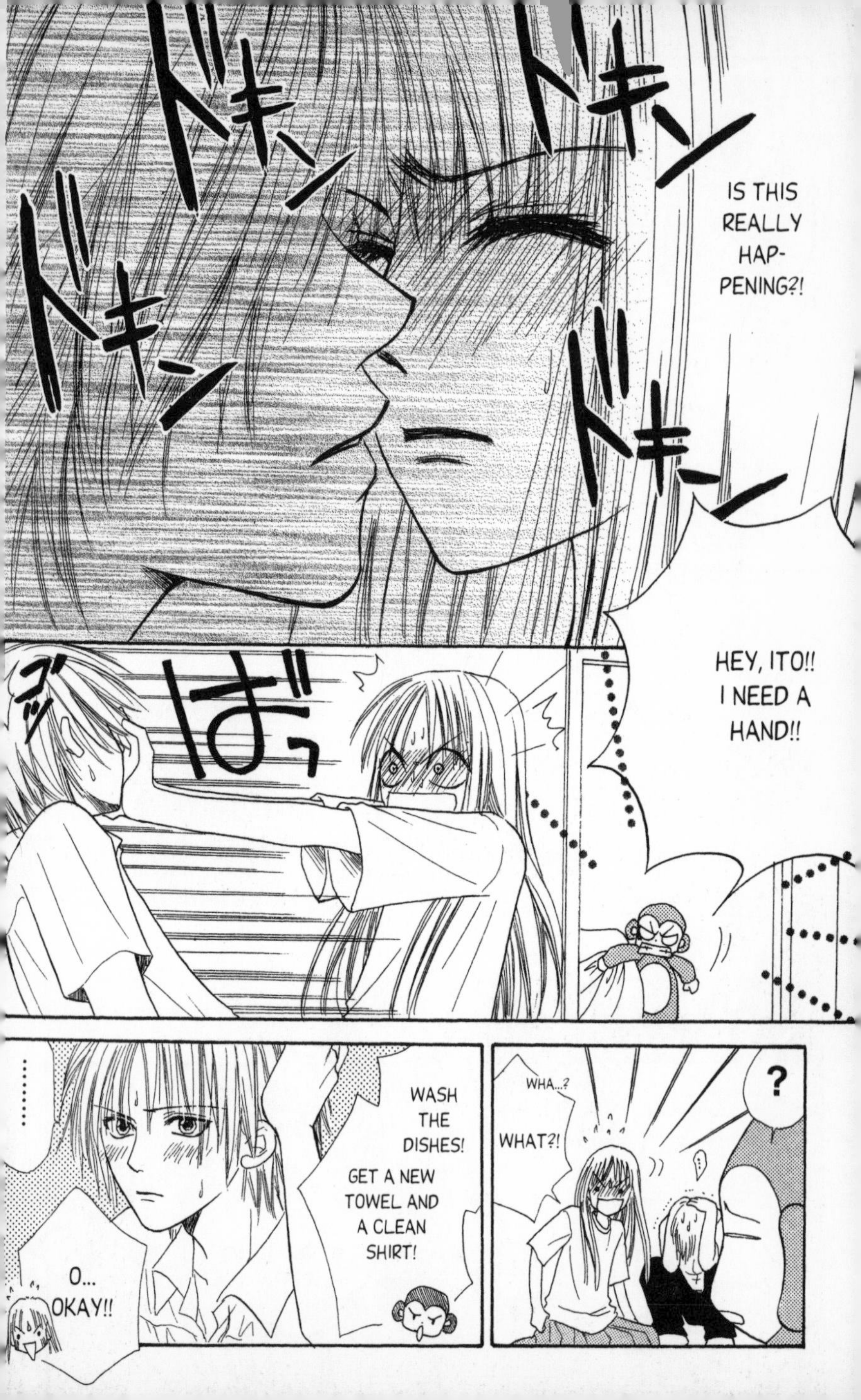
IS THIS REALLY HAP-PENING?!
ドキン
ドキン
ドキン
ドキン
HEY, ITO!! I NEED A HAND!!
ゴッ
ばっ
WHA...?
WHAT?!
?
WASH THE DISHES!
GET A NEW TOWEL AND A CLEAN SHIRT!
....
O... OKAY!!

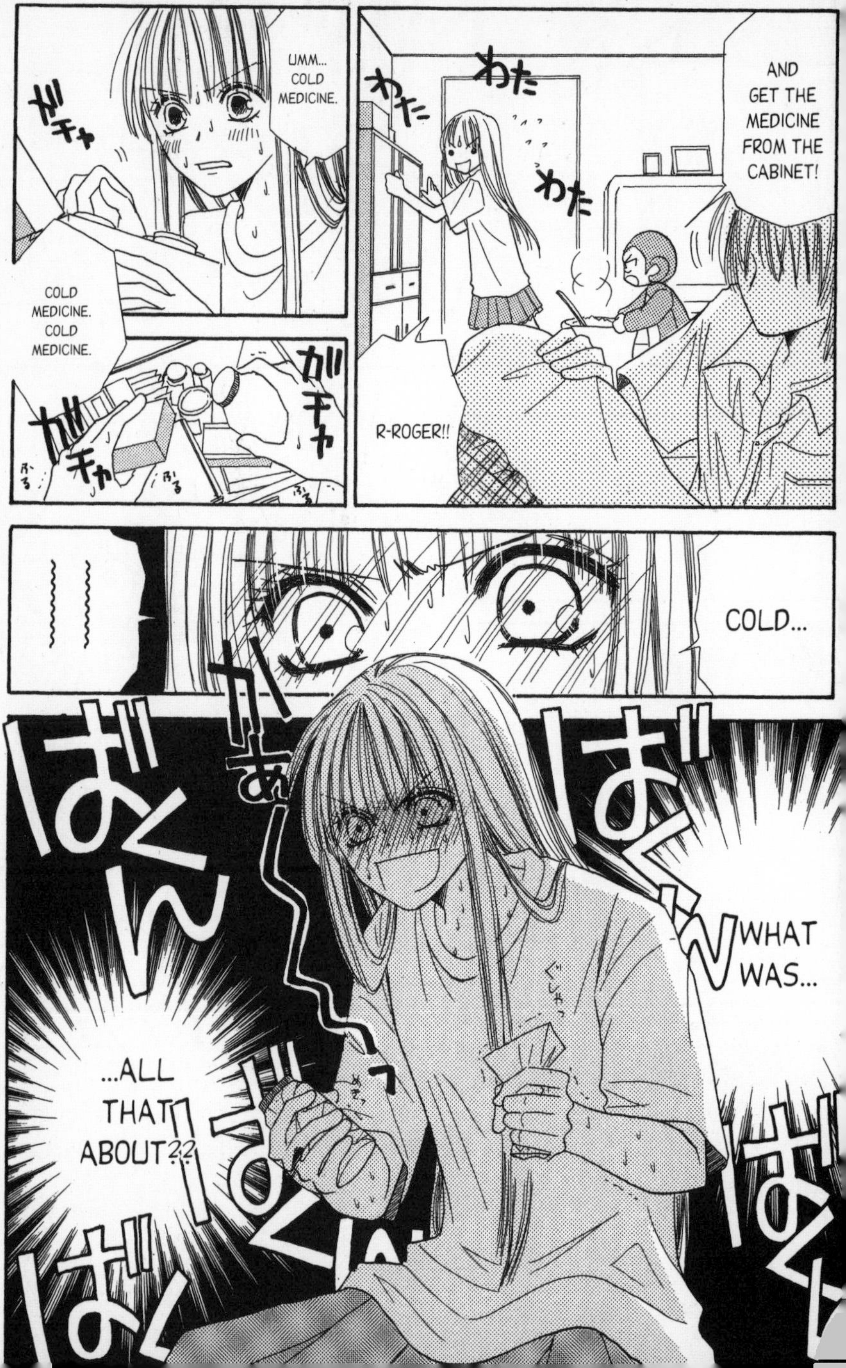
AND GET THE MEDICINE FROM THE CABINET!
わた
わた
R-ROGER!!
UMM... COLD MEDICINE.
ガチャ
COLD MEDICINE. COLD MEDICINE.
ガチャ
ガチャ
COLD...
～～
かぁ
ばくん
WHAT WAS...
...ALL THAT ABOUT??
ばくん
ばくん
ばくん

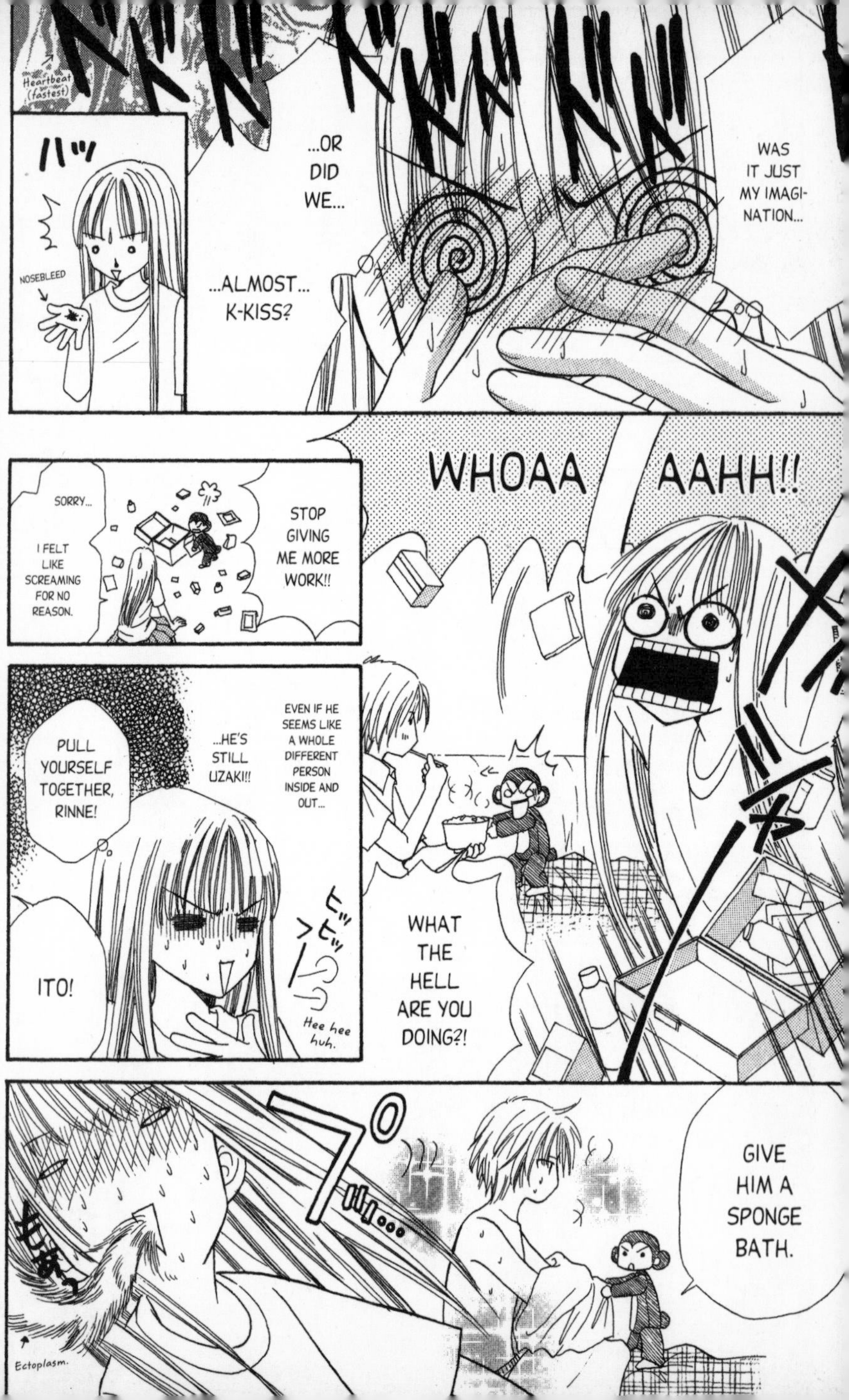

WAS IT JUST MY IMAGINATION...
...OR DID WE...
...ALMOST... K-KISS?
Heartbeat (fastest)
ハッ
NOSEBLEED
WHOAA AAHH!!
WHAT THE HELL ARE YOU DOING?!
STOP GIVING ME MORE WORK!!
SORRY...
I FELT LIKE SCREAMING FOR NO REASON.
EVEN IF HE SEEMS LIKE A WHOLE DIFFERENT PERSON INSIDE AND OUT...
...HE'S STILL UZAKI!!
PULL YOURSELF TOGETHER, RINNE!
ITO!
ヒッヒッ
Hee hee huh.
GIVE HIM A SPONGE BATH.
Ectoplasm.

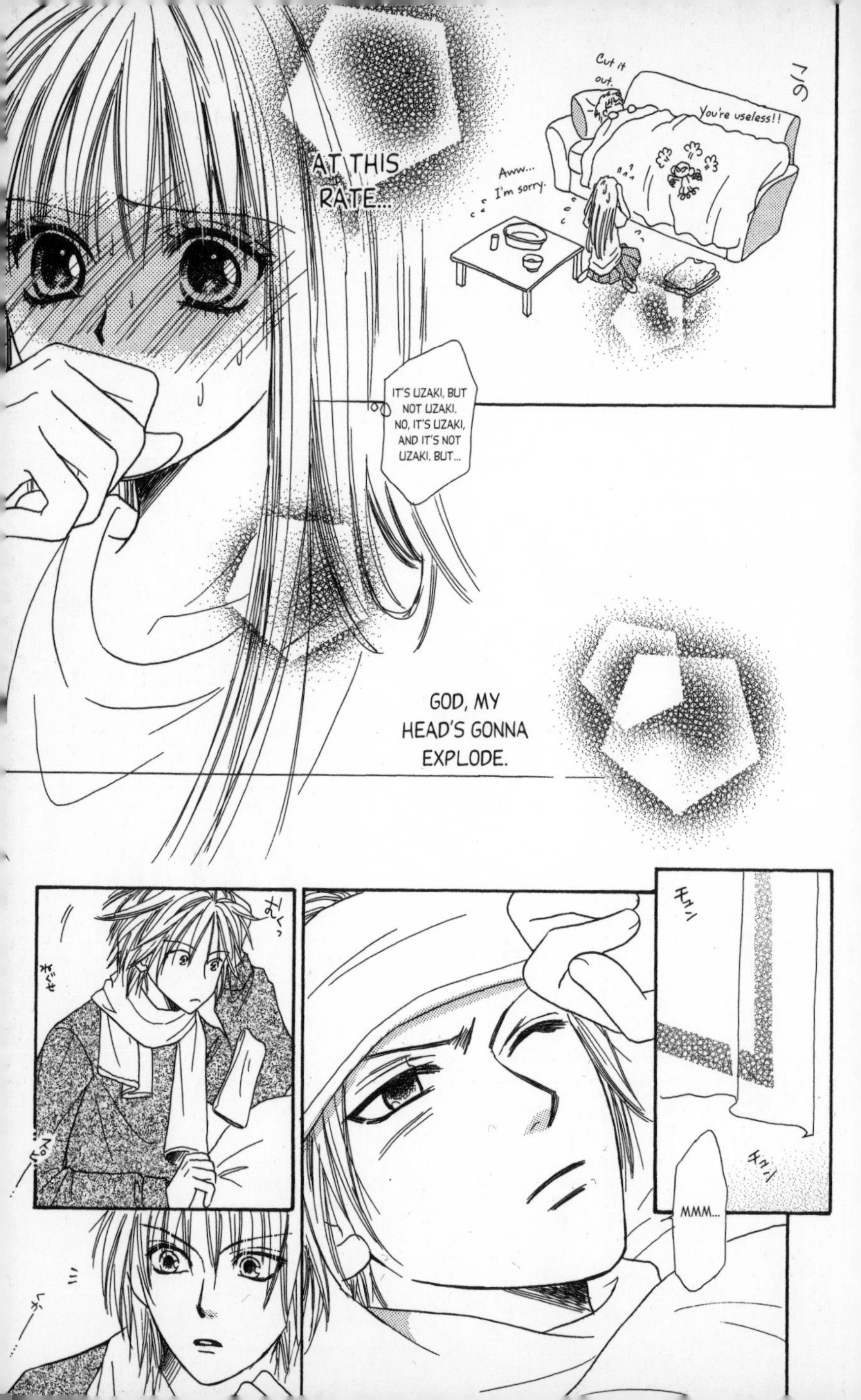
Cut it out.
You're useless!!
Aww... I'm sorry.
AT THIS RATE...
IT'S UZAKI, BUT NOT UZAKI. NO, IT'S UZAKI, AND IT'S NOT UZAKI. BUT...
GOD, MY HEAD'S GONNA EXPLODE.
MMM...

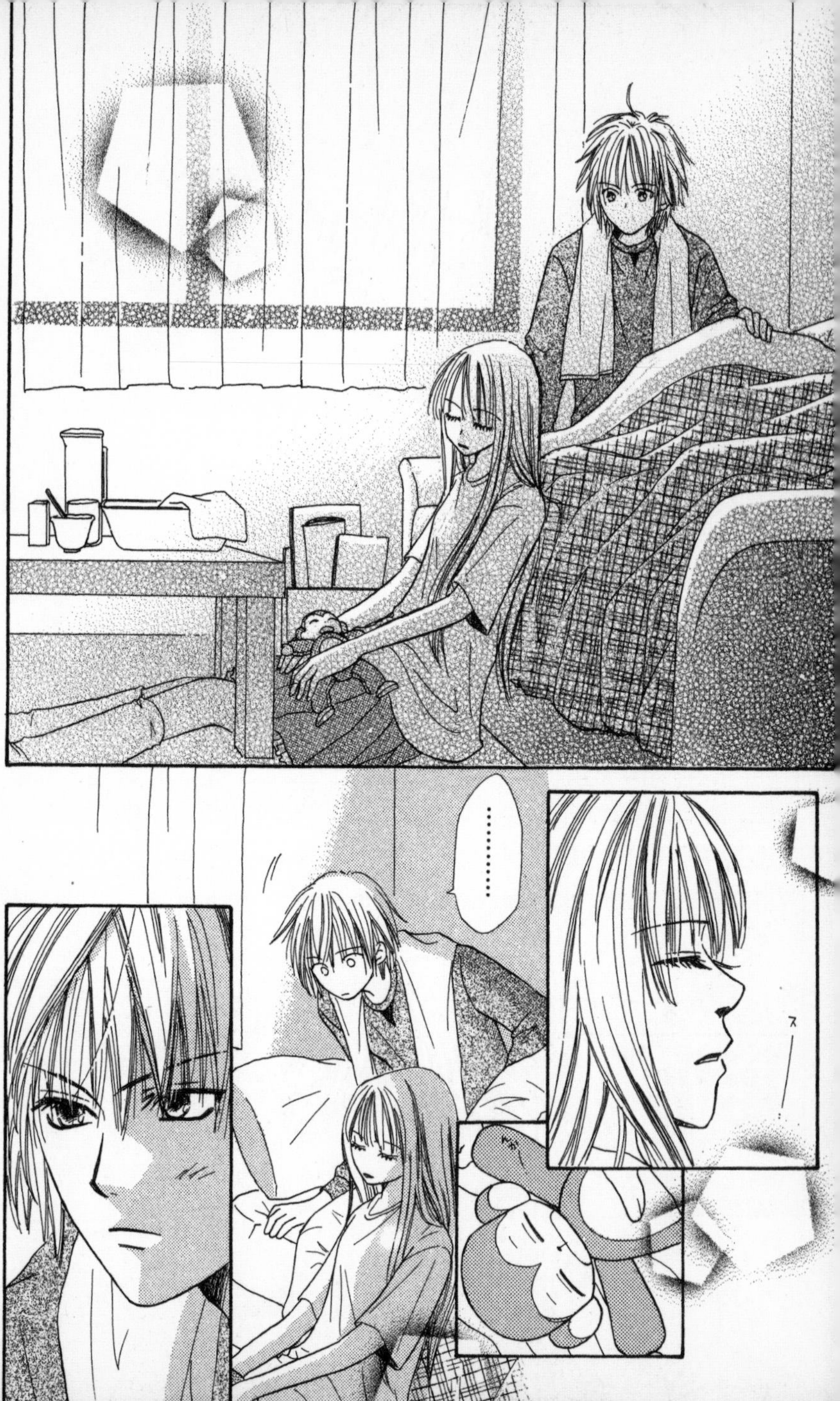
スー…
…………

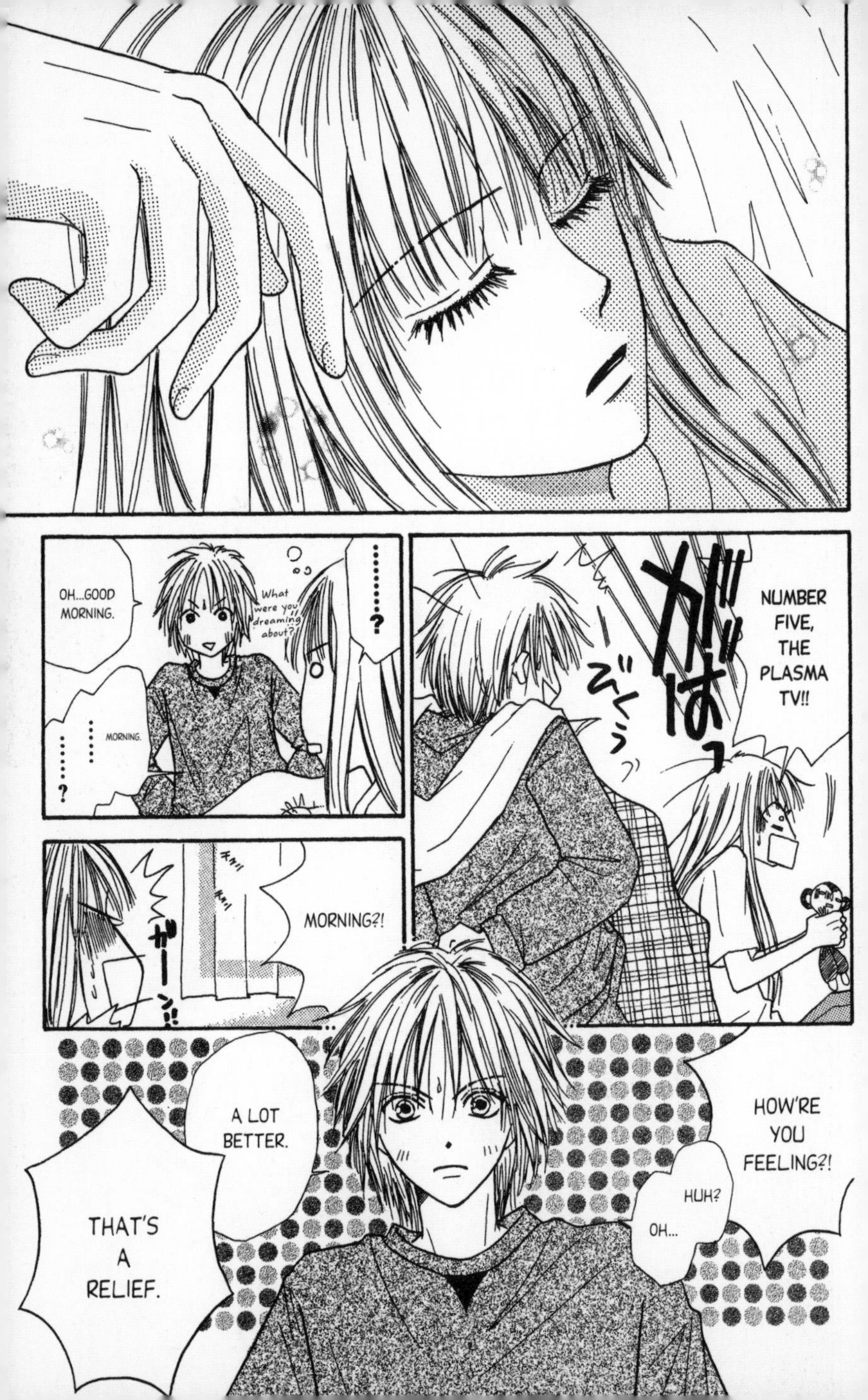
NUMBER FIVE, THE PLASMA TV!!
ガバッ
びくっ
……?
OH...GOOD MORNING.
What were you dreaming about?
MORNING.
……?
MORNING?!
ガーン!!
HOW'RE YOU FEELING?!
HUH?
OH...
A LOT BETTER.
THAT'S A RELIEF.

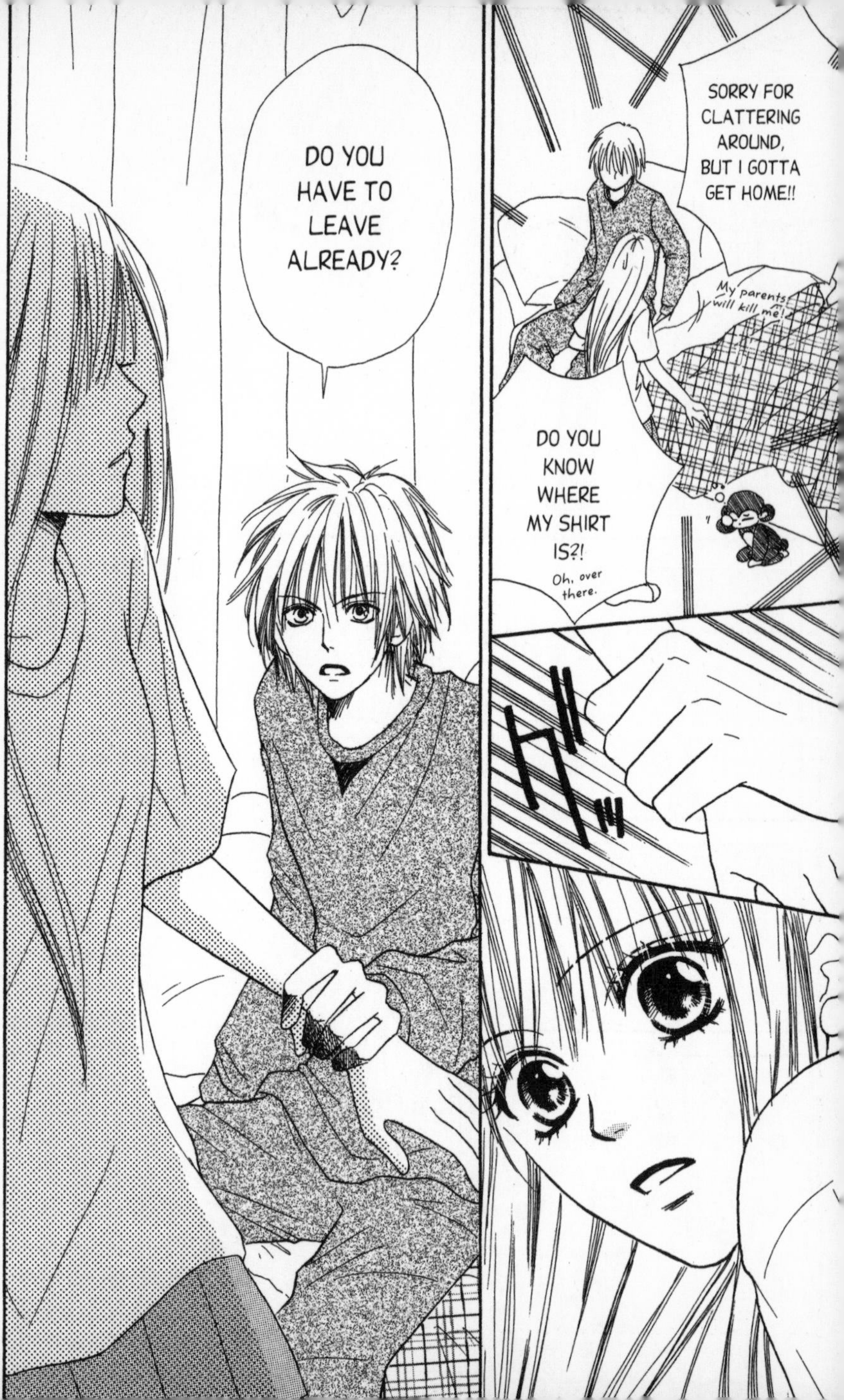
SORRY FOR CLATTERING AROUND, BUT I GOTTA GET HOME!!
My parents will kill me!
DO YOU KNOW WHERE MY SHIRT IS?!
Oh, over there.
DO YOU HAVE TO LEAVE ALREADY?

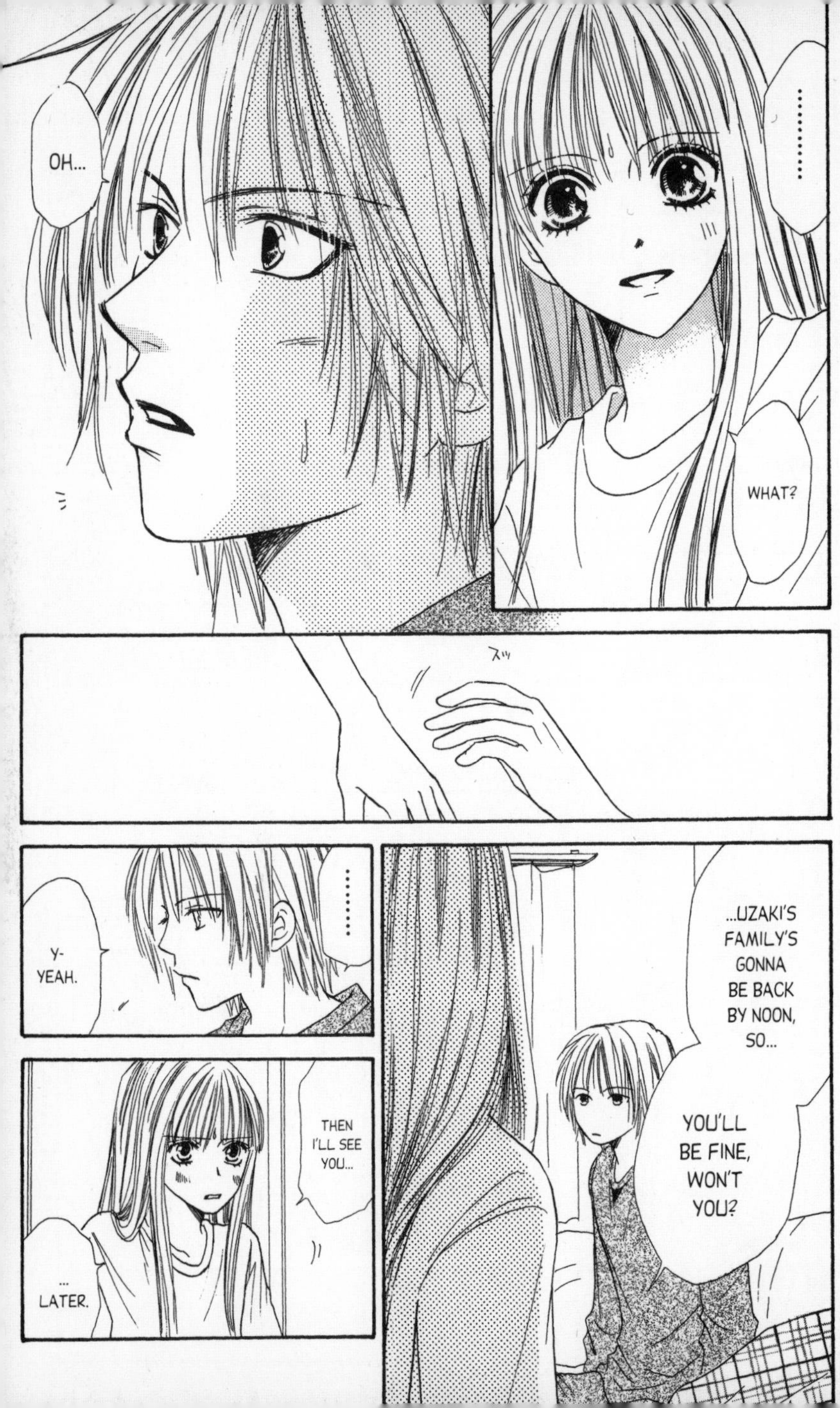
......
WHAT?
OH...
スッ
...UZAKI'S FAMILY'S GONNA BE BACK BY NOON, SO...
YOU'LL BE FINE, WON'T YOU?
......
Y- YEAH.
THEN I'LL SEE YOU...
... LATER.

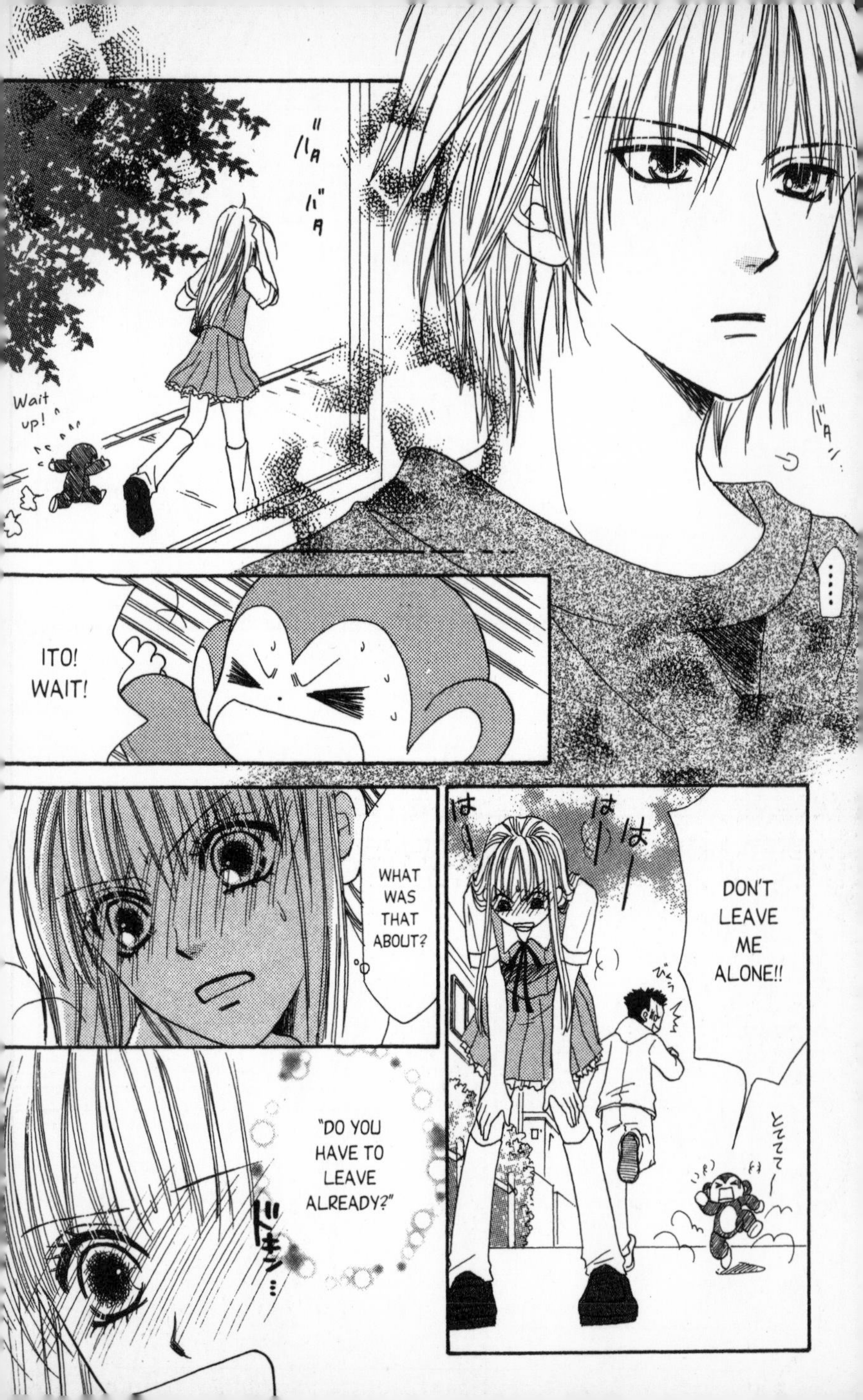
バッ
......
バタバタ
Wait up!
ITO! WAIT!
はーはーはー
DON'T LEAVE ME ALONE!!
びくっ
とてててー
WHAT WAS THAT ABOUT?
"DO YOU HAVE TO LEAVE ALREADY?"
ドキン...

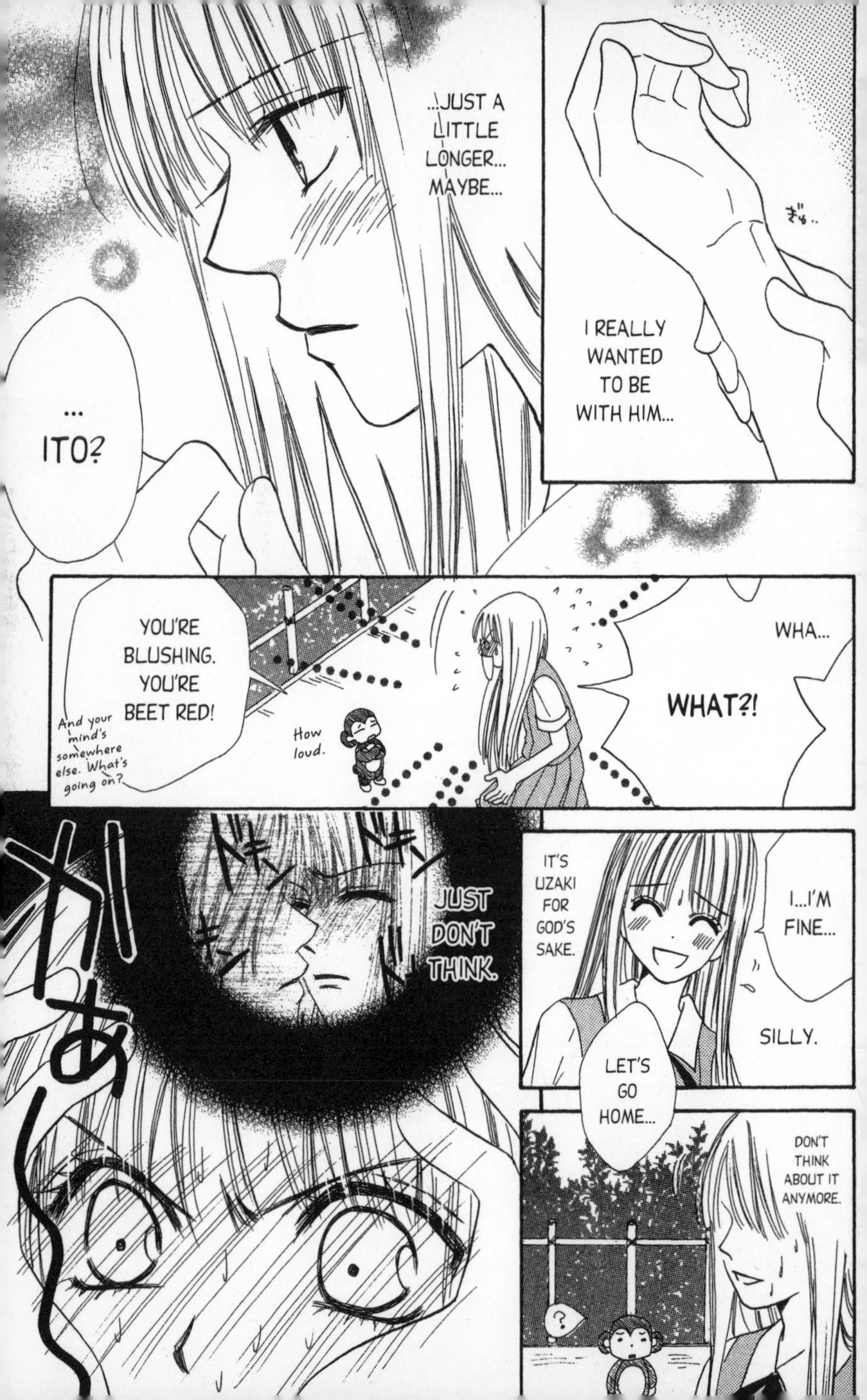
I REALLY WANTED TO BE WITH HIM...
...JUST A LITTLE LONGER... MAYBE...
... ITO?
WHA...
WHAT?!
YOU'RE BLUSHING. YOU'RE BEET RED!
And your mind's somewhere else. What's going on?
How loud.
I...I'M FINE...
SILLY.
IT'S UZAKI FOR GOD'S SAKE.
JUST DON'T THINK.
LET'S GO HOME...
DON'T THINK ABOUT IT ANYMORE.

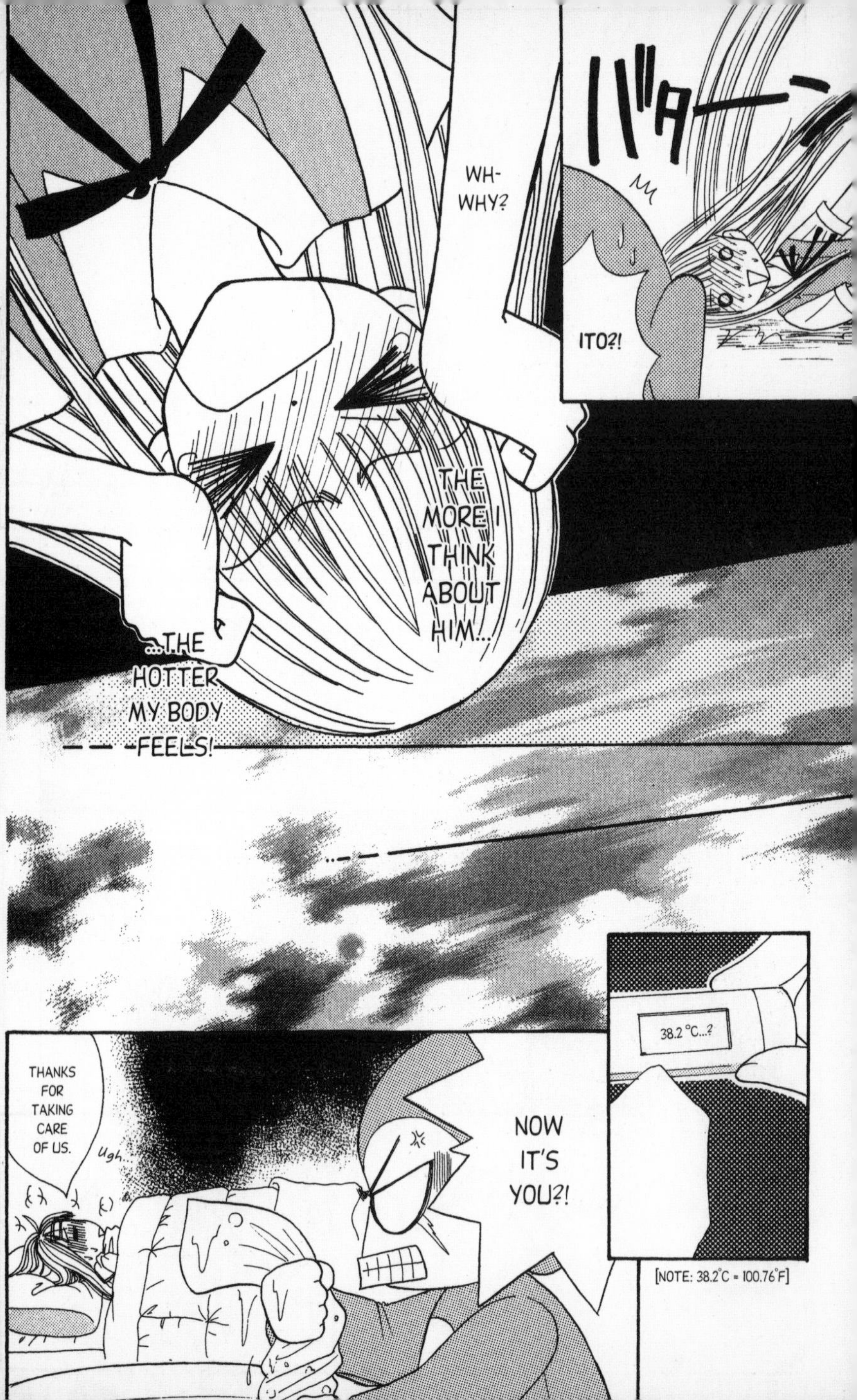
バタ―ン
ITO?!
WH- WHY?
THE MORE I THINK ABOUT HIM...
...THE HOTTER MY BODY FEELS!
38.2 °C...?
NOW IT'S YOU?!
THANKS FOR TAKING CARE OF US.
Ugh...
[NOTE: 38.2°C = 100.76°F]

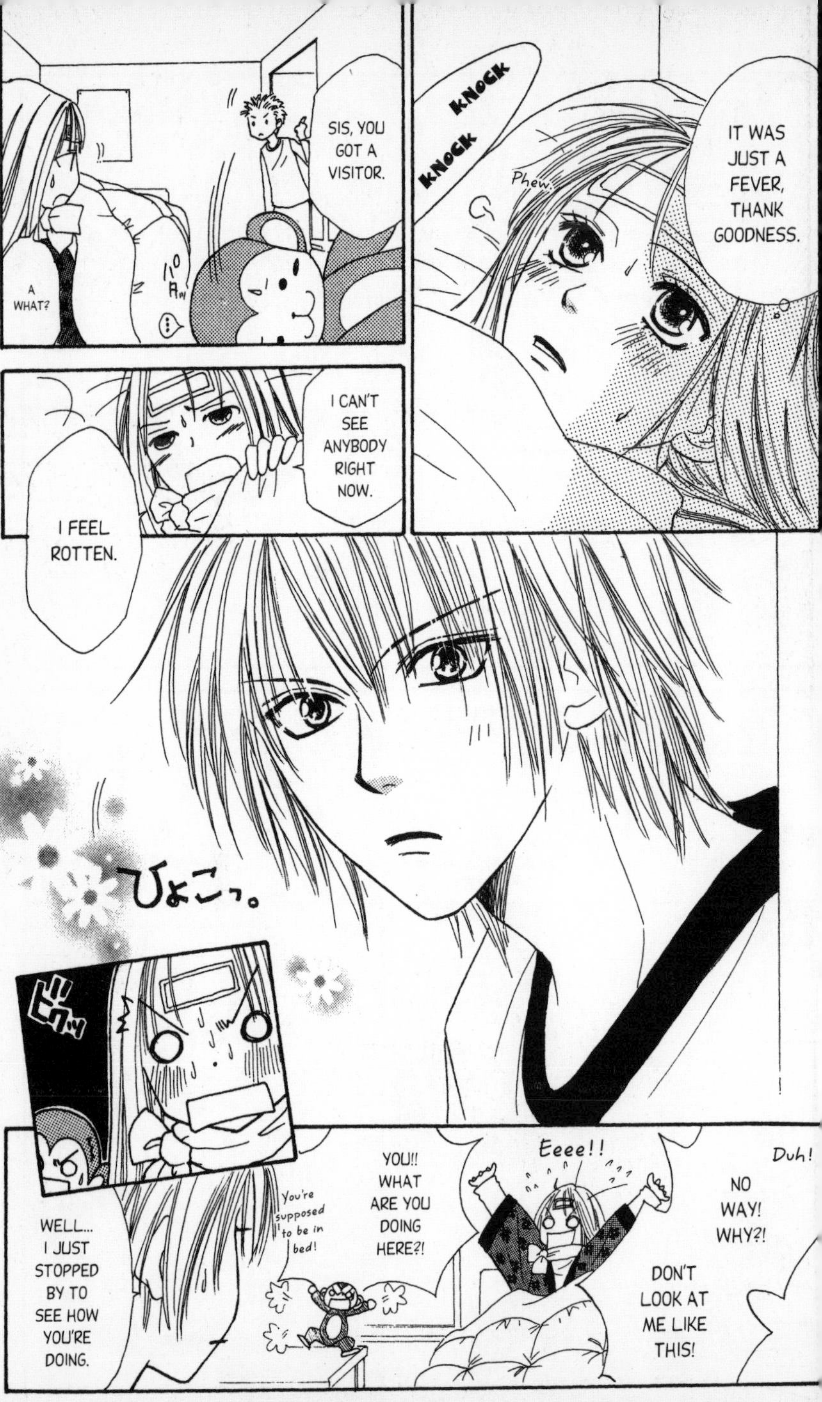
IT WAS JUST A FEVER, THANK GOODNESS.
Phew.
KNOCK KNOCK
SIS, YOU GOT A VISITOR.
A WHAT?
I CAN'T SEE ANYBODY RIGHT NOW.
I FEEL ROTTEN.
ひよこっ。
Duh!
NO WAY! WHY?!
DON'T LOOK AT ME LIKE THIS!
Eeee!!
YOU!! WHAT ARE YOU DOING HERE?!
You're supposed to be in bed!
WELL... I JUST STOPPED BY TO SEE HOW YOU'RE DOING.

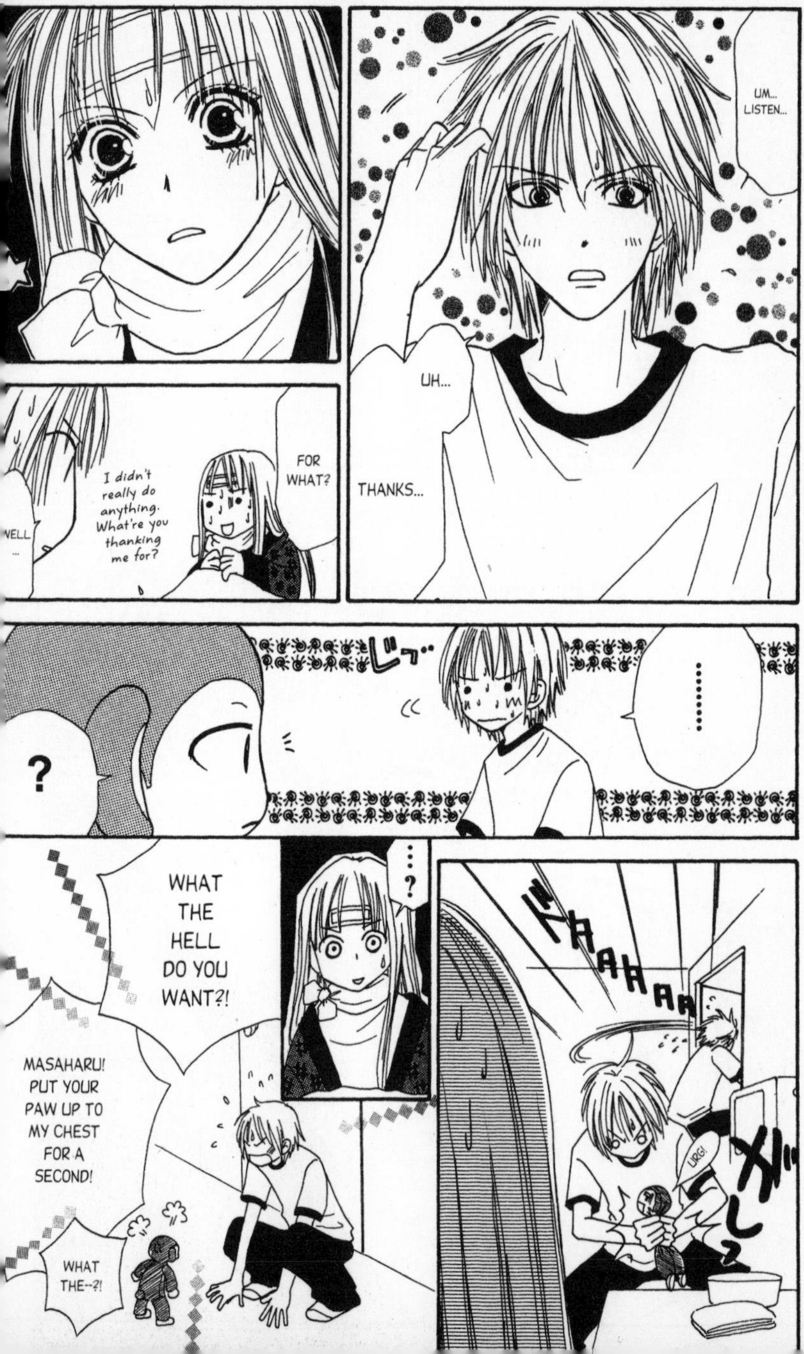
UM... LISTEN...
UH...
THANKS...
FOR WHAT?
I didn't really do anything. What're you thanking me for?
WELL ...
....
?
...?
WHAT THE HELL DO YOU WANT?!
MASAHARU! PUT YOUR PAW UP TO MY CHEST FOR A SECOND!
WHAT THE--?!
URG!

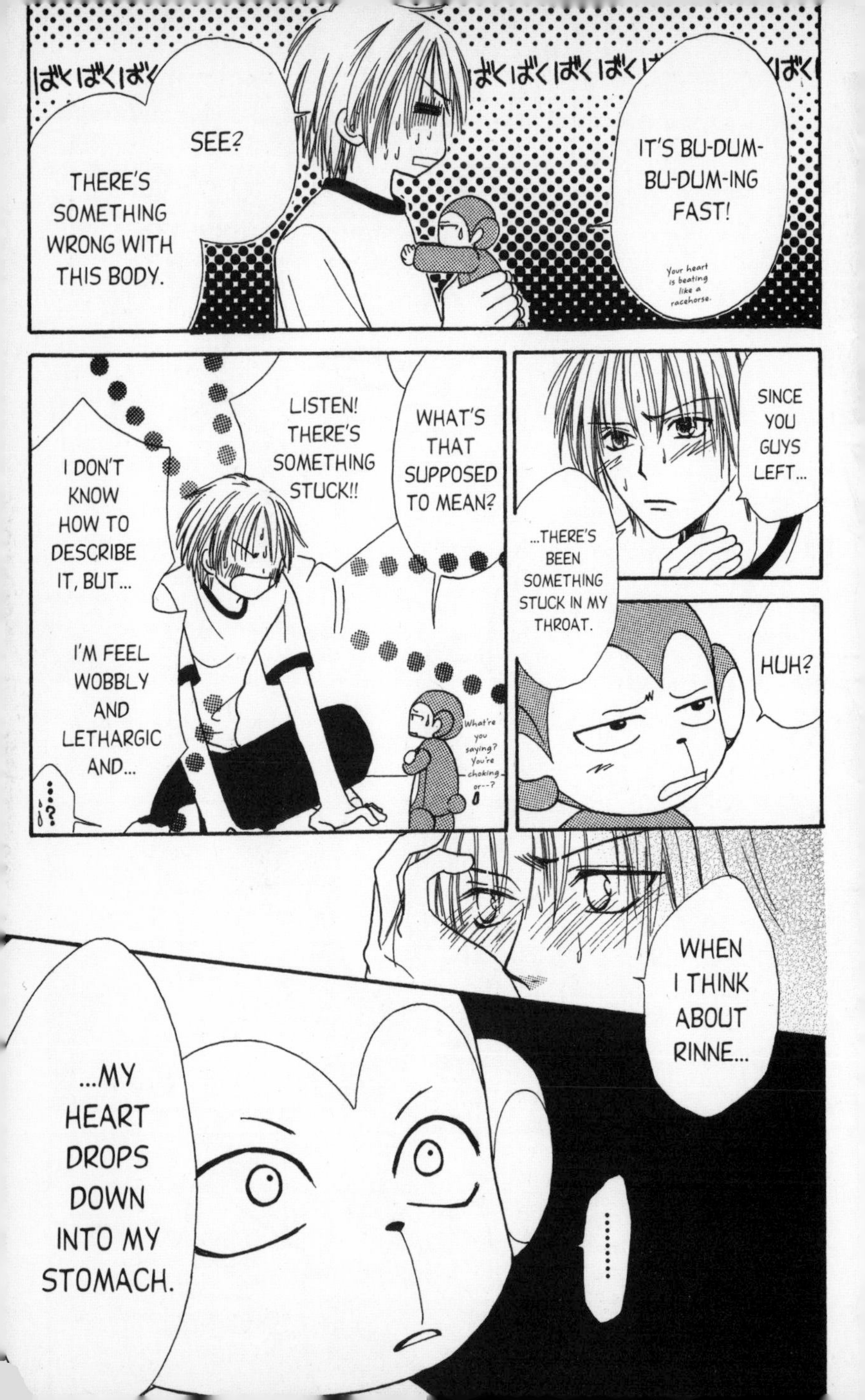
ばくばくばくばく
IT'S BU-DUM-BU-DUM-ING FAST!
Your heart is beating like a racehorse.
ばくばくばく
SEE?
THERE'S SOMETHING WRONG WITH THIS BODY.
SINCE YOU GUYS LEFT...
...THERE'S BEEN SOMETHING STUCK IN MY THROAT.
HUH?
WHAT'S THAT SUPPOSED TO MEAN?
LISTEN! THERE'S SOMETHING STUCK!!
I DON'T KNOW HOW TO DESCRIBE IT, BUT...
I'M FEEL WOBBLY AND LETHARGIC AND...
What're you saying? You're choking or--?
...?
WHEN I THINK ABOUT RINNE...
...MY HEART DROPS DOWN INTO MY STOMACH.
....

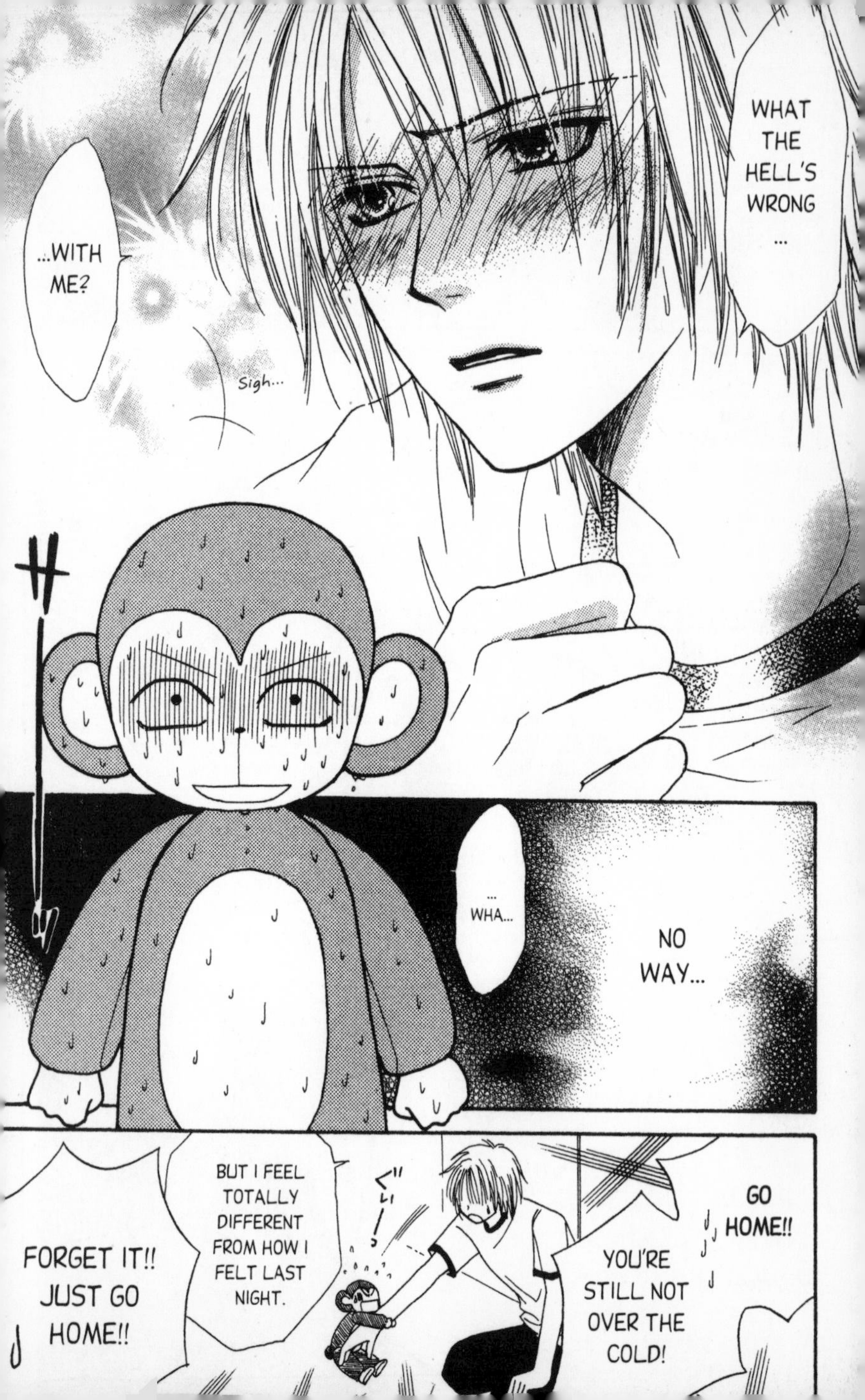
WHAT THE HELL'S WRONG ...
...WITH ME?
Sigh...
... WHA...
NO WAY...
GO HOME!!
YOU'RE STILL NOT OVER THE COLD!
BUT I FEEL TOTALLY DIFFERENT FROM HOW I FELT LAST NIGHT.
FORGET IT!! JUST GO HOME!!

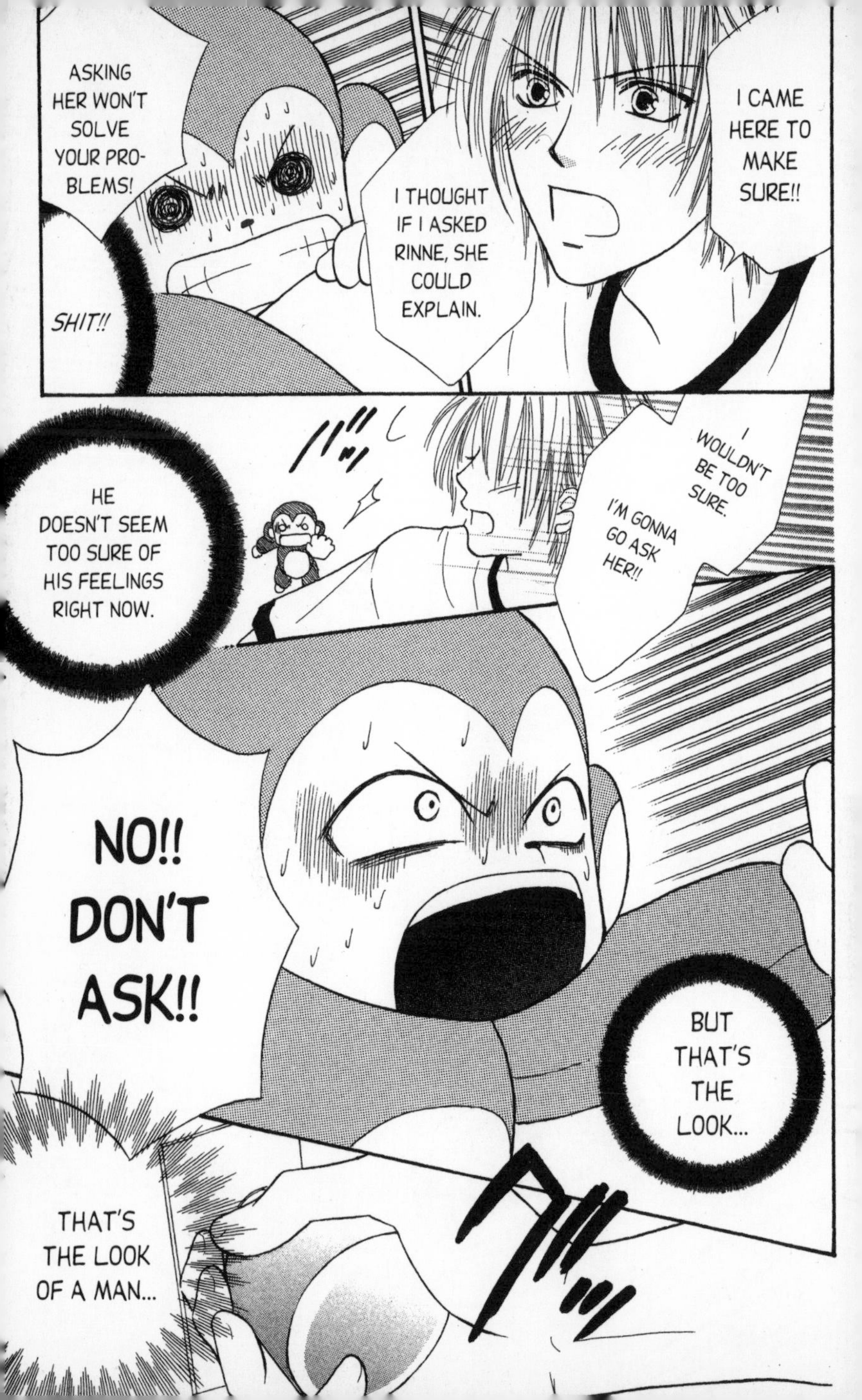
I CAME HERE TO MAKE SURE!!
I THOUGHT IF I ASKED RINNE, SHE COULD EXPLAIN.
ASKING HER WON'T SOLVE YOUR PRO-BLEMS!
SHIT!!
I WOULDN'T BE TOO SURE.
I'M GONNA GO ASK HER!!
HE DOESN'T SEEM TOO SURE OF HIS FEELINGS RIGHT NOW.
NO!! DON'T ASK!!
BUT THAT'S THE LOOK...
THAT'S THE LOOK OF A MAN...

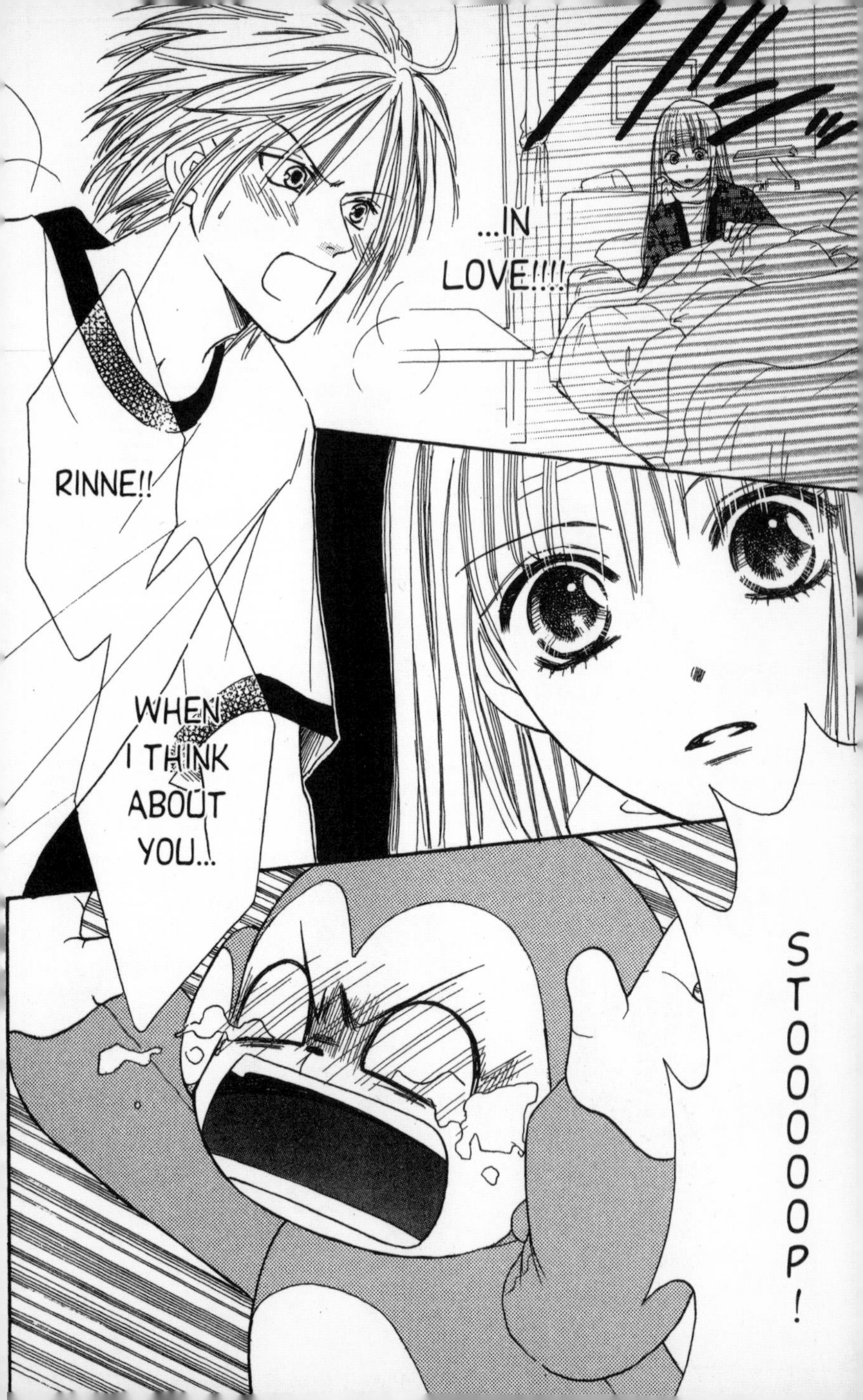
...IN LOVE!!!!
RINNE!!
WHEN I THINK ABOUT YOU...
STOOOOOOP!

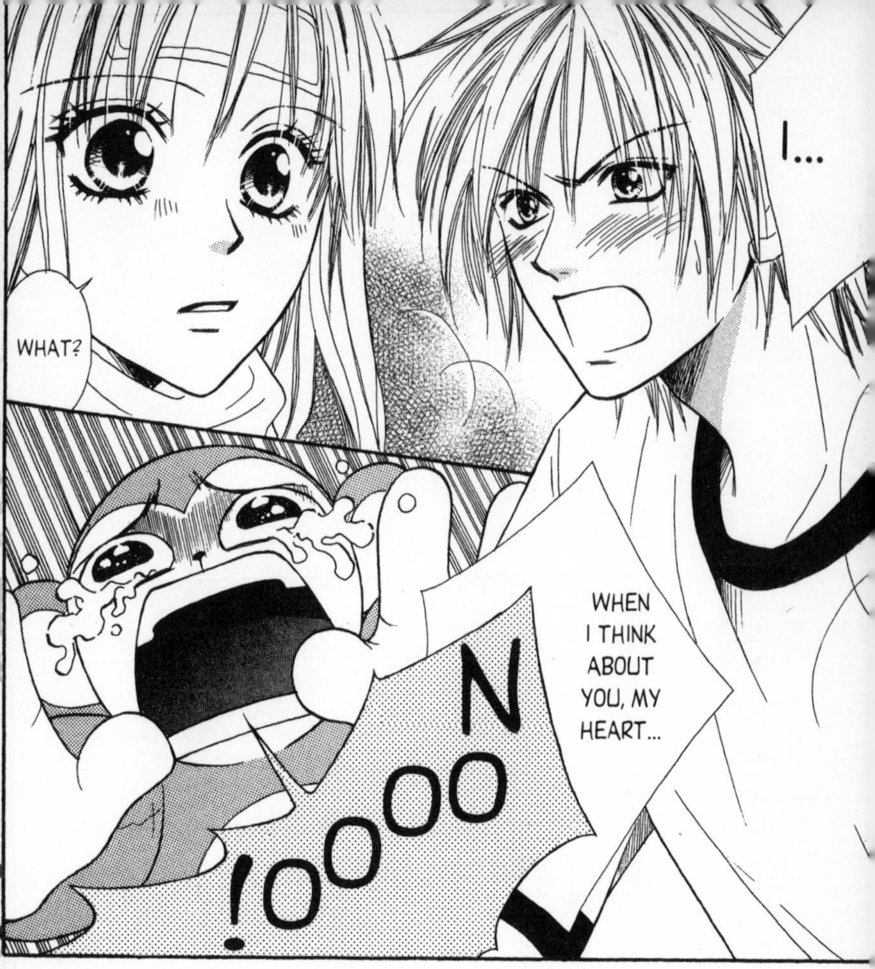
I...
WHAT?
WHEN I THINK ABOUT YOU, MY HEART...
NOOOOO!

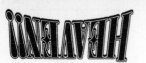

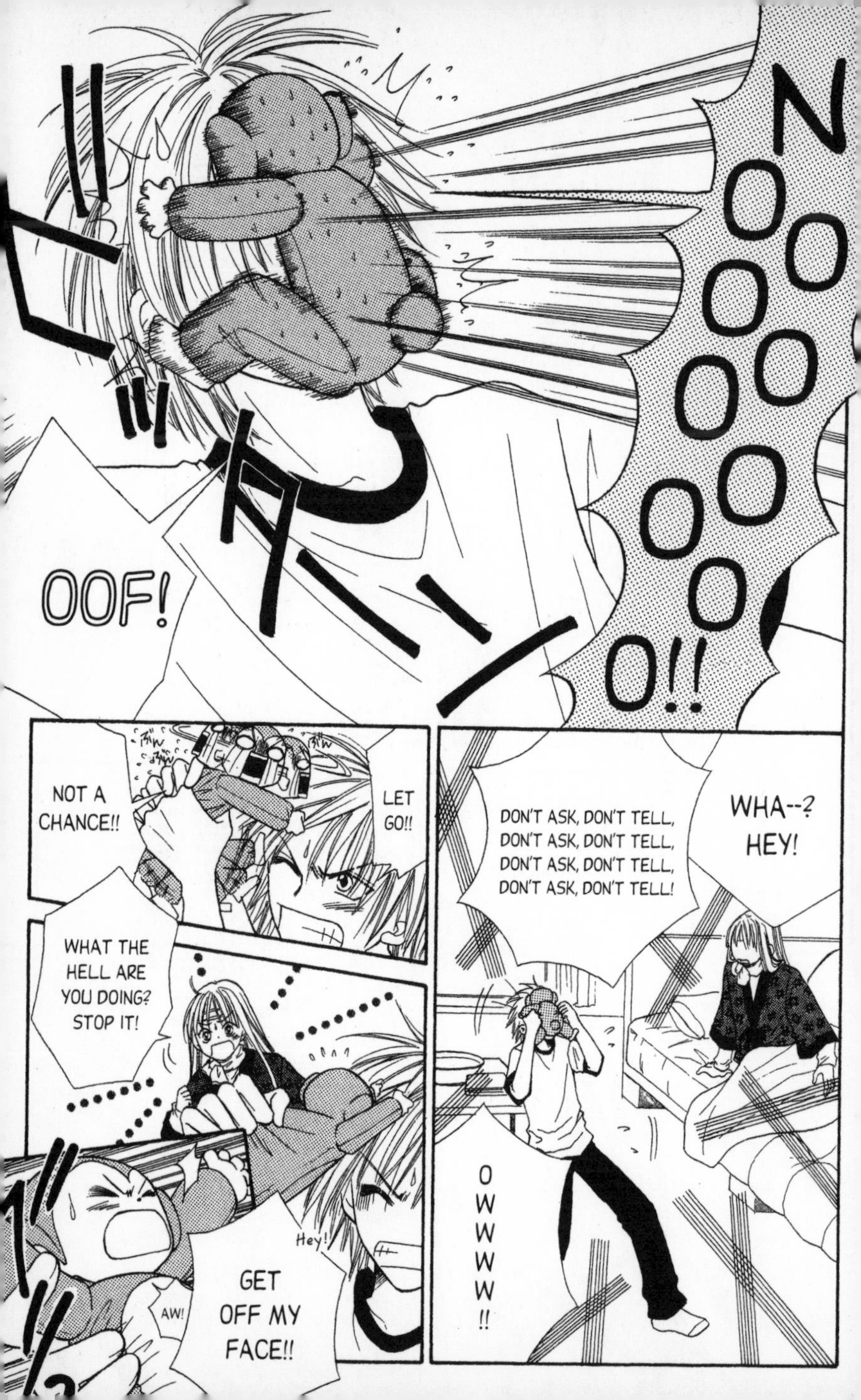
NOOOOOOOOOOOO!!
OOF!
WHA--? HEY!
DON'T ASK, DON'T TELL, DON'T ASK, DON'T TELL, DON'T ASK, DON'T TELL, DON'T ASK, DON'T TELL!
OWWWW!!
NOT A CHANCE!!
LET GO!!
WHAT THE HELL ARE YOU DOING? STOP IT!
Hey!
GET OFF MY FACE!!
AW!

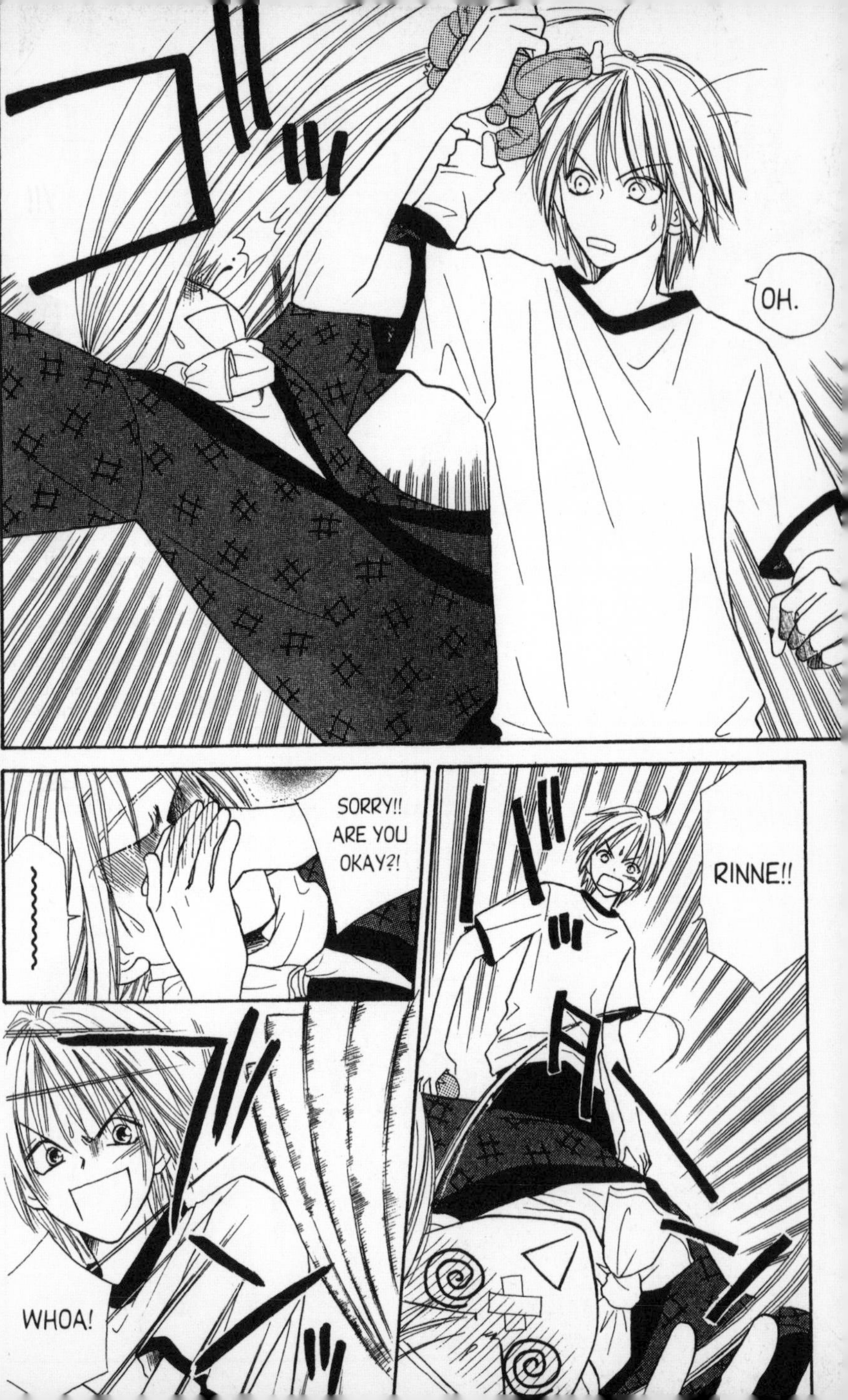
OH.
RINNE!!
SORRY!! ARE YOU OKAY?!
~~~~~~
WHOA!
~~~~~~

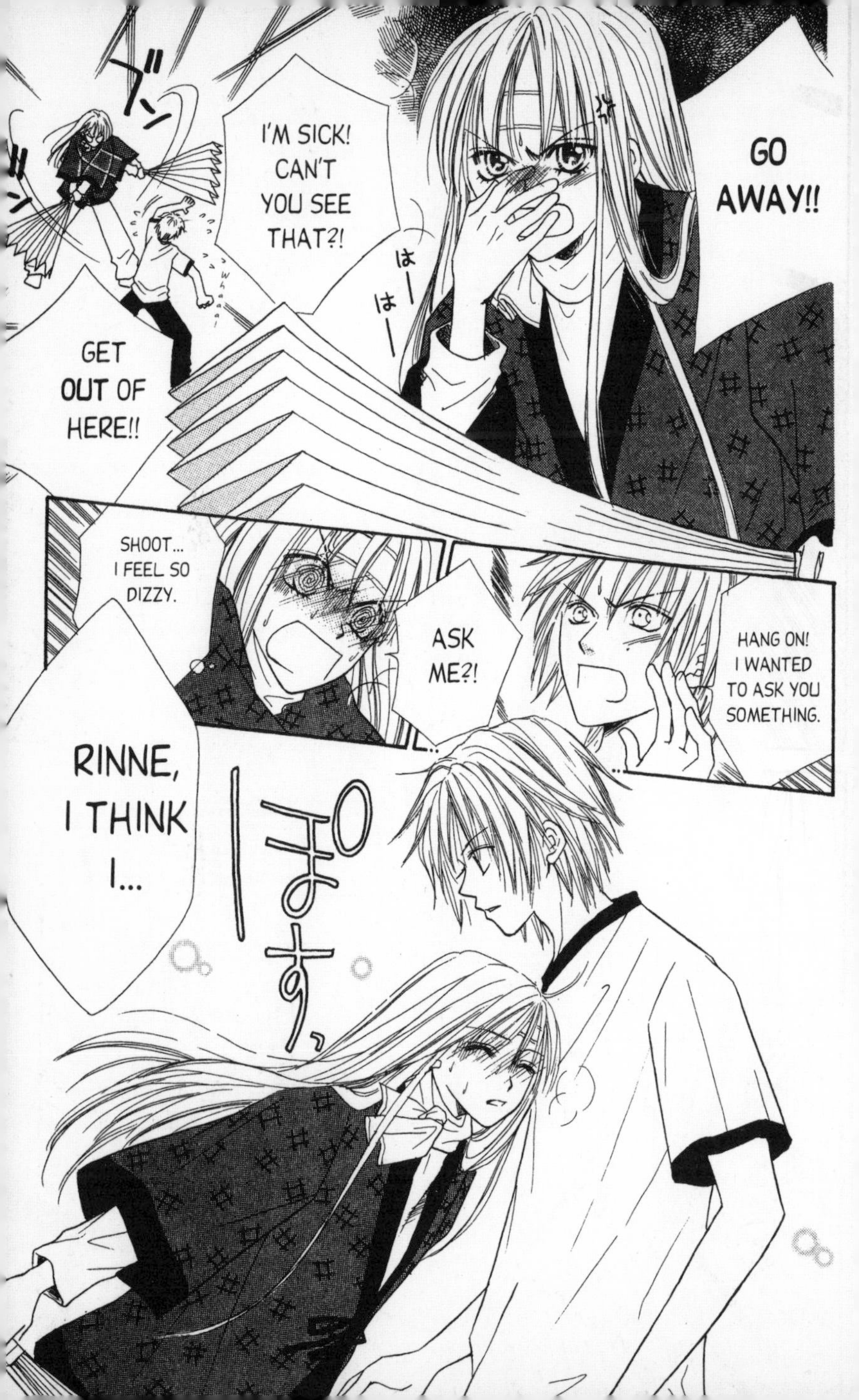
GO AWAY!!
はーはー
I'M SICK! CAN'T YOU SEE THAT?!
ズン
GET OUT OF HERE!!
HANG ON! I WANTED TO ASK YOU SOMETHING.
ASK ME?!
SHOOT... I FEEL SO DIZZY.
ぽすっ
RINNE, I THINK I...

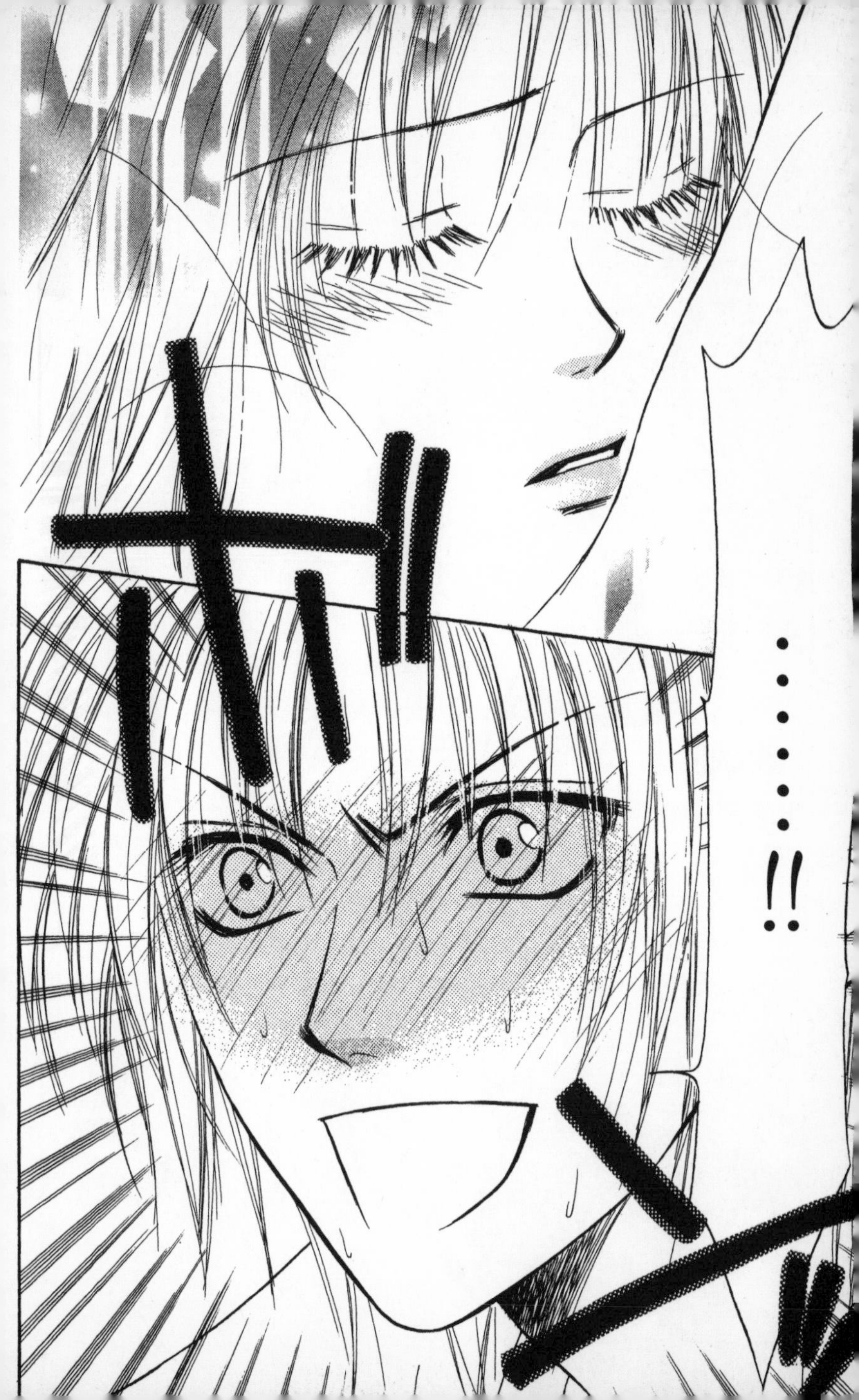
ガ
……!!

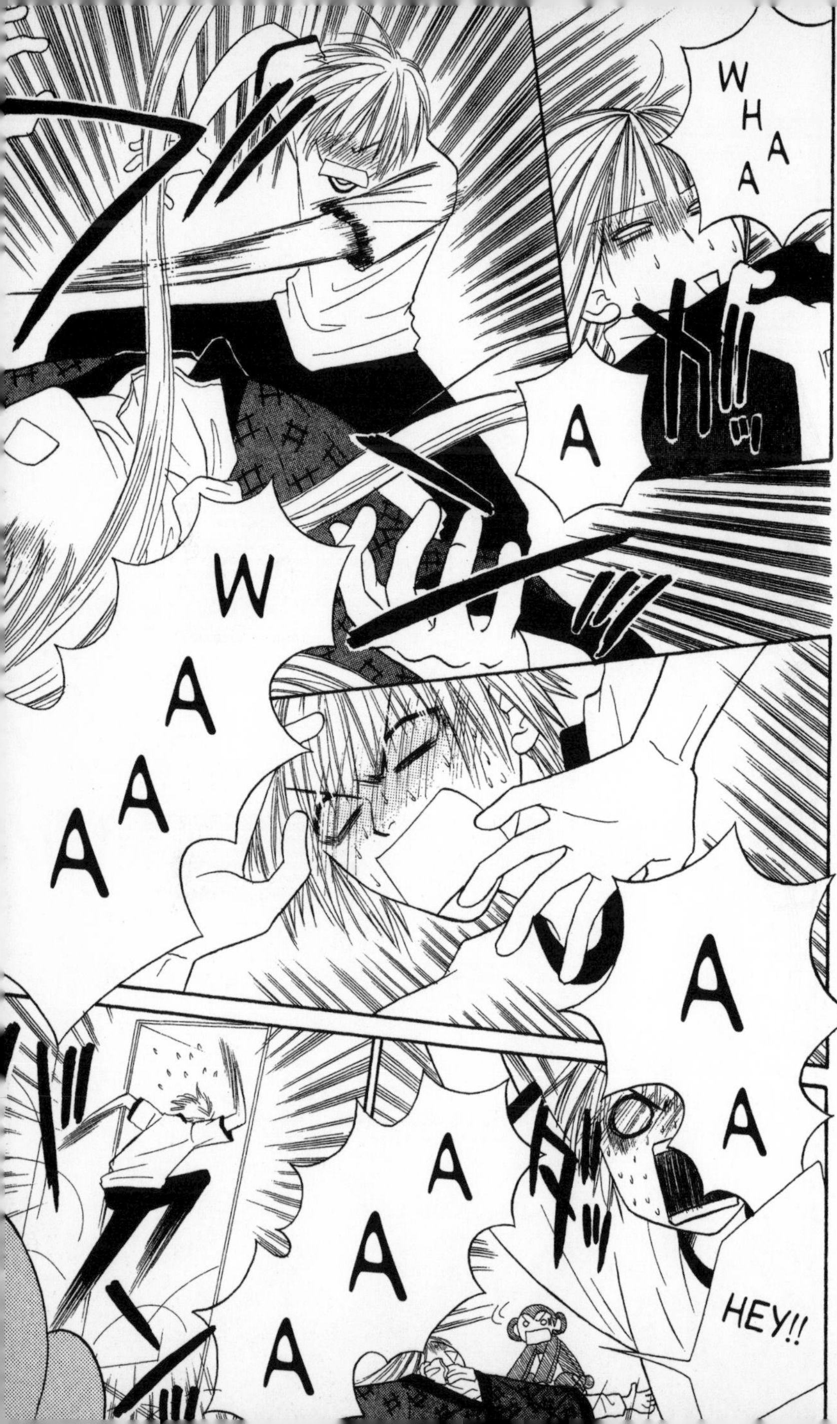
WHAA
A
WAAA
AA
AAAA
HEY!!

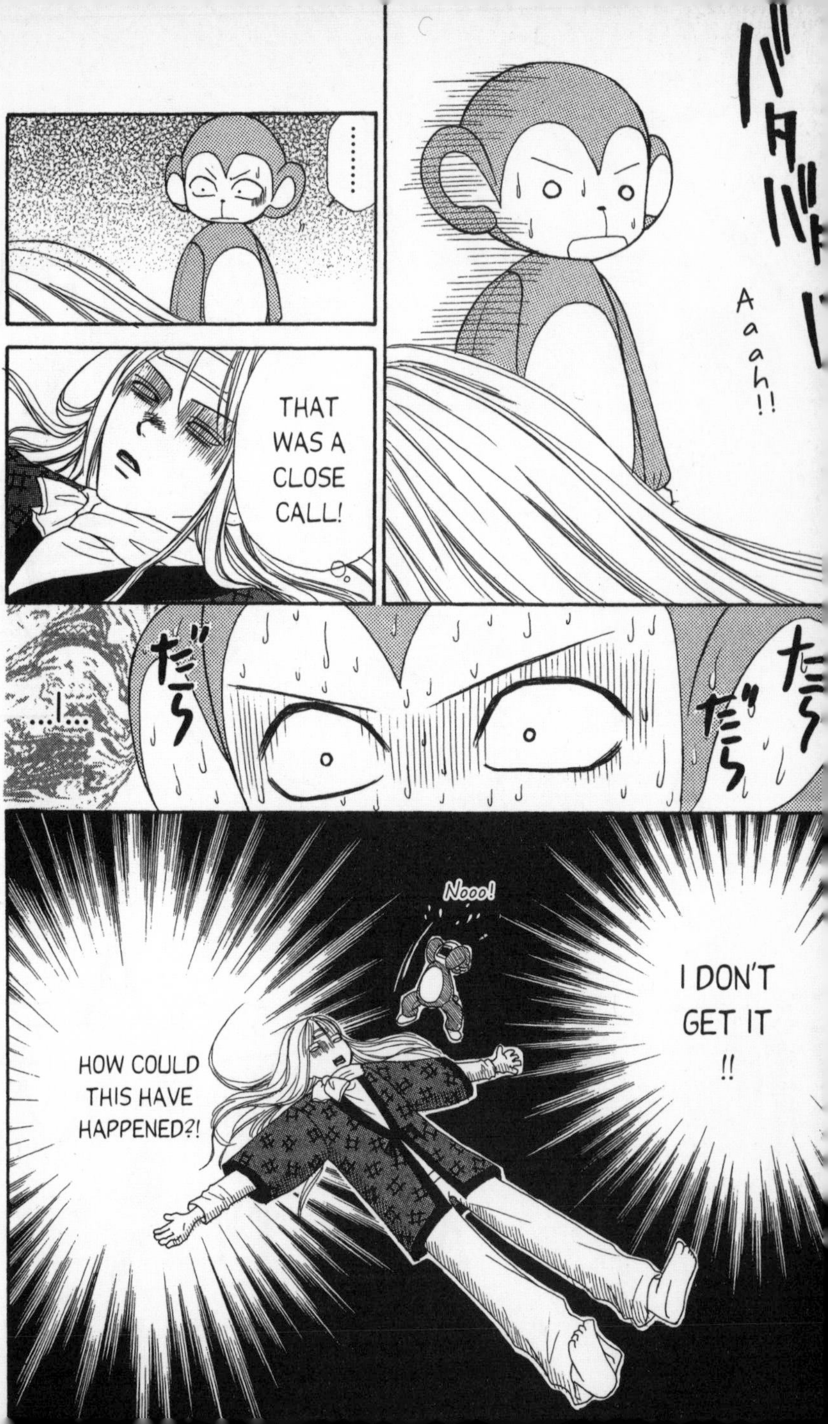
バタバ
Aaah!!
......
THAT WAS A CLOSE CALL!
だらだら
だら
...I...
I DON'T GET IT !!
Nooo!
HOW COULD THIS HAVE HAPPENED?!

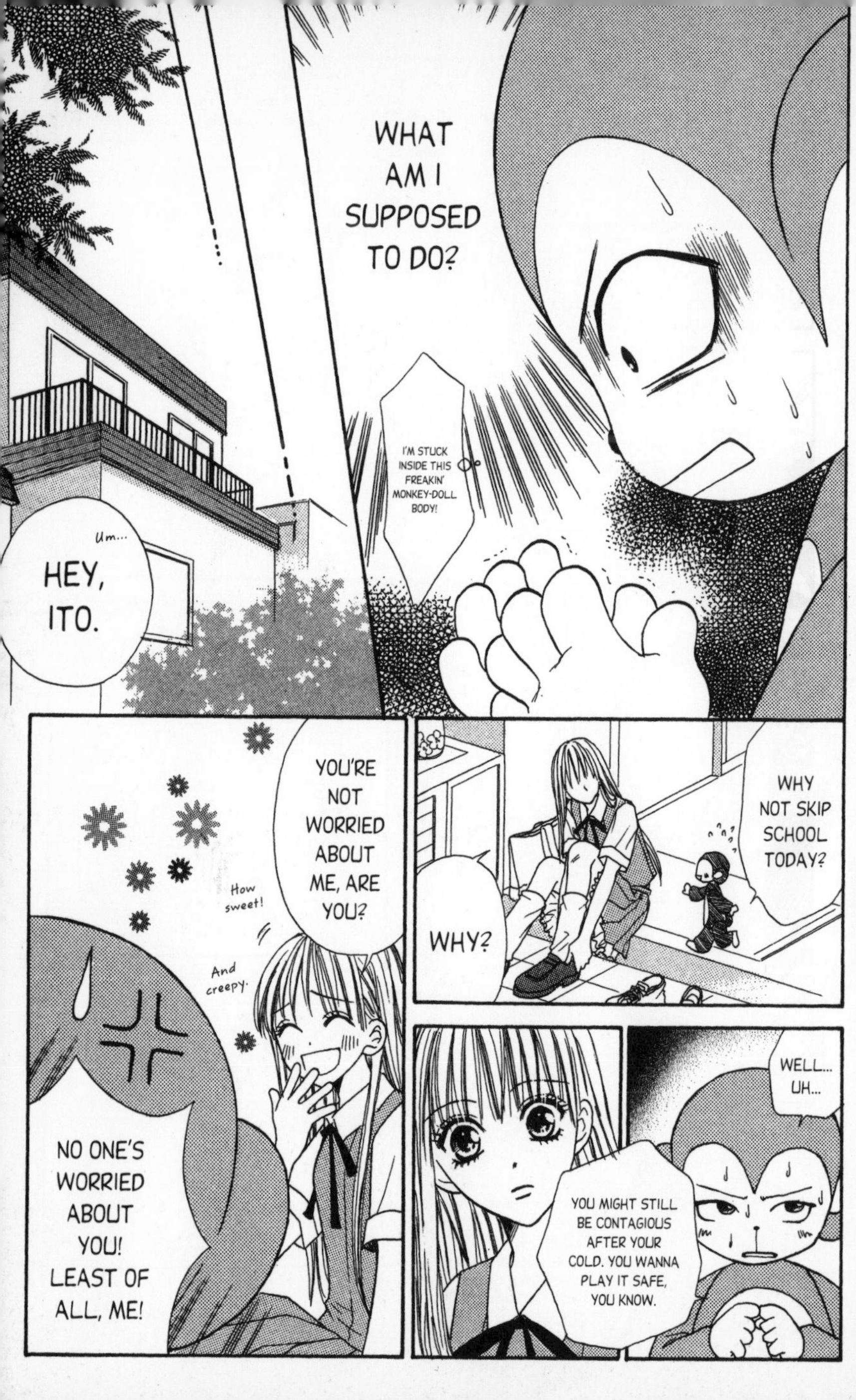
WHAT AM I SUPPOSED TO DO?
I'M STUCK INSIDE THIS FREAKIN' MONKEY-DOLL BODY!
Um...
HEY, ITO.
WHY NOT SKIP SCHOOL TODAY?
WHY?
WELL... UH...
YOU MIGHT STILL BE CONTAGIOUS AFTER YOUR COLD. YOU WANNA PLAY IT SAFE, YOU KNOW.
YOU'RE NOT WORRIED ABOUT ME, ARE YOU?
How sweet!
And creepy.
NO ONE'S WORRIED ABOUT YOU! LEAST OF ALL, ME!

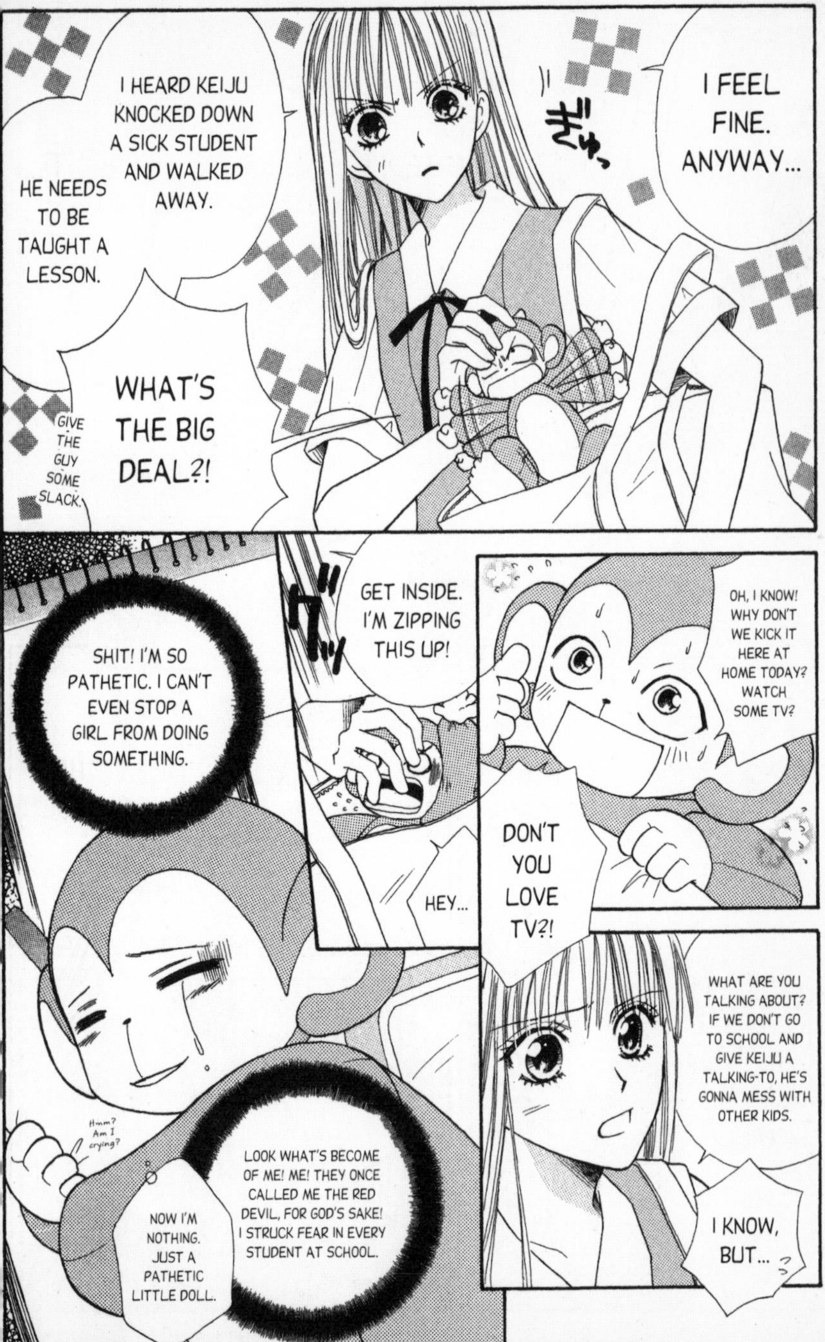
I FEEL FINE. ANYWAY...
I HEARD KEIJU KNOCKED DOWN A SICK STUDENT AND WALKED AWAY.
HE NEEDS TO BE TAUGHT A LESSON.
WHAT'S THE BIG DEAL?!
GIVE THE GUY SOME SLACK.
OH, I KNOW! WHY DON'T WE KICK IT HERE AT HOME TODAY? WATCH SOME TV?
DON'T YOU LOVE TV?!
WHAT ARE YOU TALKING ABOUT? IF WE DON'T GO TO SCHOOL AND GIVE KEIJU A TALKING-TO, HE'S GONNA MESS WITH OTHER KIDS.
I KNOW, BUT...
GET INSIDE. I'M ZIPPING THIS UP!
HEY...
SHIT! I'M SO PATHETIC. I CAN'T EVEN STOP A GIRL FROM DOING SOMETHING.
LOOK WHAT'S BECOME OF ME! ME! THEY ONCE CALLED ME THE RED DEVIL, FOR GOD'S SAKE! I STRUCK FEAR IN EVERY STUDENT AT SCHOOL.
NOW I'M NOTHING. JUST A PATHETIC LITTLE DOLL.
Hmm? Am I crying?

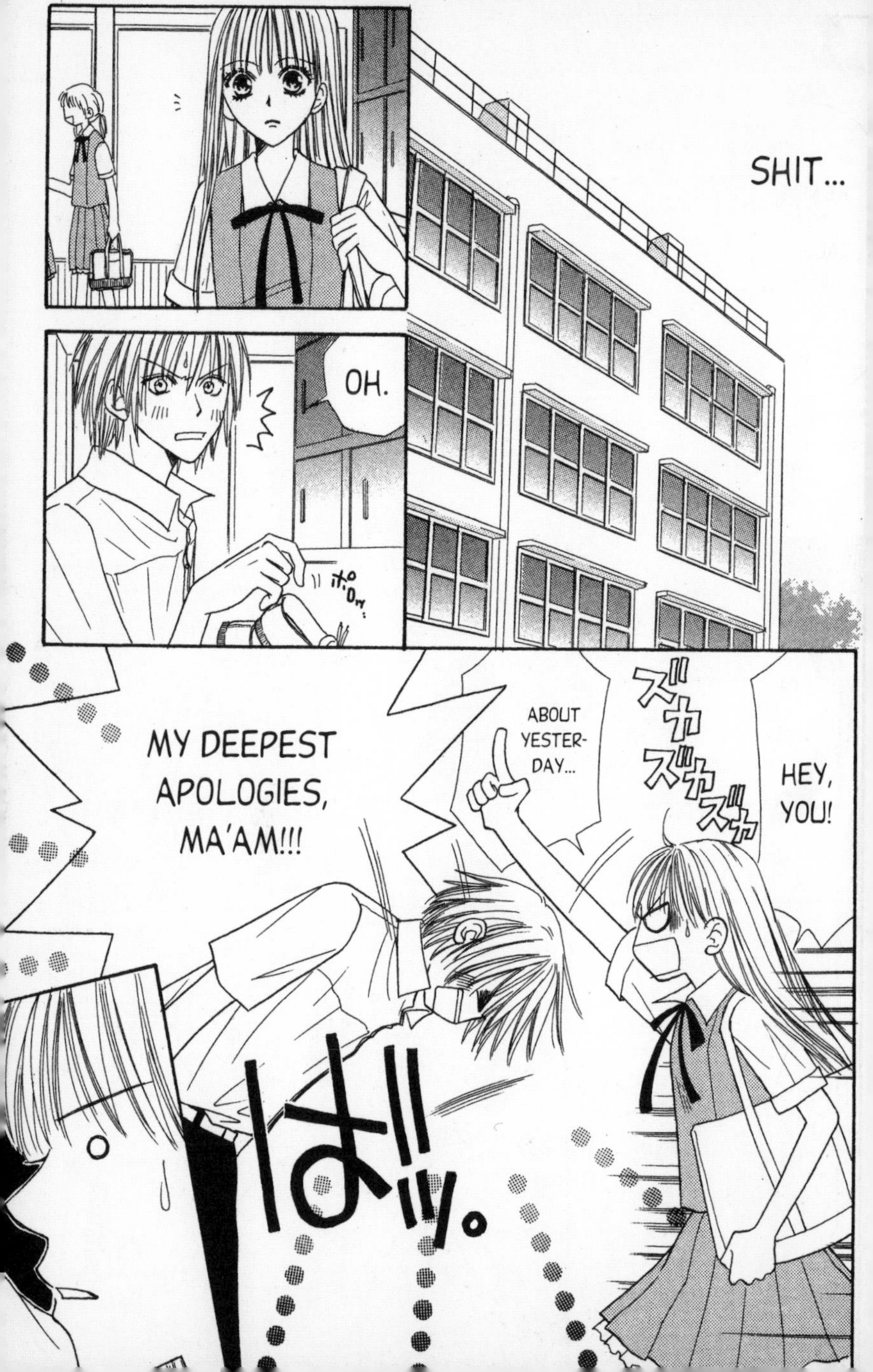
SHIT...
OH.
HEY, YOU!
ズカズカズカ
ABOUT YESTER-DAY...
MY DEEPEST APOLOGIES, MA'AM!!!
は!!。

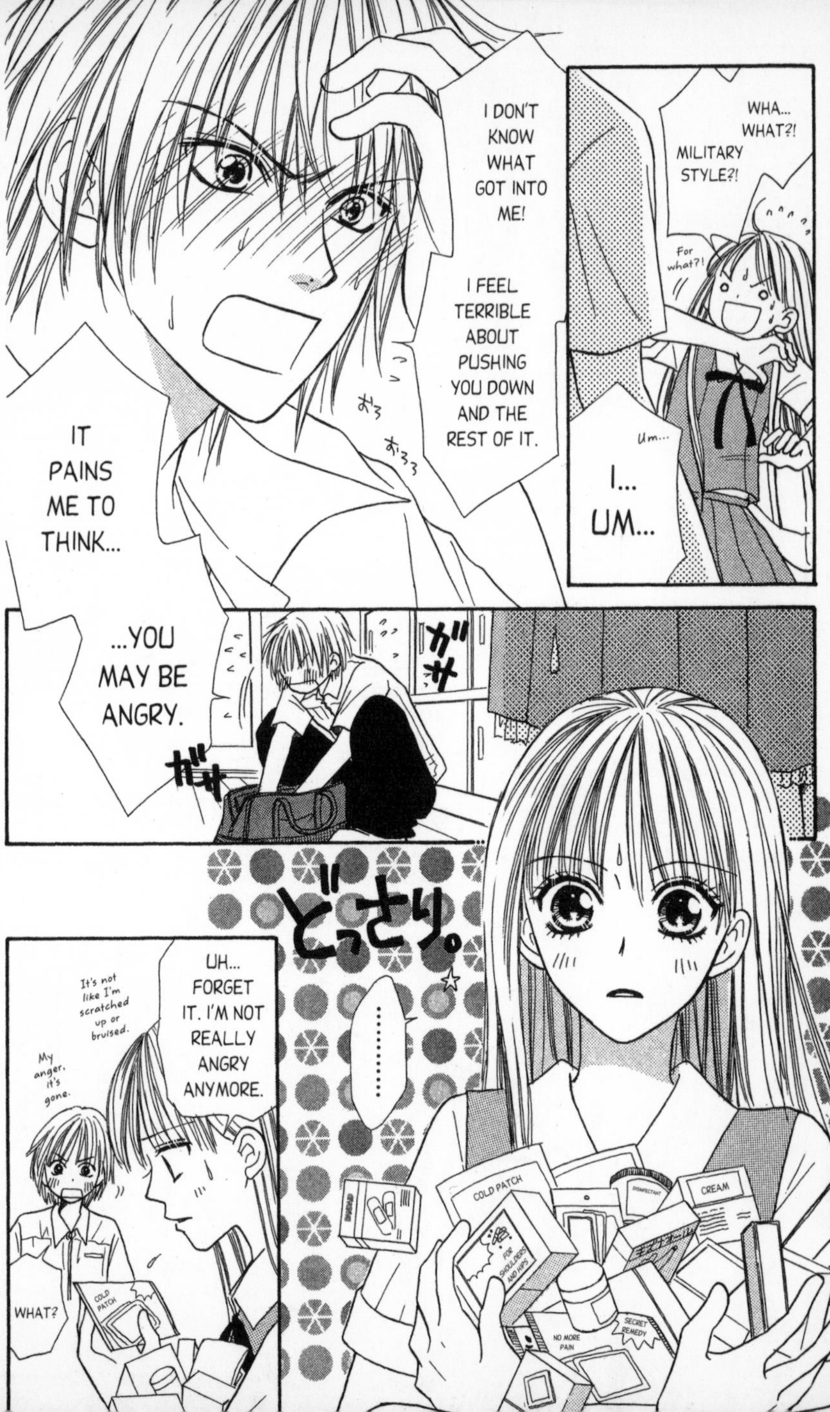
WHA... WHAT?!
MILITARY STYLE?!
For what?!
Um...
I... UM...
I DON'T KNOW WHAT GOT INTO ME!
I FEEL TERRIBLE ABOUT PUSHING YOU DOWN AND THE REST OF IT.
IT PAINS ME TO THINK...
...YOU MAY BE ANGRY.
どっさり。
......
UH... FORGET IT. I'M NOT REALLY ANGRY ANYMORE.
It's not like I'm scratched up or bruised.
My anger, it's gone.
WHAT?
COLD PATCH
CREAM
DISINFECTANT
FOR SHOULDERS AND HIPS
NO MORE PAIN
SECRET REMEDY

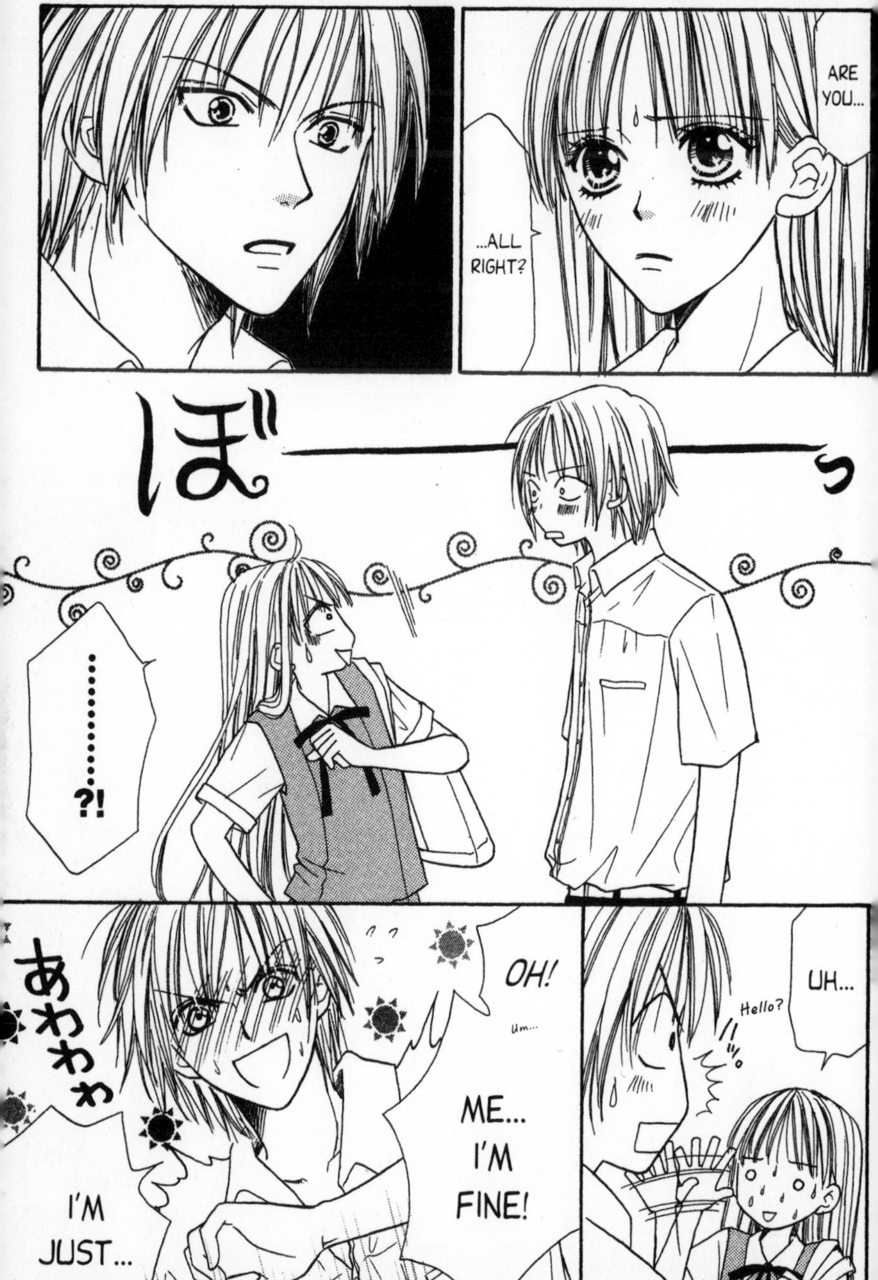
ARE YOU...
...ALL RIGHT?
ぼーーっ
......?!
UH...
Hello?
OH!
Um...
ME... I'M FINE!
あわわゎ
I'M JUST... UH...

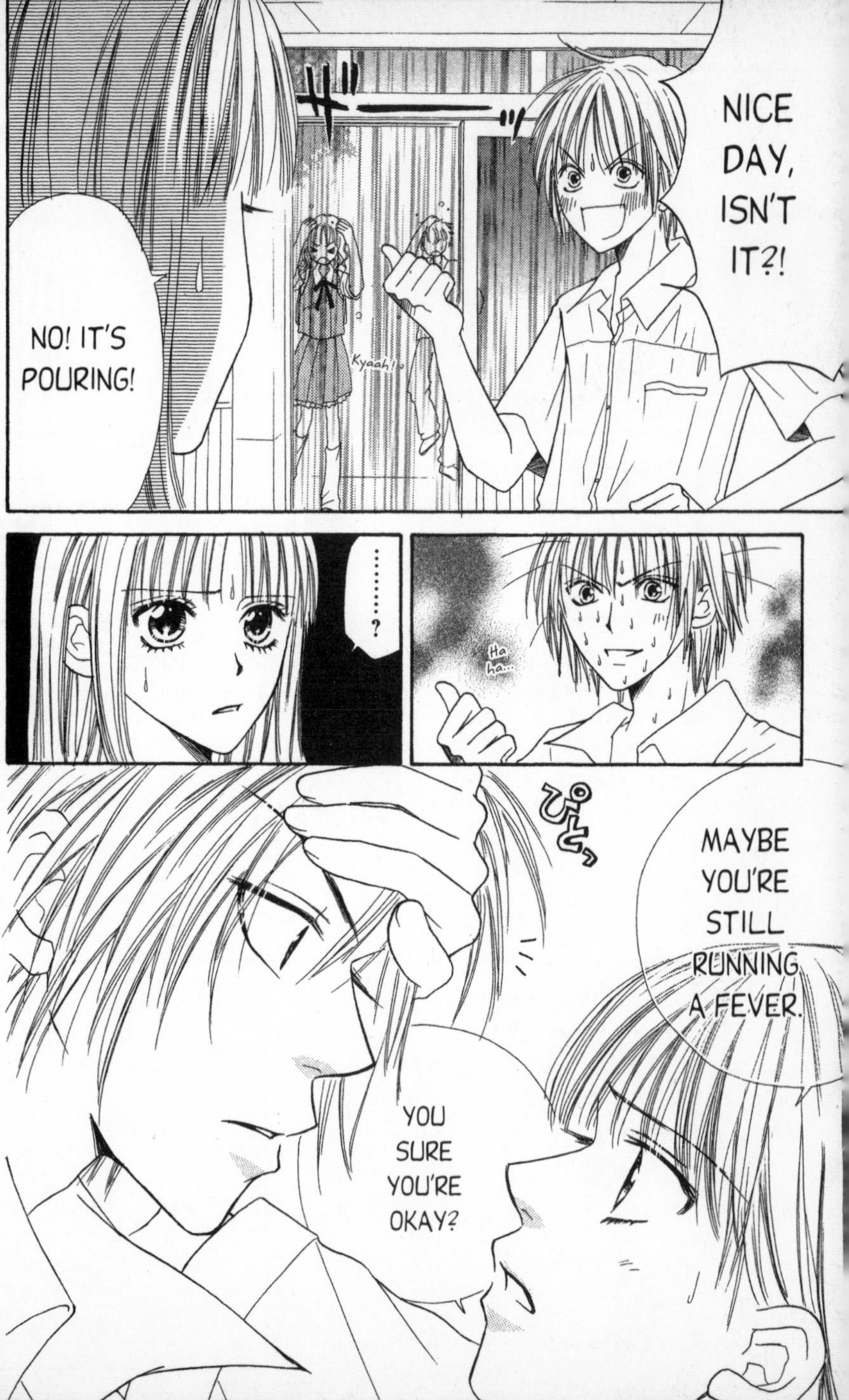
NICE DAY, ISN'T IT?!
Kyaah!♪
NO! IT'S POURING!
Ha ha...
......?
MAYBE YOU'RE STILL RUNNING A FEVER.
ぴとっ
YOU SURE YOU'RE OKAY?

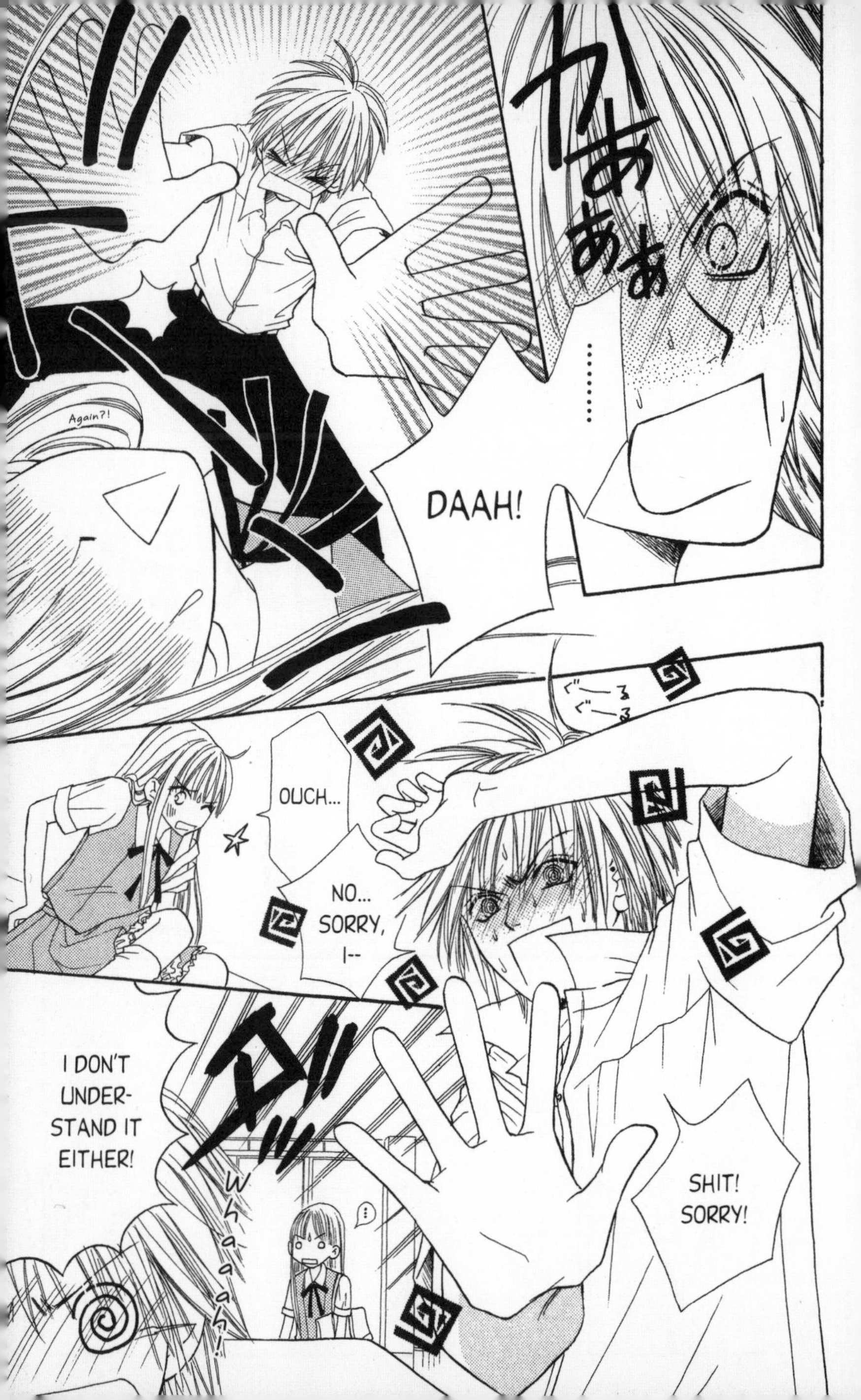
......
DAAH!
Again?!
OUCH...
NO... SORRY, I--
SHIT! SORRY!
ダッ
Whaaaah!
I DON'T UNDER-STAND IT EITHER!

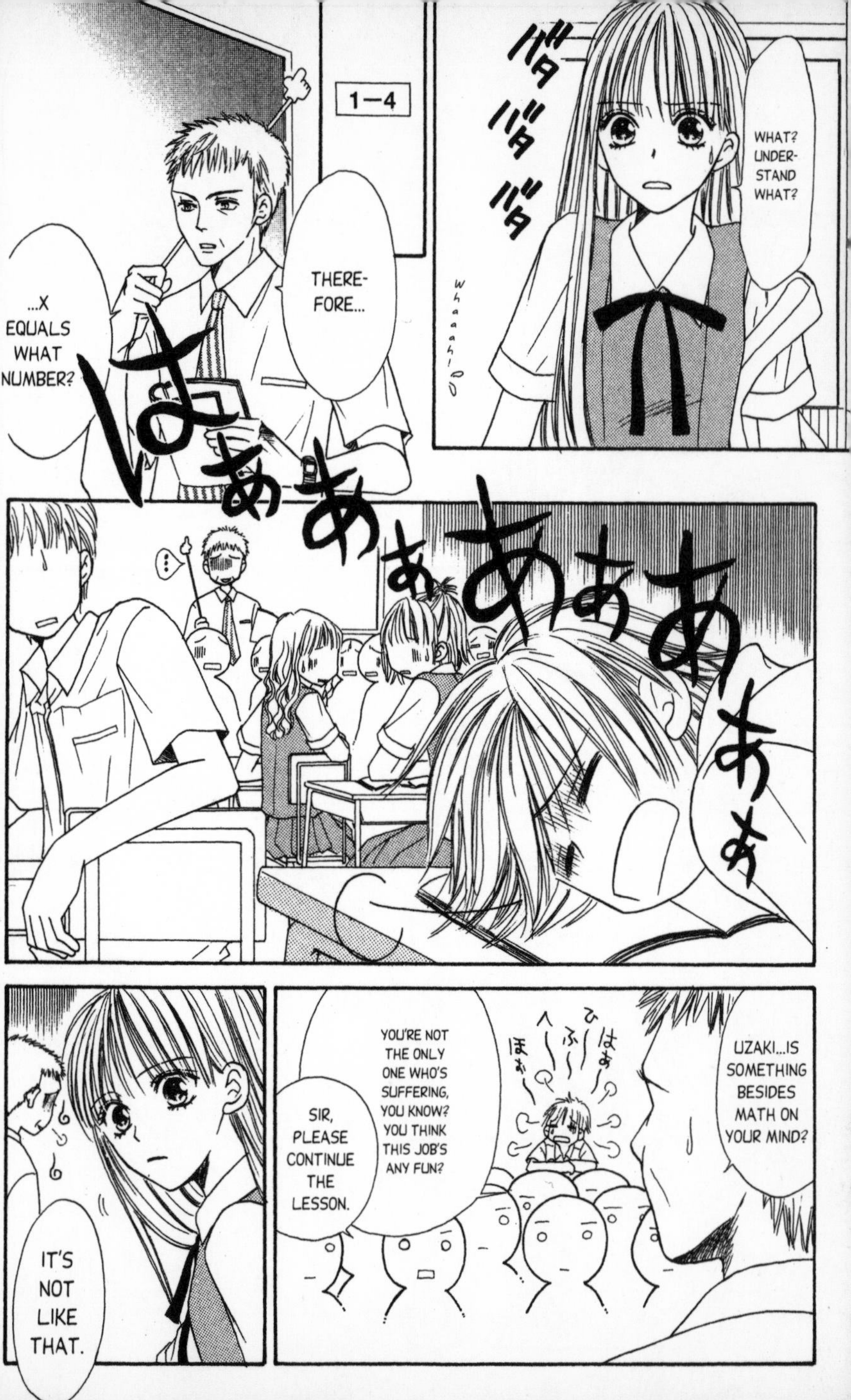

WHAT? UNDER-STAND WHAT?
バタバタバタ
Whaaaah!
1—4
THERE-FORE...
...X EQUALS WHAT NUMBER?
はぁぁぁぁぁぁぁ
...
UZAKI...IS SOMETHING BESIDES MATH ON YOUR MIND?
はぁ～ ひ～ ふ～ へ～ ほぉ～
YOU'RE NOT THE ONLY ONE WHO'S SUFFERING, YOU KNOW? YOU THINK THIS JOB'S ANY FUN?
SIR, PLEASE CONTINUE THE LESSON.
IT'S NOT LIKE THAT.

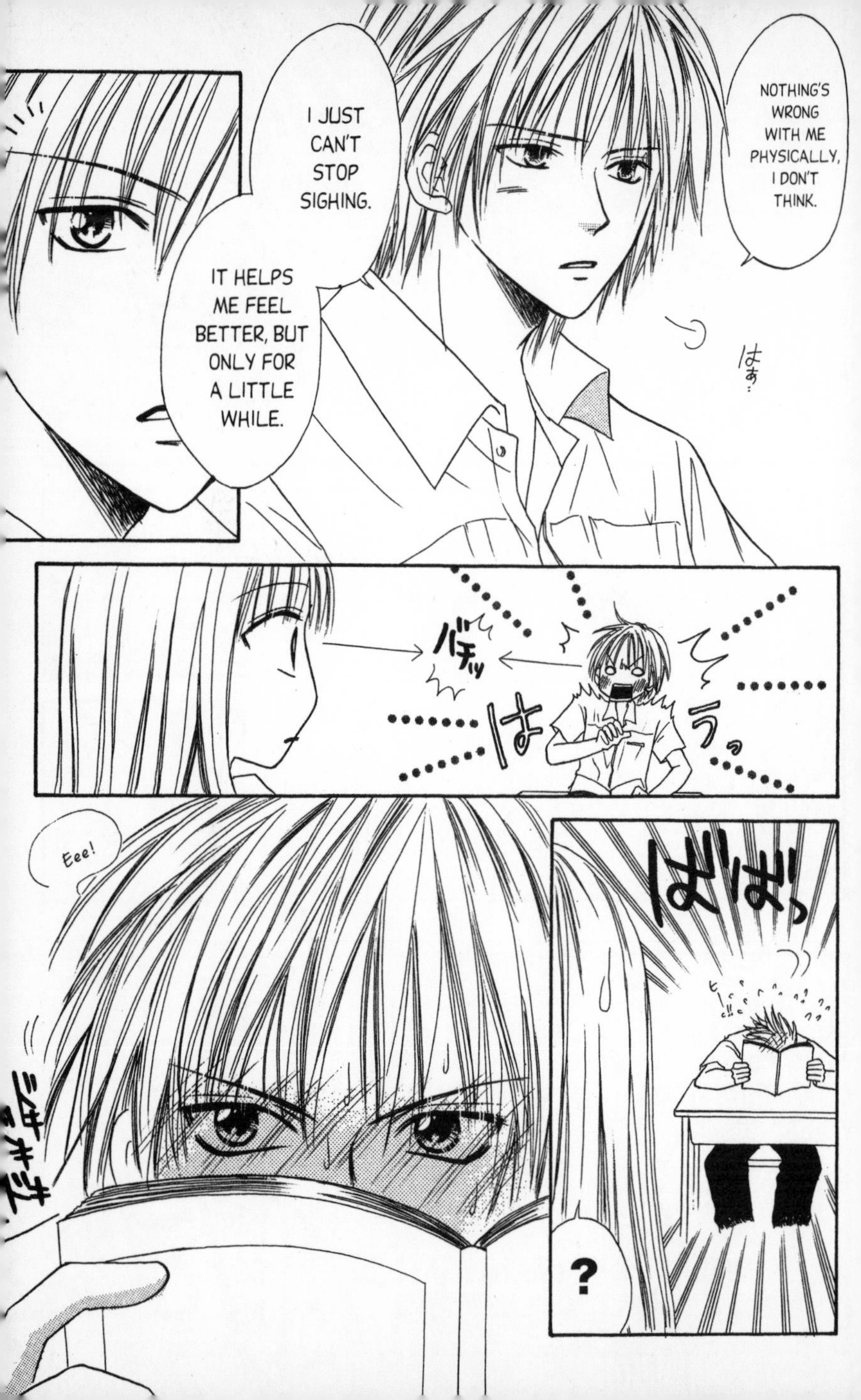
NOTHING'S WRONG WITH ME PHYSICALLY, I DON'T THINK.
はぁ…
I JUST CAN'T STOP SIGHING.
IT HELPS ME FEEL BETTER, BUT ONLY FOR A LITTLE WHILE.
はうっ
バチッ
ばばっ
?
Eee!

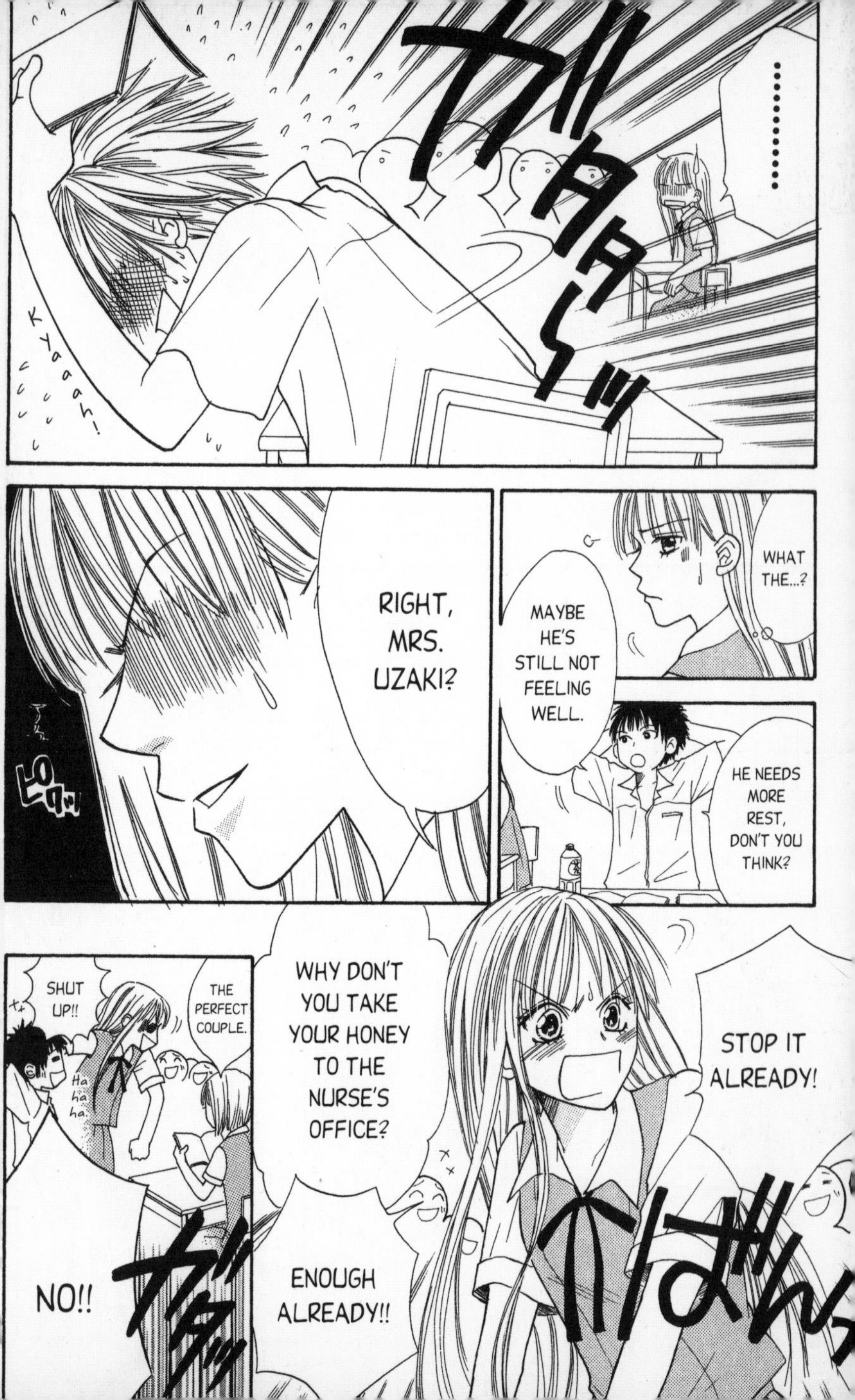
Kyaaaah!
....
WHAT THE...?
MAYBE HE'S STILL NOT FEELING WELL.
HE NEEDS MORE REST, DON'T YOU THINK?
RIGHT, MRS. UZAKI?
STOP IT ALREADY!
WHY DON'T YOU TAKE YOUR HONEY TO THE NURSE'S OFFICE?
ENOUGH ALREADY!!
THE PERFECT COUPLE.
SHUT UP!!
Ha ha ha.
NO!!

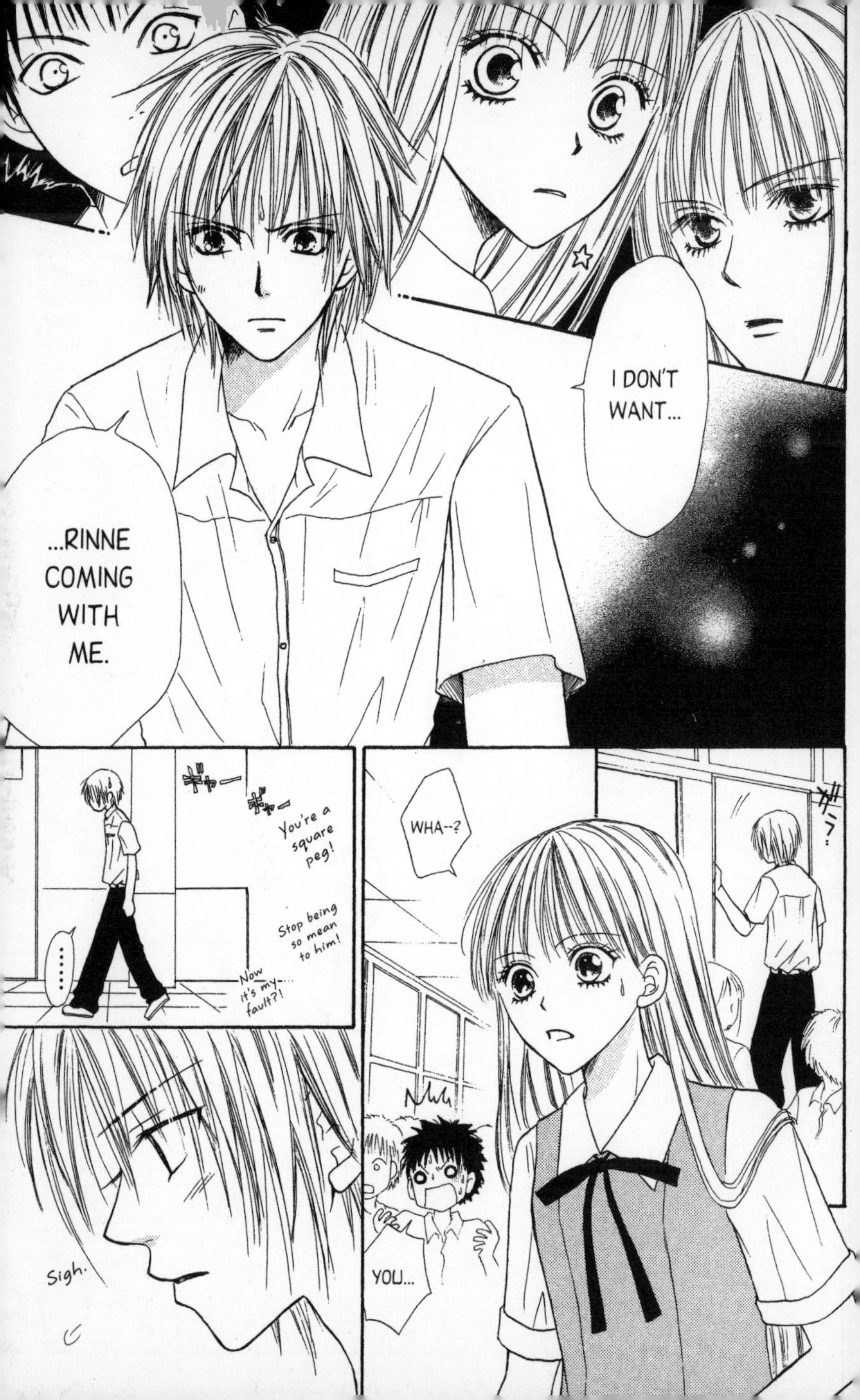
I DON'T WANT...
...RINNE COMING WITH ME.
WHA--?
YOU...
You're a square peg!
Stop being so mean to him!
Now it's my... fault?!
......
Sigh.

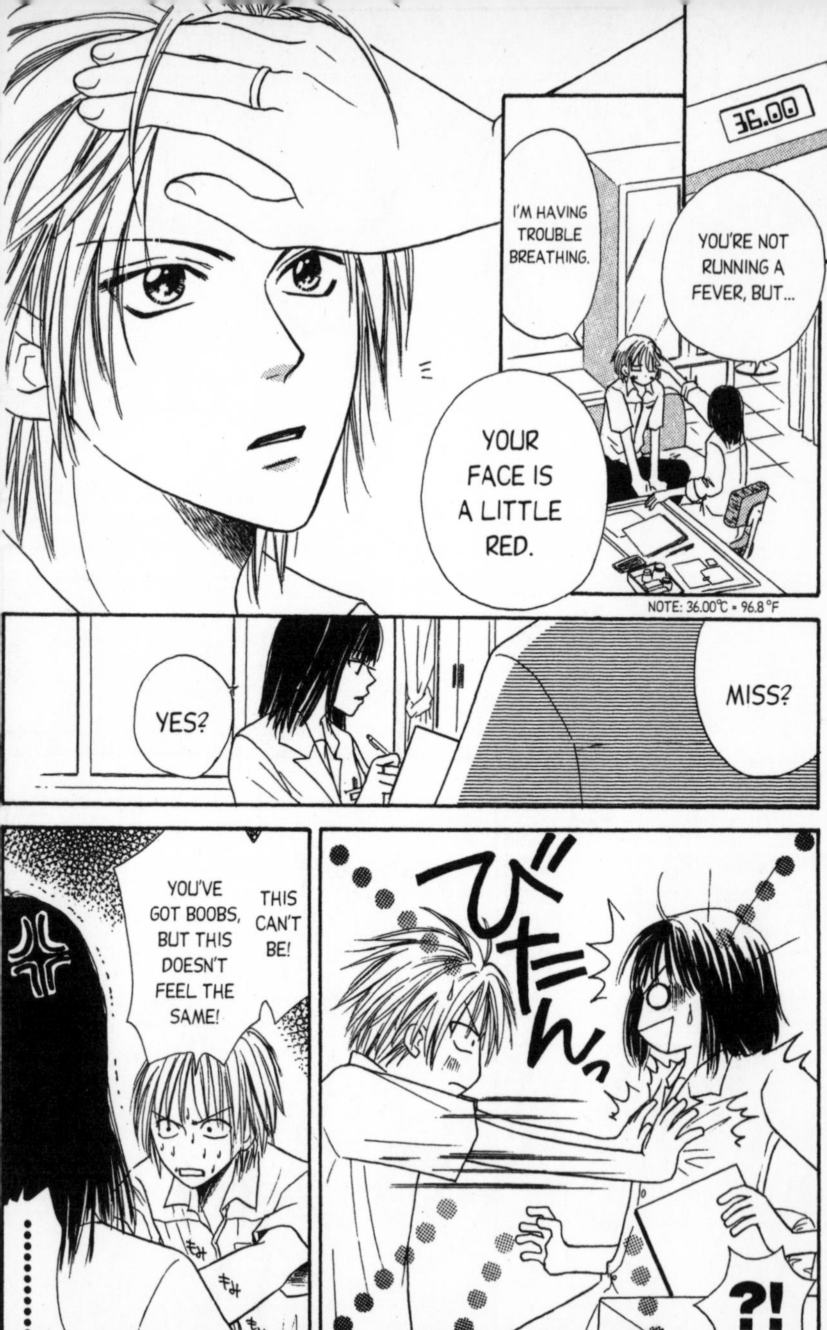
36.00
YOU'RE NOT RUNNING A FEVER, BUT...
I'M HAVING TROUBLE BREATHING.
YOUR FACE IS A LITTLE RED.
NOTE: 36.00°C = 96.8°F
MISS?
YES?
びたん
?!
THIS CAN'T BE!
YOU'VE GOT BOOBS, BUT THIS DOESN'T FEEL THE SAME!
もみ
もみ
もみ
....

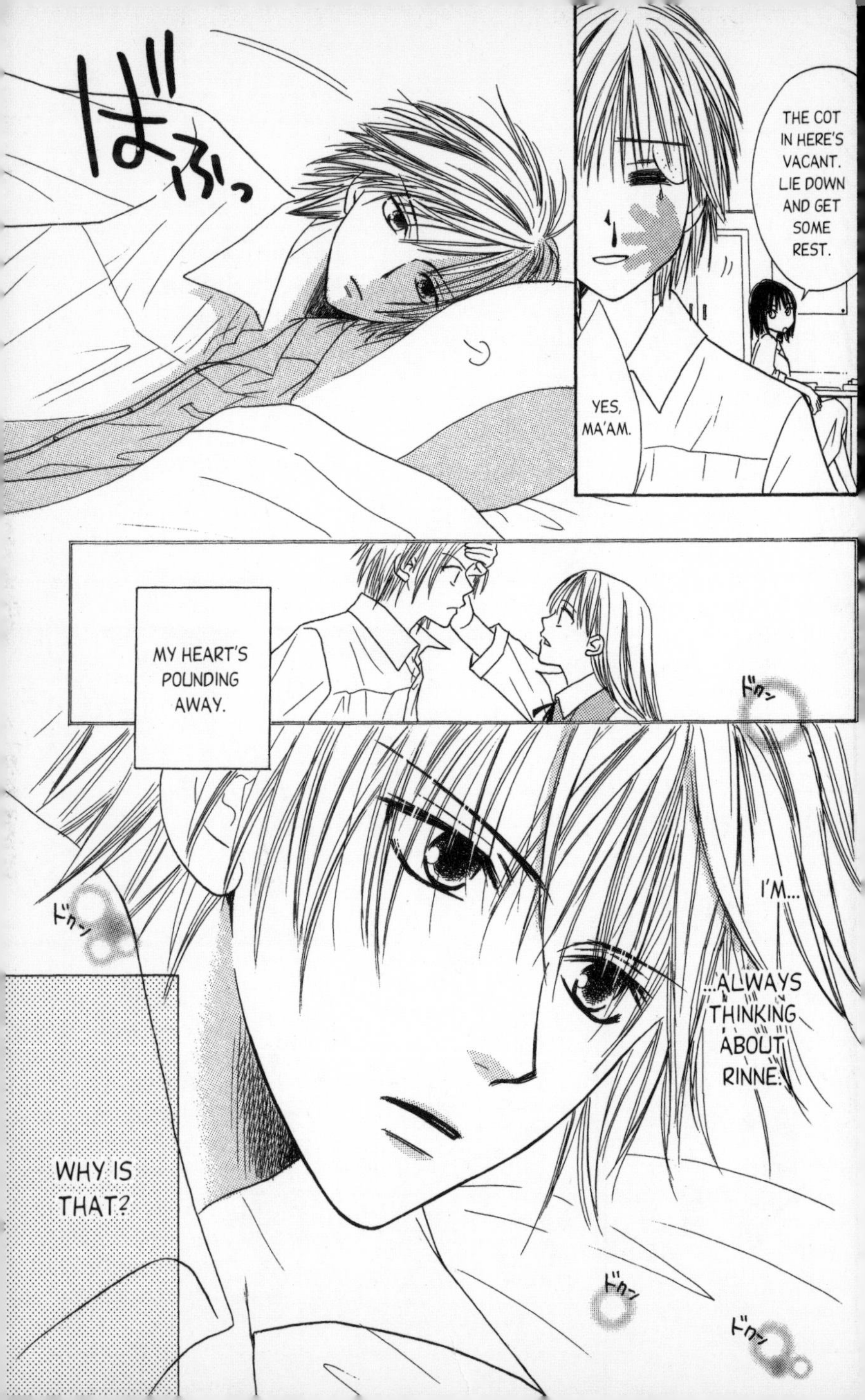
THE COT IN HERE'S VACANT. LIE DOWN AND GET SOME REST.
YES, MA'AM.
ばふっ
MY HEART'S POUNDING AWAY.
ドクン
I'M...
...ALWAYS THINKING ABOUT RINNE.
ドクン
WHY IS THAT?
ドクン
ドクン

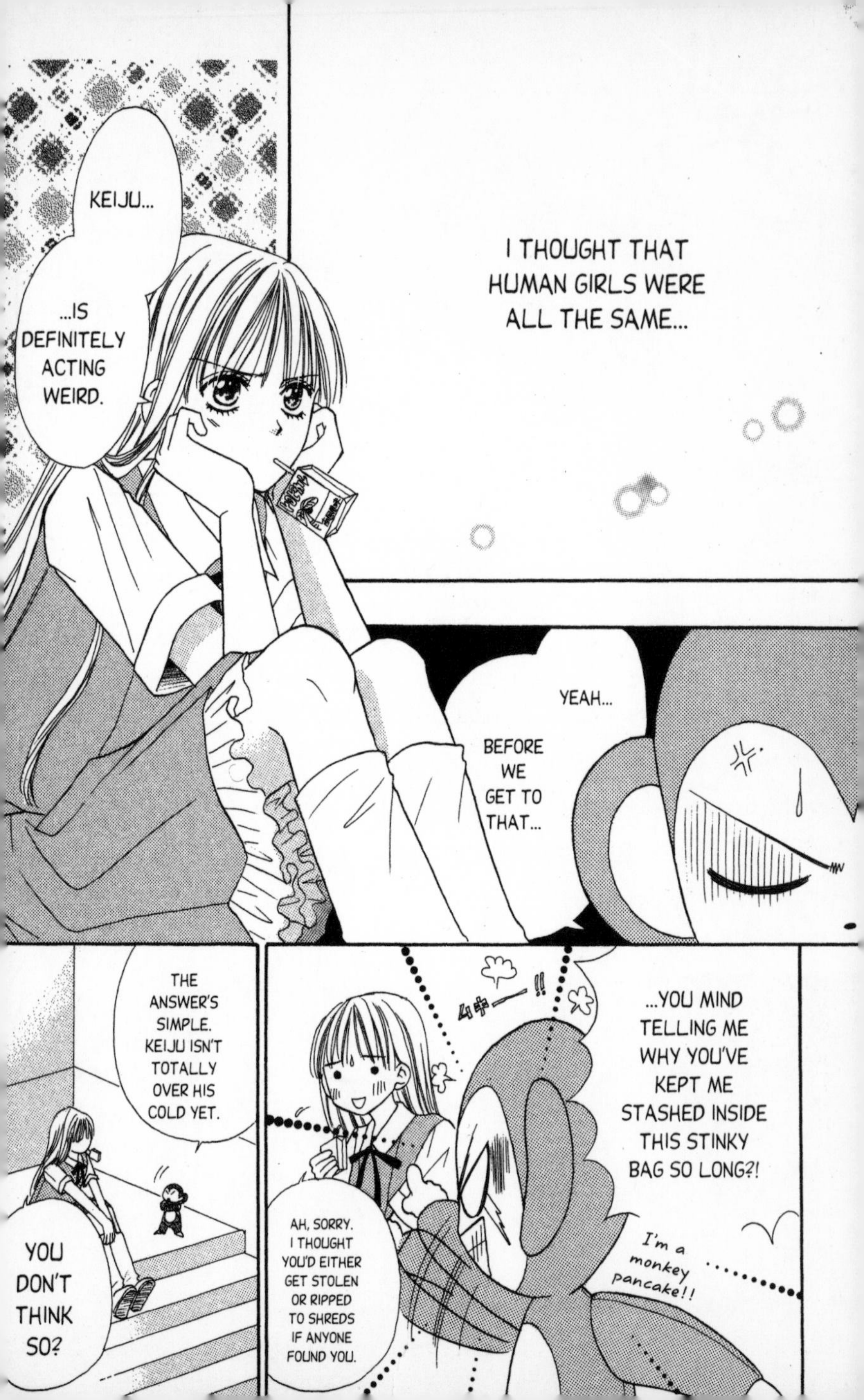
I THOUGHT THAT HUMAN GIRLS WERE ALL THE SAME...
KEIJU...
...IS DEFINITELY ACTING WEIRD.
YEAH...
BEFORE WE GET TO THAT...
...YOU MIND TELLING ME WHY YOU'VE KEPT ME STASHED INSIDE THIS STINKY BAG SO LONG?!
ムキー!!
AH, SORRY. I THOUGHT YOU'D EITHER GET STOLEN OR RIPPED TO SHREDS IF ANYONE FOUND YOU.
I'm a monkey pancake!!
YOU DON'T THINK SO?
THE ANSWER'S SIMPLE. KEIJU ISN'T TOTALLY OVER HIS COLD YET.

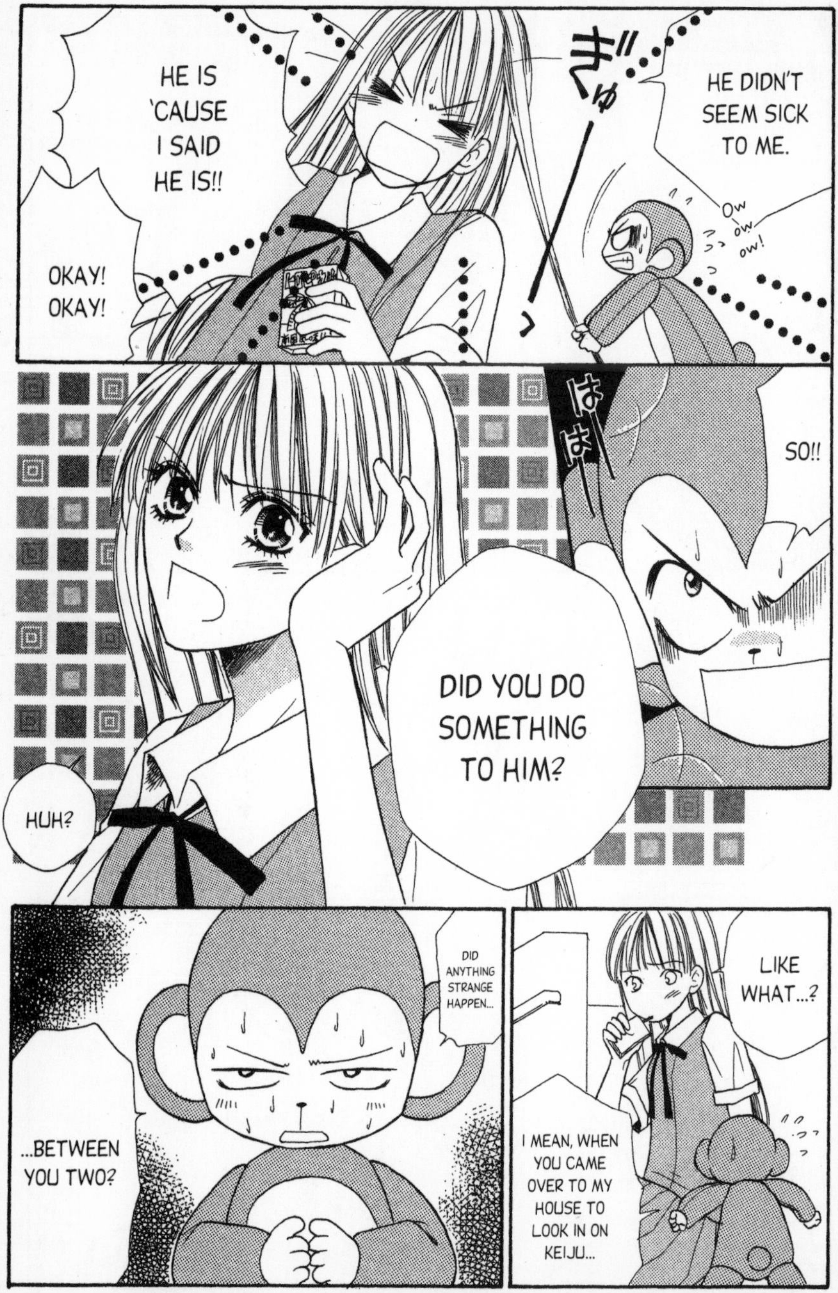
HE DIDN'T SEEM SICK TO ME.
ぎゅ
Ow ow ow!
HE IS 'CAUSE I SAID HE IS!!
OKAY! OKAY!
SO!!
はは
DID YOU DO SOMETHING TO HIM?
HUH?
LIKE WHAT...?
I MEAN, WHEN YOU CAME OVER TO MY HOUSE TO LOOK IN ON KEIJU...
DID ANYTHING STRANGE HAPPEN...
...BETWEEN YOU TWO?

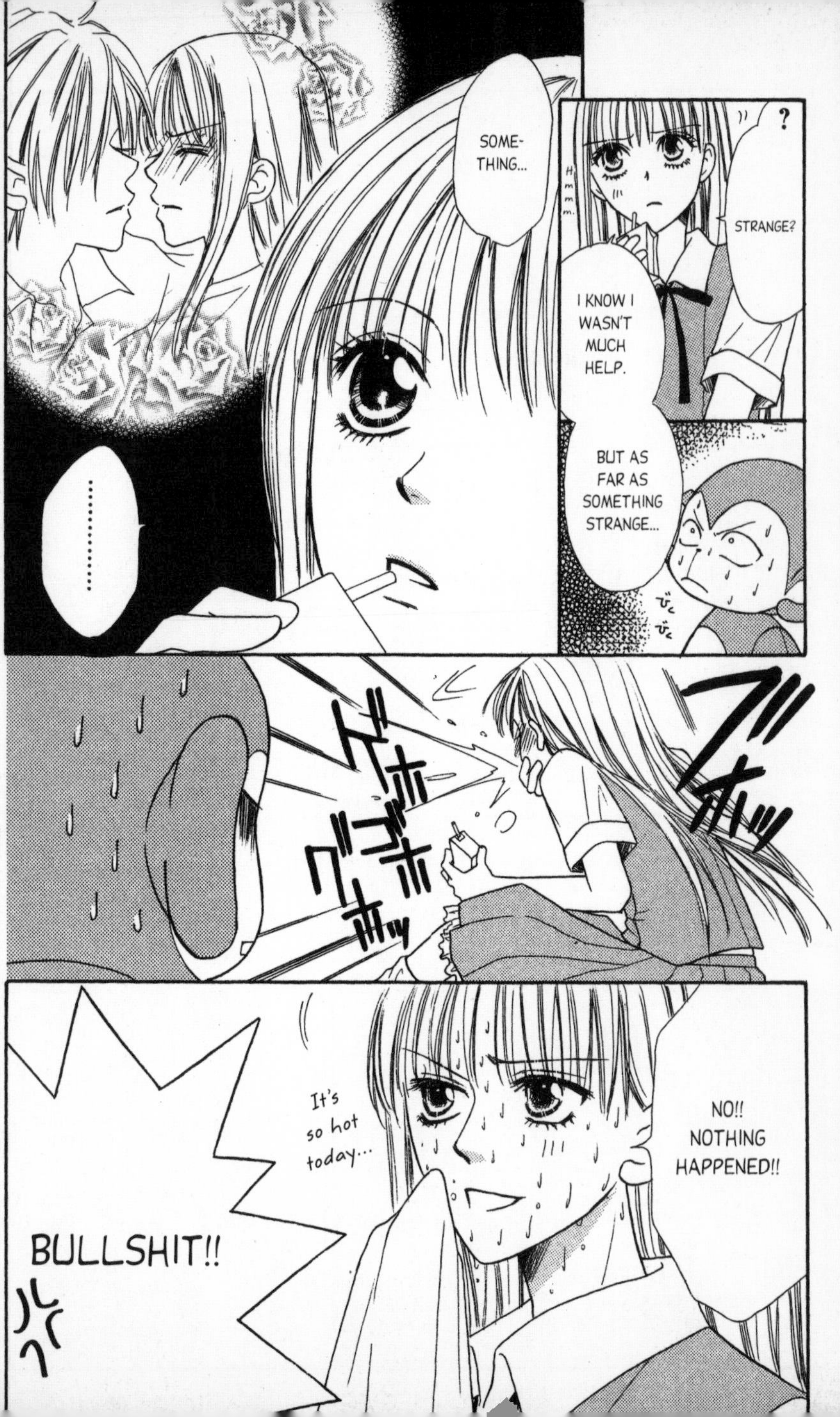
?
STRANGE?
Hmmm.
I KNOW I WASN'T MUCH HELP.
BUT AS FAR AS SOMETHING STRANGE...
びくびく
SOME-THING...
......
ブフォッ
ゲホゴホゲホッ
NO!! NOTHING HAPPENED!!
It's so hot today...
BULLSHIT!!

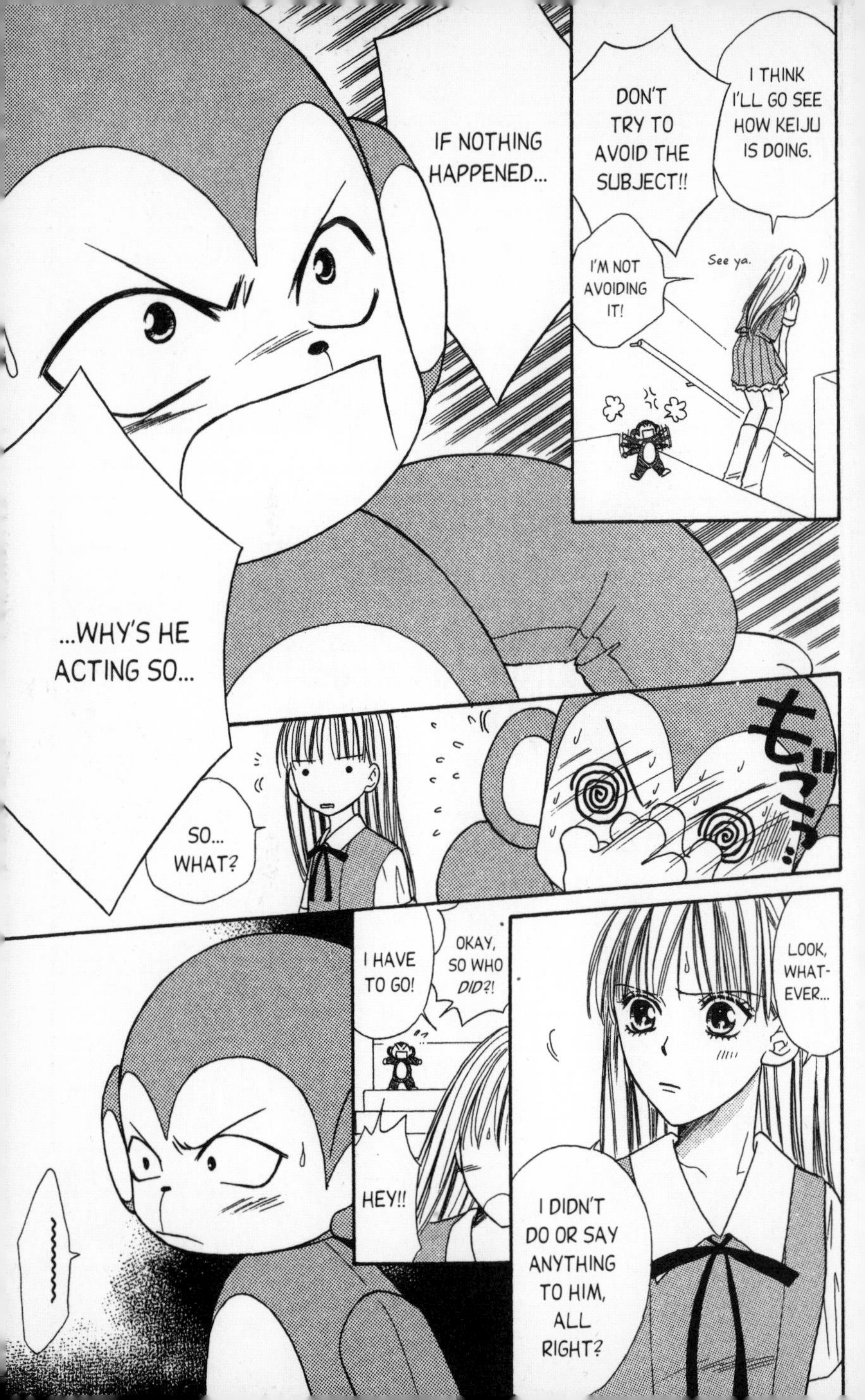
I THINK I'LL GO SEE HOW KEIJU IS DOING.
DON'T TRY TO AVOID THE SUBJECT!!
I'M NOT AVOIDING IT!
See ya.
IF NOTHING HAPPENED...
...WHY'S HE ACTING SO...
もごう
SO... WHAT?
LOOK, WHAT-EVER...
I DIDN'T DO OR SAY ANYTHING TO HIM, ALL RIGHT?
OKAY, SO WHO DID?!
I HAVE TO GO!
HEY!!
...

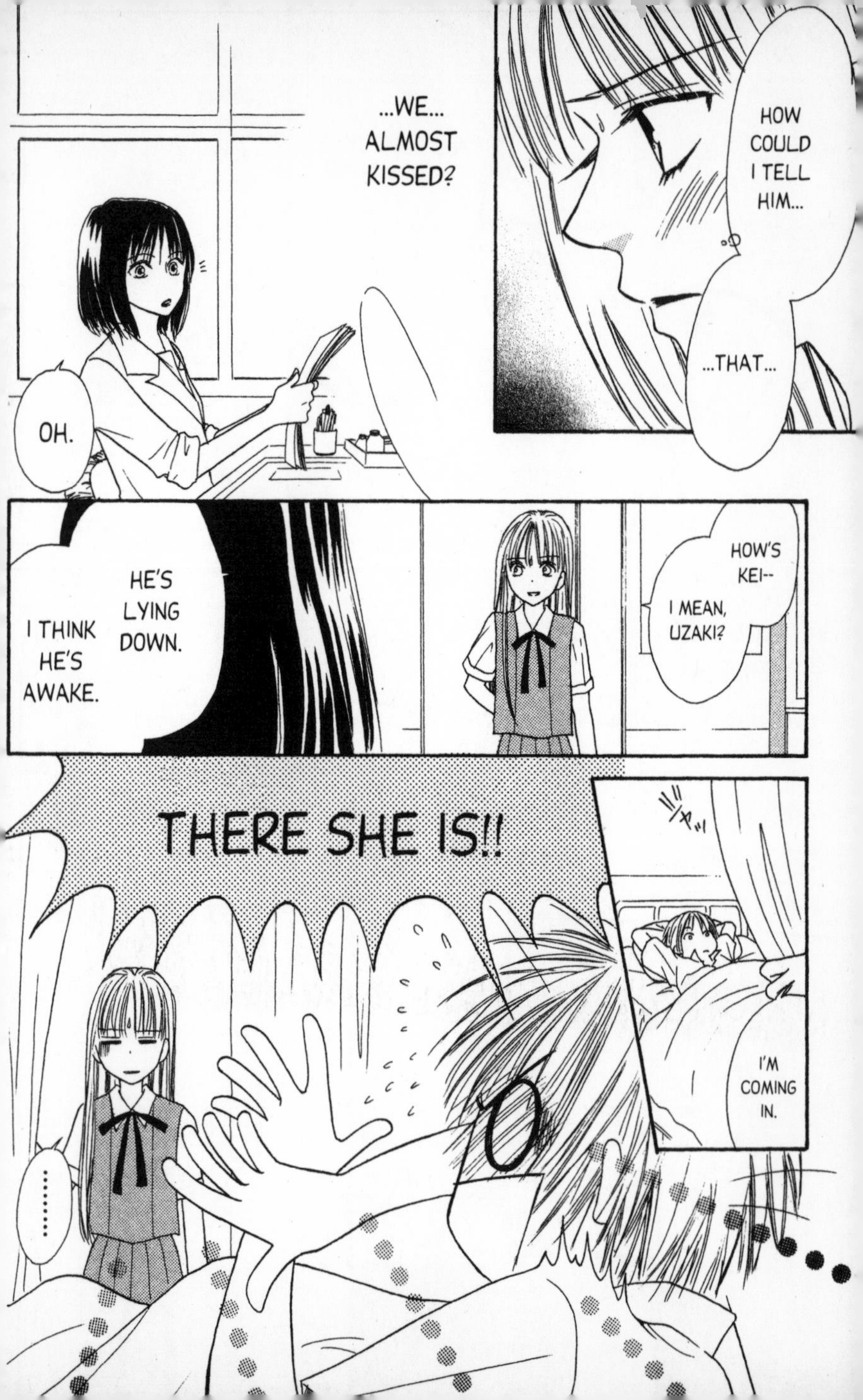
HOW COULD I TELL HIM...
...THAT...
...WE... ALMOST KISSED?
OH.
HOW'S KEI-- I MEAN, UZAKI?
HE'S LYING DOWN.
I THINK HE'S AWAKE.
I'M COMING IN.
THERE SHE IS!!
......
...

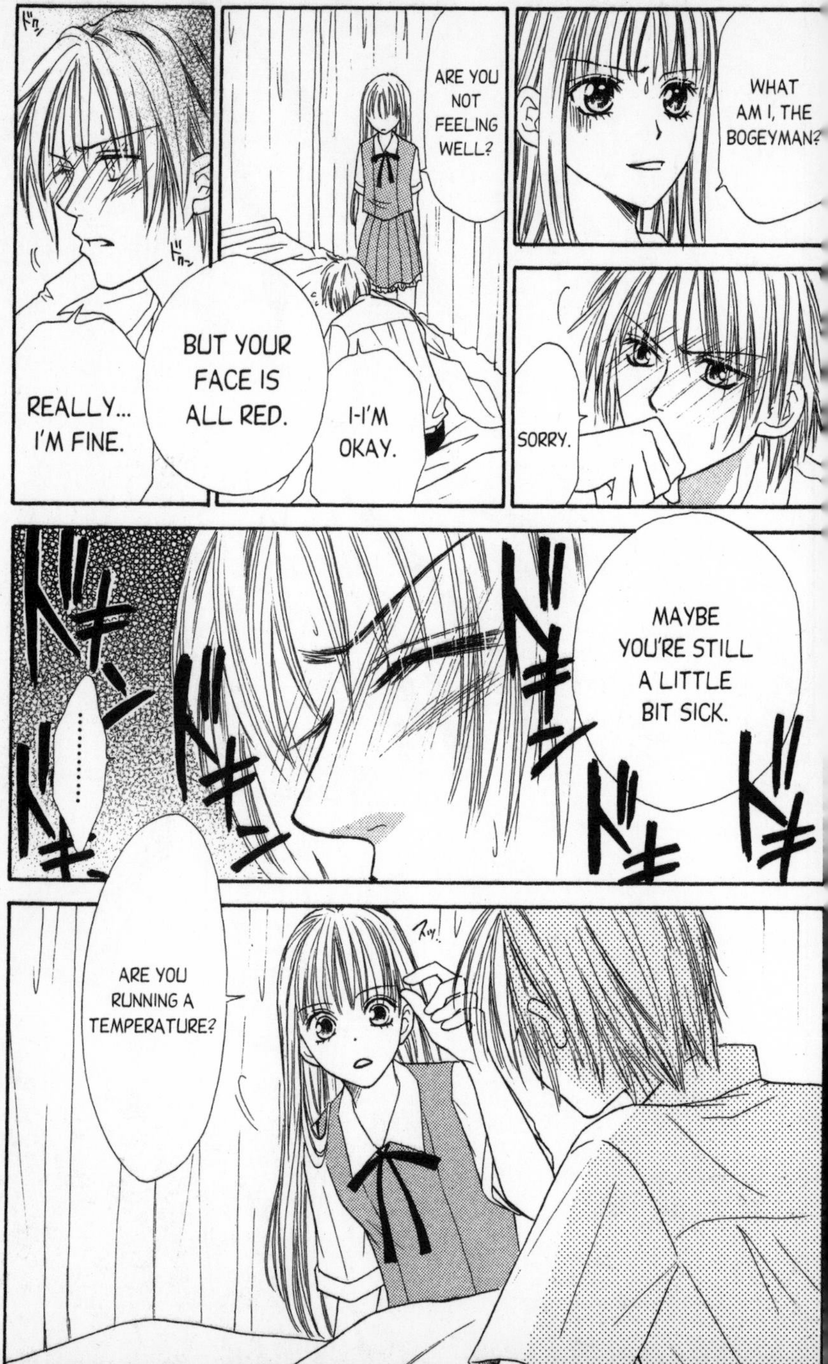
WHAT AM I, THE BOGEYMAN?
SORRY.
ARE YOU NOT FEELING WELL?
I-I'M OKAY.
BUT YOUR FACE IS ALL RED.
REALLY... I'M FINE.
MAYBE YOU'RE STILL A LITTLE BIT SICK.
......
ARE YOU RUNNING A TEMPERATURE?

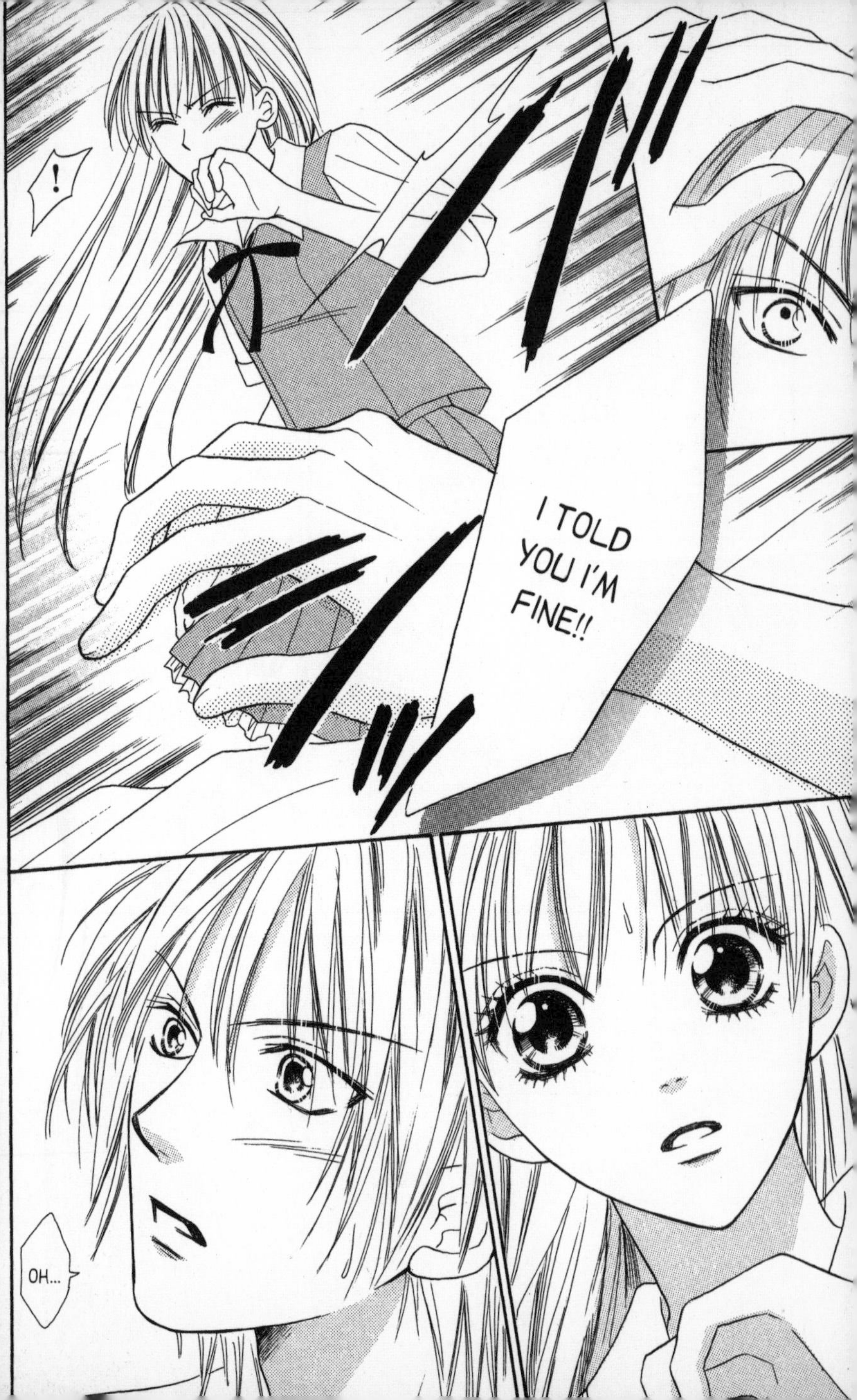
I TOLD YOU I'M FINE!!
!
OH...

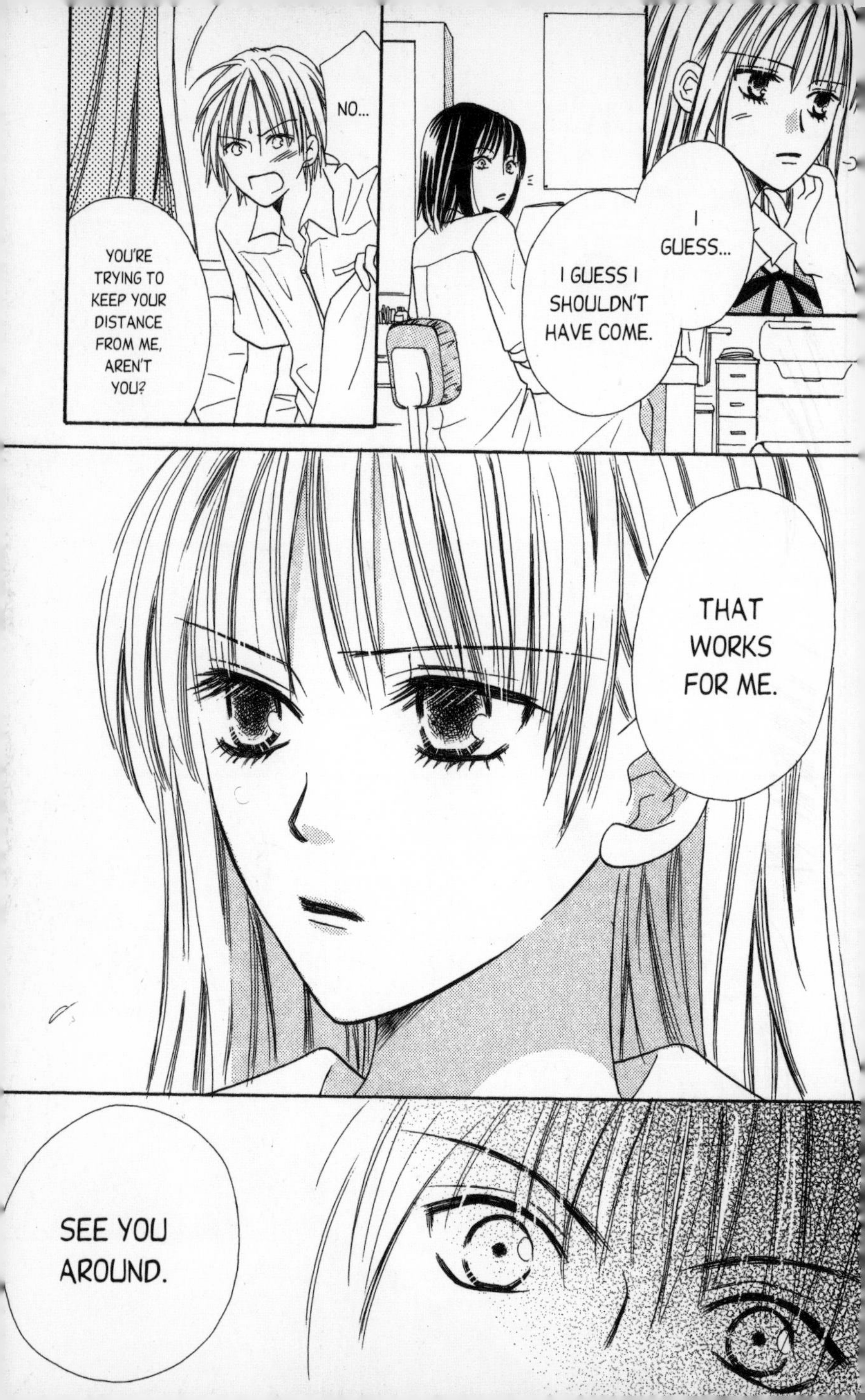
I GUESS...
I GUESS I SHOULDN'T HAVE COME.
NO...
YOU'RE TRYING TO KEEP YOUR DISTANCE FROM ME, AREN'T YOU?
THAT WORKS FOR ME.
SEE YOU AROUND.

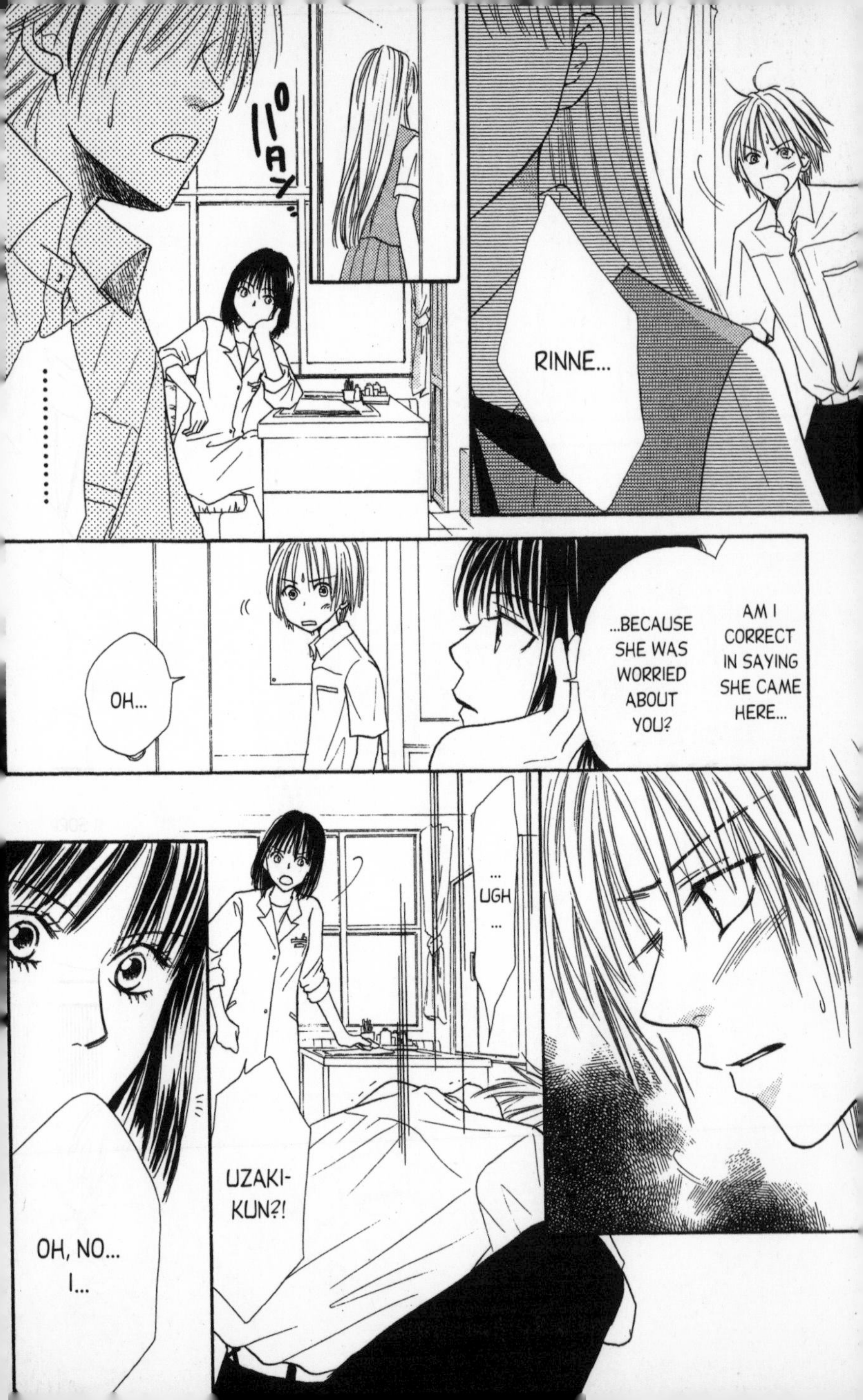
RINNE...
パタン
......
AM I CORRECT IN SAYING SHE CAME HERE...
...BECAUSE SHE WAS WORRIED ABOUT YOU?
OH...
... UGH ...
UZAKI-KUN?!
OH, NO... I...

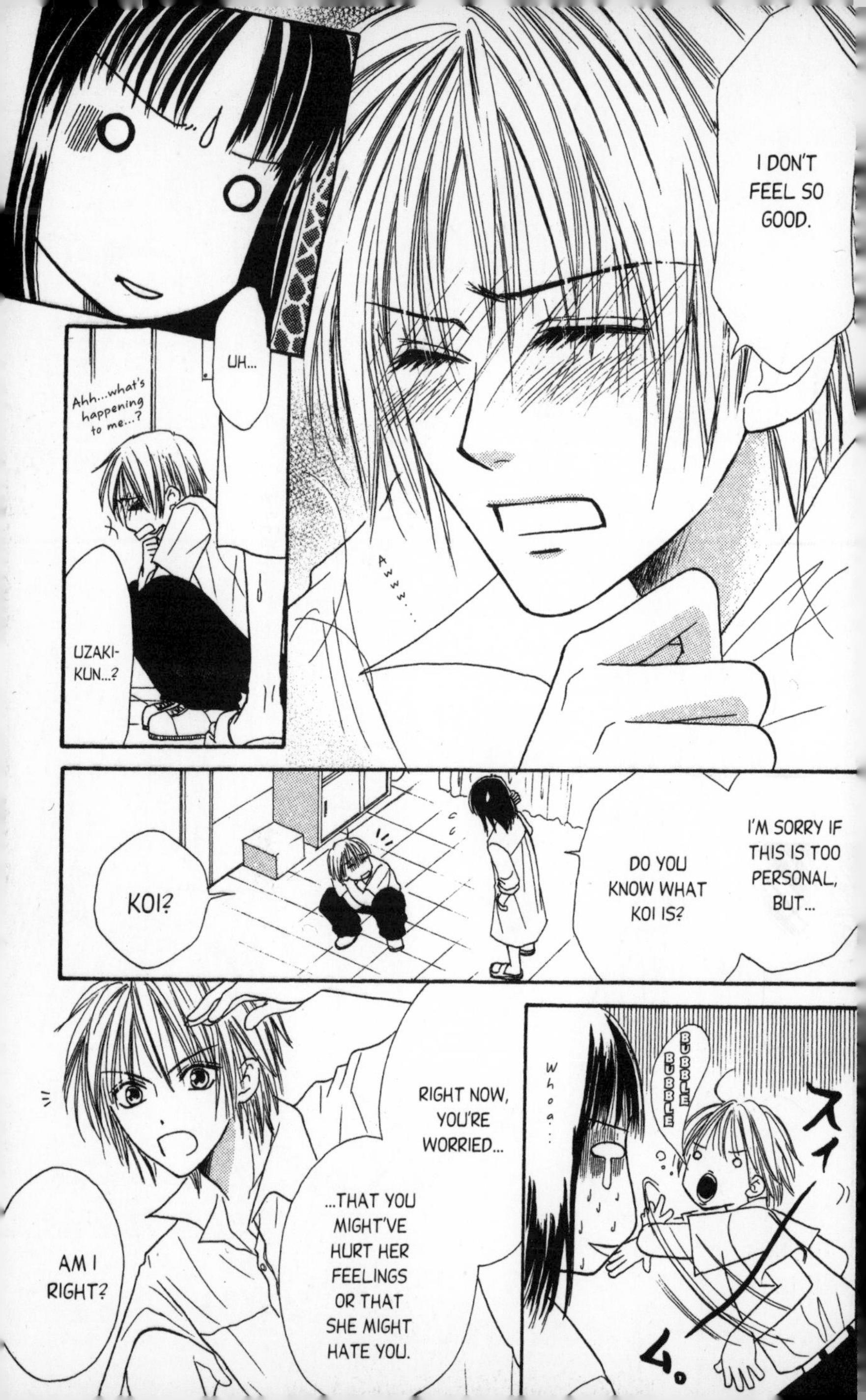
I DON'T FEEL SO GOOD.
Awww...
UH...
UZAKI-KUN...?
Ahh...what's happening to me...?
I'M SORRY IF THIS IS TOO PERSONAL, BUT...
DO YOU KNOW WHAT KOI IS?
KOI?
BUBBLE BUBBLE
Whoa...
RIGHT NOW, YOU'RE WORRIED...
...THAT YOU MIGHT'VE HURT HER FEELINGS OR THAT SHE MIGHT HATE YOU.
AM I RIGHT?

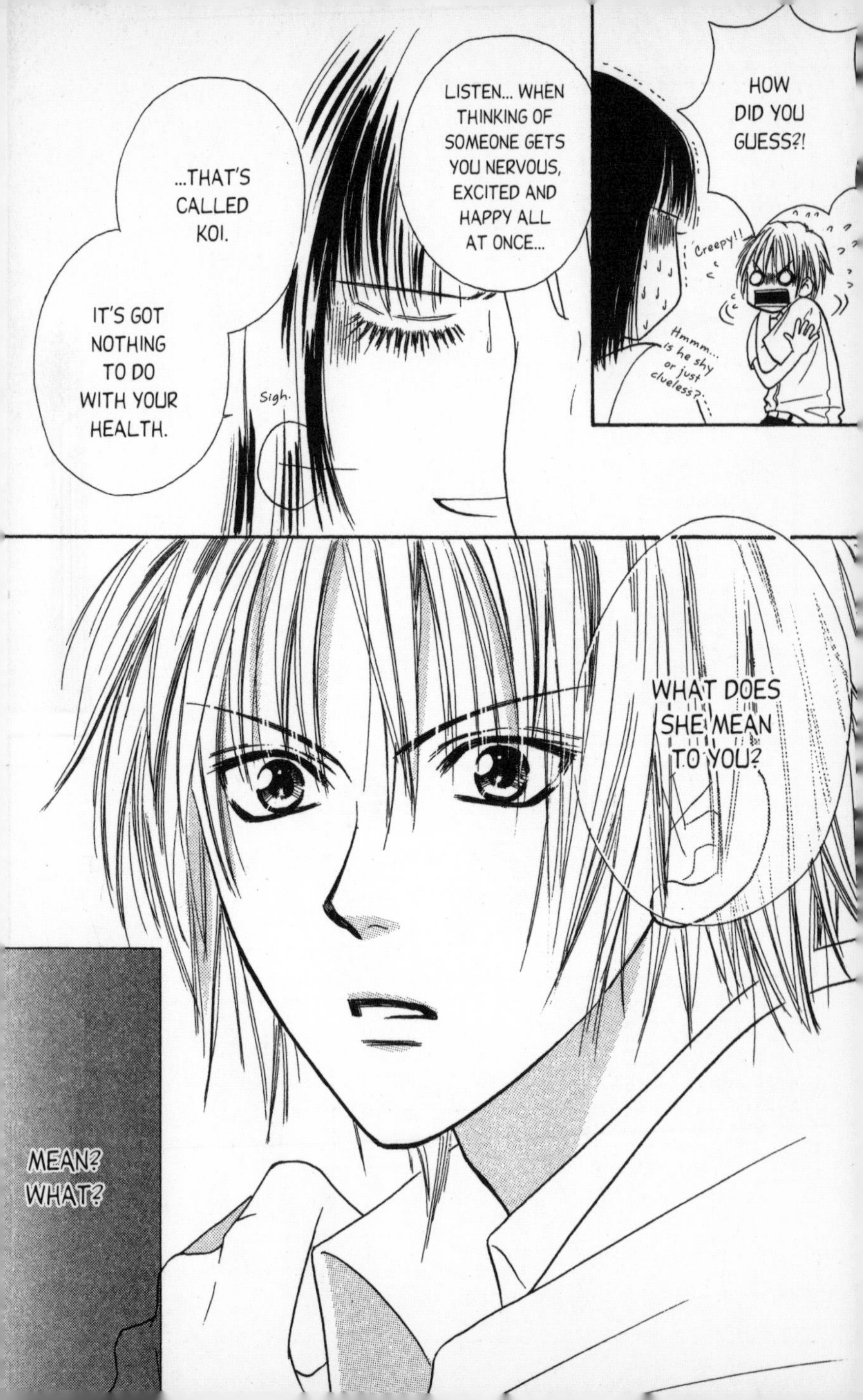
HOW DID YOU GUESS?!
Creepy!!
Hmmm... is he shy or just clueless?
LISTEN... WHEN THINKING OF SOMEONE GETS YOU NERVOUS, EXCITED AND HAPPY ALL AT ONCE...
...THAT'S CALLED KOI.
IT'S GOT NOTHING TO DO WITH YOUR HEALTH.
Sigh.
WHAT DOES SHE MEAN TO YOU?
MEAN? WHAT?

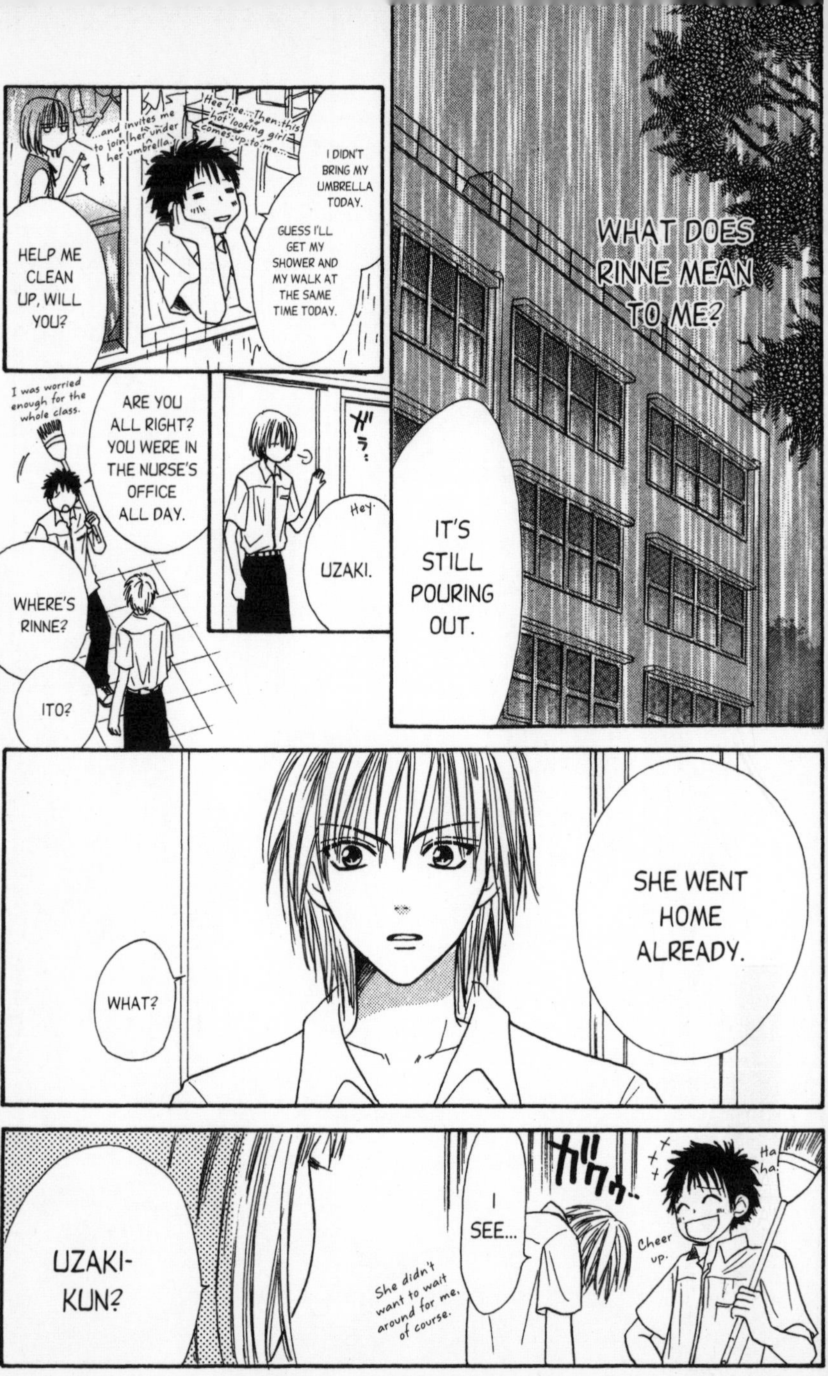
WHAT DOES RINNE MEAN TO ME?
IT'S STILL POURING OUT.
I DIDN'T BRING MY UMBRELLA TODAY.
GUESS I'LL GET MY SHOWER AND MY WALK AT THE SAME TIME TODAY.
Hee hee... Then this hot looking girl comes up to me...
...and invites me to join her under her umbrella.
HELP ME CLEAN UP, WILL YOU?
ガラ
Hey.
UZAKI.
ARE YOU ALL RIGHT? YOU WERE IN THE NURSE'S OFFICE ALL DAY.
I was worried enough for the whole class.
WHERE'S RINNE?
ITO?
SHE WENT HOME ALREADY.
WHAT?
UZAKI-KUN?
I SEE...
She didn't want to wait around for me, of course.
ガクゥ
Ha ha.
Cheer up.

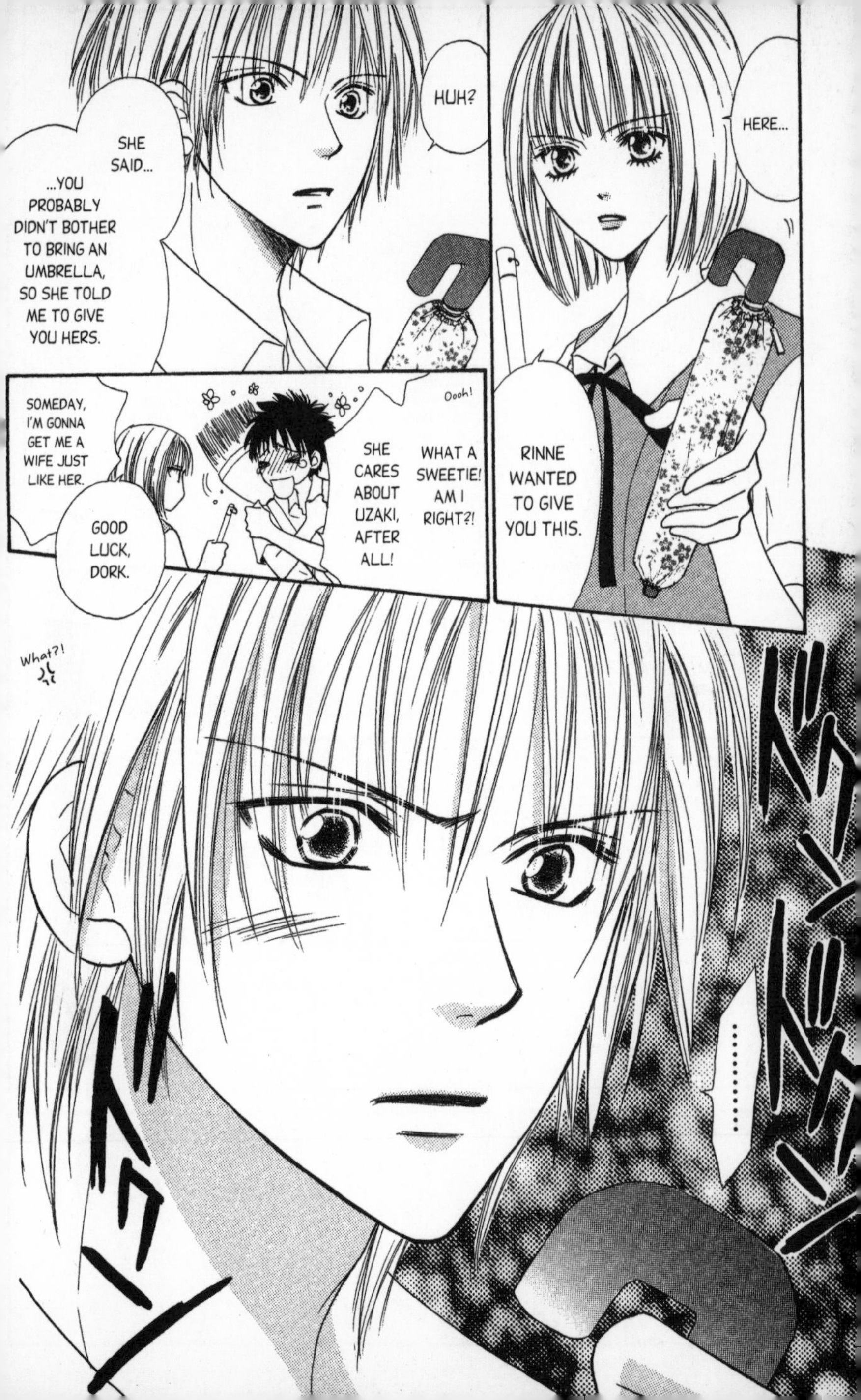
HERE...
RINNE WANTED TO GIVE YOU THIS.
HUH?
SHE SAID...
...YOU PROBABLY DIDN'T BOTHER TO BRING AN UMBRELLA, SO SHE TOLD ME TO GIVE YOU HERS.
Oooh!
WHAT A SWEETIE! AM I RIGHT?!
SHE CARES ABOUT UZAKI, AFTER ALL!
SOMEDAY, I'M GONNA GET ME A WIFE JUST LIKE HER.
GOOD LUCK, DORK.
What?!
......

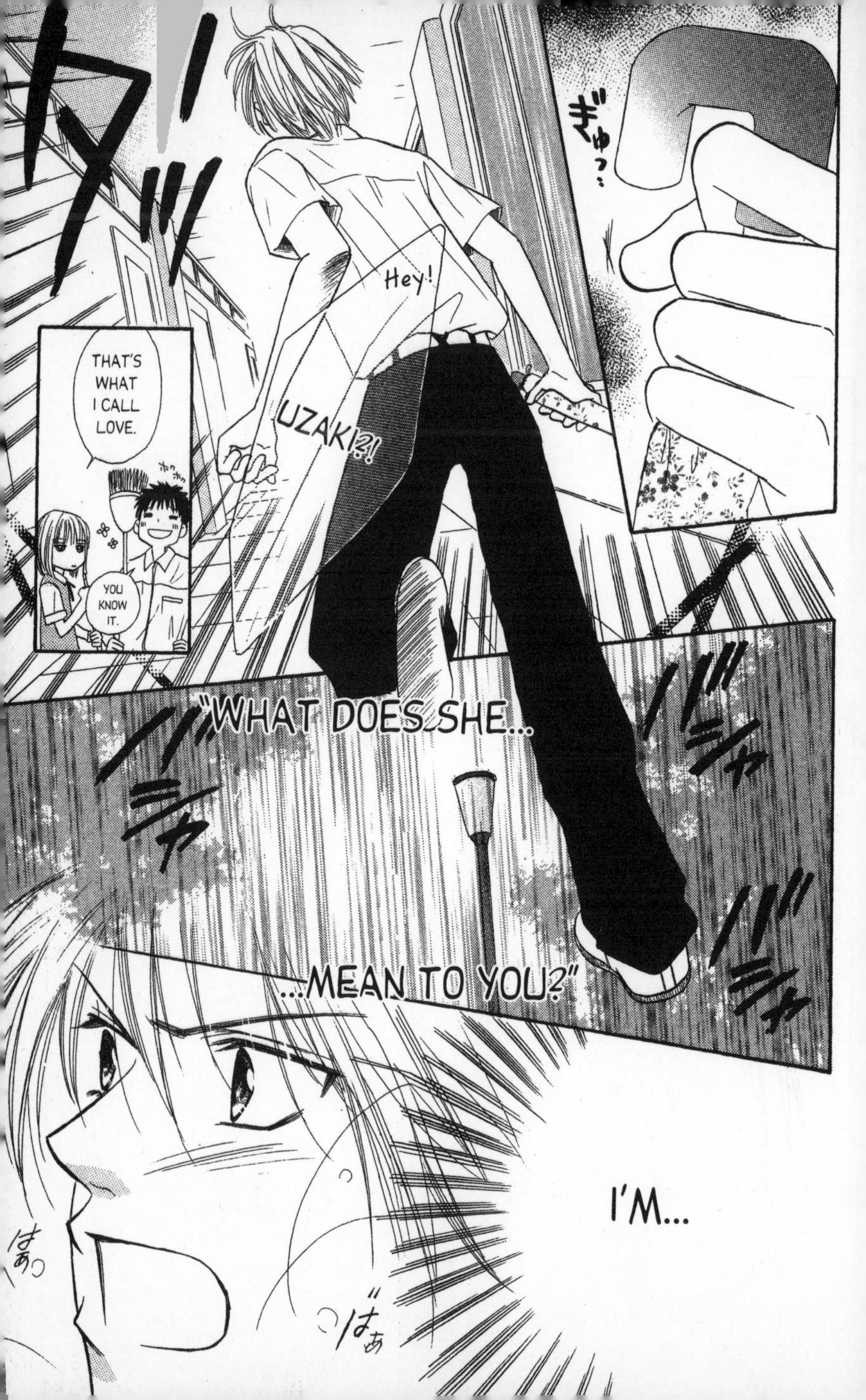
ぎゅっ
Hey!
UZAKI?!
THAT'S WHAT I CALL LOVE.
YOU KNOW IT.
"WHAT DOES SHE...
...MEAN TO YOU?"
I'M...
はぁ
はぁ

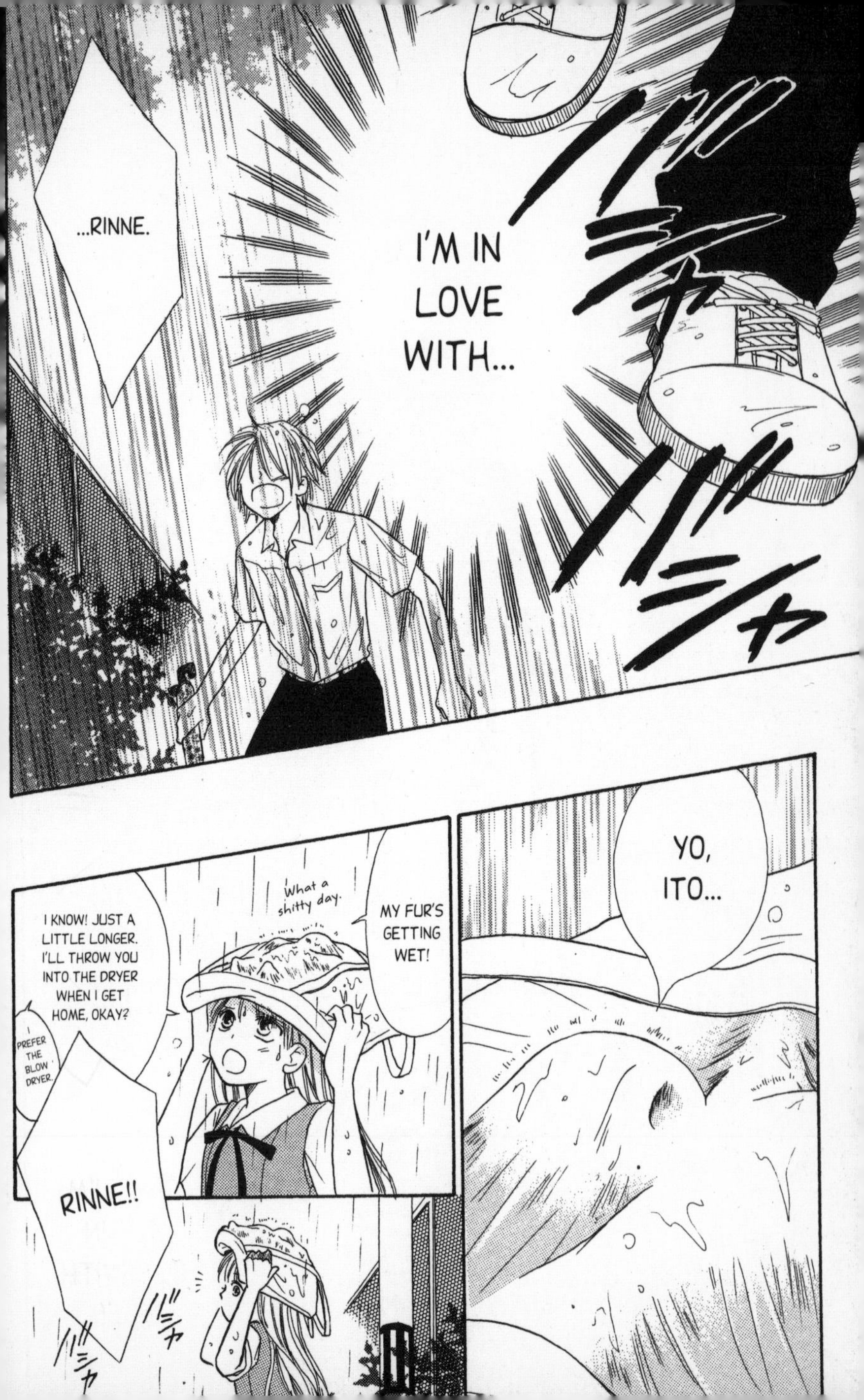
バシャ
I'M IN LOVE WITH...
...RINNE.
YO, ITO...
MY FUR'S GETTING WET!
What a shitty day.
I KNOW! JUST A LITTLE LONGER. I'LL THROW YOU INTO THE DRYER WHEN I GET HOME, OKAY?
I PREFER THE BLOW DRYER.
RINNE!!
バシャ
バシャ

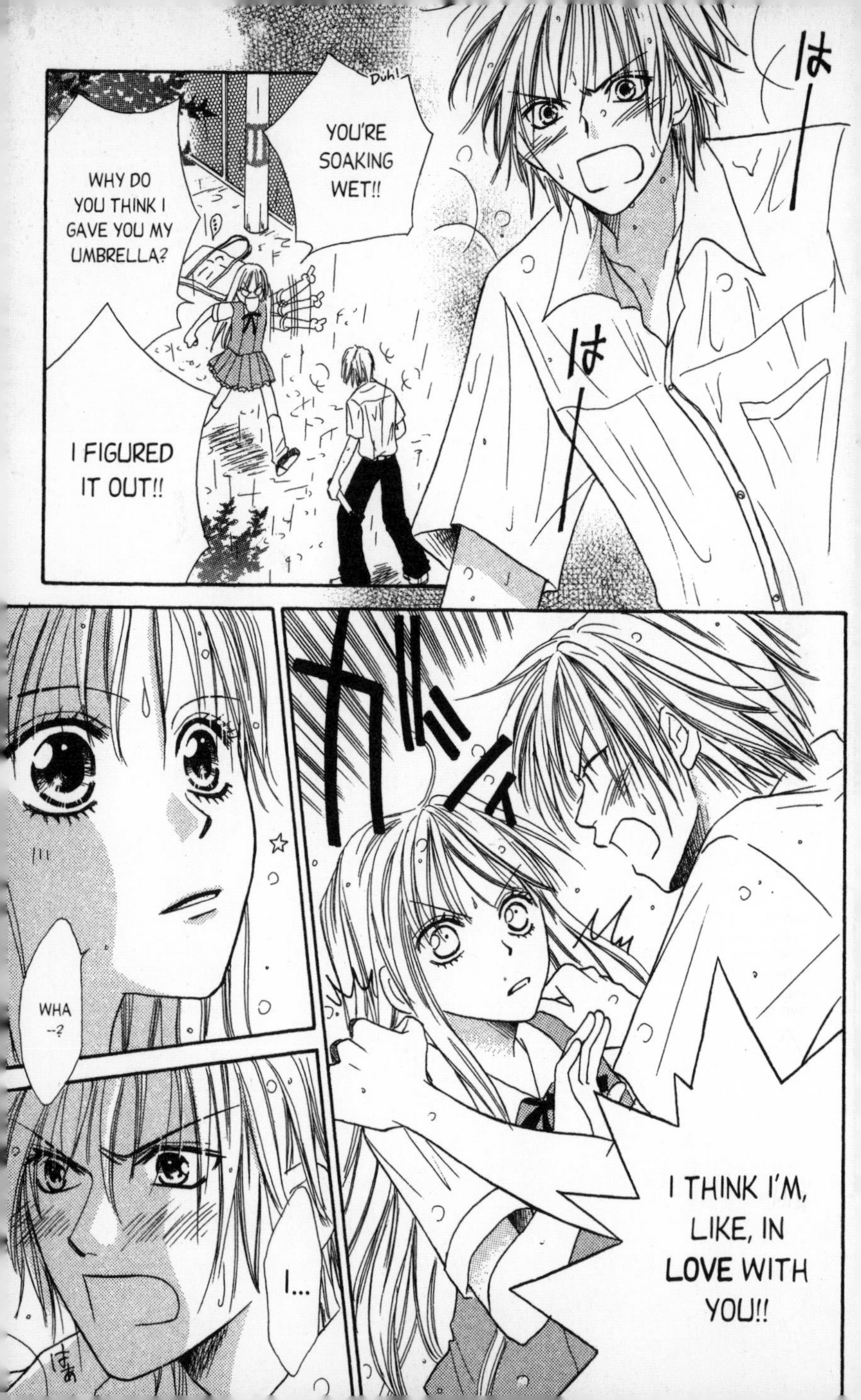
はーはー
Duh!
YOU'RE SOAKING WET!!
WHY DO YOU THINK I GAVE YOU MY UMBRELLA?
I FIGURED IT OUT!!
ガバ
I THINK I'M, LIKE, IN LOVE WITH YOU!!
WHA --?
I...
はぁ

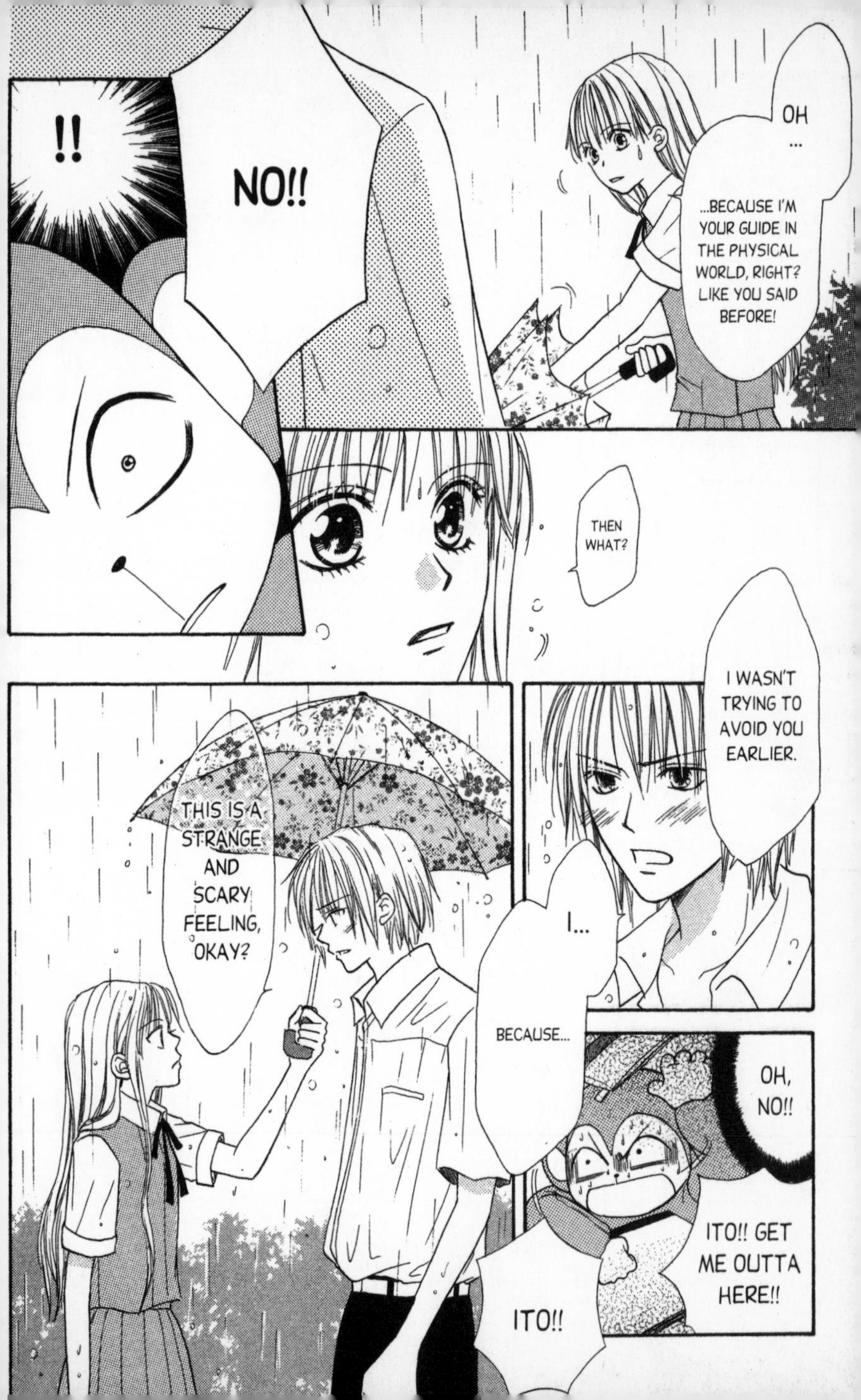
OH ...
...BECAUSE I'M YOUR GUIDE IN THE PHYSICAL WORLD, RIGHT? LIKE YOU SAID BEFORE!
!!
NO!!
THEN WHAT?
I WASN'T TRYING TO AVOID YOU EARLIER.
I...
BECAUSE...
OH, NO!!
ITO!! GET ME OUTTA HERE!!
THIS IS A STRANGE AND SCARY FEELING, OKAY?
ITO!!

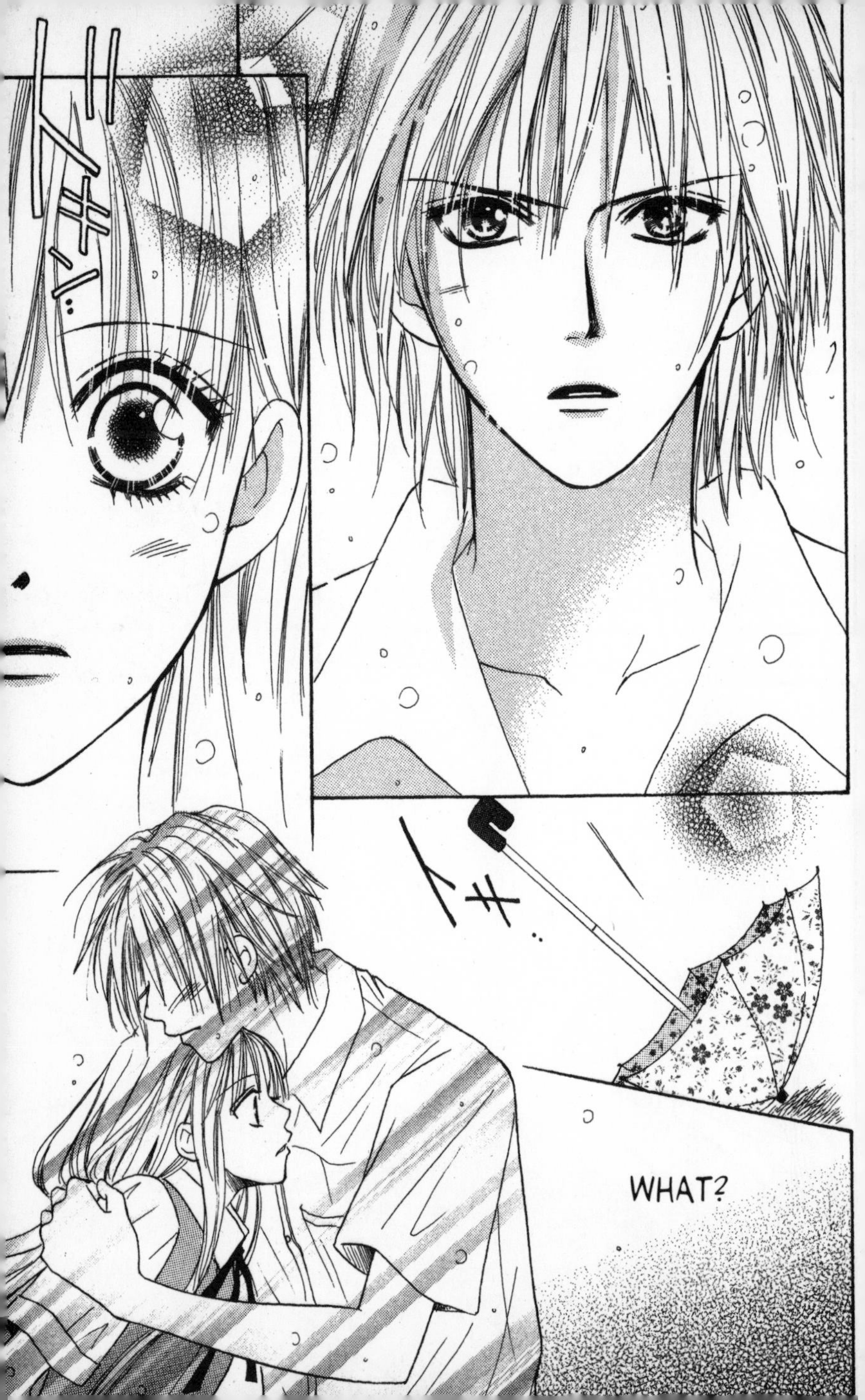
ドキン…
ギュ…
WHAT?

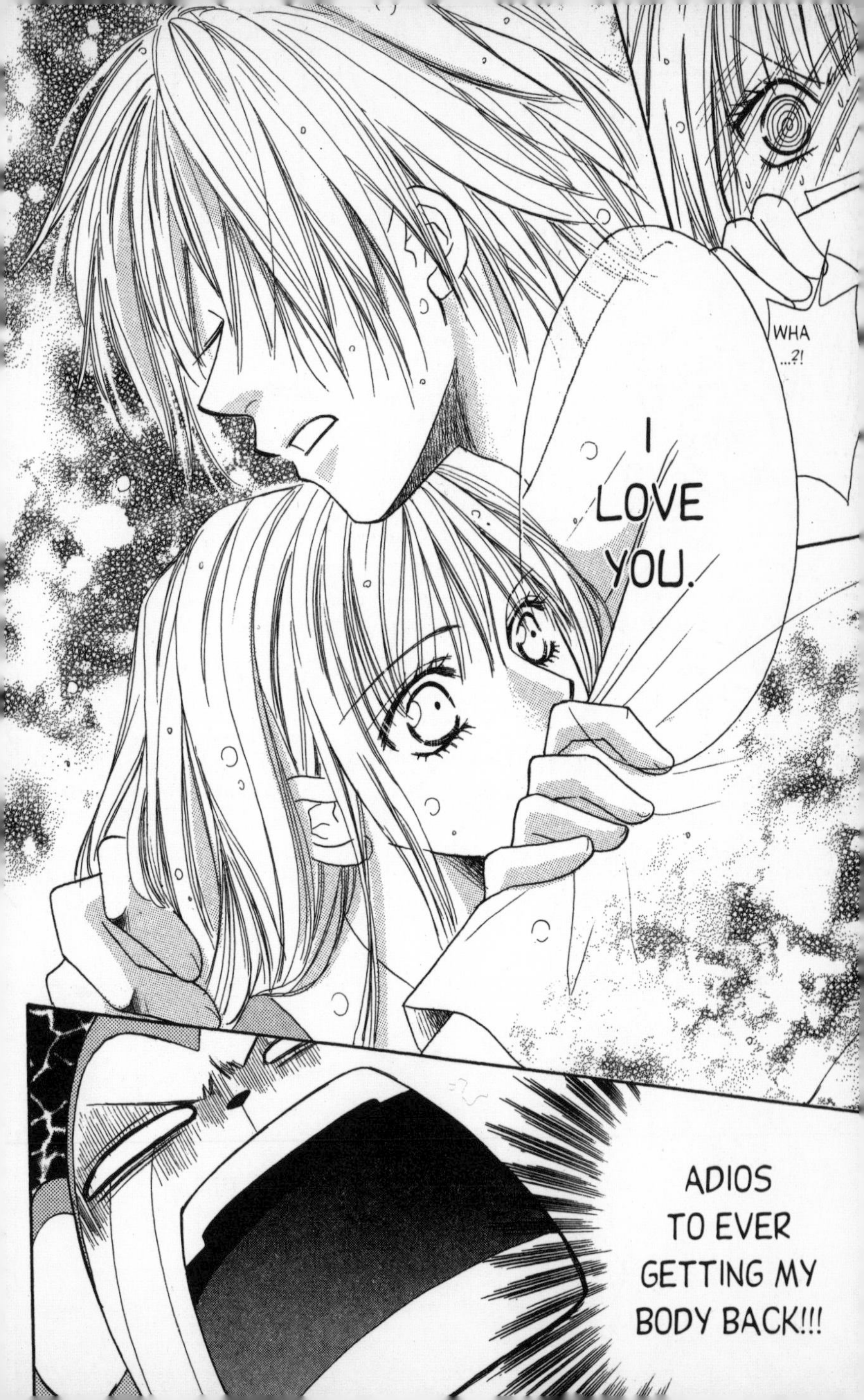
WHA ...?!
I LOVE YOU.
ADIOS TO EVER GETTING MY BODY BACK!!!

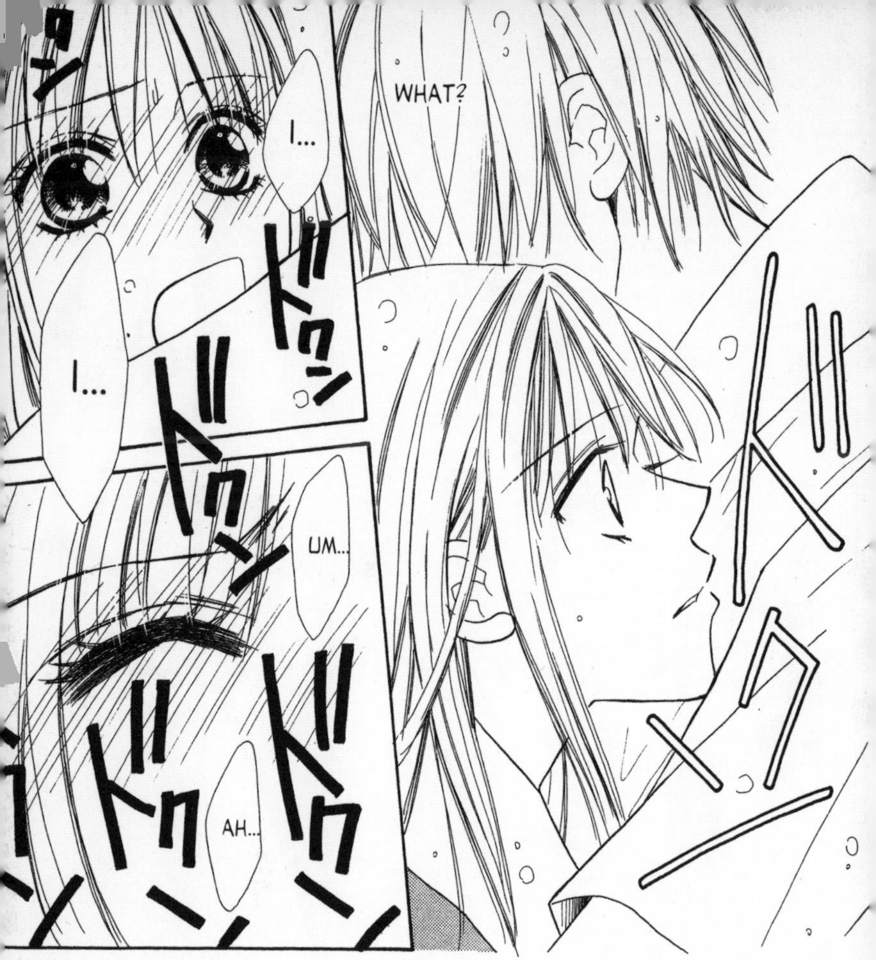
WHAT?
I...
I...
UM...
AH...

HEAVEN!!

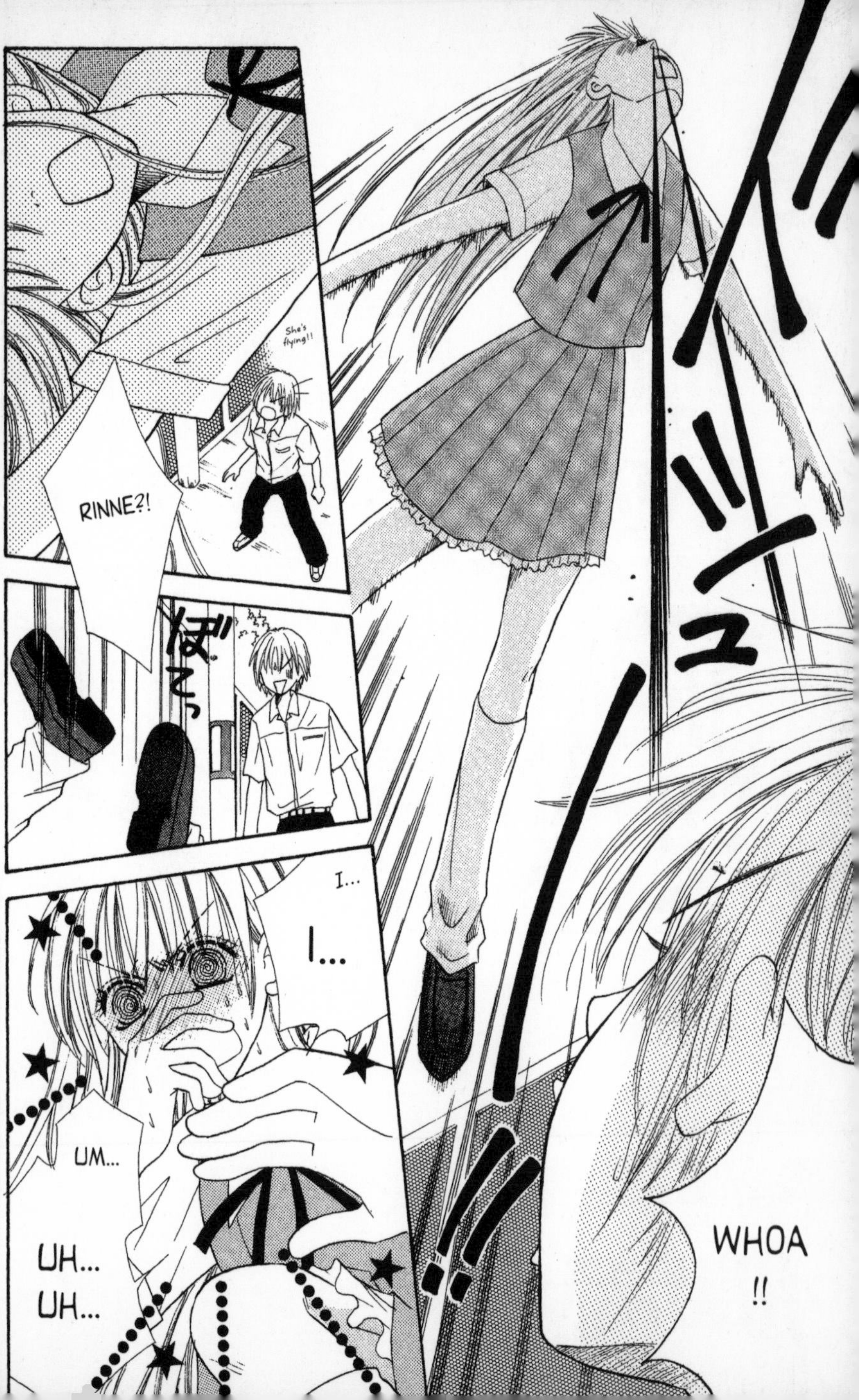
WHOA
!!
She's flying!!
RINNE?!
I...
I...
UM...
UH...
UH...

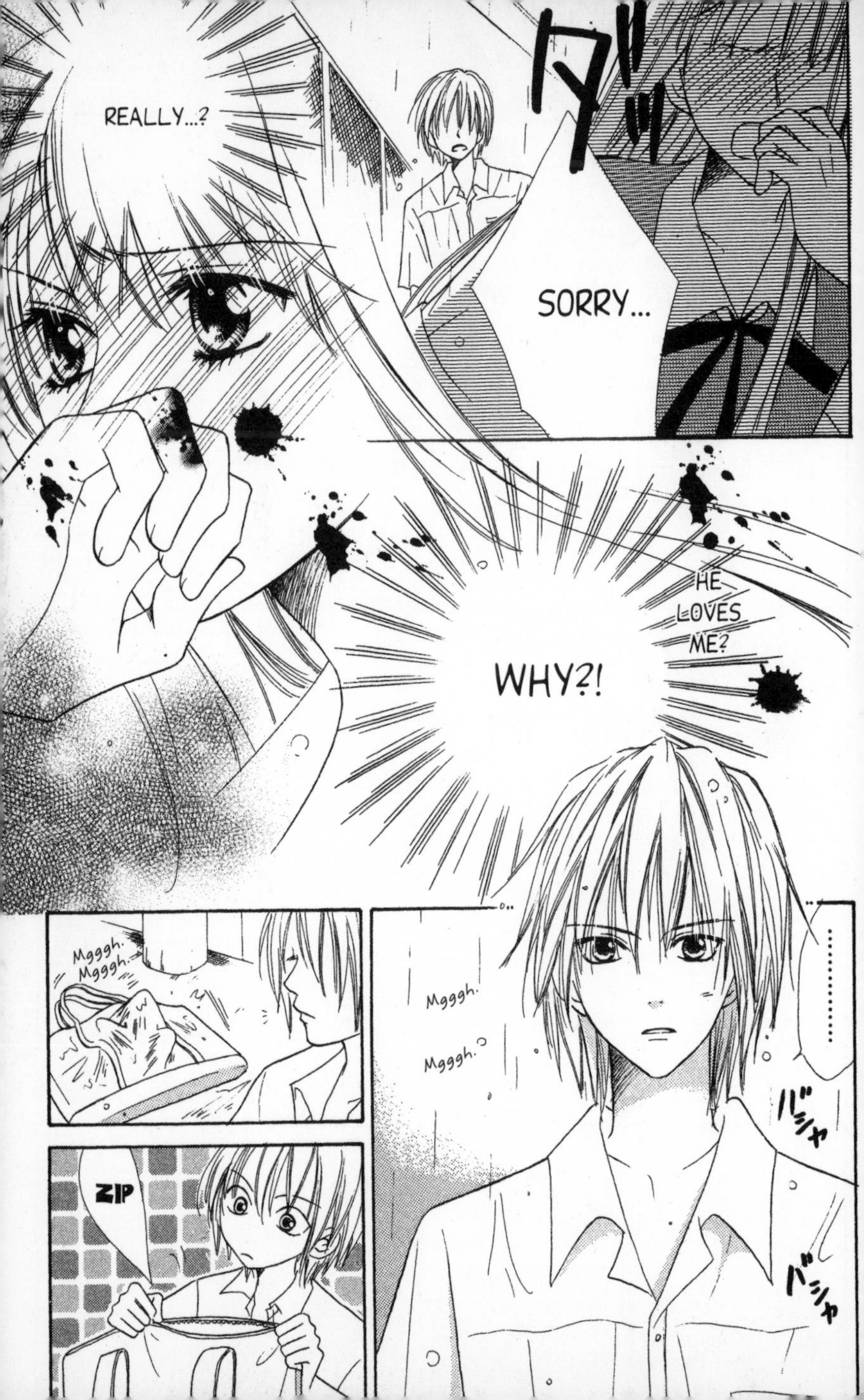
ダッ
SORRY...
REALLY...?
HE LOVES ME?
WHY?!
......
Mgggh.
Mgggh.
バシャ
バシャ
Mgggh.
Mgggh.
ZIP

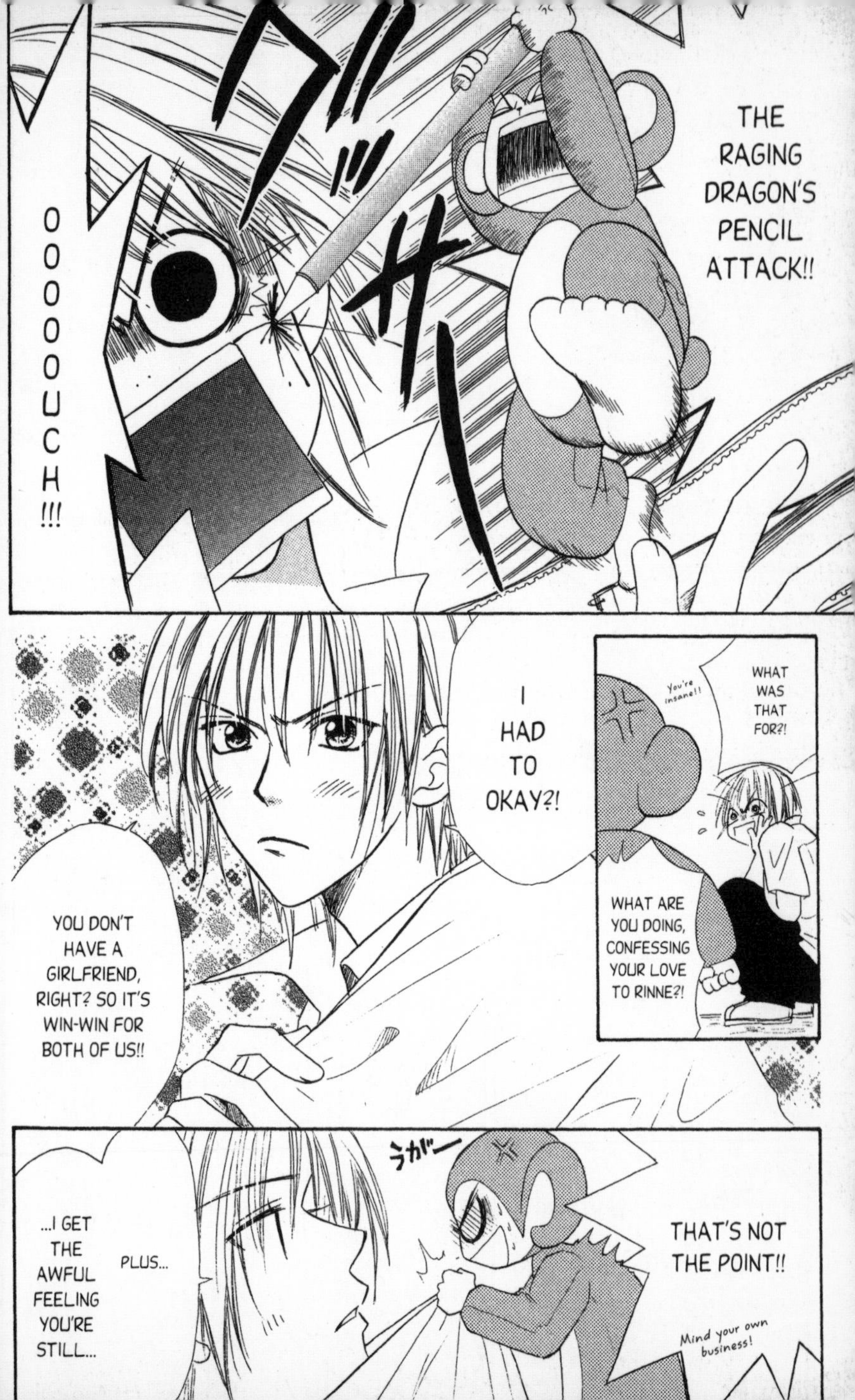
THE RAGING DRAGON'S PENCIL ATTACK!!
OOOOOOUCH!!!
WHAT WAS THAT FOR?!
You're insane!!
WHAT ARE YOU DOING, CONFESSING YOUR LOVE TO RINNE?!
I HAD TO OKAY?!
YOU DON'T HAVE A GIRLFRIEND, RIGHT? SO IT'S WIN-WIN FOR BOTH OF US!!
THAT'S NOT THE POINT!!
Mind your own business!
PLUS...
...I GET THE AWFUL FEELING YOU'RE STILL...

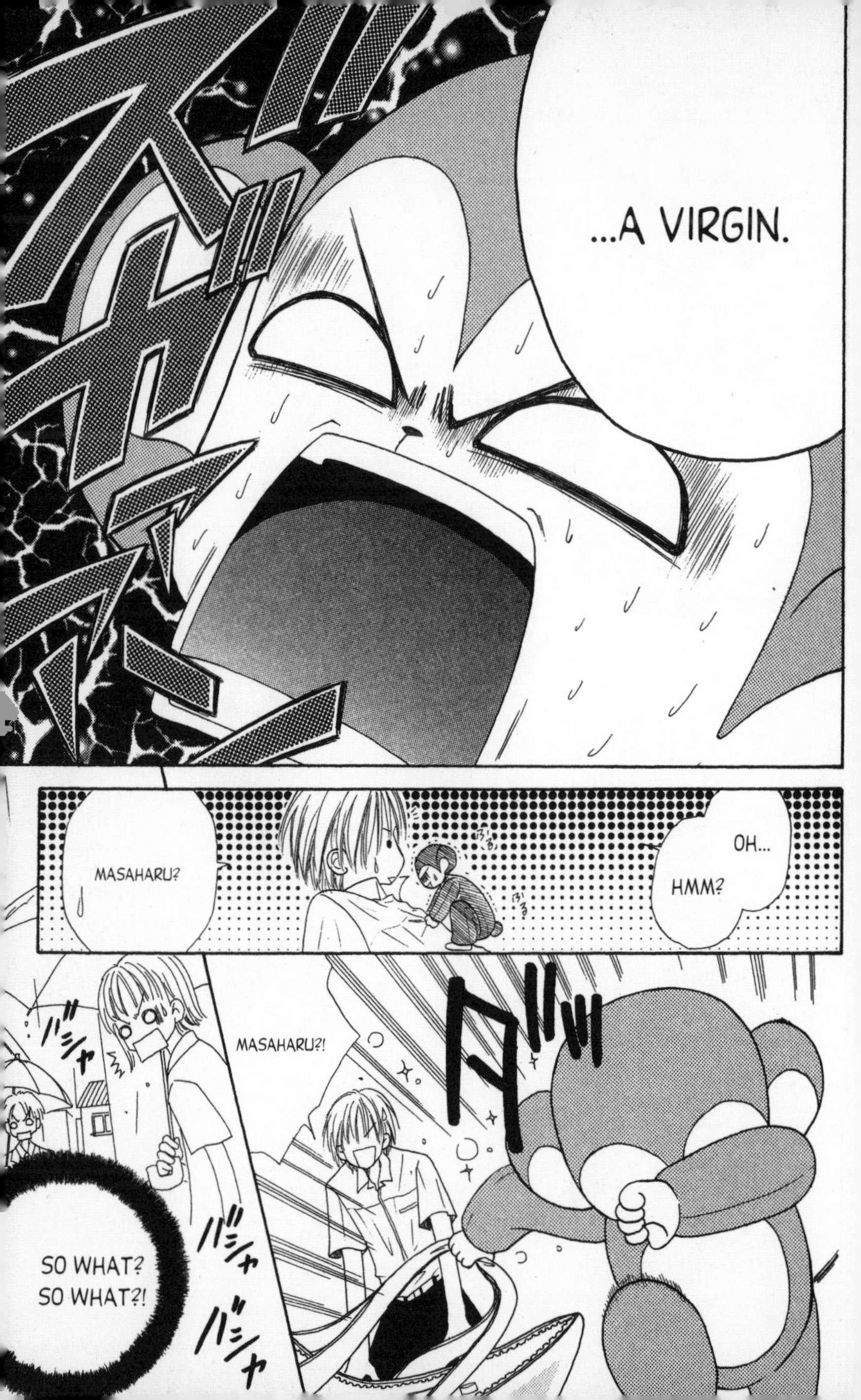
...A VIRGIN.
OH... HMM?
MASAHARU?
MASAHARU?!
SO WHAT? SO WHAT?!

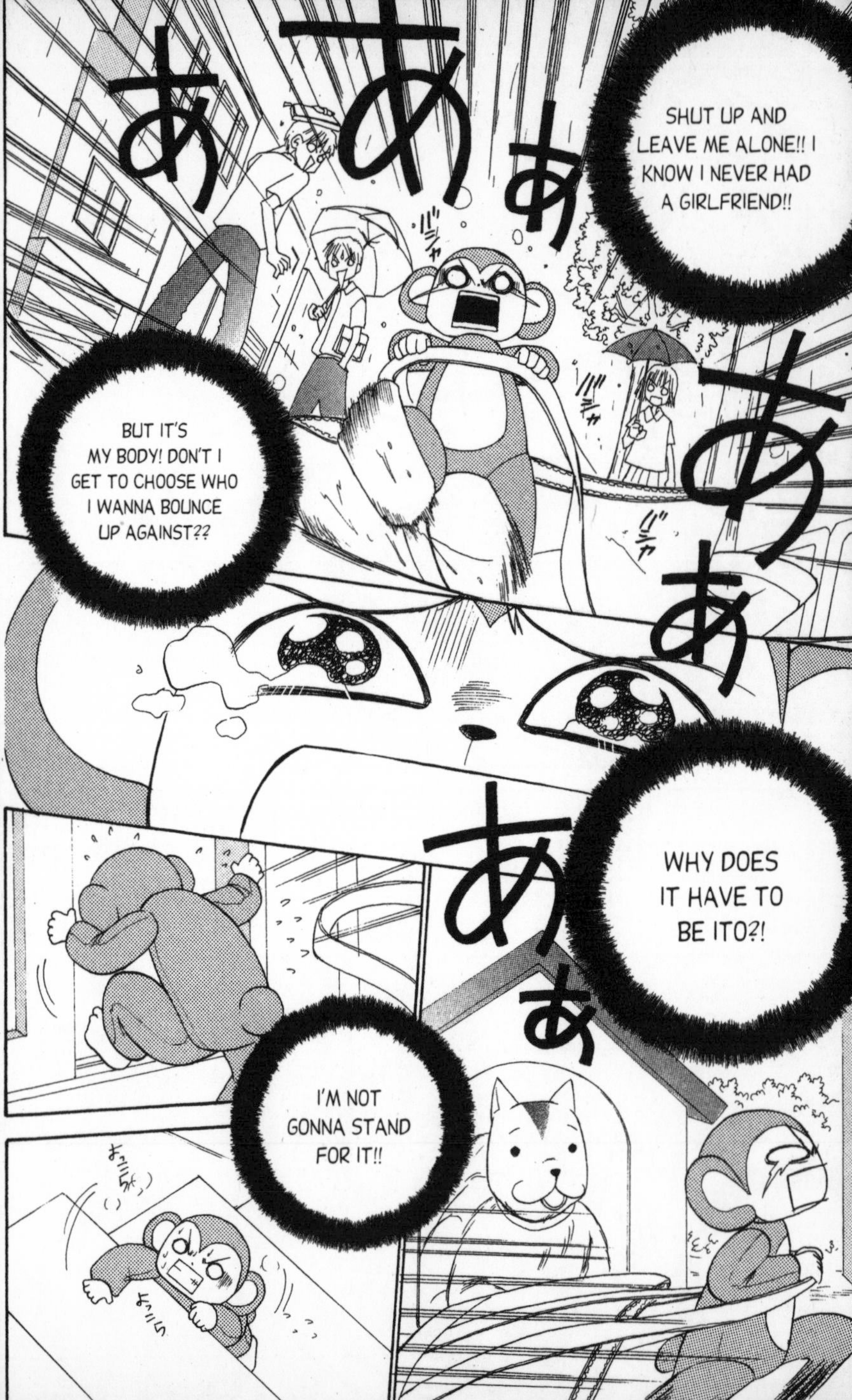
SHUT UP AND LEAVE ME ALONE!! I KNOW I NEVER HAD A GIRLFRIEND!!
BUT IT'S MY BODY! DON'T I GET TO CHOOSE WHO I WANNA BOUNCE UP AGAINST??
WHY DOES IT HAVE TO BE ITO?!
I'M NOT GONNA STAND FOR IT!!

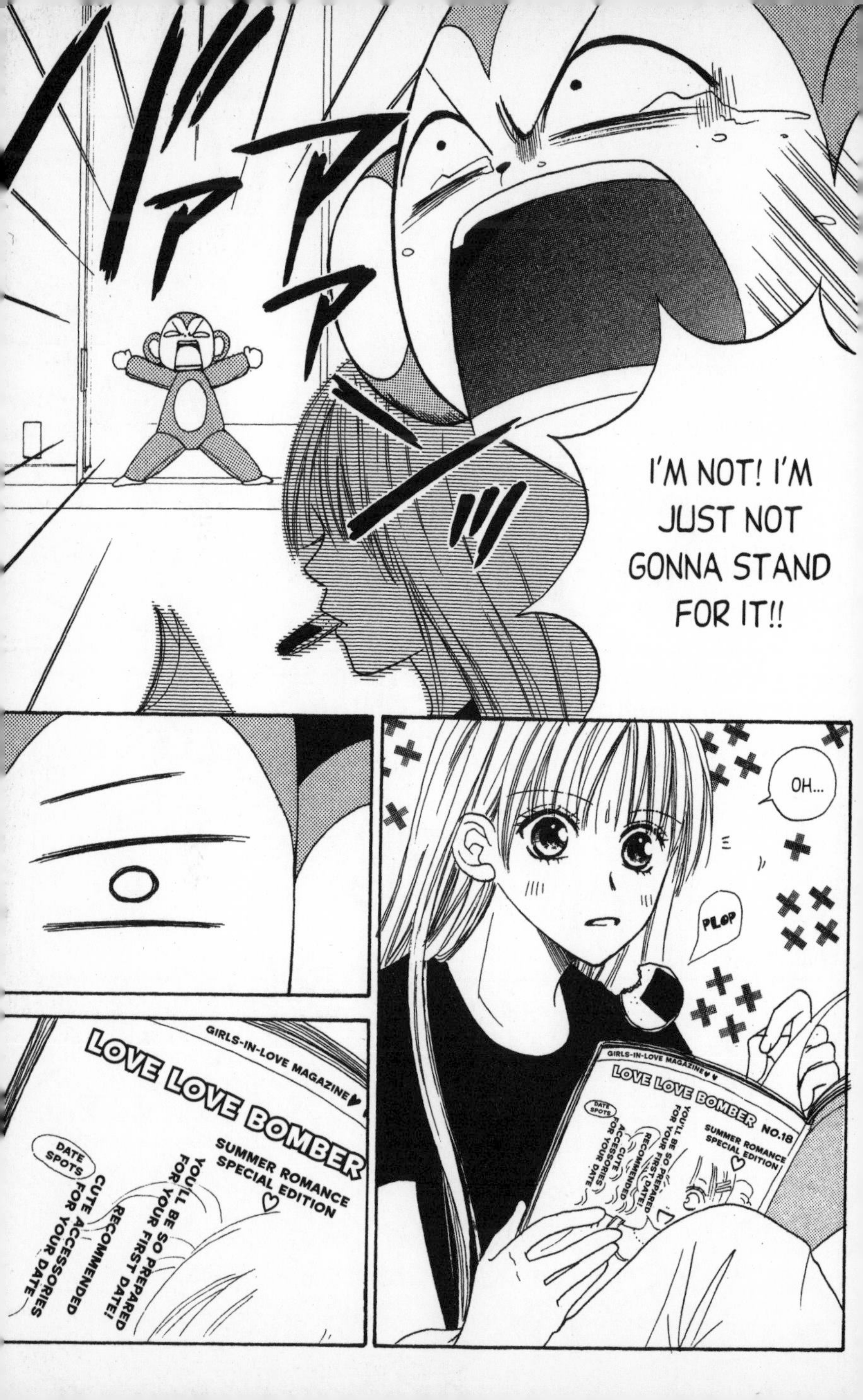
I'M NOT! I'M JUST NOT GONNA STAND FOR IT!!
OH...
PLOP
GIRLS-IN-LOVE MAGAZINE♥♥
LOVE LOVE BOMBER NO.18
SUMMER ROMANCE SPECIAL EDITION
YOU'LL BE SO PREPARED FOR YOUR FIRST DATE!
RECOMMENDED
CUTE ACCESSORIES FOR YOUR DATE
DATE SPOTS
GIRLS-IN-LOVE MAGAZINE♥
LOVE LOVE BOMBER
SUMMER ROMANCE SPECIAL EDITION
YOU'LL BE SO PREPARED FOR YOUR FIRST DATE!
RECOMMENDED
CUTE ACCESSORIES FOR YOUR DATE
DATE SPOTS

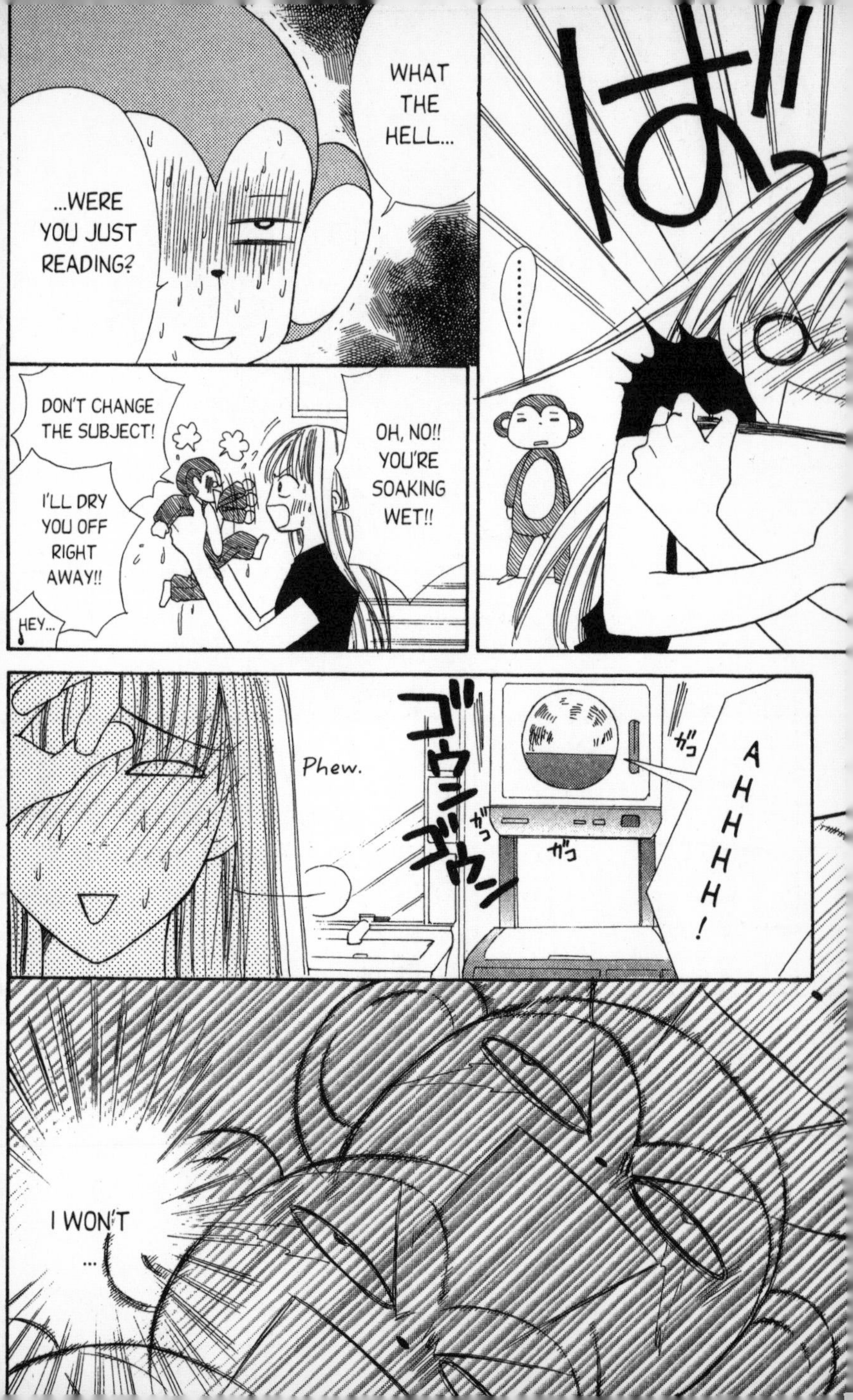
……
WHAT THE HELL...
...WERE YOU JUST READING?
OH, NO!! YOU'RE SOAKING WET!!
DON'T CHANGE THE SUBJECT!
I'LL DRY YOU OFF RIGHT AWAY!!
HEY...
AHHHHH!
Phew.
I WON'T ...

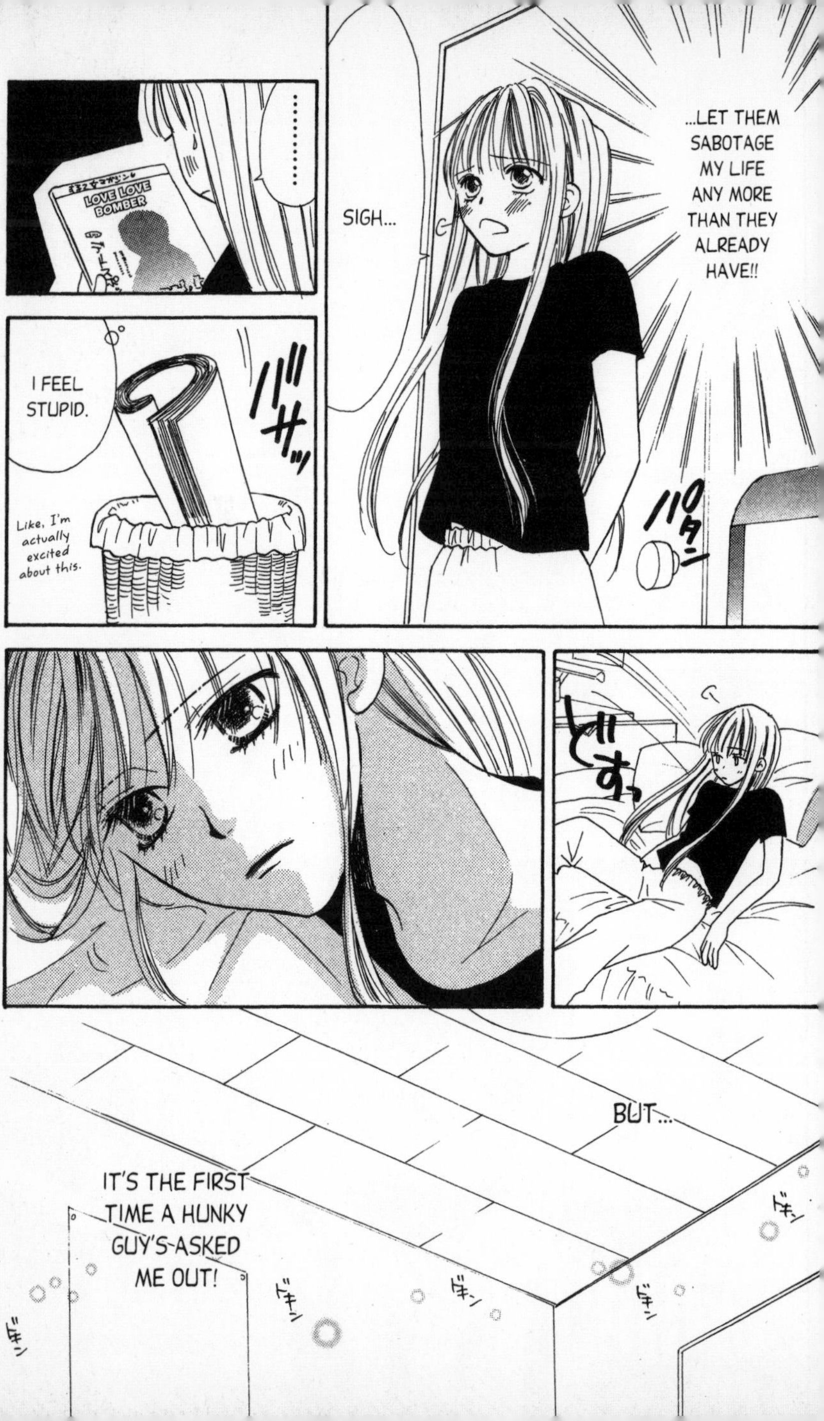
...LET THEM SABOTAGE MY LIFE ANY MORE THAN THEY ALREADY HAVE!!
SIGH...
パタン
......
LOVE LOVE BOMBER
I FEEL STUPID.
バサッ
Like, I'm actually excited about this.
どすっ
BUT...
IT'S THE FIRST TIME A HUNKY GUY'S-ASKED ME OUT!
ドキン
ドキン
ドキン
ドキン
ドキン

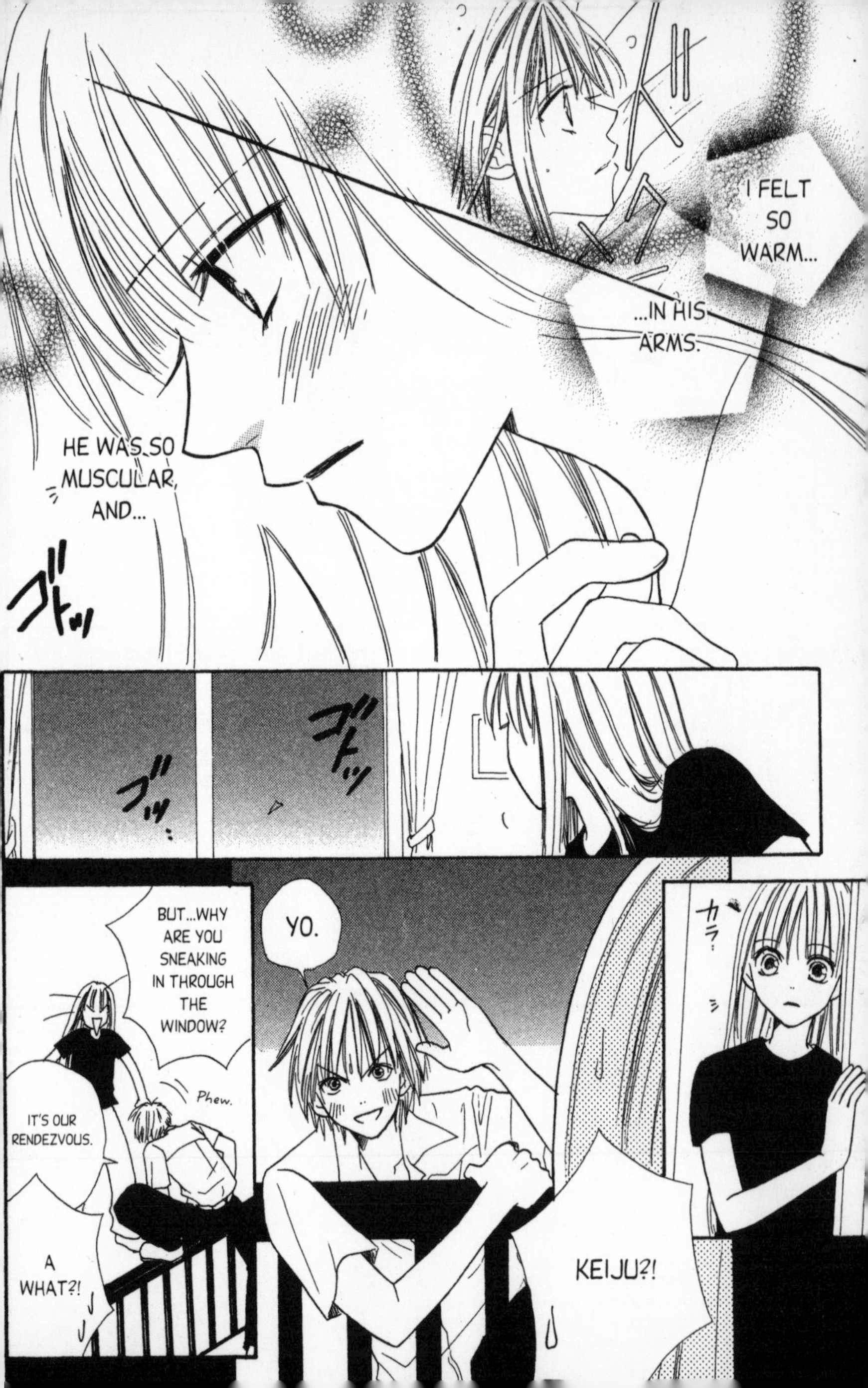
I FELT SO WARM...
...IN HIS ARMS.
HE WAS SO MUSCULAR, AND...
ゴトッ
ゴトッ
ゴッ...
カラ...
KEIJU?!
YO.
BUT...WHY ARE YOU SNEAKING IN THROUGH THE WINDOW?
Phew.
IT'S OUR RENDEZVOUS.
A WHAT?!

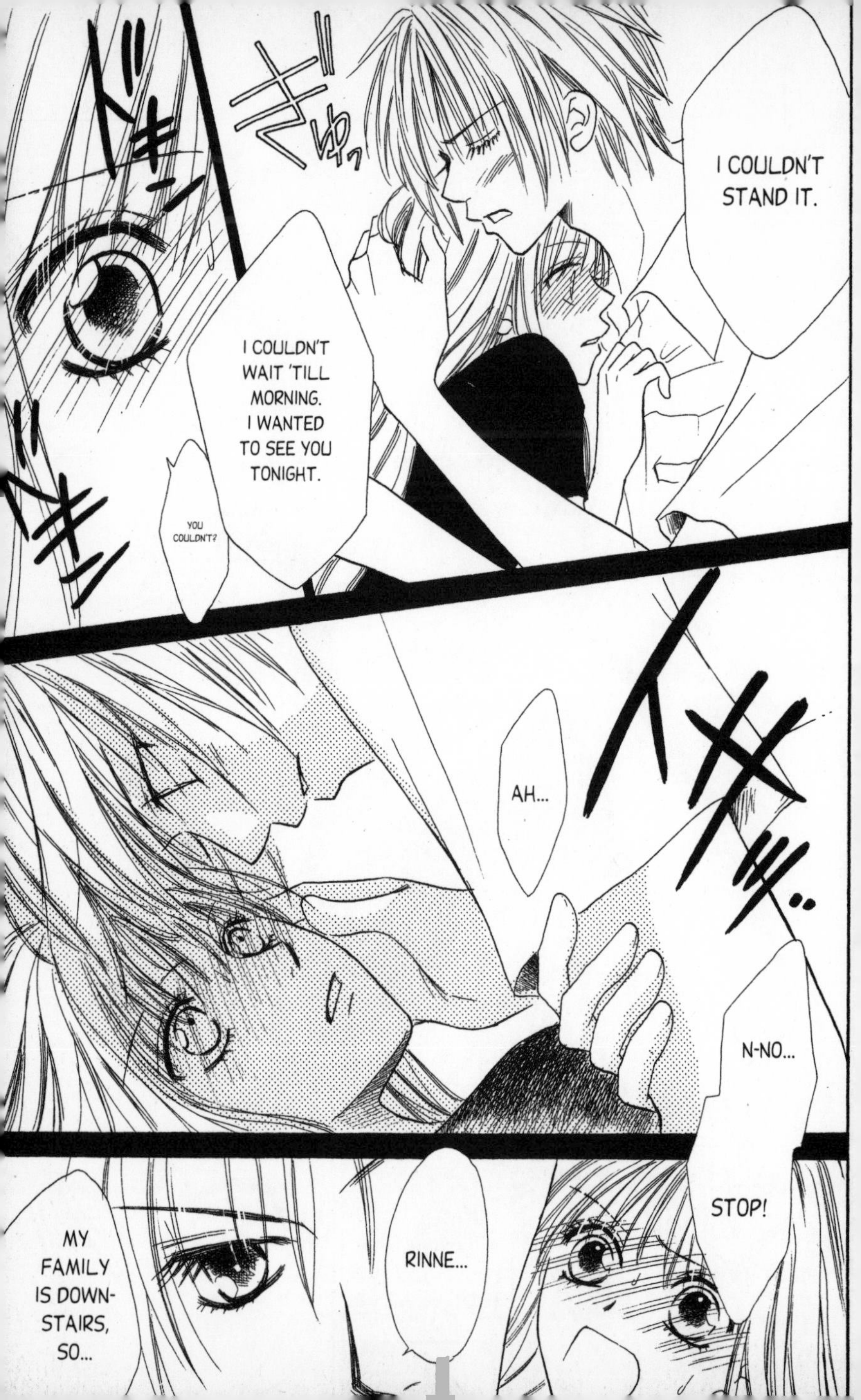
I COULDN'T STAND IT.
I COULDN'T WAIT 'TILL MORNING. I WANTED TO SEE YOU TONIGHT.
YOU COULDN'T?
AH...
N-NO...
STOP!
RINNE...
MY FAMILY IS DOWN-STAIRS, SO...

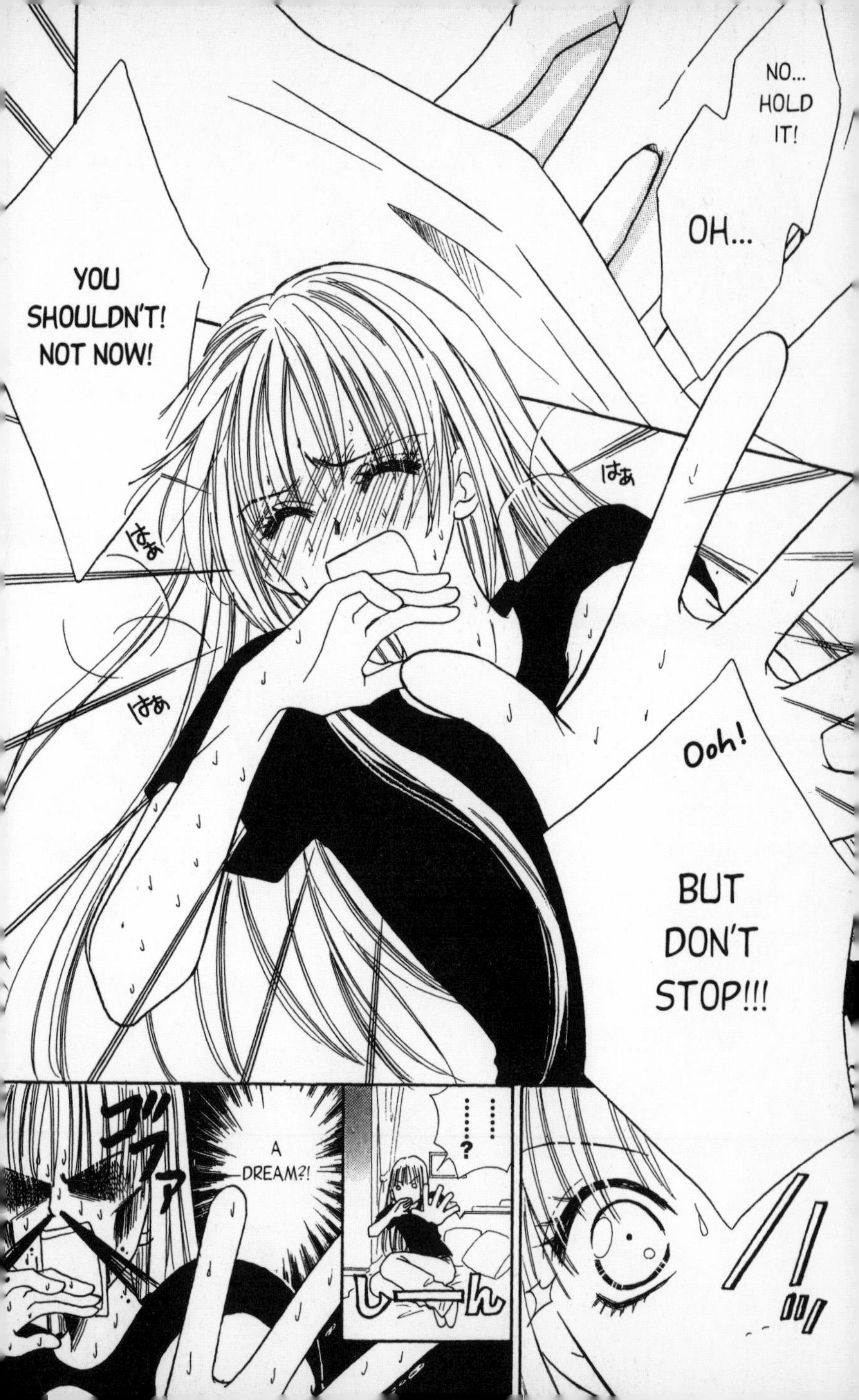
NO... HOLD IT!
OH...
YOU SHOULDN'T! NOT NOW!
はぁ
はぁ
はぁ
Ooh!
BUT DON'T STOP!!!
......?
しーん
A DREAM?!
ゴァ

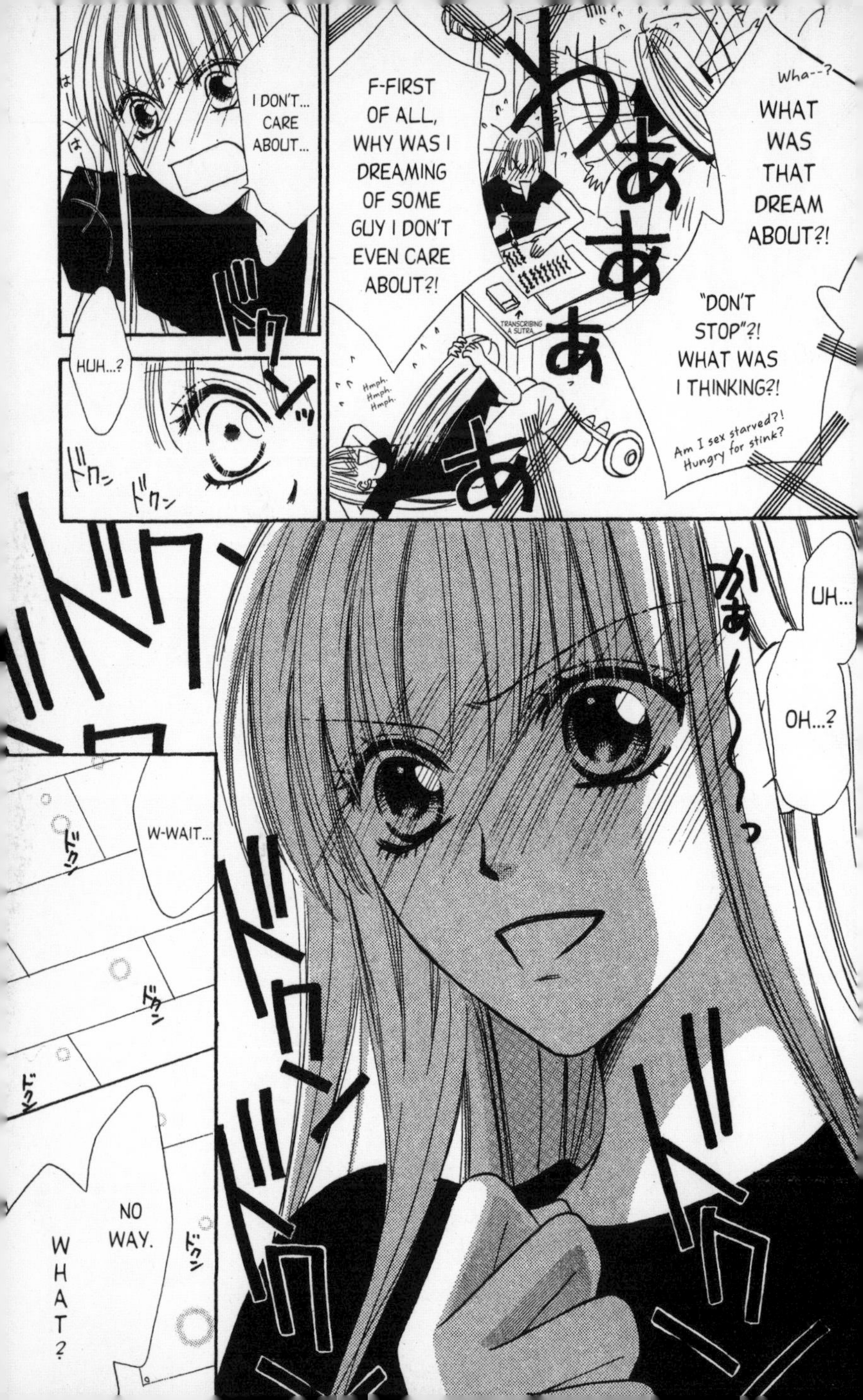
Wha--?
WHAT WAS THAT DREAM ABOUT?!
わぁあああ
F-FIRST OF ALL, WHY WAS I DREAMING OF SOME GUY I DON'T EVEN CARE ABOUT?!
TRANSCRIBING A SUTRA
Hmph. Hmph. Hmph.
"DON'T STOP"?! WHAT WAS I THINKING?!
Am I sex starved?! Hungry for stink?
はー
は
I DON'T... CARE ABOUT...
ドクン
HUH...?
ドクン
ドクン ドクン
ドクン
UH...
かぁ~っ
OH...?
ドクン
ドクン ドクン
W-WAIT...
ドクン
ドクン
NO WAY.
ドクン
WHAT?

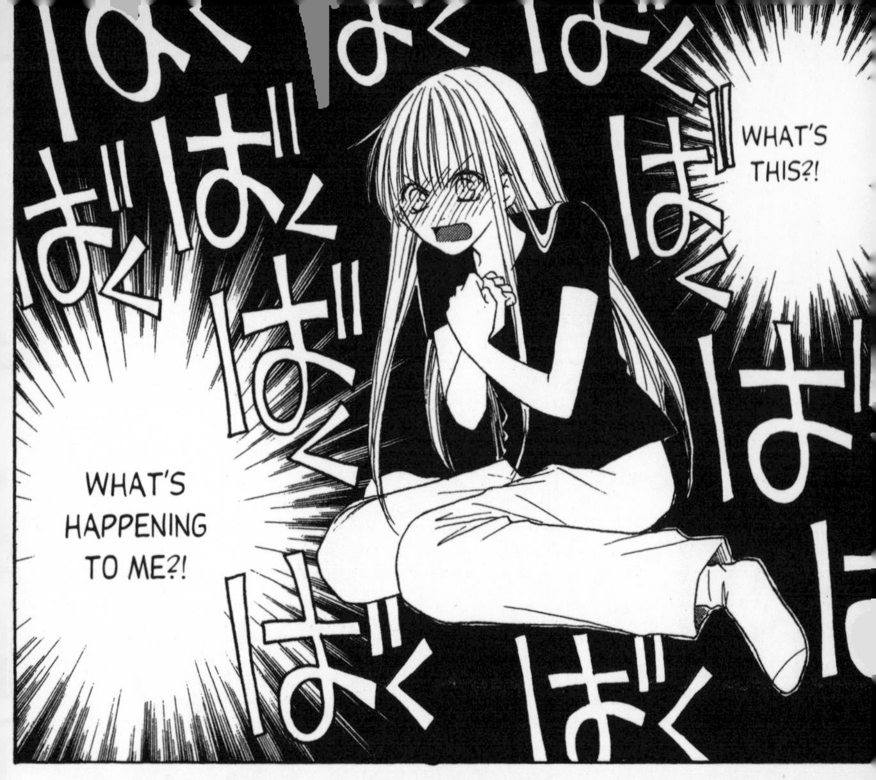
WHAT'S THIS?!
WHAT'S HAPPENING TO ME?!
ばくばくばくばくばくばくばくばく

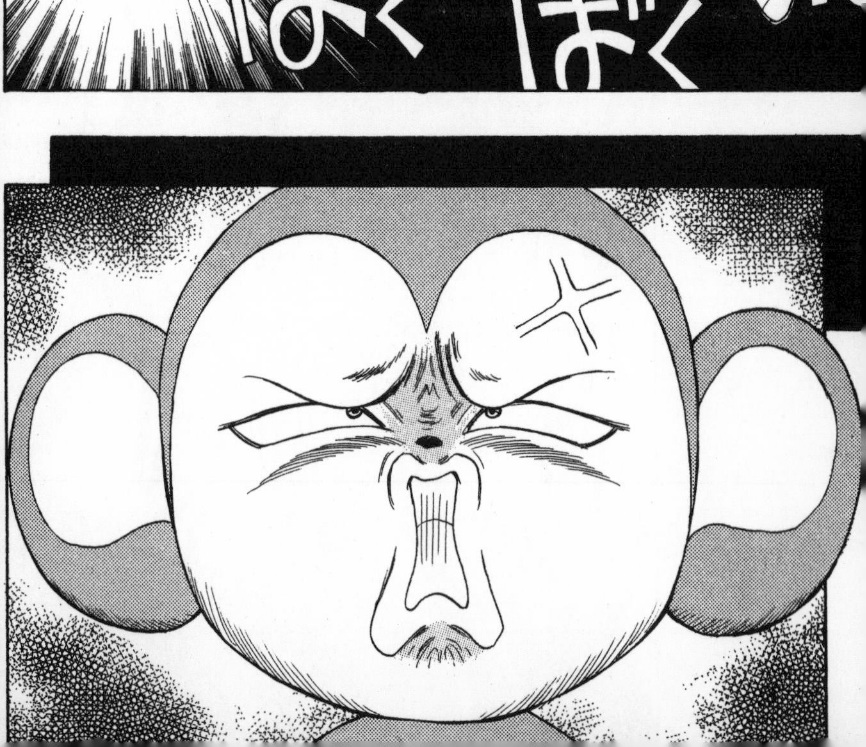

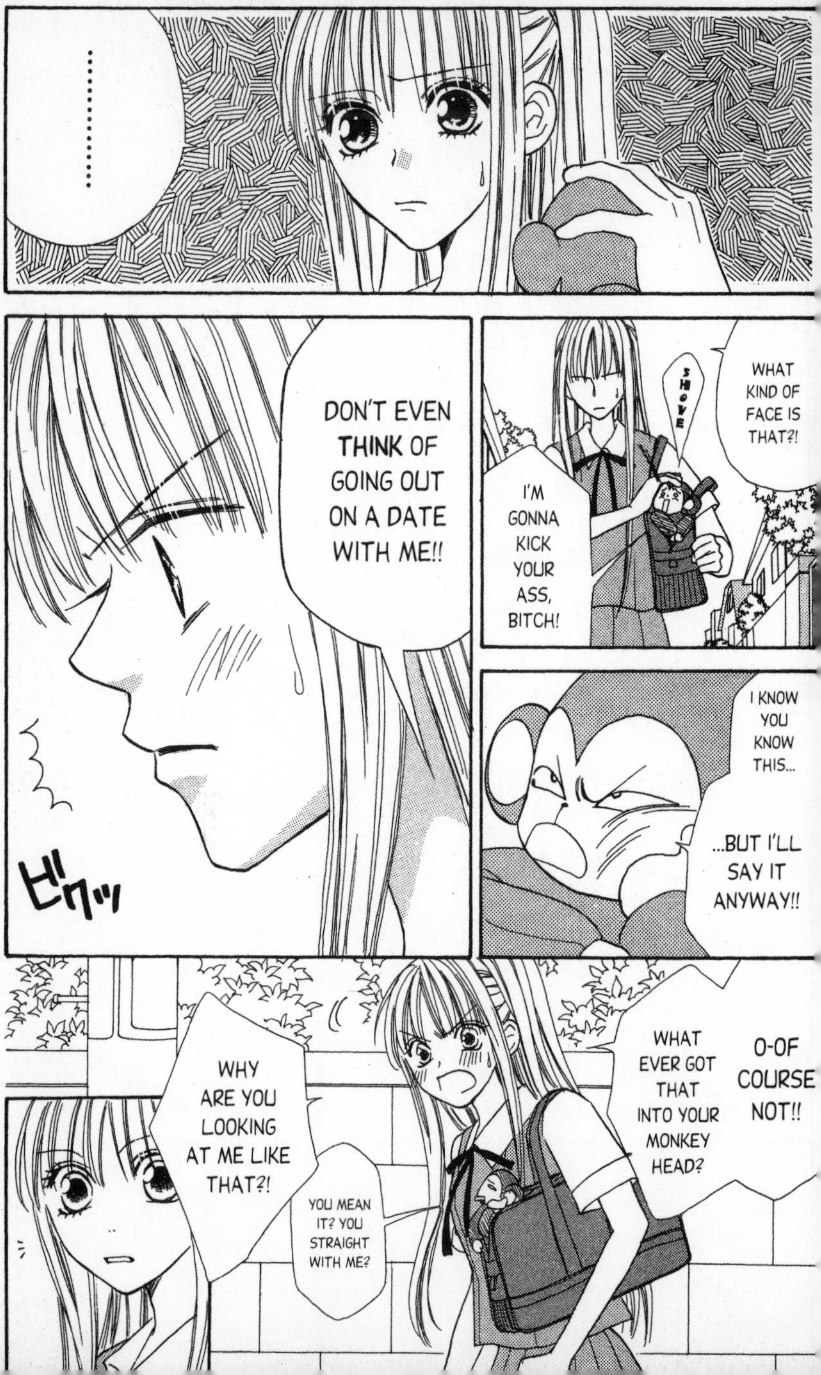
....
WHAT KIND OF FACE IS THAT?!
SHOVE
I'M GONNA KICK YOUR ASS, BITCH!
I KNOW YOU KNOW THIS...
...BUT I'LL SAY IT ANYWAY!!
DON'T EVEN THINK OF GOING OUT ON A DATE WITH ME!!
O-OF COURSE NOT!!
WHAT EVER GOT THAT INTO YOUR MONKEY HEAD?
WHY ARE YOU LOOKING AT ME LIKE THAT?!
YOU MEAN IT? YOU STRAIGHT WITH ME?

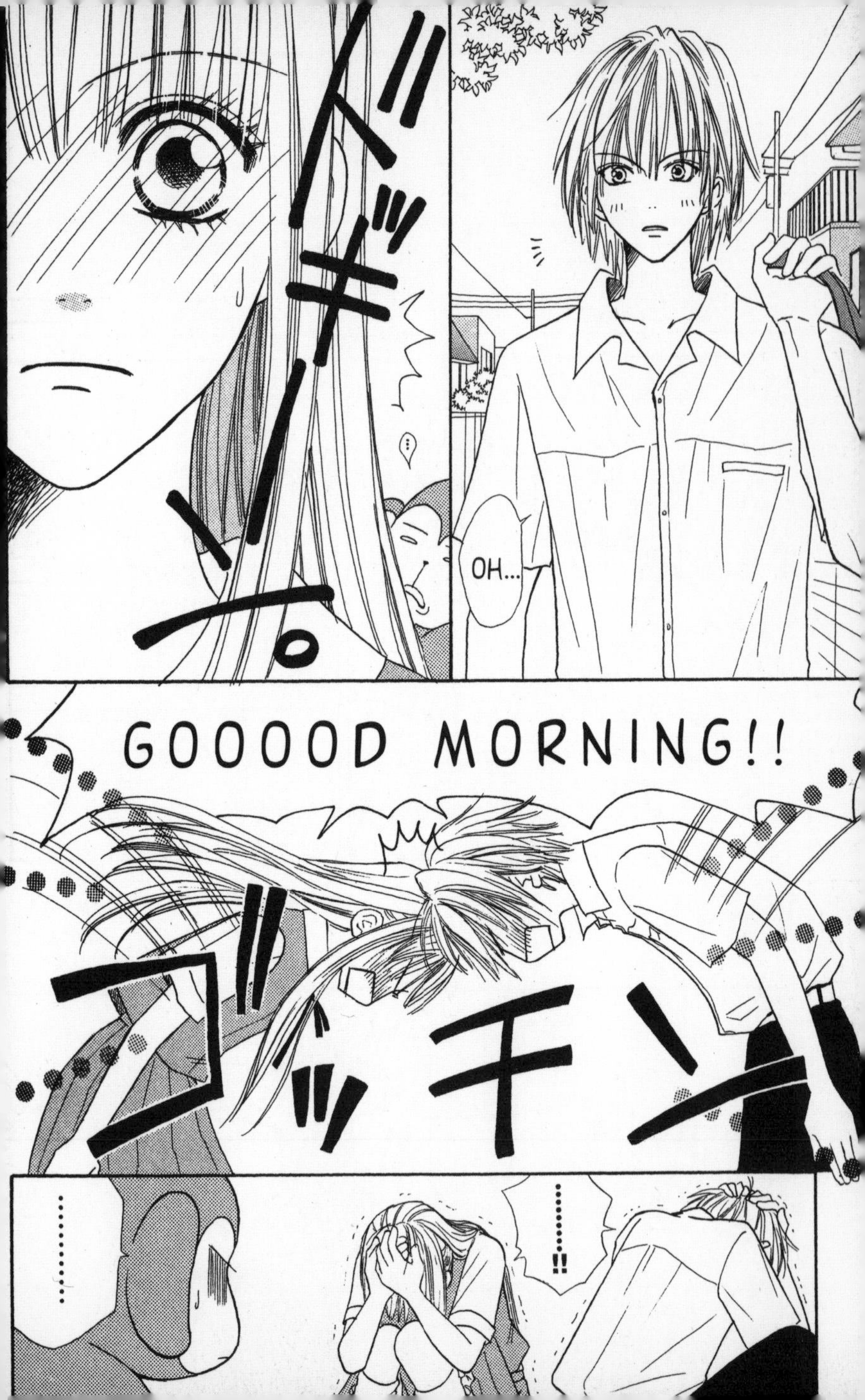
OH...
ドッキーン
GOOOOD MORNING!!
ゴッチン
.........!!
....

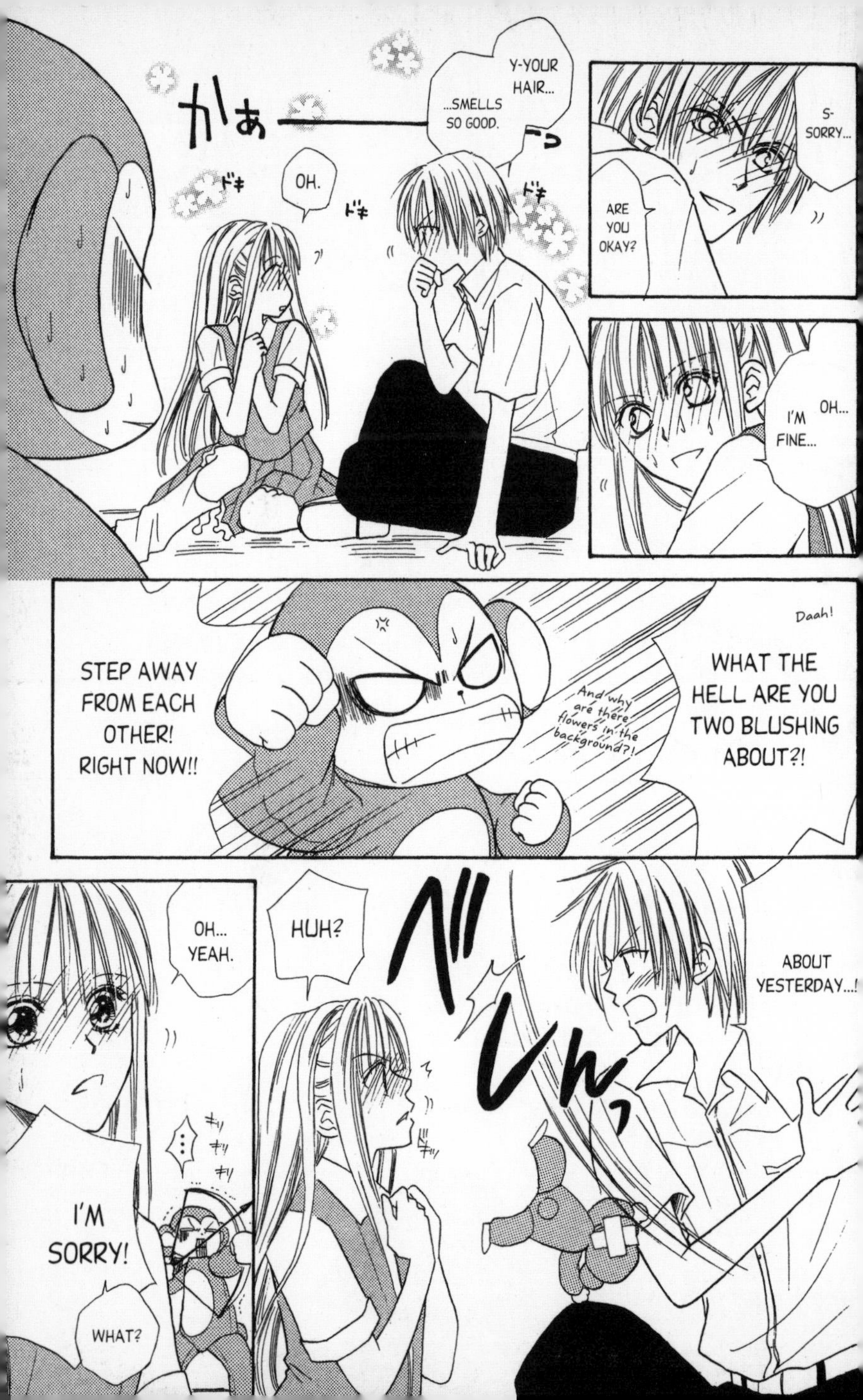
S-SORRY...
ARE YOU OKAY?
OH... I'M FINE...
Y-YOUR HAIR...
...SMELLS SO GOOD.
かぁーーーっ
OH.
ドキ
ドキ
ドキ
WHAT THE HELL ARE YOU TWO BLUSHING ABOUT?!
Daah!
And why are there flowers in the background?!
STEP AWAY FROM EACH OTHER! RIGHT NOW!!
ABOUT YESTERDAY...!
べしんっ
HUH?
OH... YEAH.
...!
キリ キリ キリ
I'M SORRY!
WHAT?

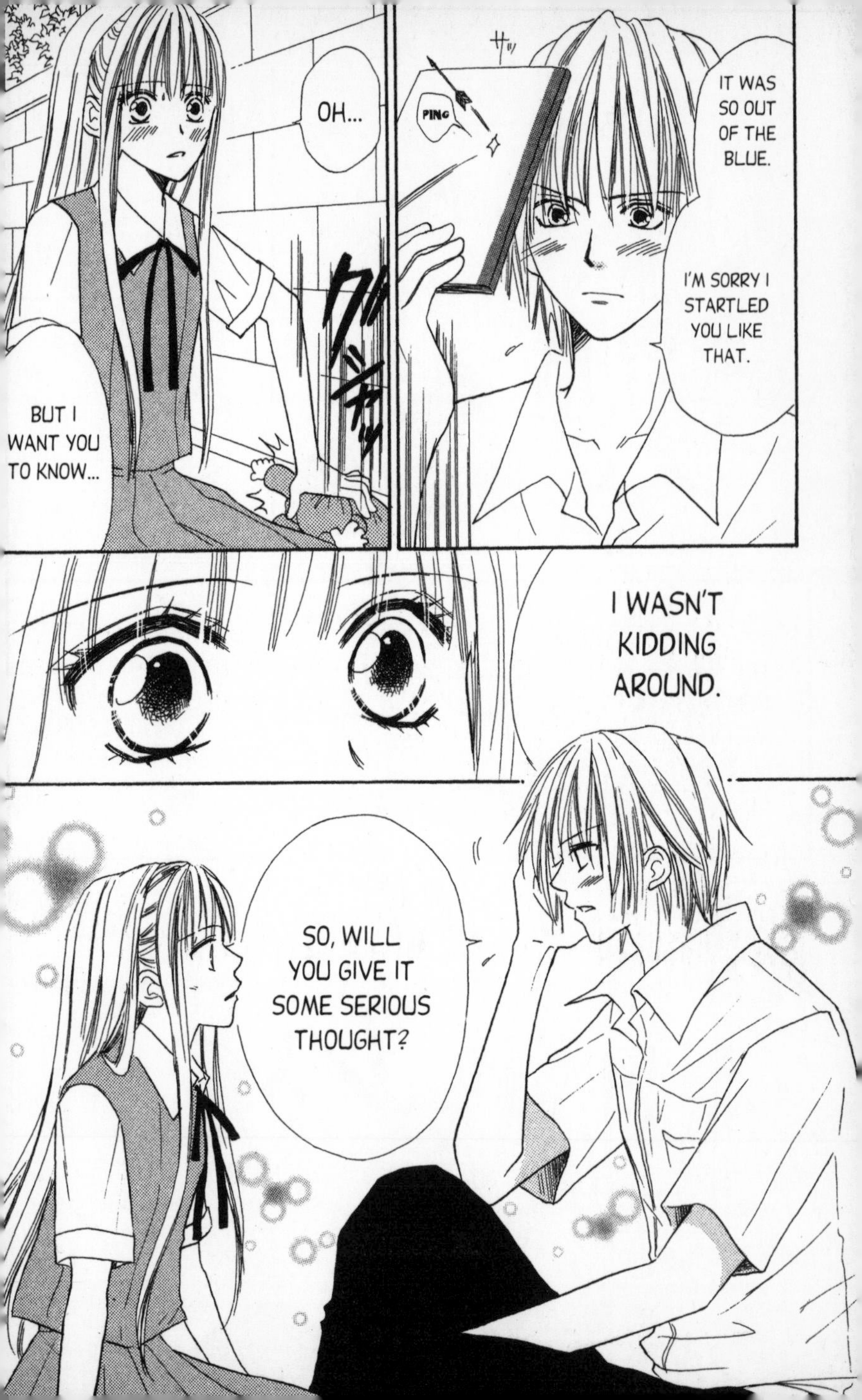
IT WAS SO OUT OF THE BLUE.
PING
I'M SORRY I STARTLED YOU LIKE THAT.
OH...
BUT I WANT YOU TO KNOW...
I WASN'T KIDDING AROUND.
SO, WILL YOU GIVE IT SOME SERIOUS THOUGHT?

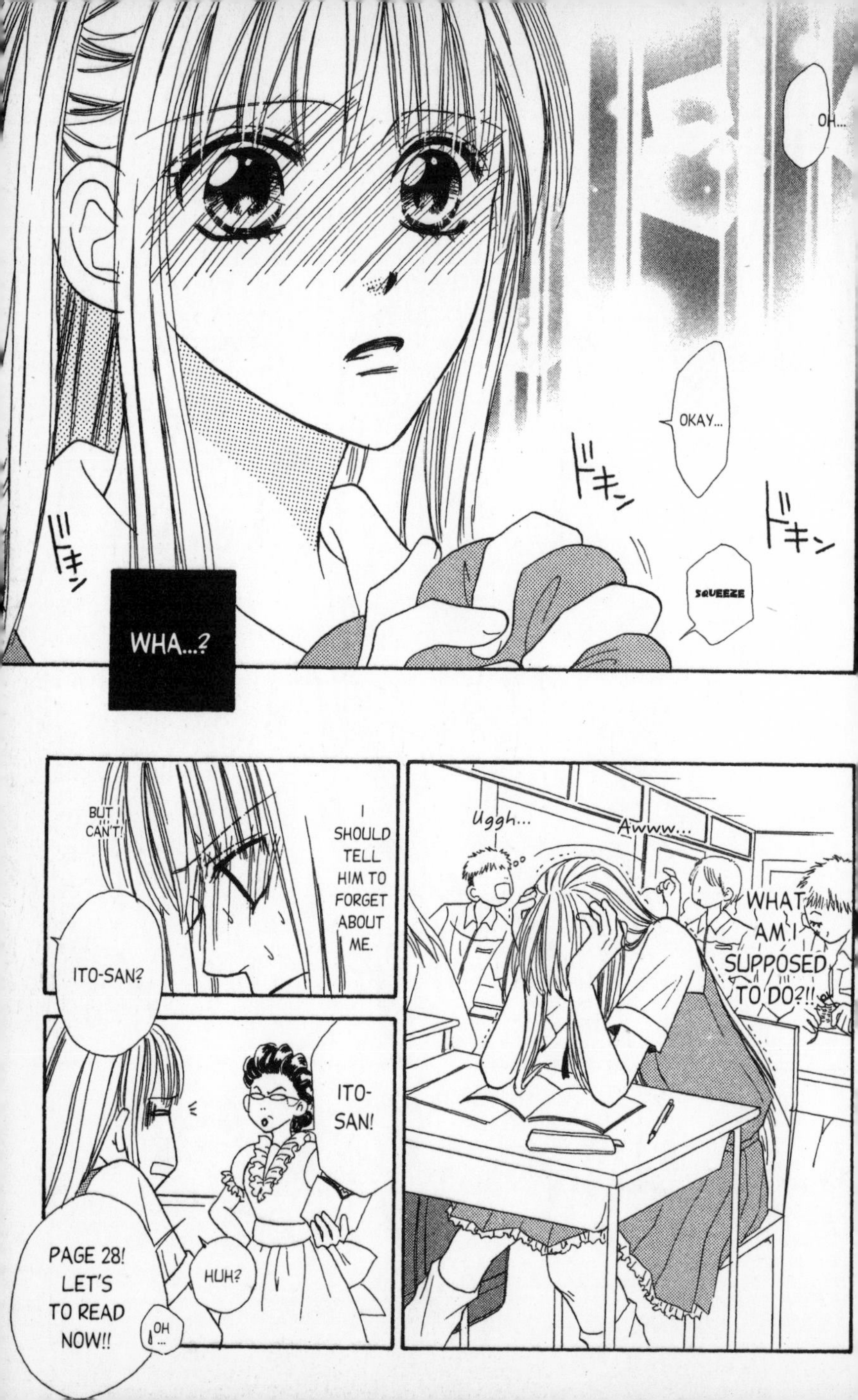
OH...
OKAY...
ドキン
ドキン
SQUEEZE
ドキン
WHA...?
Uggh...
Awww...
WHAT AM I SUPPOSED TO DO?!!
I SHOULD TELL HIM TO FORGET ABOUT ME.
BUT I CAN'T!
ITO-SAN?
ITO-SAN!
HUH?
PAGE 28! LET'S TO READ NOW!!
OH...

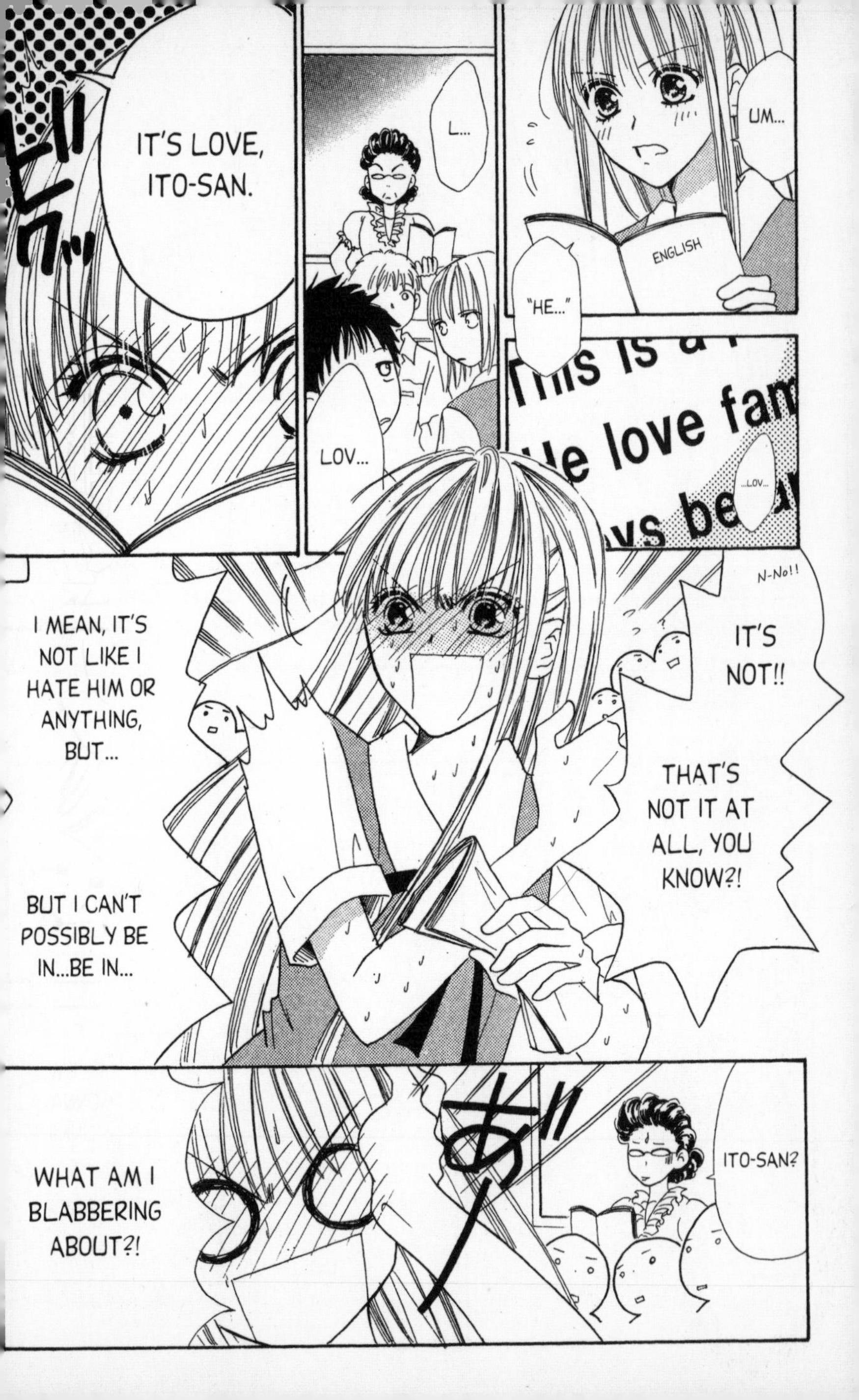

UM...
ENGLISH
"HE..."
This is
love
...LOV...
L...
LOV...
IT'S LOVE, ITO-SAN.
N-No!!
IT'S NOT!!
THAT'S NOT IT AT ALL, YOU KNOW?!
I MEAN, IT'S NOT LIKE I HATE HIM OR ANYTHING, BUT...
BUT I CAN'T POSSIBLY BE IN...BE IN...
ITO-SAN?
あっ
WHAT AM I BLABBERING ABOUT?!

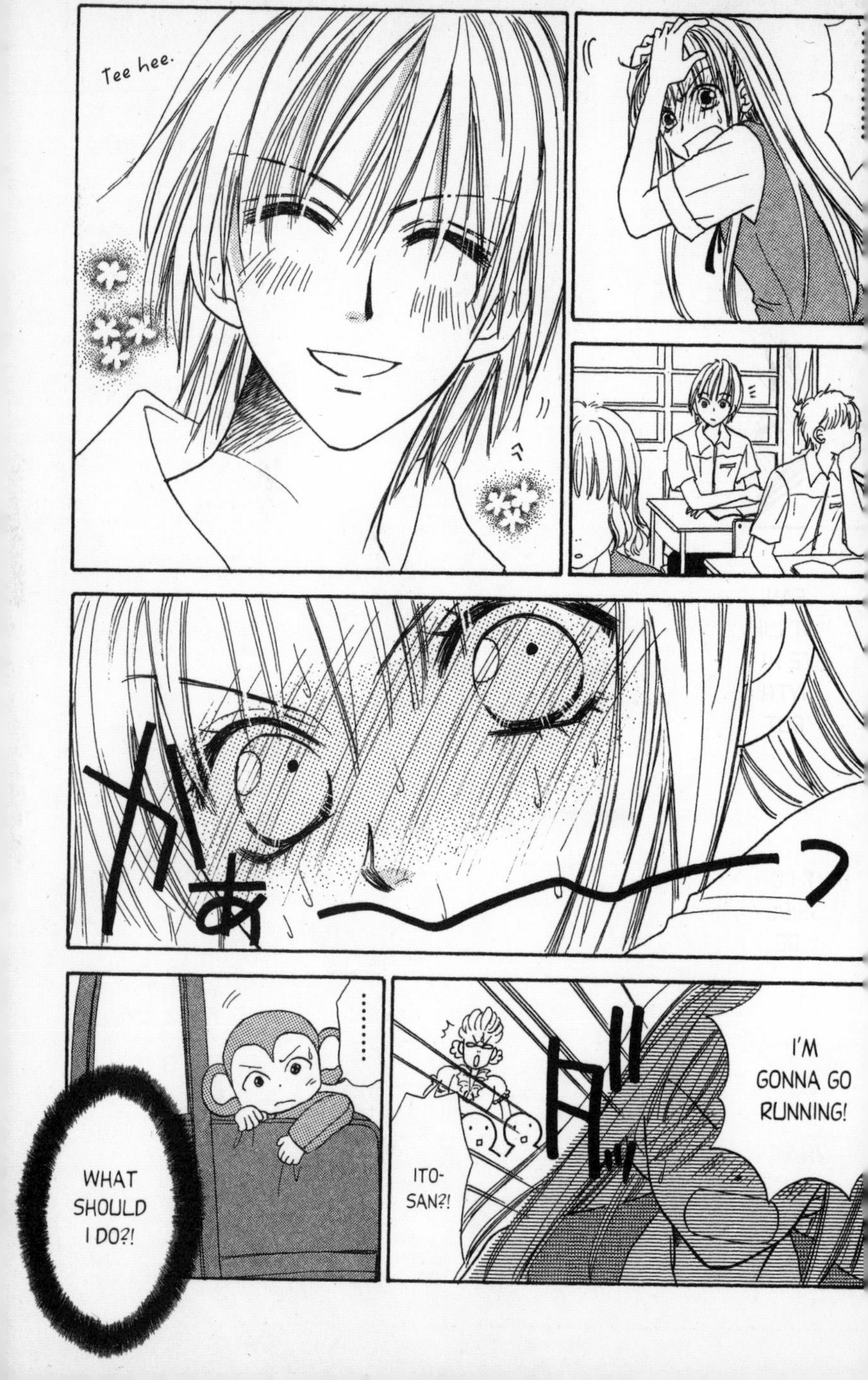
Tee hee.
かあ〜〜っ
I'M GONNA GO RUNNING!
ITO-SAN?!
......
WHAT SHOULD I DO?!

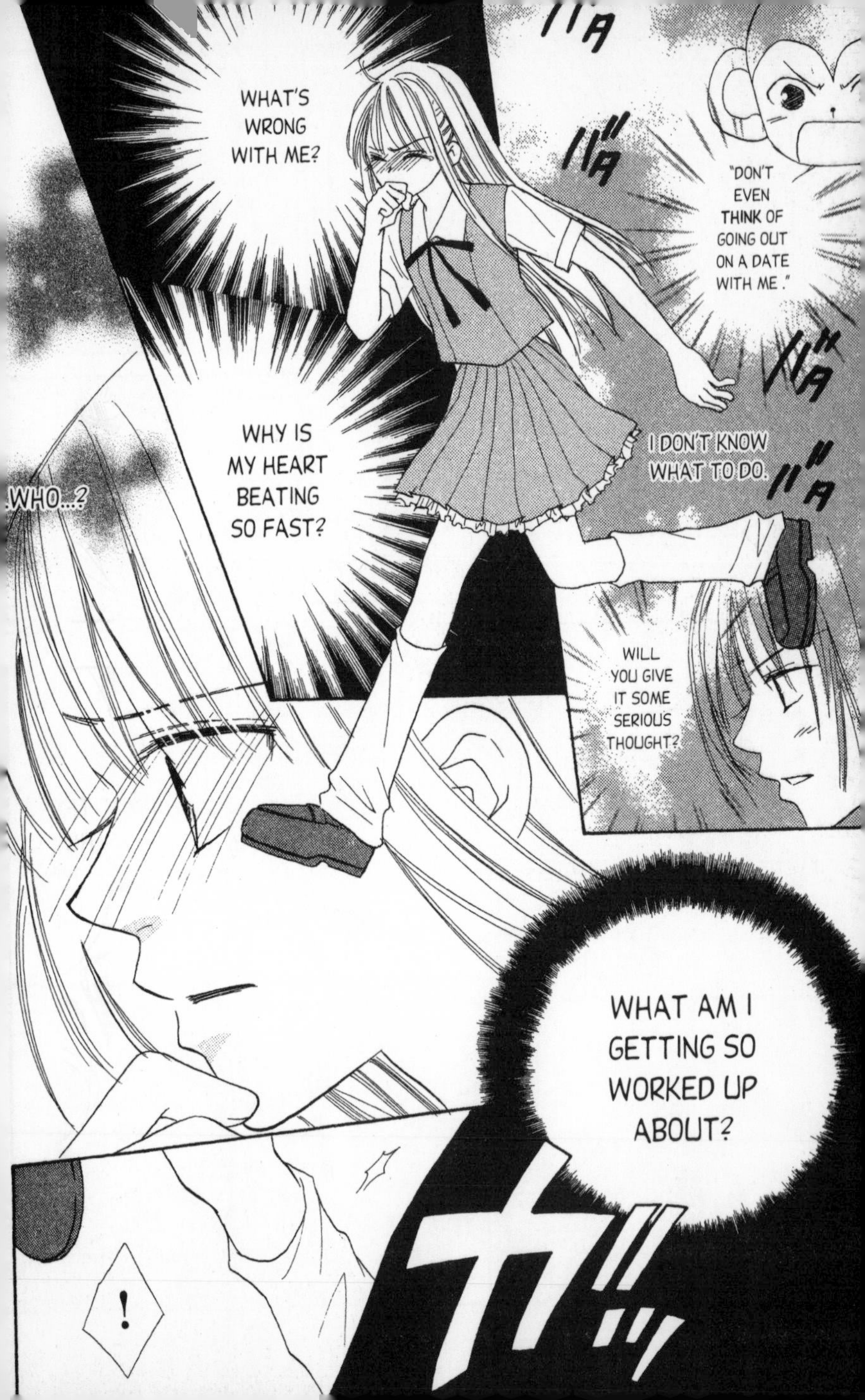
HA
HA
"DON'T EVEN THINK OF GOING OUT ON A DATE WITH ME."
WHAT'S WRONG WITH ME?
HA
HA
I DON'T KNOW WHAT TO DO.
WHY IS MY HEART BEATING SO FAST?
WILL YOU GIVE IT SOME SERIOUS THOUGHT?
...WHO...?
WHAT AM I GETTING SO WORKED UP ABOUT?
!

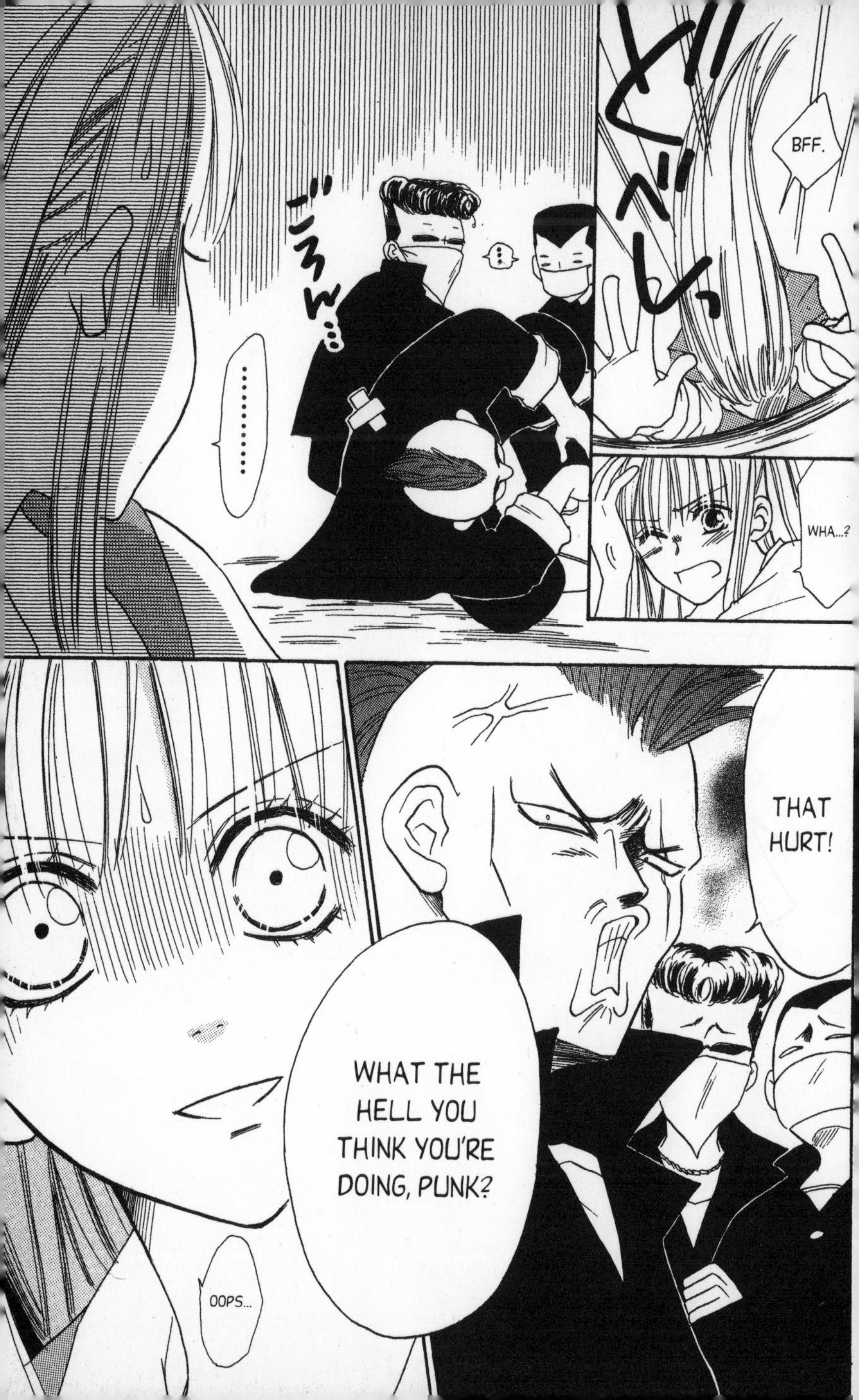
BFF.
WHA...?
......
ごろん…
...
THAT HURT!
WHAT THE HELL YOU THINK YOU'RE DOING, PUNK?
OOPS...

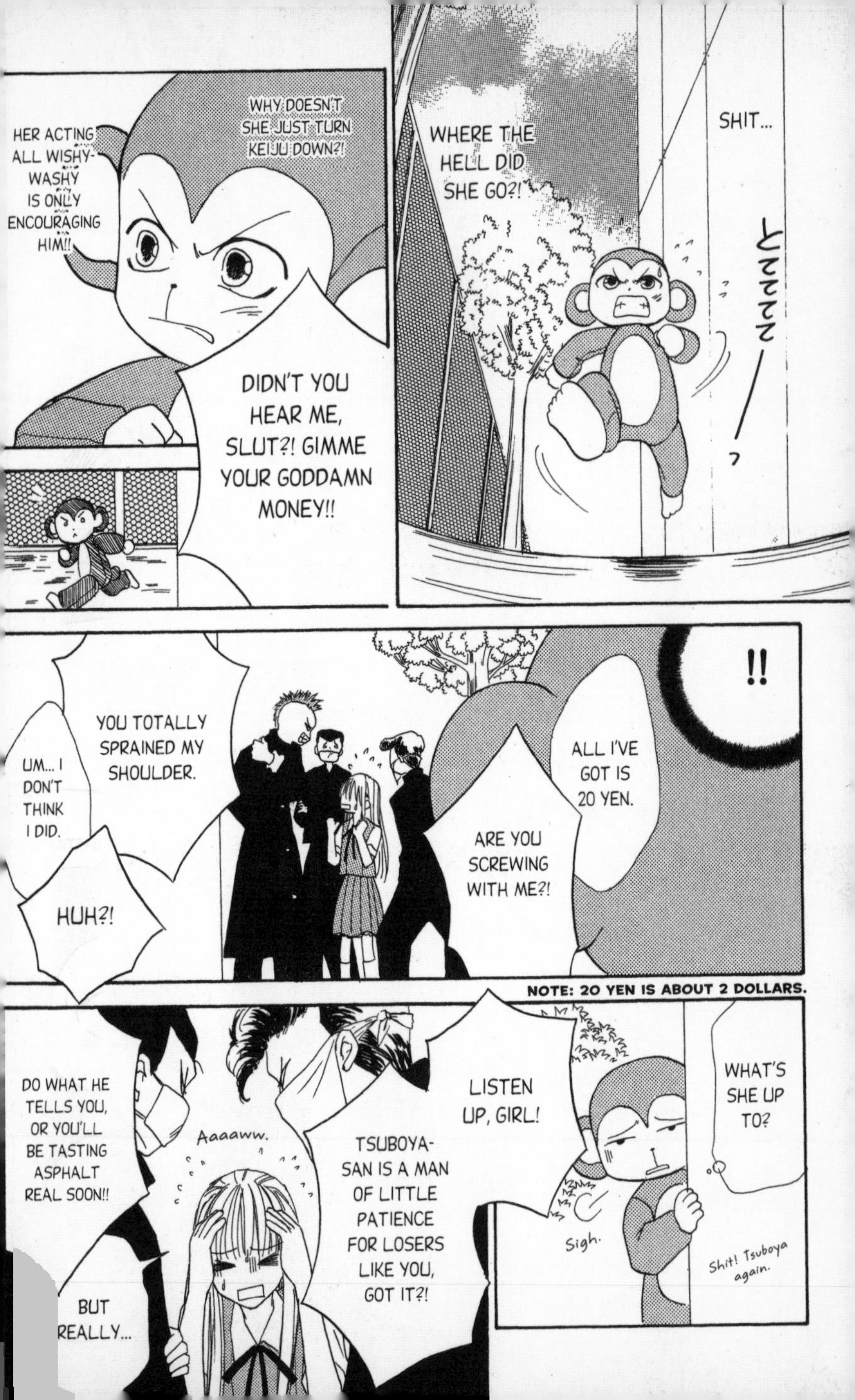
SHIT...
WHERE THE HELL DID SHE GO?!
WHY DOESN'T SHE JUST TURN KEIJU DOWN?!
HER ACTING ALL WISHY-WASHY IS ONLY ENCOURAGING HIM!!
DIDN'T YOU HEAR ME, SLUT?! GIMME YOUR GODDAMN MONEY!!
!!
ALL I'VE GOT IS 20 YEN.
ARE YOU SCREWING WITH ME?!
YOU TOTALLY SPRAINED MY SHOULDER.
UM... I DON'T THINK I DID.
HUH?!
WHAT'S SHE UP TO?
Sigh.
Shit! Tsuboya again.
LISTEN UP, GIRL!
TSUBOYA-SAN IS A MAN OF LITTLE PATIENCE FOR LOSERS LIKE YOU, GOT IT?!
Aaaaww.
DO WHAT HE TELLS YOU, OR YOU'LL BE TASTING ASPHALT REAL SOON!!
BUT REALLY...
NOTE: 20 YEN IS ABOUT 2 DOLLARS.

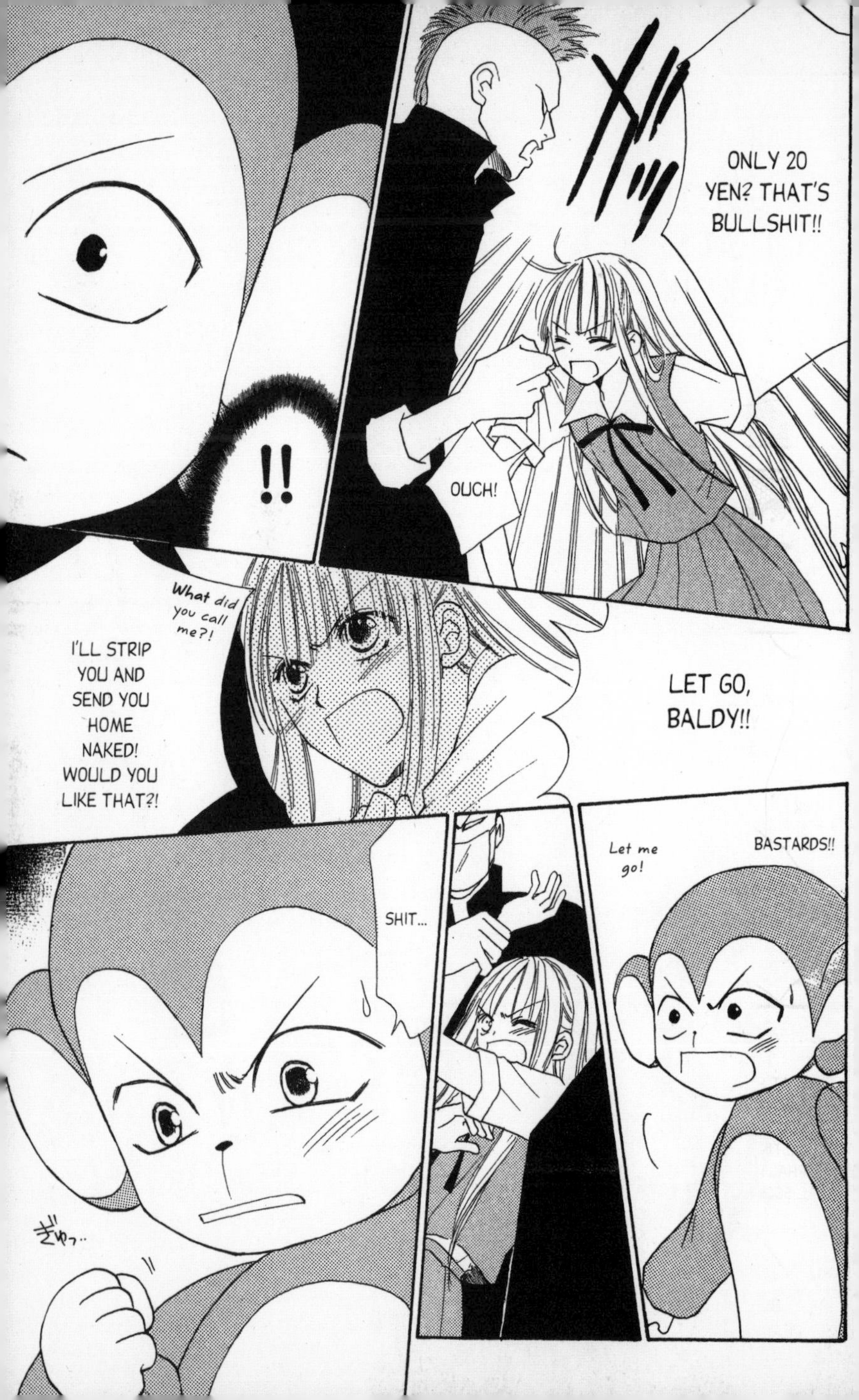
ONLY 20 YEN? THAT'S BULLSHIT!!
OUCH!
!!
LET GO, BALDY!!
What did you call me?!
I'LL STRIP YOU AND SEND YOU HOME NAKED! WOULD YOU LIKE THAT?!
BASTARDS!!
Let me go!
SHIT...
ぎゅっ..

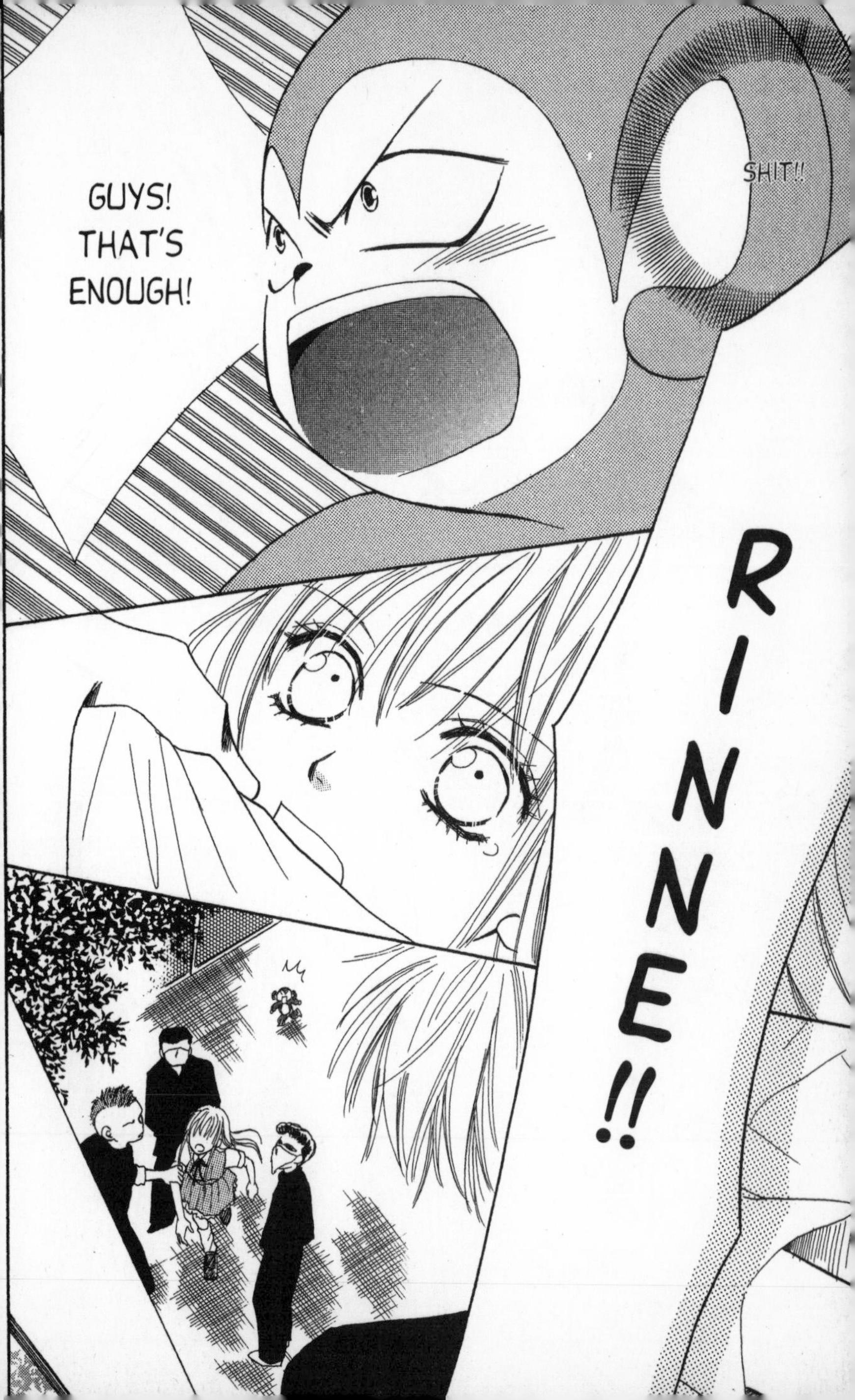
SHIT!!
GUYS! THAT'S ENOUGH!
RINNE!!

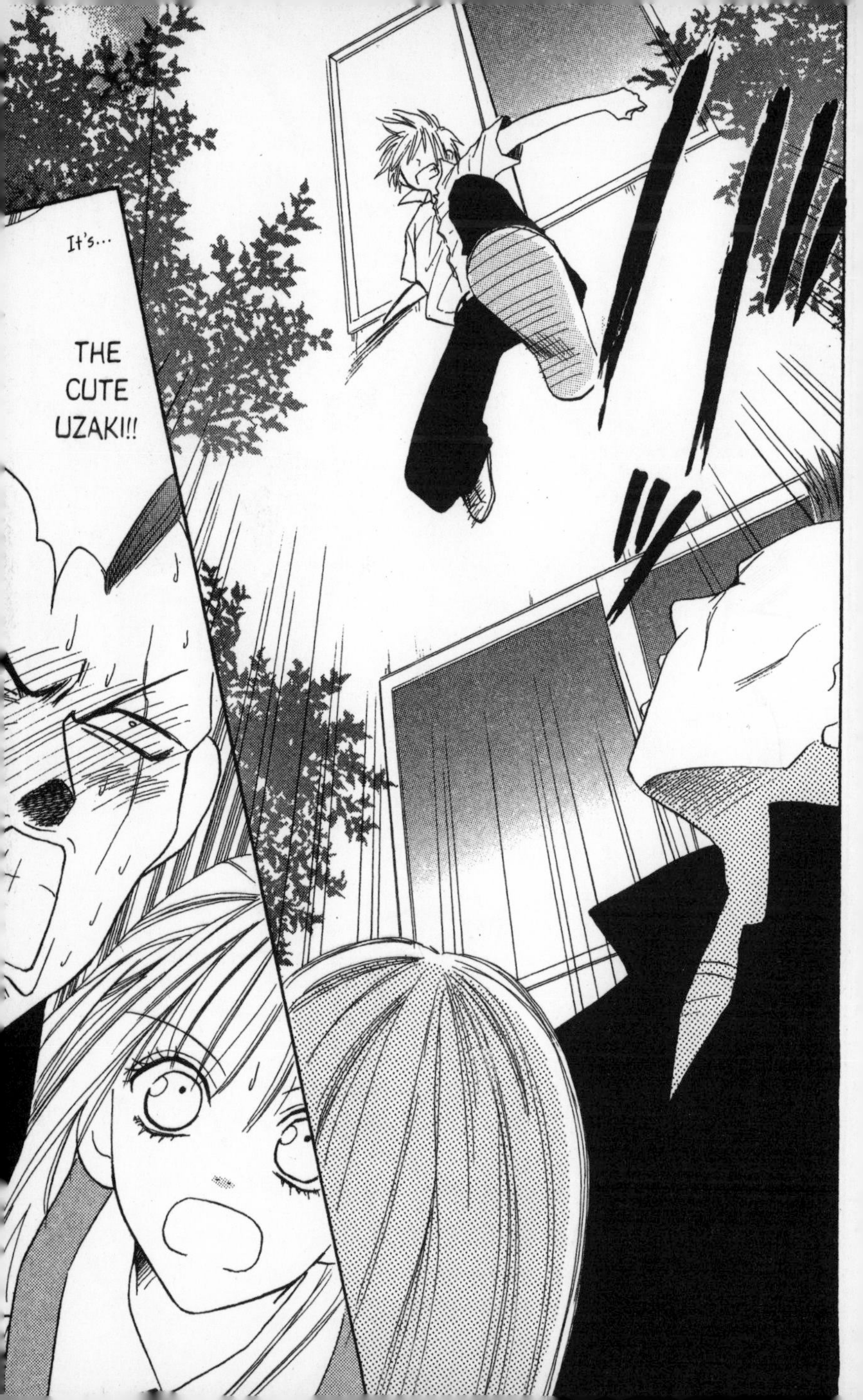
It's...
THE CUTE UZAKI!!

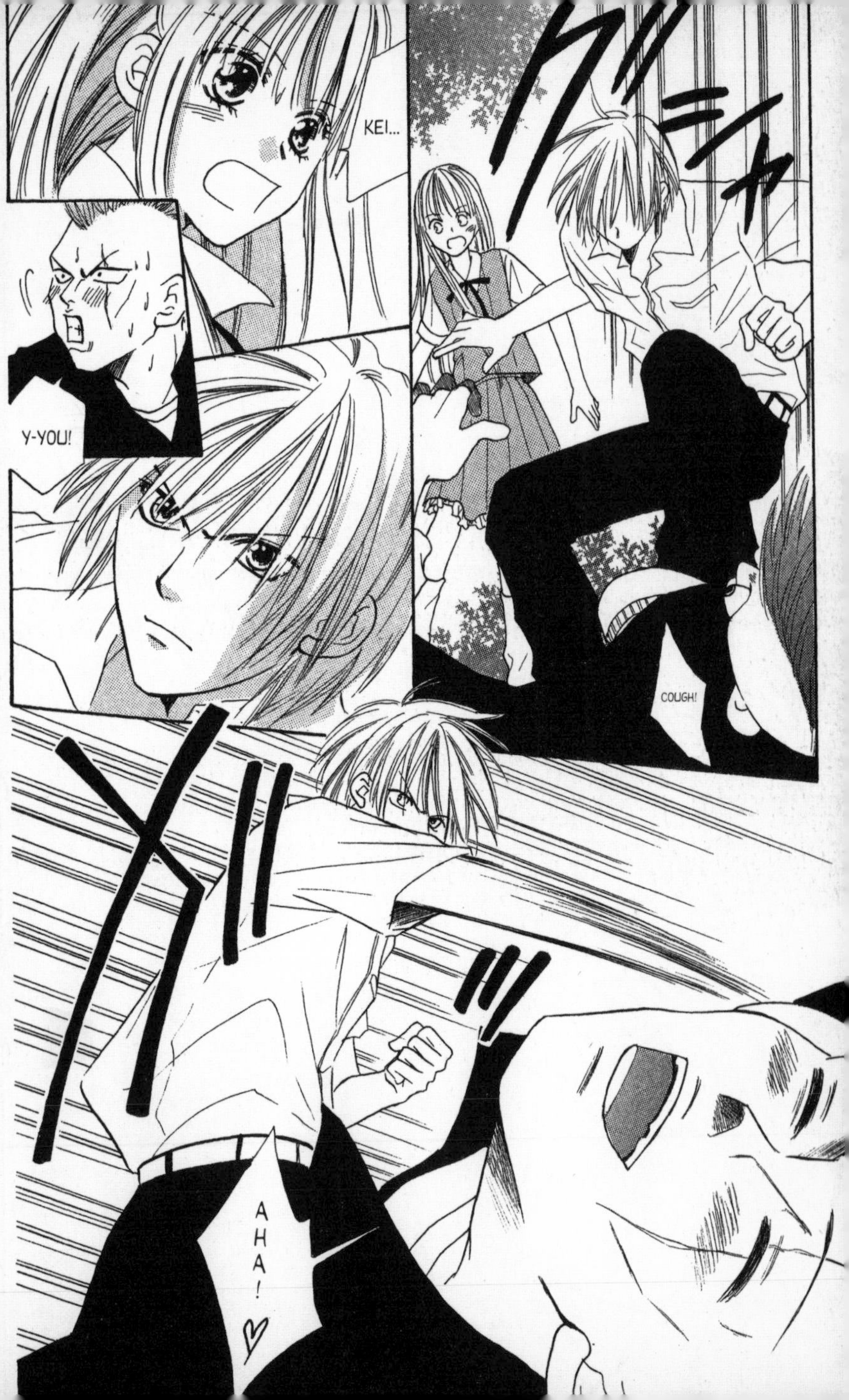
COUGH!
KEI...
Y-YOU!
AHA! ♥

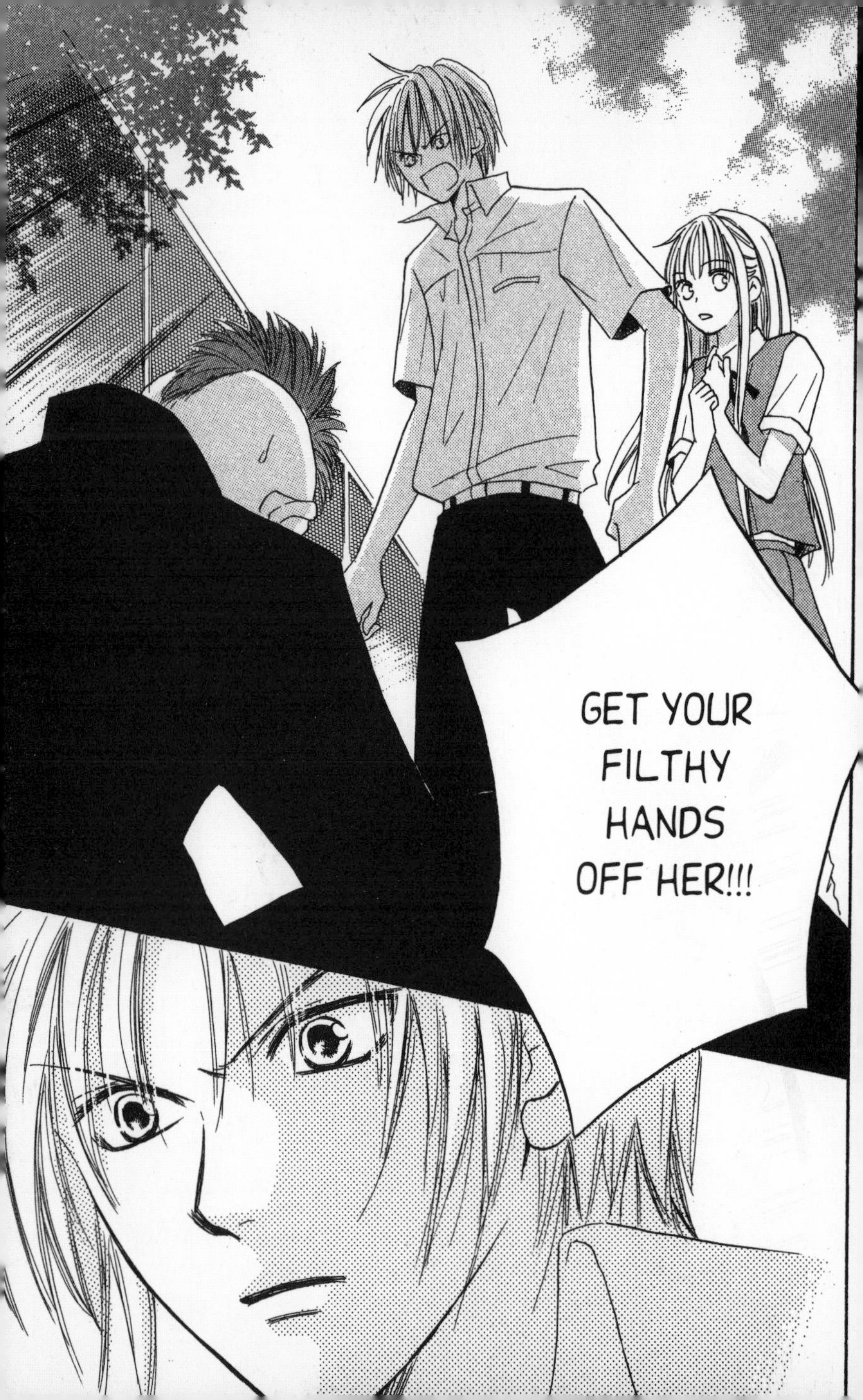
GET YOUR FILTHY HANDS OFF HER!!!

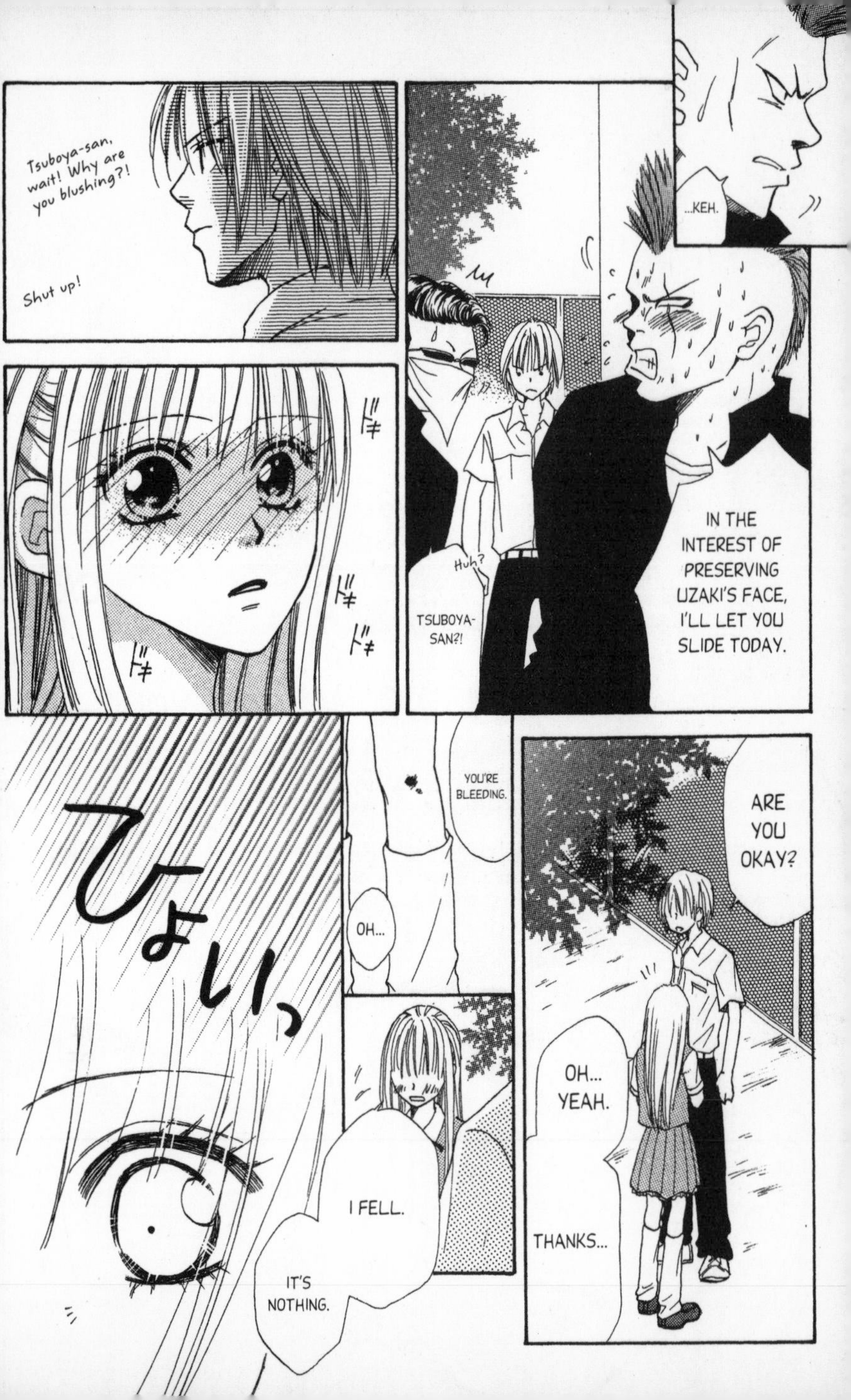
...KEH.
IN THE INTEREST OF PRESERVING UZAKI'S FACE, I'LL LET YOU SLIDE TODAY.
Huh?
TSUBOYA-SAN?!
Tsuboya-san, wait! Why are you blushing?!
Shut up!
ドキ
ドキ
ドキ
ドキ
ARE YOU OKAY?
OH... YEAH.
THANKS...
YOU'RE BLEEDING.
OH...
I FELL.
IT'S NOTHING.
ひょいっ

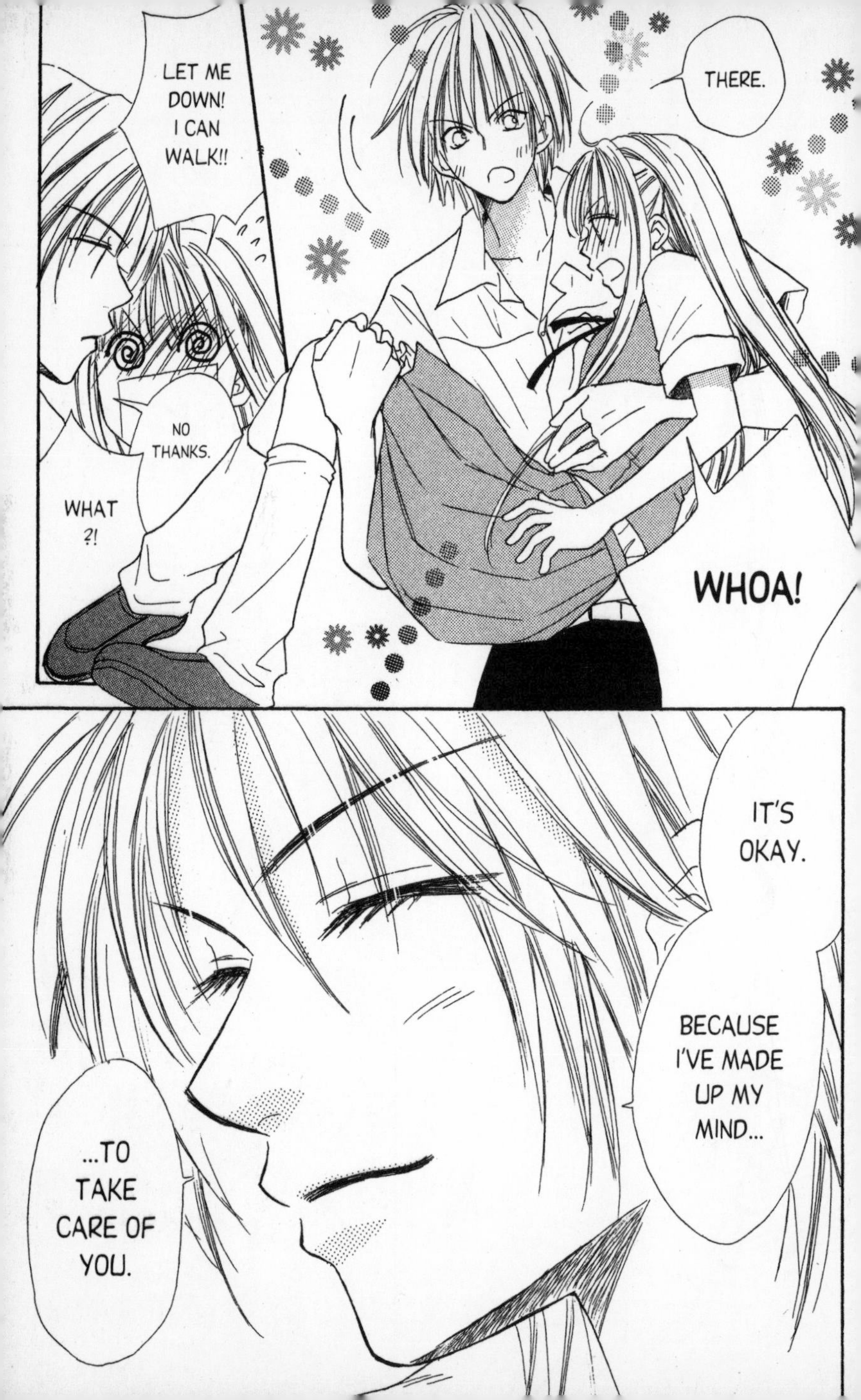
THERE.
WHOA!
LET ME DOWN! I CAN WALK!!
NO THANKS.
WHAT ?!
IT'S OKAY.
BECAUSE I'VE MADE UP MY MIND...
...TO TAKE CARE OF YOU.

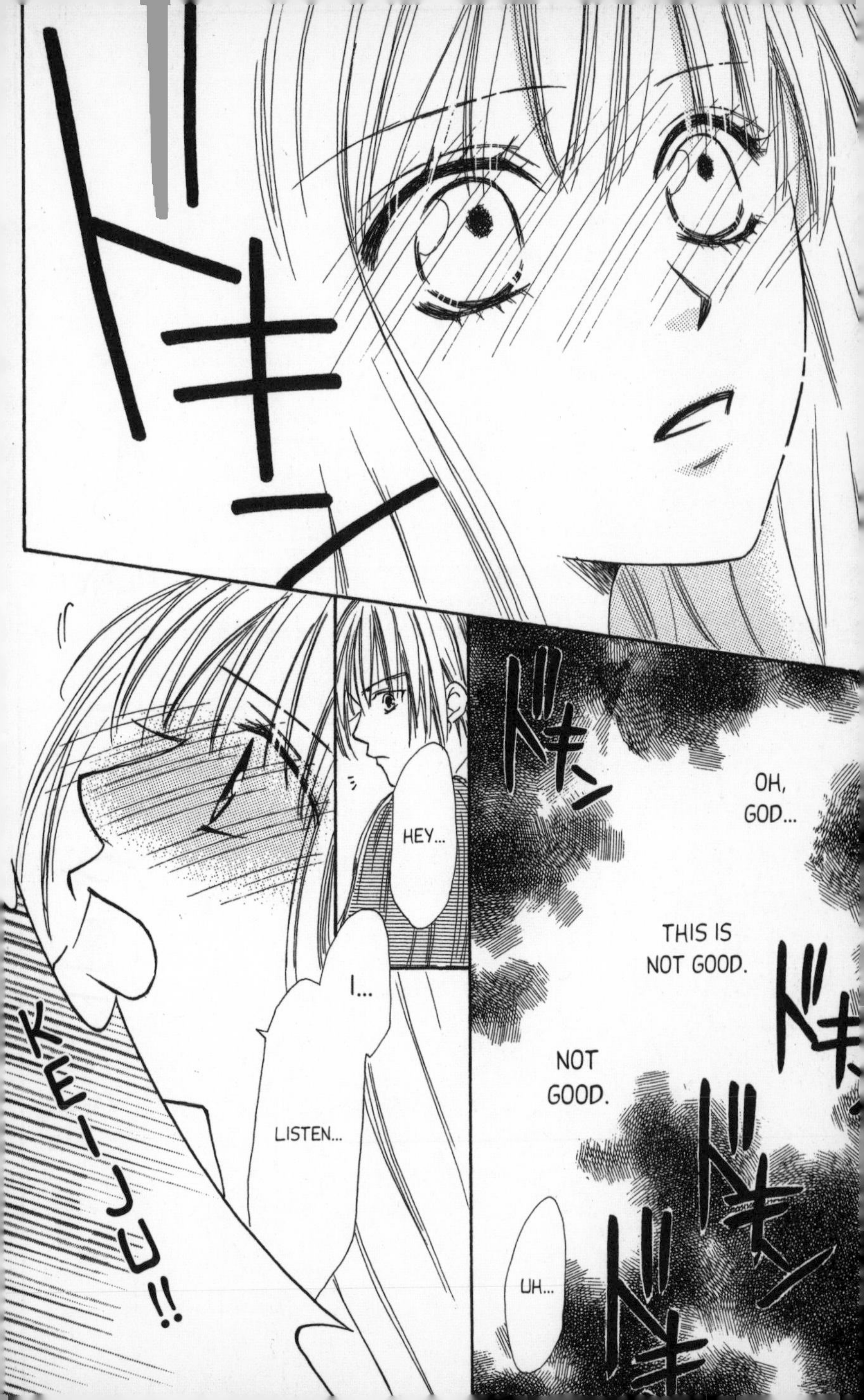
ドキーン
ドキン
OH, GOD...
THIS IS NOT GOOD.
NOT GOOD.
UH...
HEY...
I...
LISTEN...
KE--JU!!

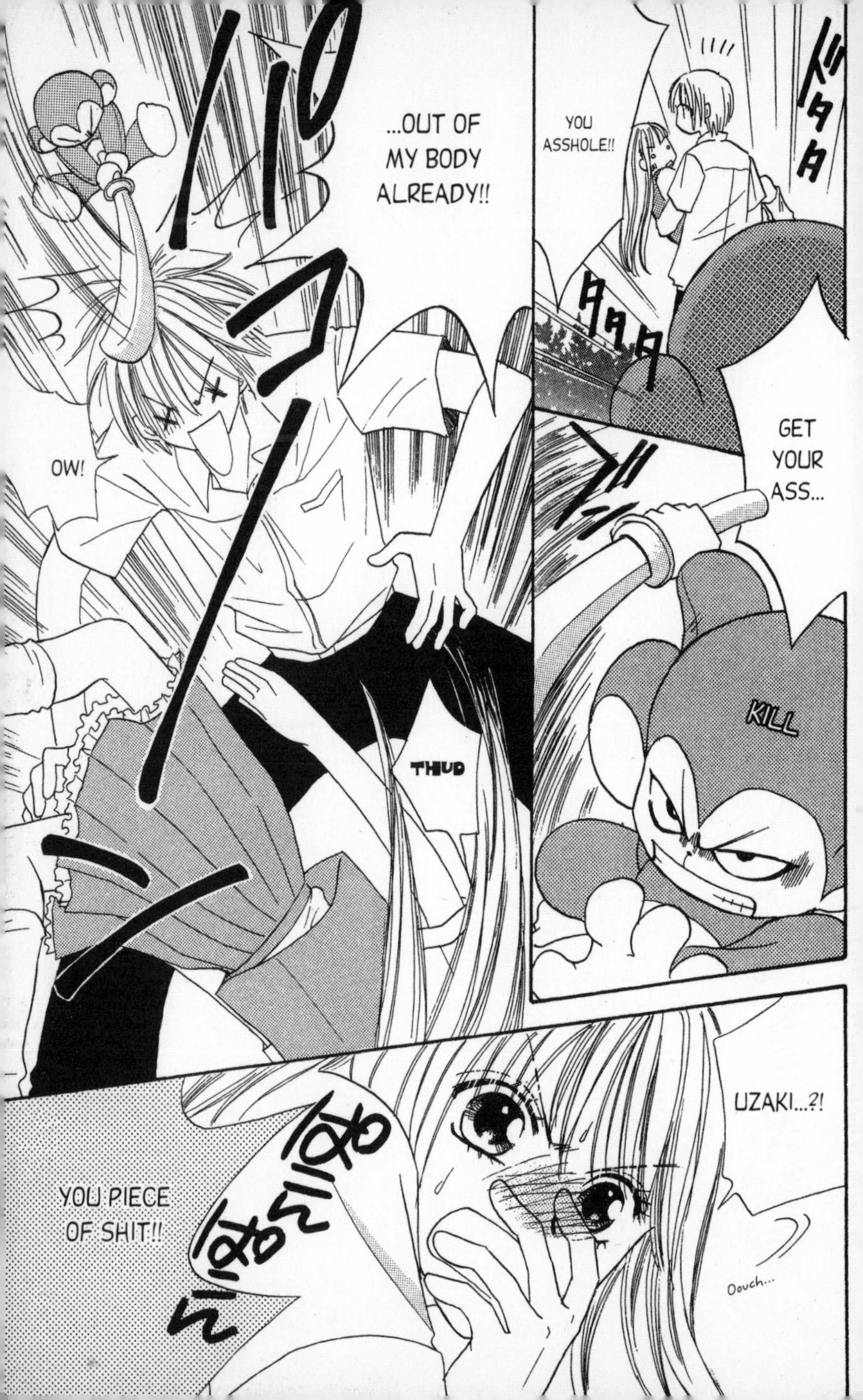
ドタタタ
YOU ASSHOLE!!
タタタ
GET YOUR ASS...
KILL
...OUT OF MY BODY ALREADY!!
OW!
THUD
UZAKI...?!
Oouch...
YOU PIECE OF SHIT!!

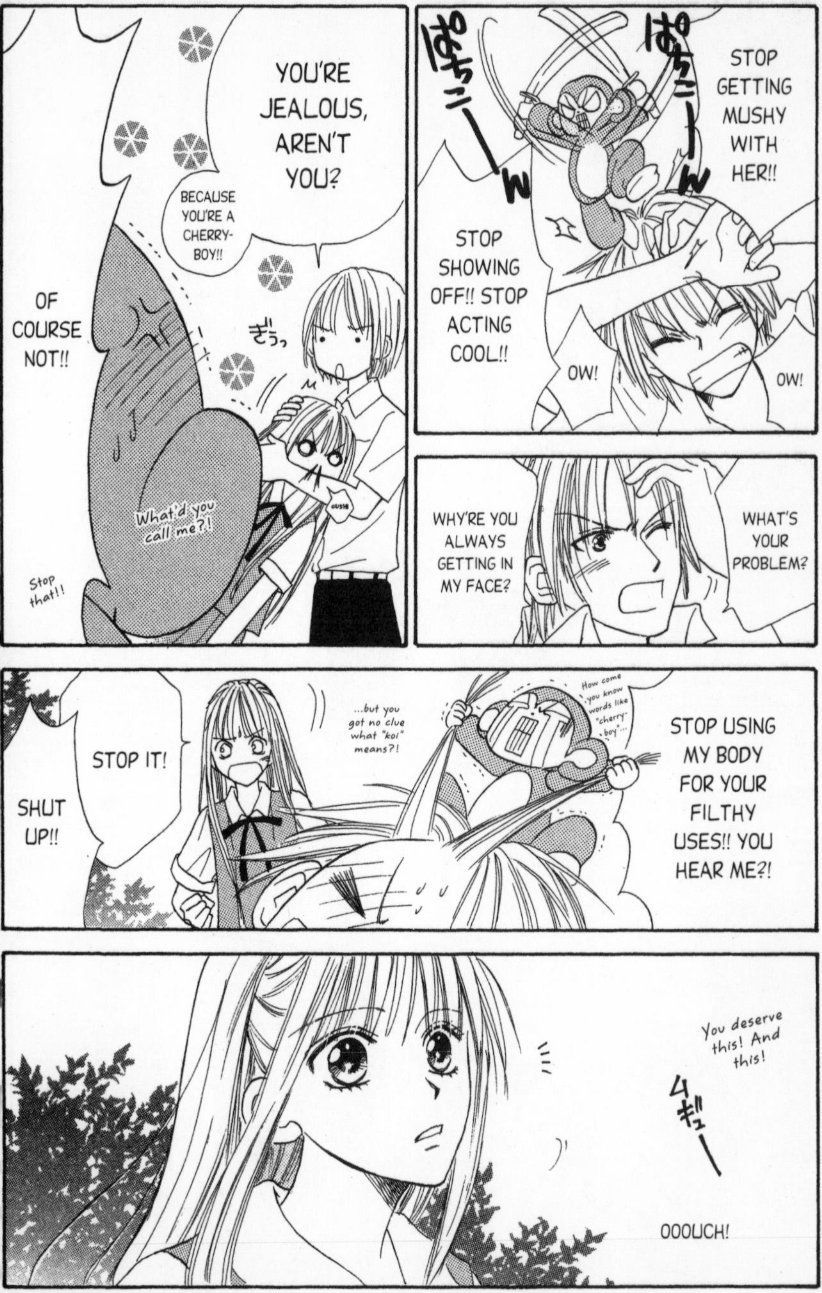
ぱちこーん
ぱちこーん
STOP GETTING MUSHY WITH HER!!
STOP SHOWING OFF!! STOP ACTING COOL!!
OW!
OW!
WHAT'S YOUR PROBLEM?
WHY'RE YOU ALWAYS GETTING IN MY FACE?
YOU'RE JEALOUS, AREN'T YOU?
BECAUSE YOU'RE A CHERRY-BOY!!
OF COURSE NOT!!
What'd you call me?!
Stop that!!
STOP USING MY BODY FOR YOUR FILTHY USES!! YOU HEAR ME?!
How come you know words like "cherry-boy"...
...but you got no clue what "koi" means?!
STOP IT!
SHUT UP!!
You deserve this! And this!
ムギュー
OOOUCH!

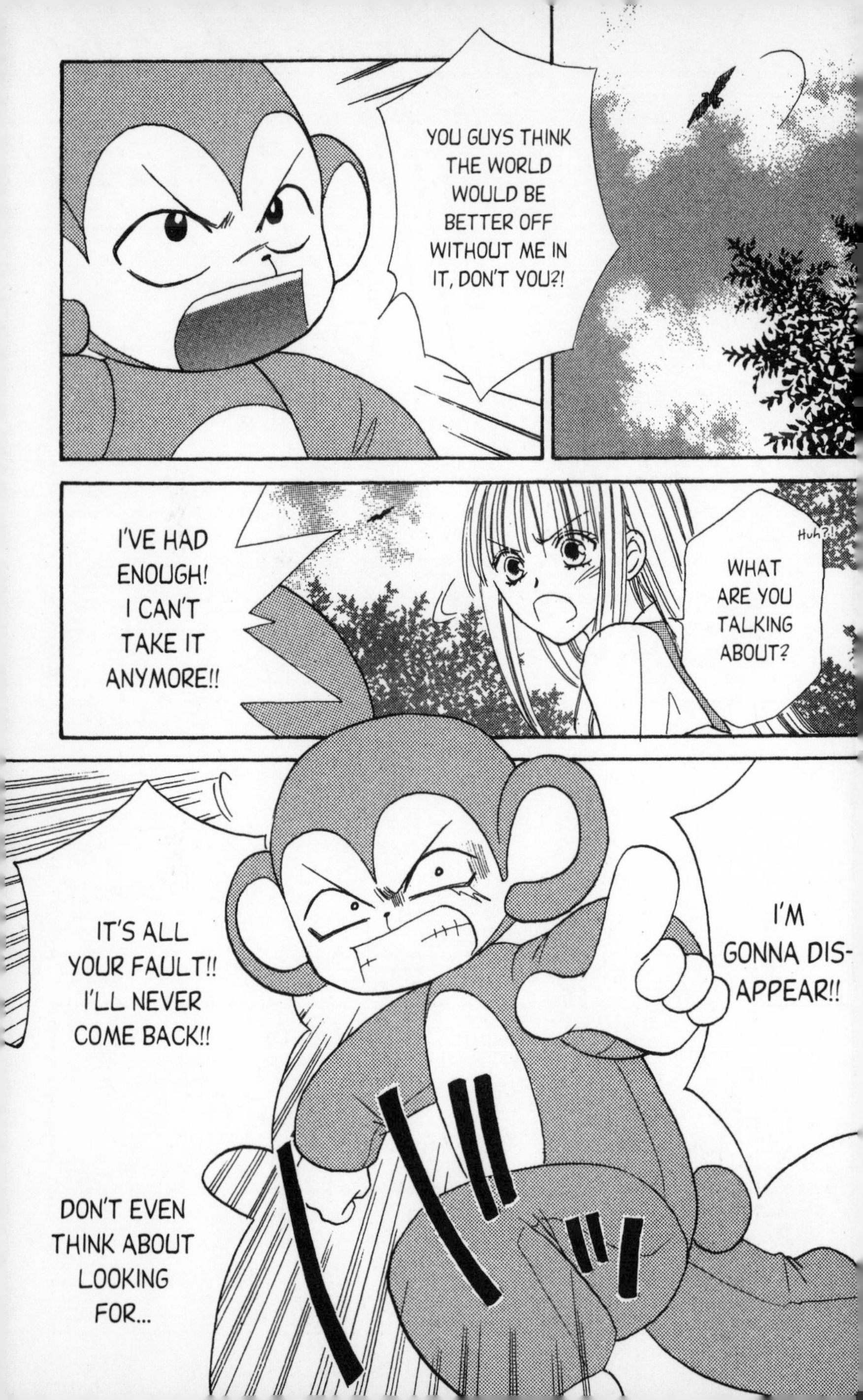
YOU GUYS THINK THE WORLD WOULD BE BETTER OFF WITHOUT ME IN IT, DON'T YOU?!
Huh?!
WHAT ARE YOU TALKING ABOUT?
I'VE HAD ENOUGH! I CAN'T TAKE IT ANYMORE!!
I'M GONNA DIS-APPEAR!!
IT'S ALL YOUR FAULT!! I'LL NEVER COME BACK!!
DON'T EVEN THINK ABOUT LOOKING FOR...

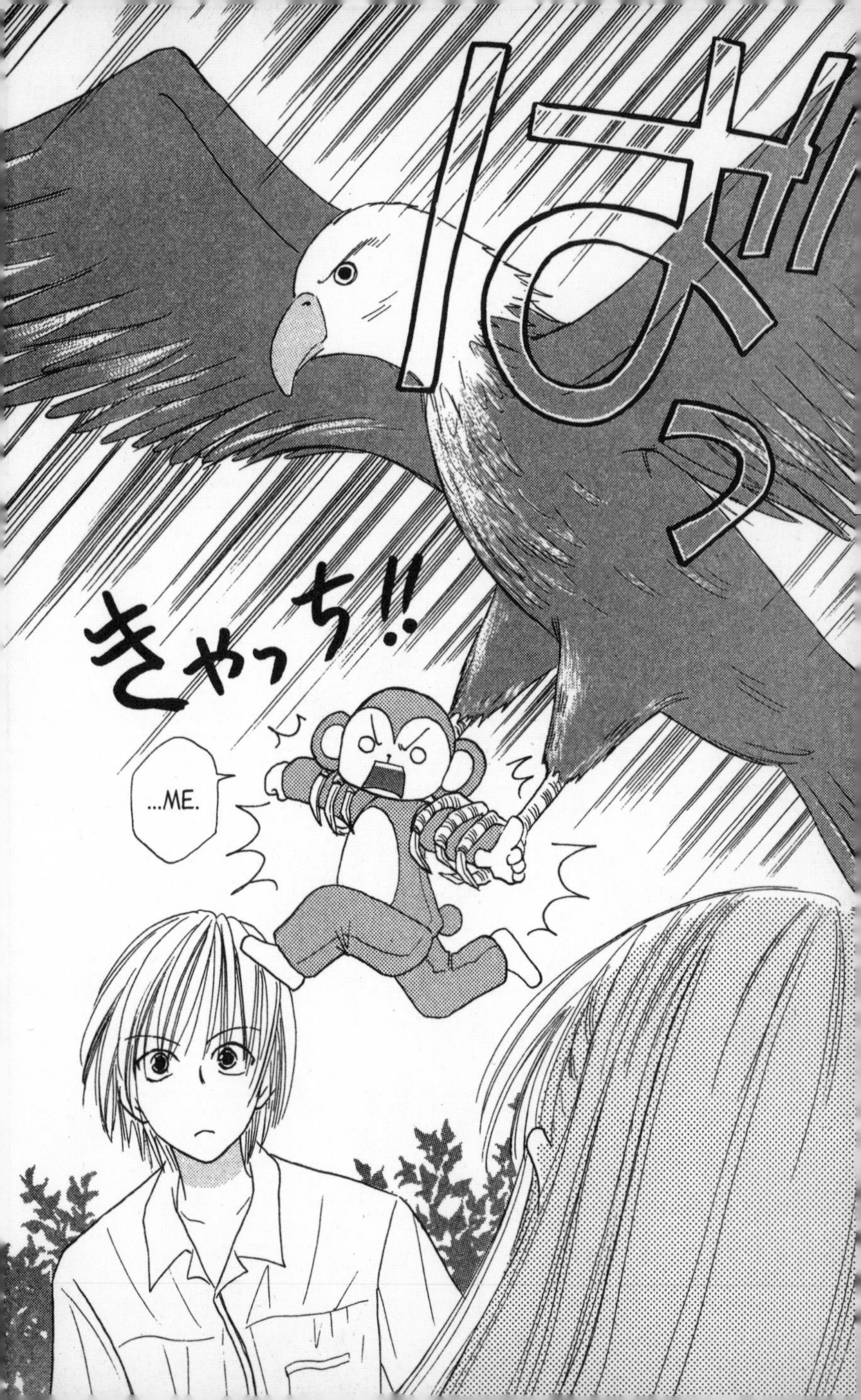
ばっ
きゃっち!!
...ME.

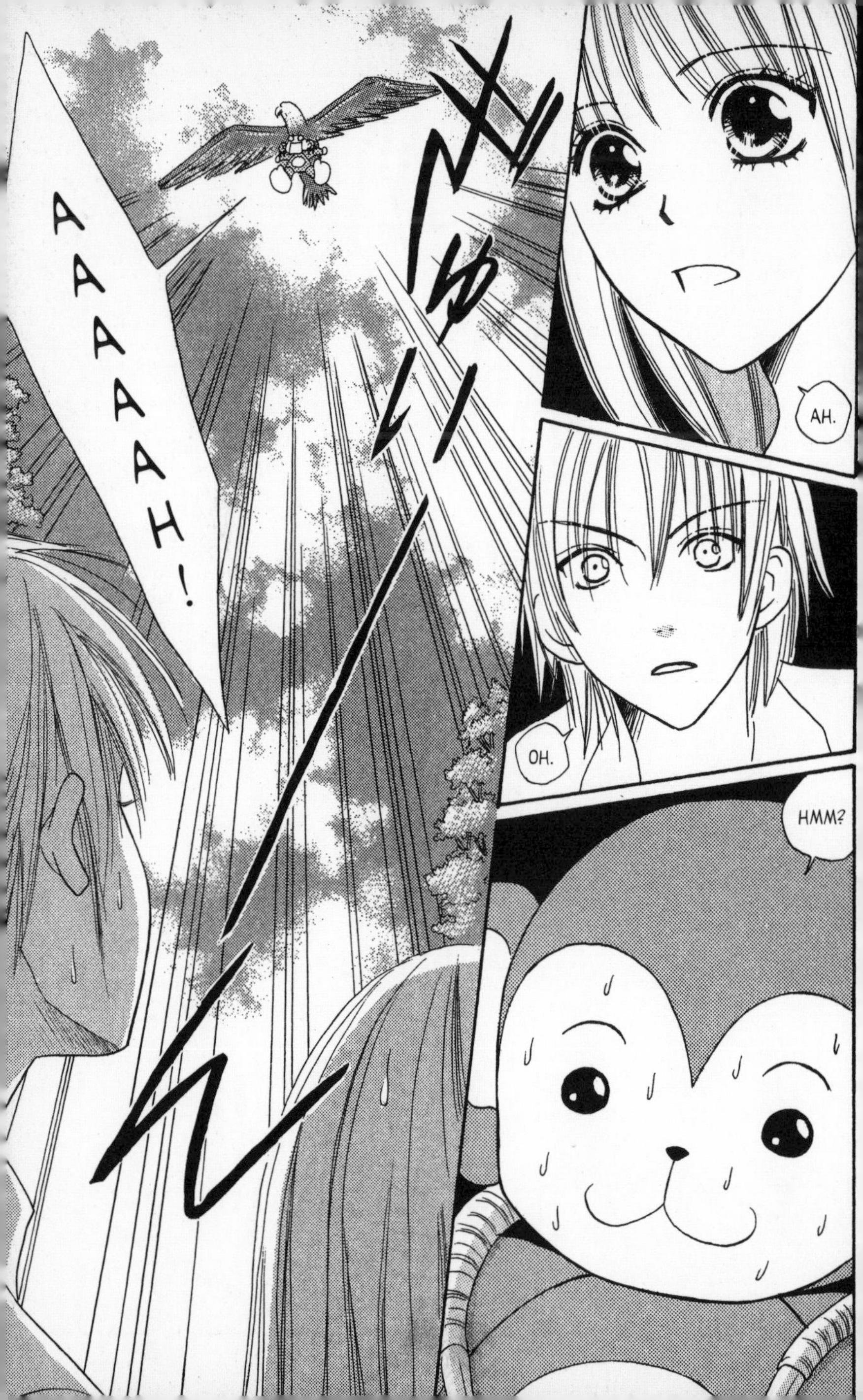
AH.
OH.
HMM?
AAAAAH!

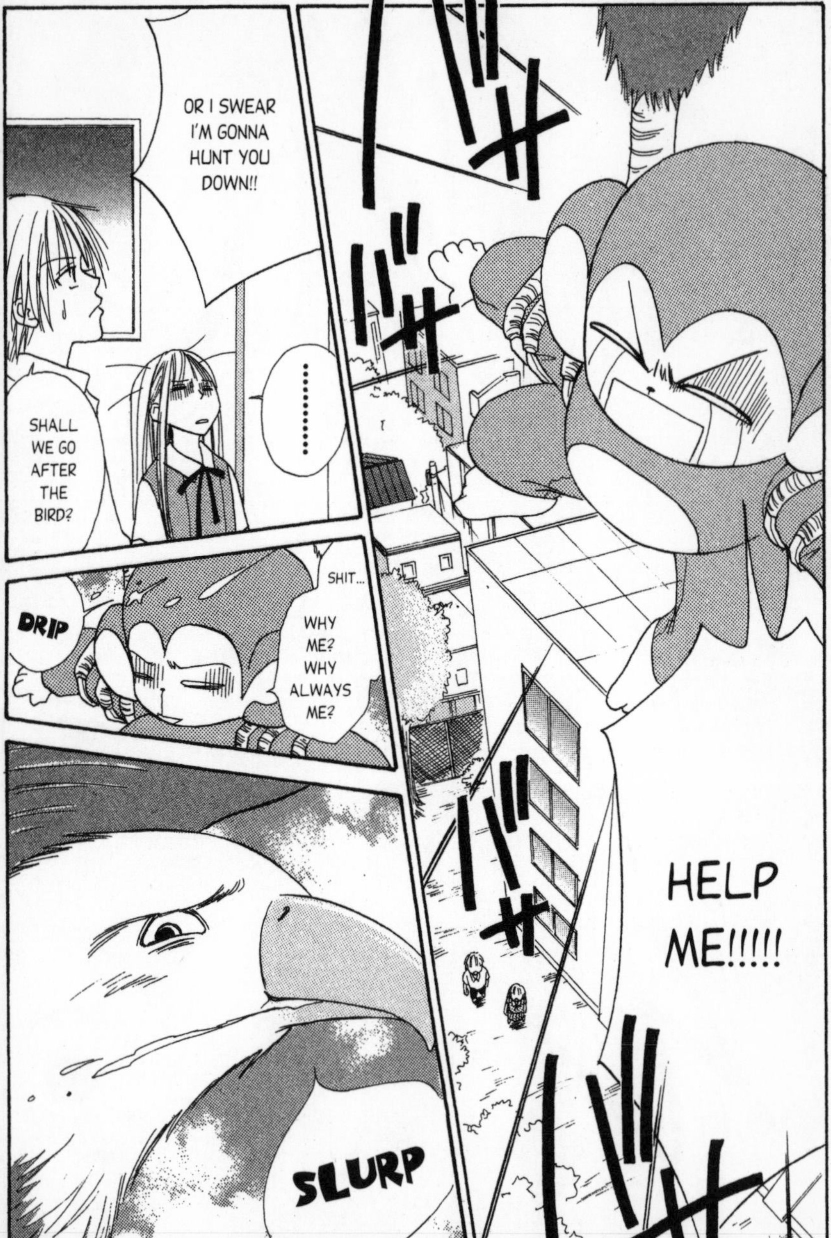
HELP ME!!!!!
OR I SWEAR I'M GONNA HUNT YOU DOWN!!
....
SHALL WE GO AFTER THE BIRD?
SHIT...
WHY ME? WHY ALWAYS ME?
DRIP
SLURP

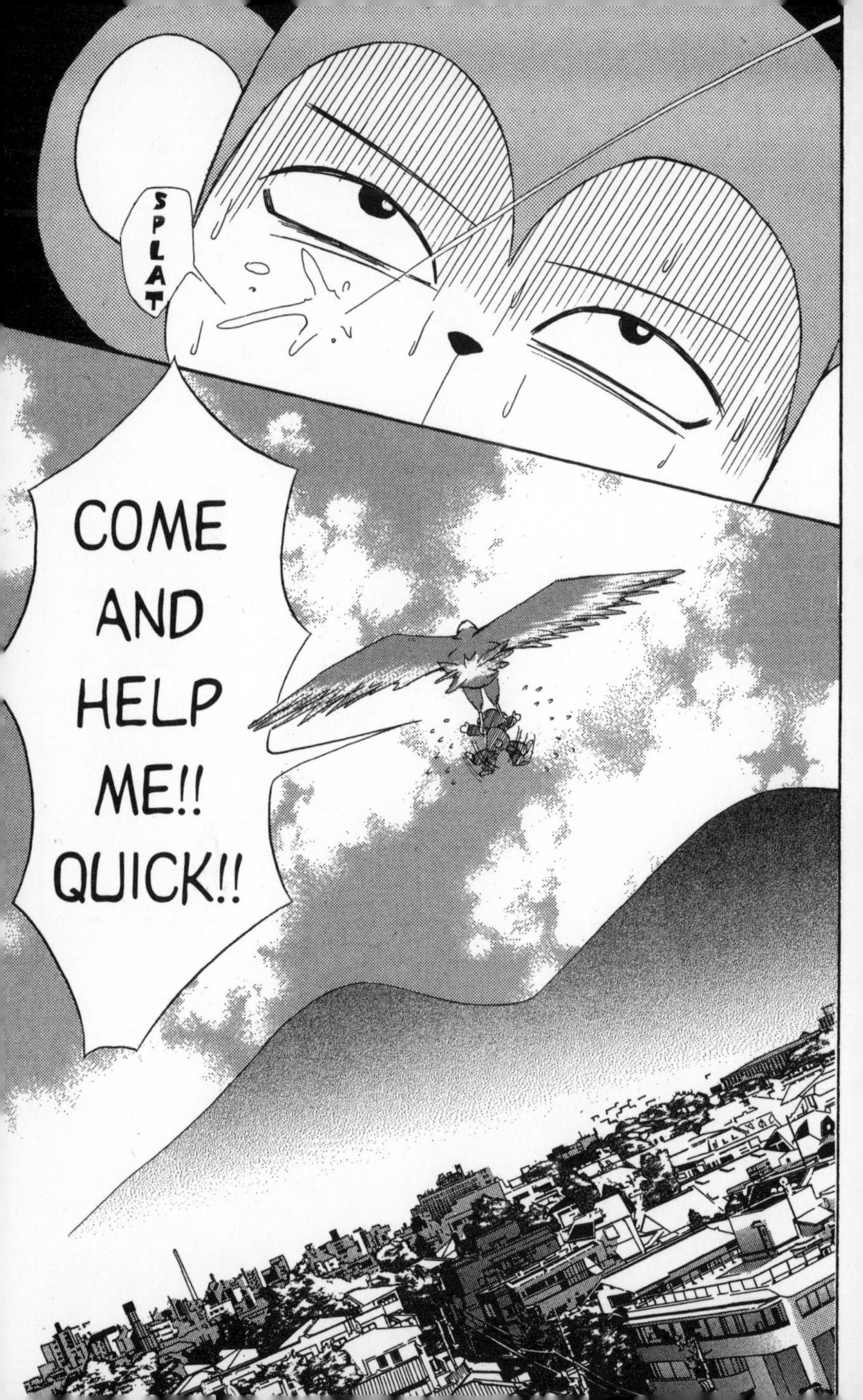
SPLAT
COME AND HELP ME!! QUICK!!

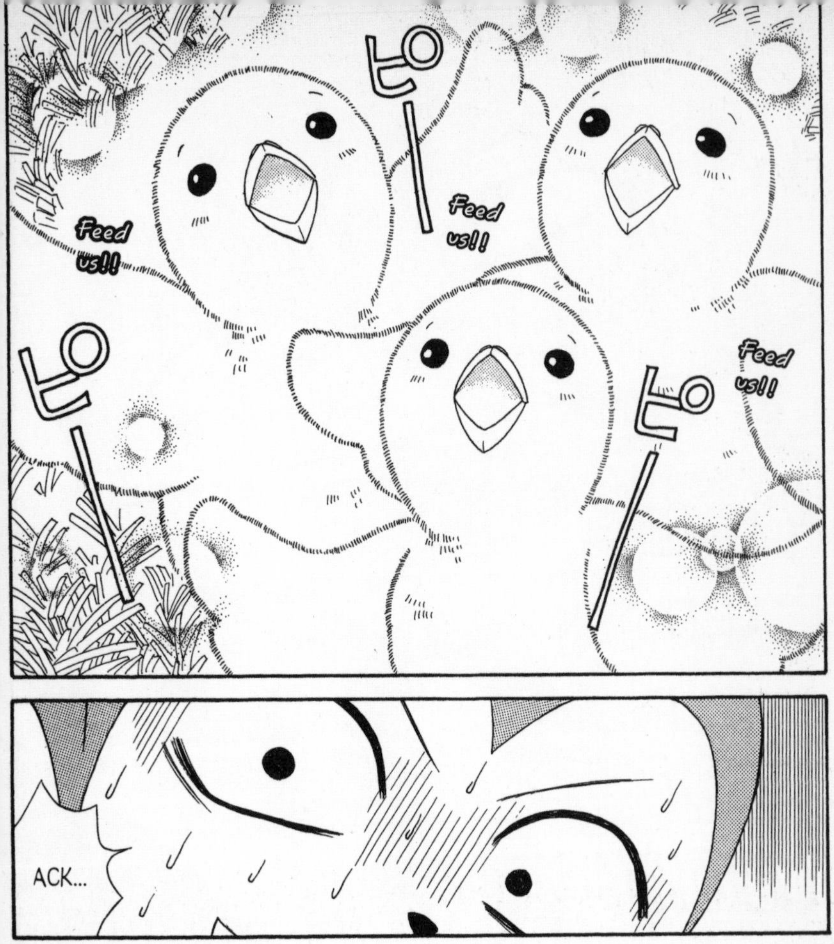
Feed us!!
Feed us!!
Feed us!!
ACK...

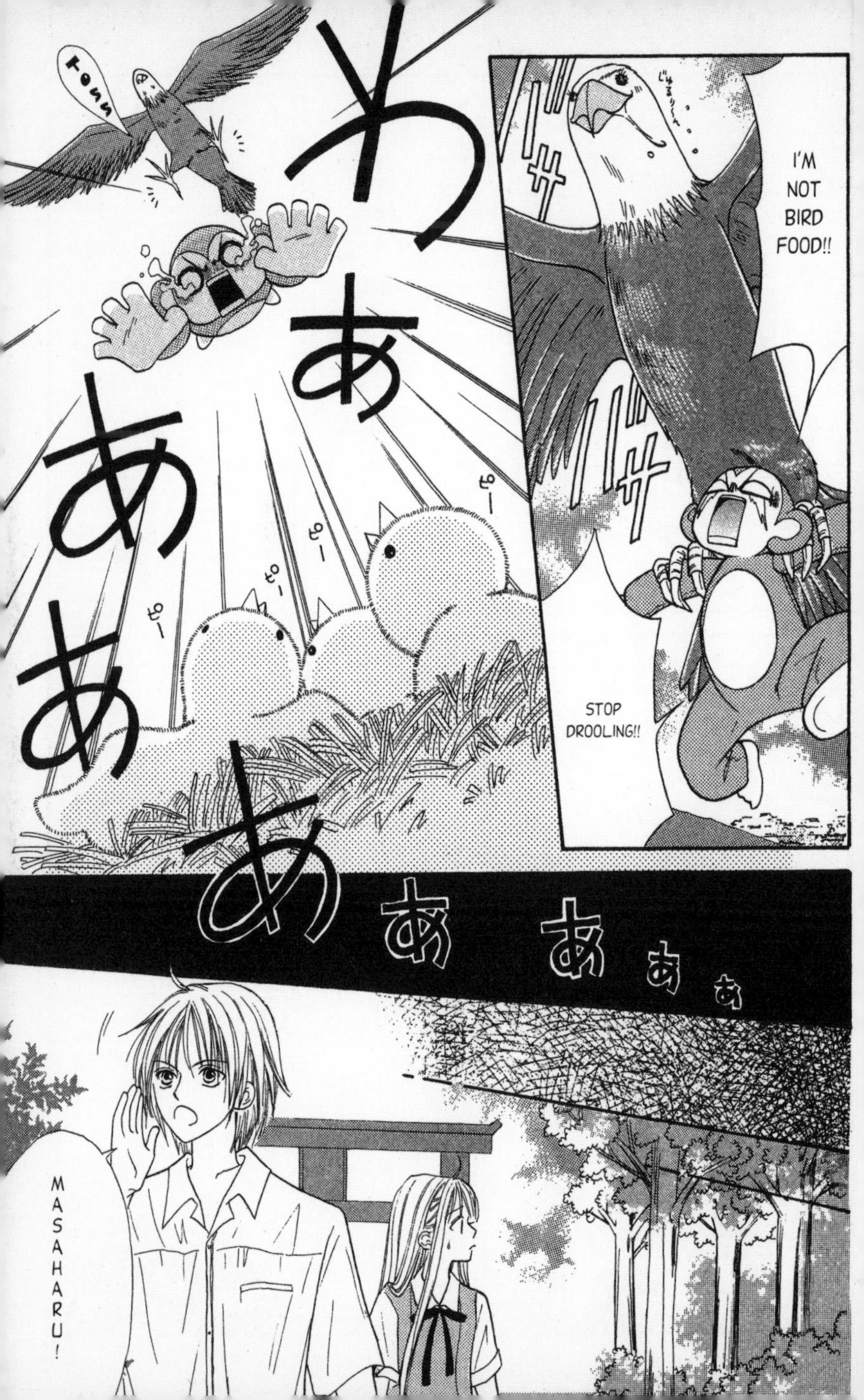
I'M NOT BIRD FOOD!!
STOP DROOLING!!
ザ
ザ
わあああああああぁぁ
TOSS
ぴー
ぴー
ぴー
ぴー
MASAHARU!

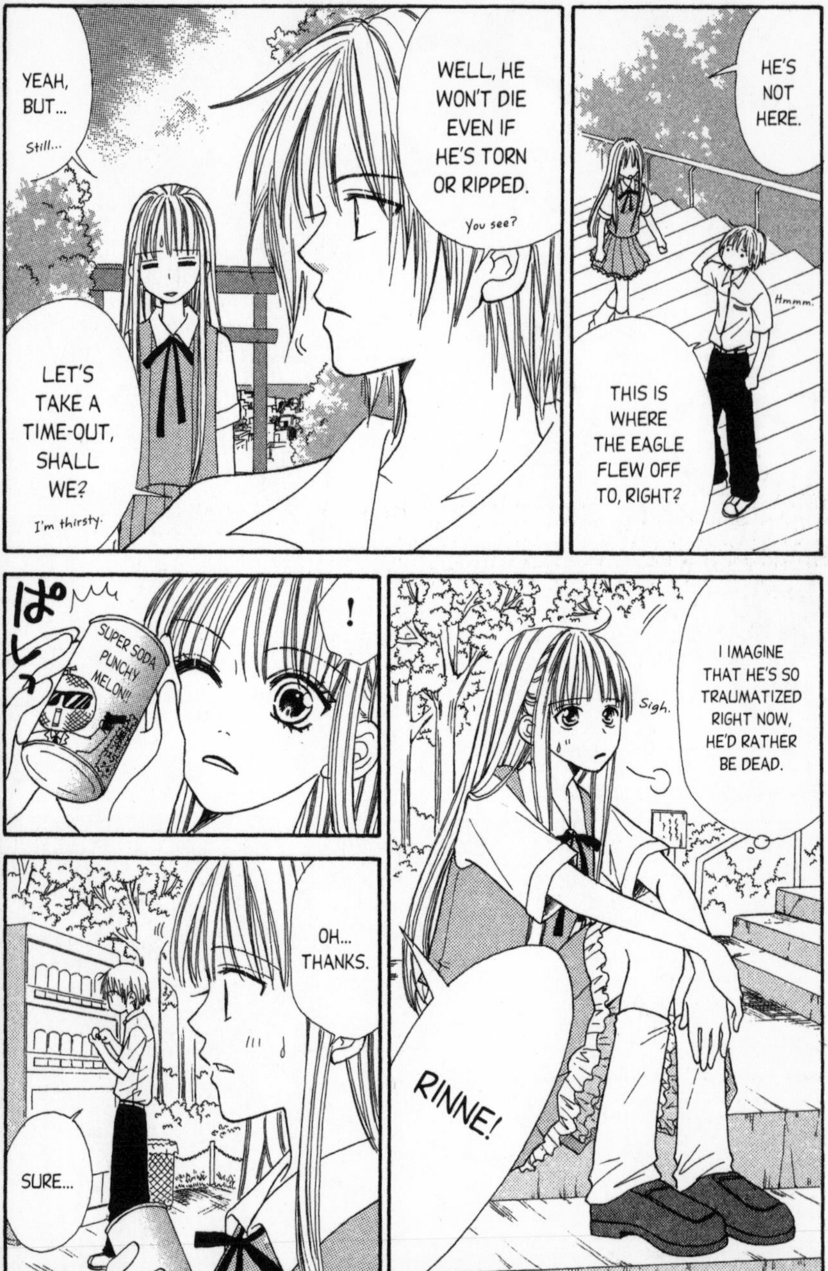
HE'S NOT HERE.
Hmmm.
THIS IS WHERE THE EAGLE FLEW OFF TO, RIGHT?
WELL, HE WON'T DIE EVEN IF HE'S TORN OR RIPPED.
You see?
YEAH, BUT...
Still...
LET'S TAKE A TIME-OUT, SHALL WE?
I'm thirsty.
I IMAGINE THAT HE'S SO TRAUMATIZED RIGHT NOW, HE'D RATHER BE DEAD.
Sigh.
RINNE!
!
SUPER SODA PUNCHY MELON!!
ぱし
OH... THANKS.
SURE...

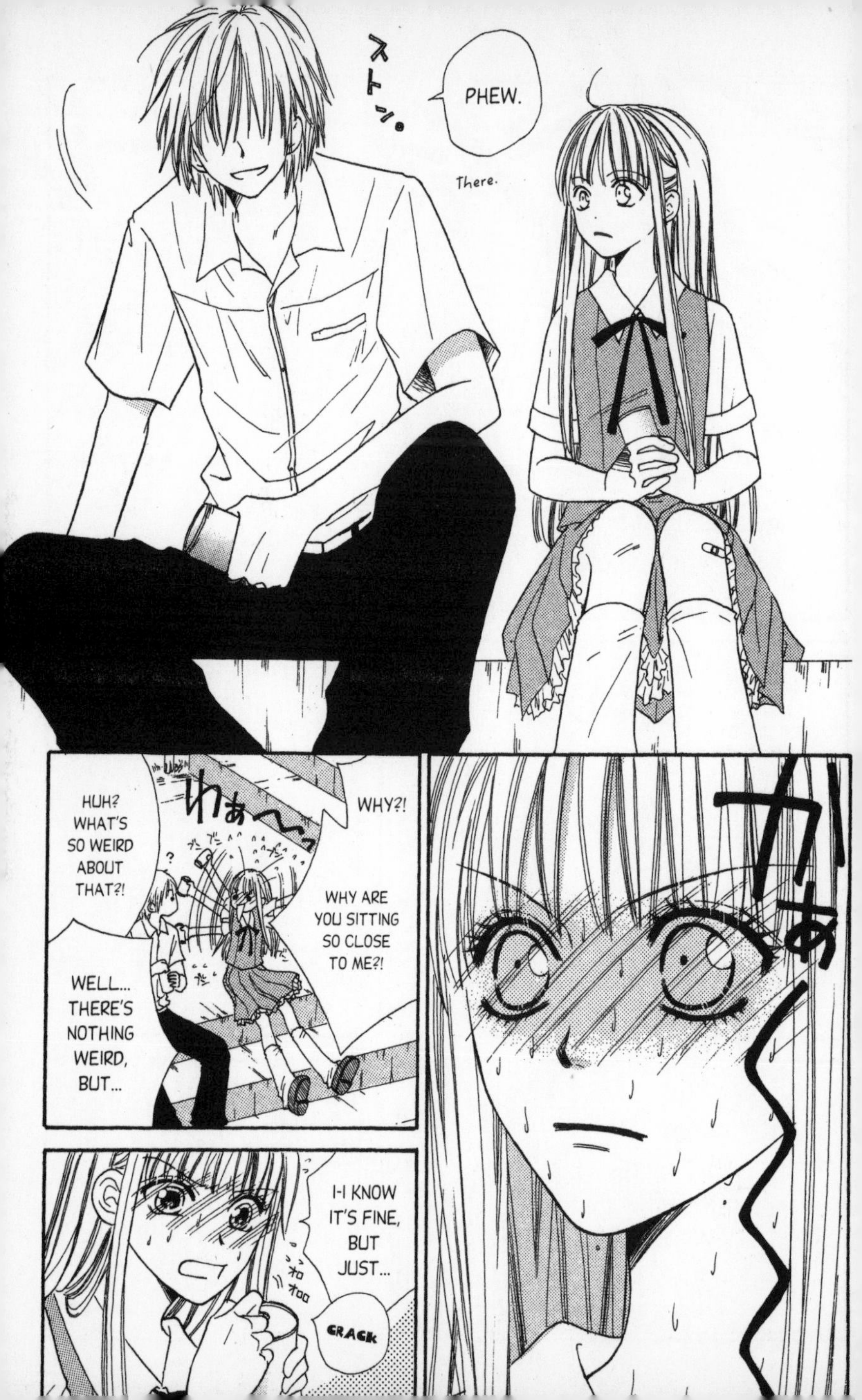

ストン。
PHEW.
There.
かぁ
WHY?!
わぁ〜〜っ
WHY ARE YOU SITTING SO CLOSE TO ME?!
HUH? WHAT'S SO WEIRD ABOUT THAT?!
WELL... THERE'S NOTHING WEIRD, BUT...
I-I KNOW IT'S FINE, BUT JUST...
オロオロ
CRACK

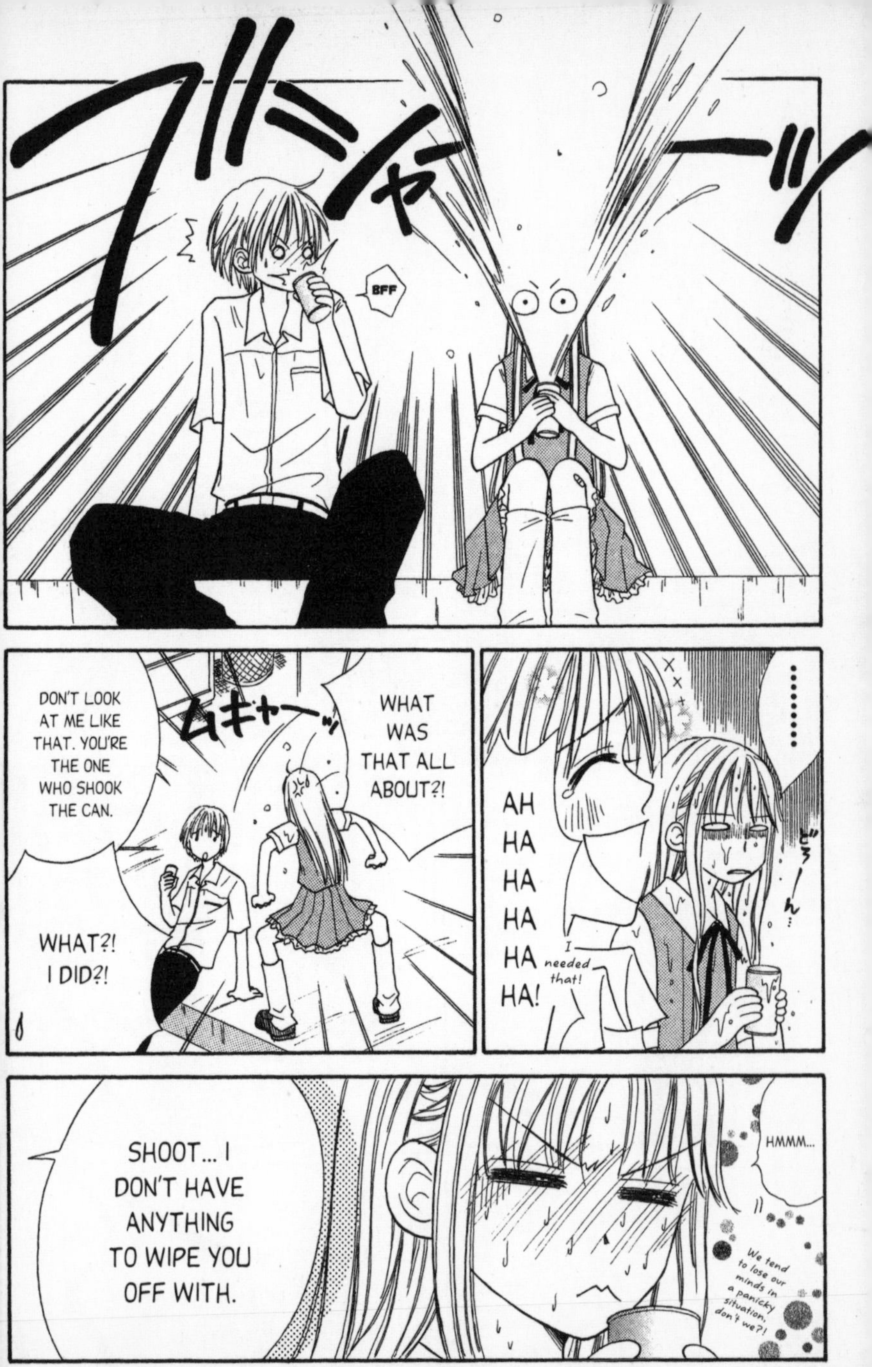

ブシャーーッ
BFF
....
AH HA HA HA HA HA!
I needed that!
びっしーん...
WHAT WAS THAT ALL ABOUT?!
ムギャーッ
DON'T LOOK AT ME LIKE THAT. YOU'RE THE ONE WHO SHOOK THE CAN.
WHAT?! I DID?!
HMMM...
We tend to lose our minds in a panicky situation, don't we?!
SHOOT... I DON'T HAVE ANYTHING TO WIPE YOU OFF WITH.

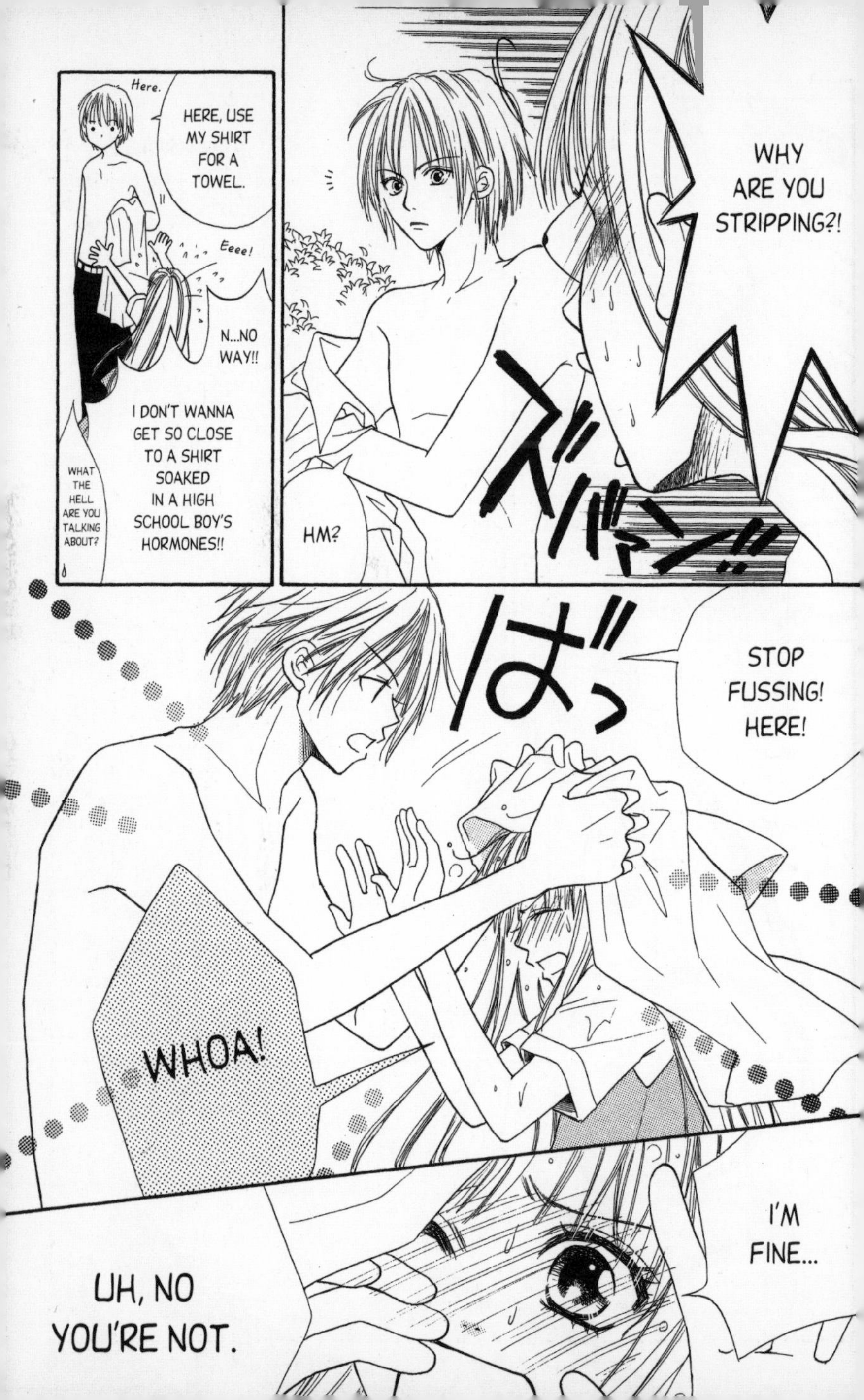
WHY ARE YOU STRIPPING?!
ズバーン!!
HM?
Here.
HERE, USE MY SHIRT FOR A TOWEL.
Eeee!
N...NO WAY!!
I DON'T WANNA GET SO CLOSE TO A SHIRT SOAKED IN A HIGH SCHOOL BOY'S HORMONES!!
WHAT THE HELL ARE YOU TALKING ABOUT?
STOP FUSSING! HERE!
ばっ
WHOA!
I'M FINE...
UH, NO YOU'RE NOT.

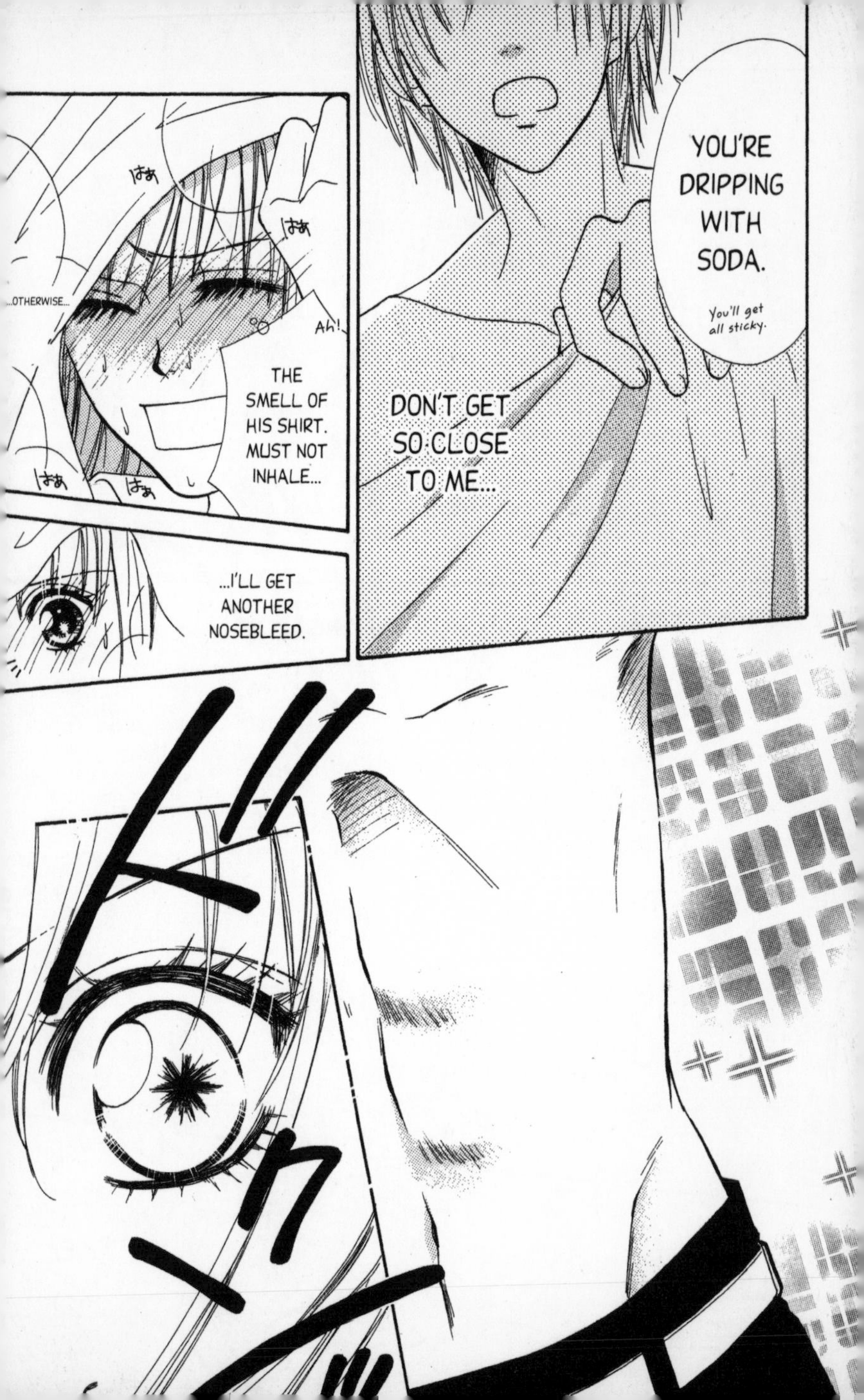
YOU'RE DRIPPING WITH SODA.
You'll get all sticky.
DON'T GET SO CLOSE TO ME...
Ah!
はあ
はあ
THE SMELL OF HIS SHIRT. MUST NOT INHALE...
はあ
はあ
...OTHERWISE...
...I'LL GET ANOTHER NOSEBLEED.

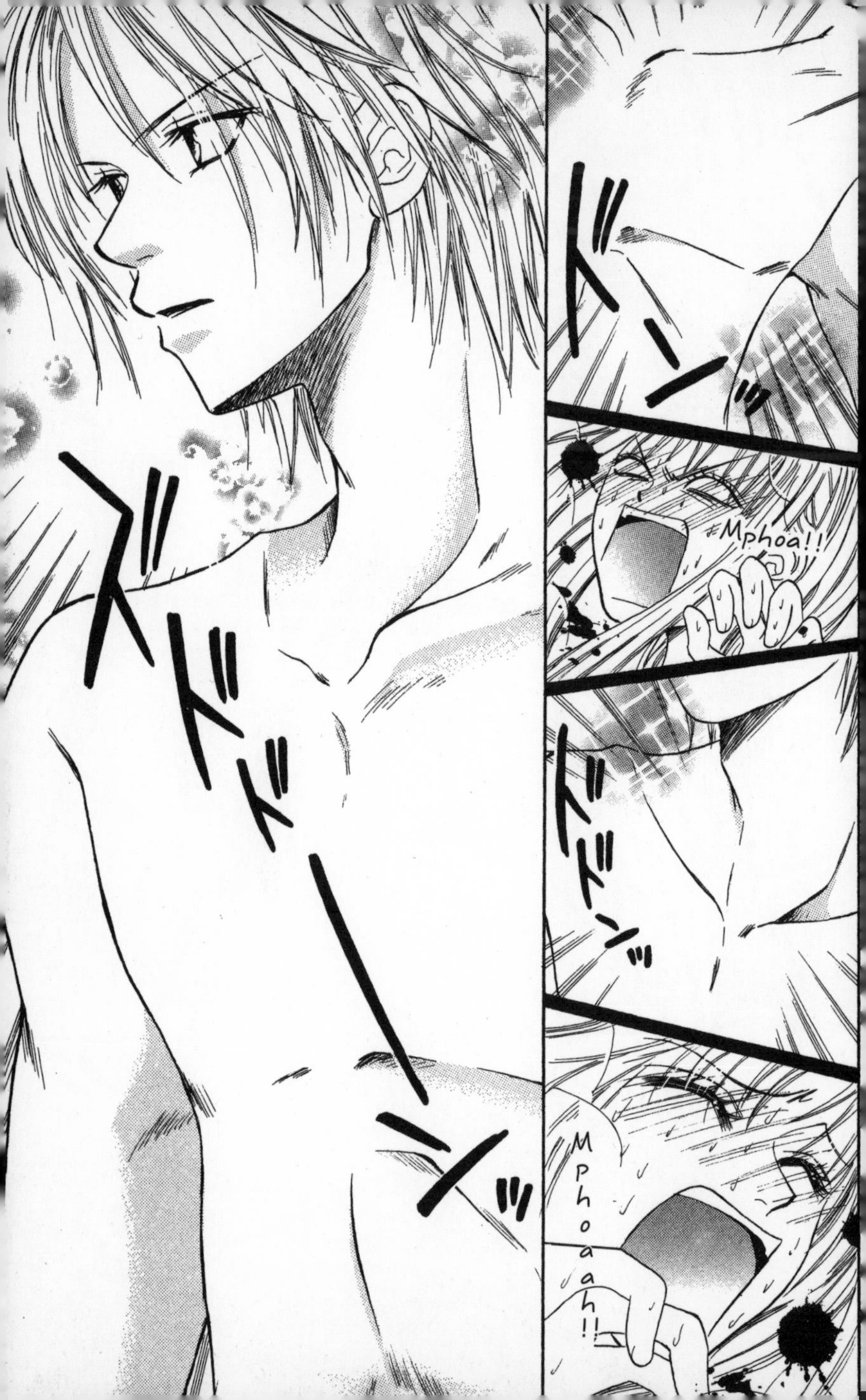
ドーンッ
Mphoa!!
ドドーンッ
Mphoaah!!
ズドドドーンッ

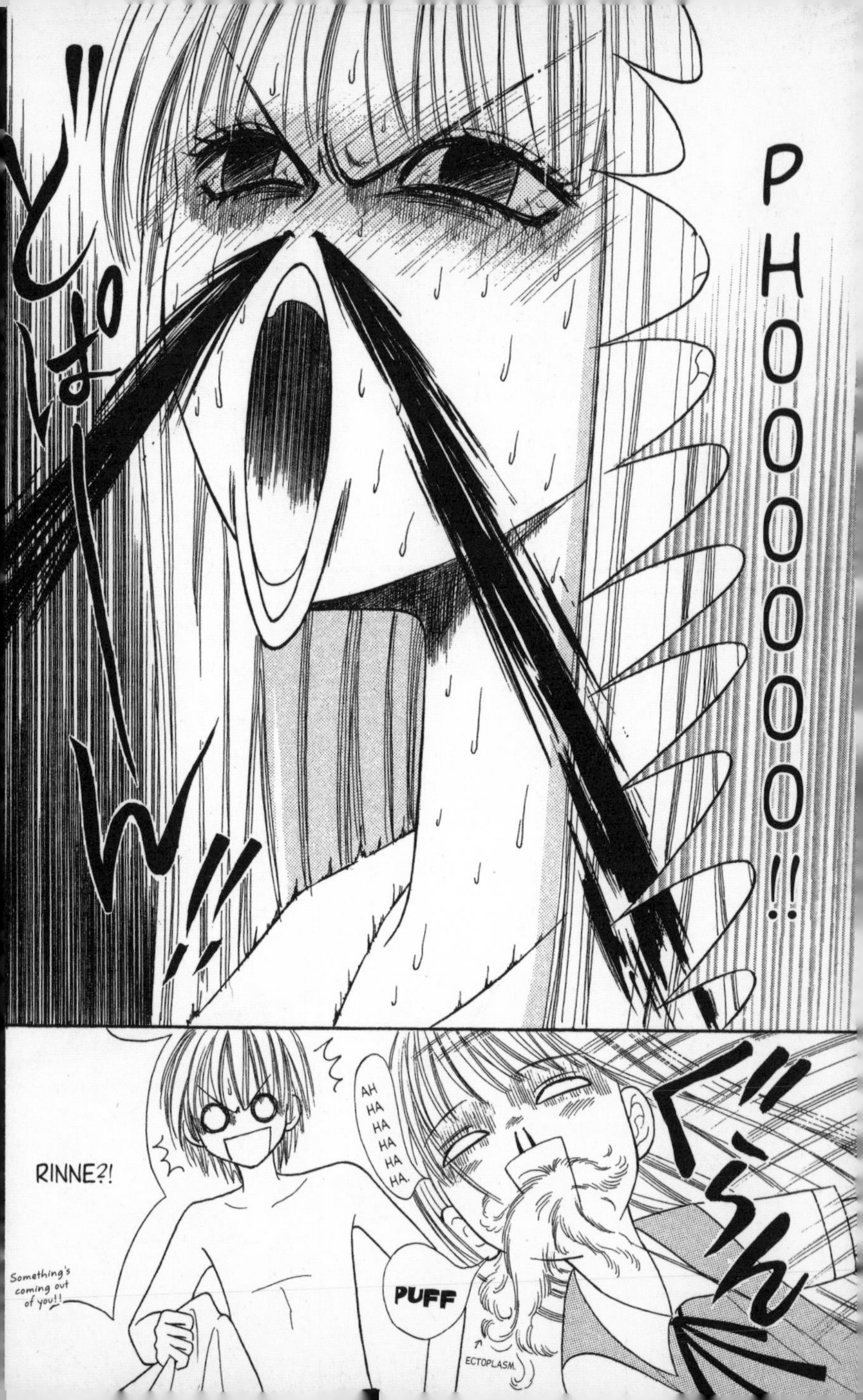
PHOOOOOOO!!
どぱーん!!
ぐらん
AH HA HA HA HA HA HA.
PUFF
ECTOPLASM.
RINNE?!
Something's coming out of you!!

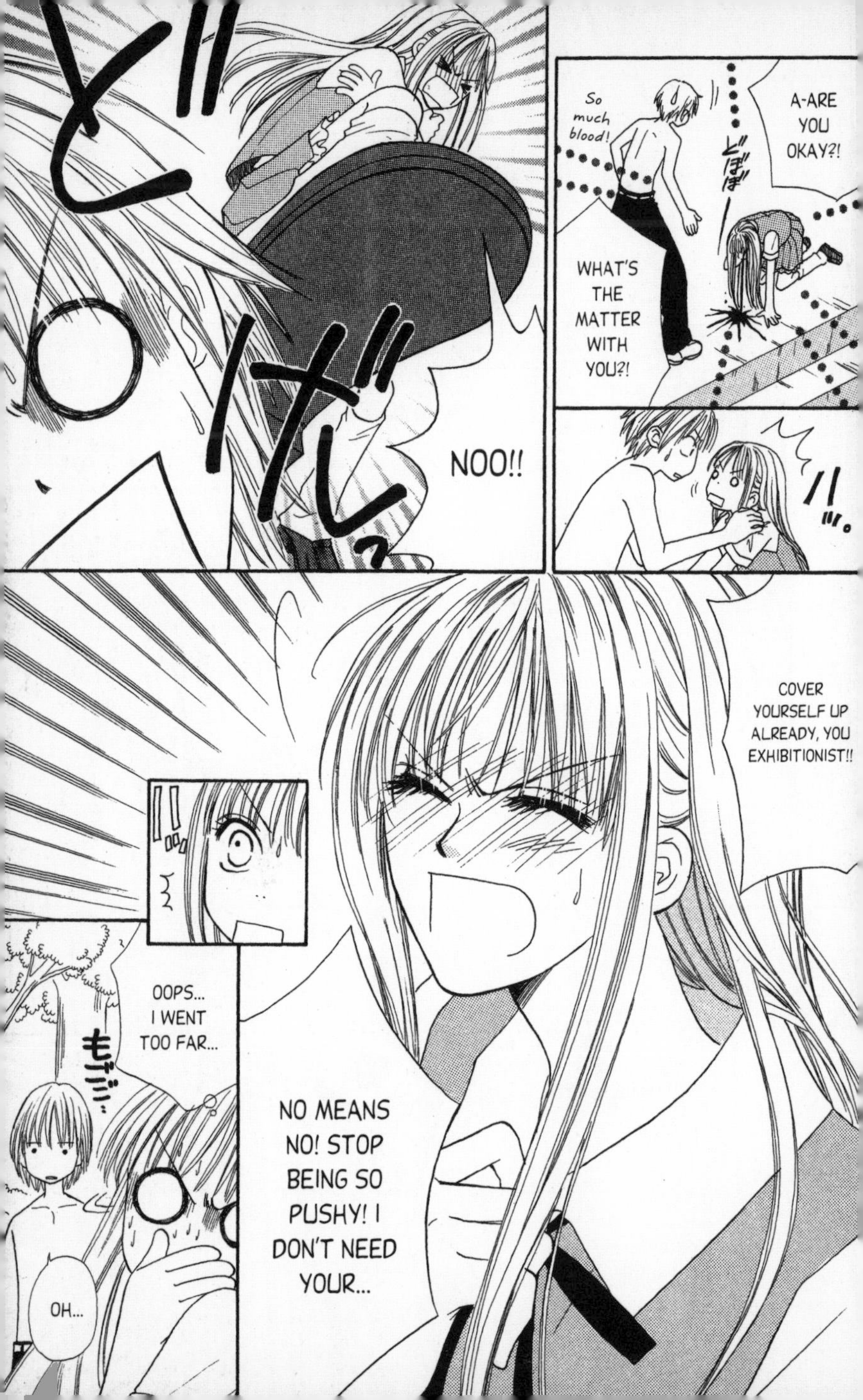

A-ARE YOU OKAY?!
So much blood!
WHAT'S THE MATTER WITH YOU?!
NOO!!
COVER YOURSELF UP ALREADY, YOU EXHIBITIONIST!!
NO MEANS NO! STOP BEING SO PUSHY! I DON'T NEED YOUR...
OOPS... I WENT TOO FAR...
OH...

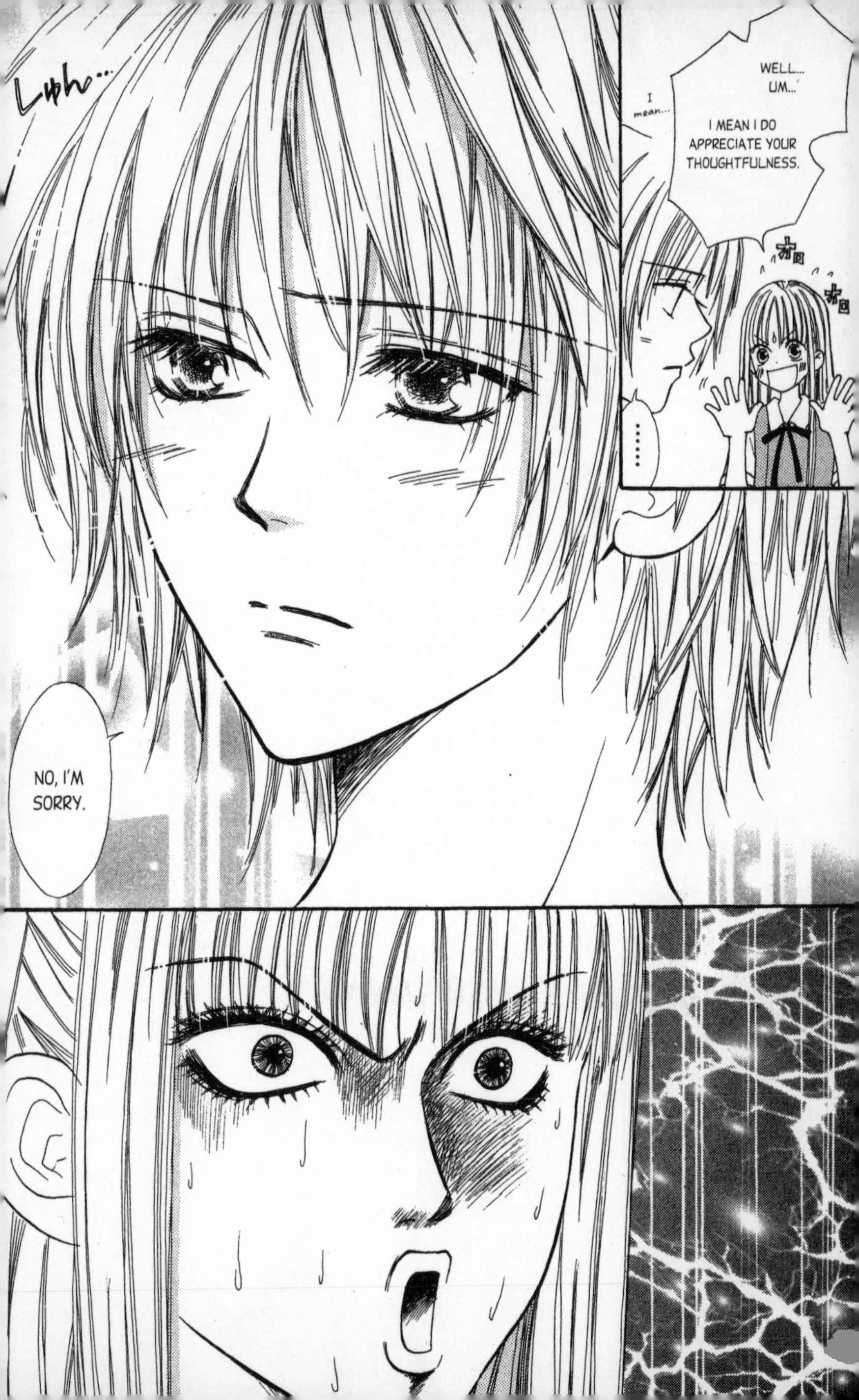
WELL... UM...
I mean...
I MEAN I DO APPRECIATE YOUR THOUGHTFULNESS.
......
しゅん...
NO, I'M SORRY.

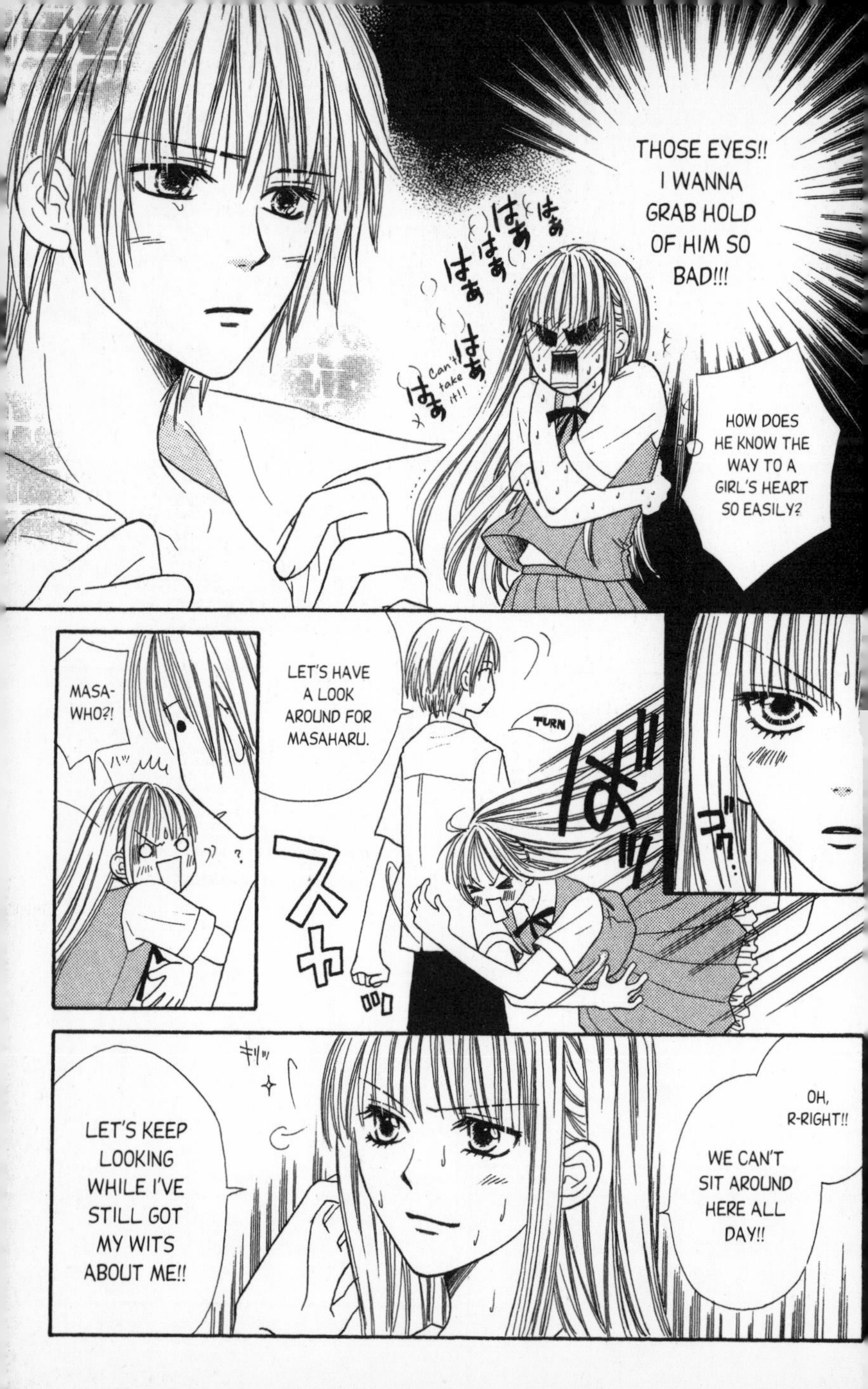
THOSE EYES!! I WANNA GRAB HOLD OF HIM SO BAD!!!
Can't take it!!
HOW DOES HE KNOW THE WAY TO A GIRL'S HEART SO EASILY?
TURN
LET'S HAVE A LOOK AROUND FOR MASAHARU.
MASA-WHO?!
OH, R-RIGHT!!
WE CAN'T SIT AROUND HERE ALL DAY!!
LET'S KEEP LOOKING WHILE I'VE STILL GOT MY WITS ABOUT ME!!

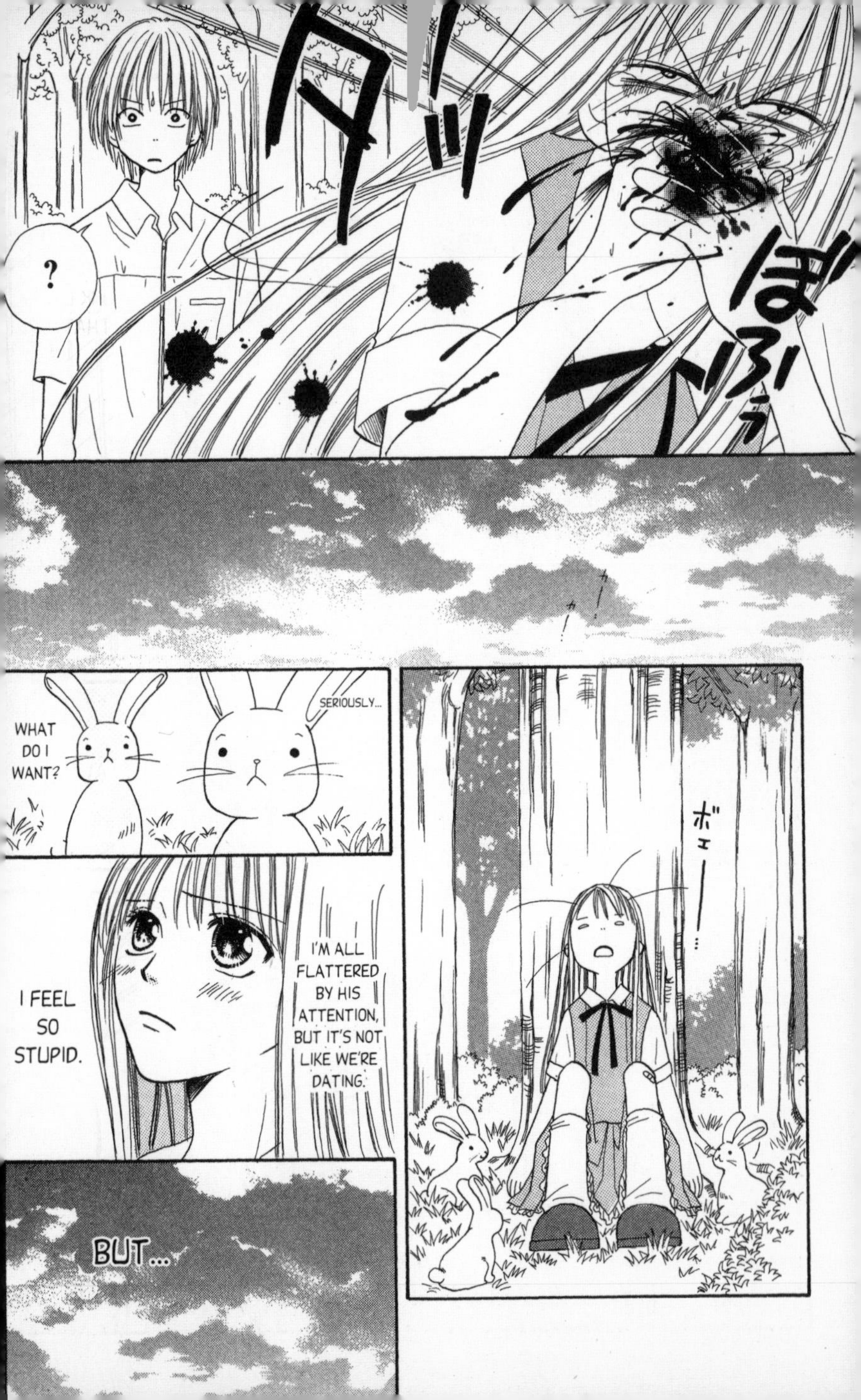
タッ
?
ボェー…
SERIOUSLY...
WHAT DO I WANT?
I'M ALL FLATTERED BY HIS ATTENTION, BUT IT'S NOT LIKE WE'RE DATING.
I FEEL SO STUPID.
BUT...

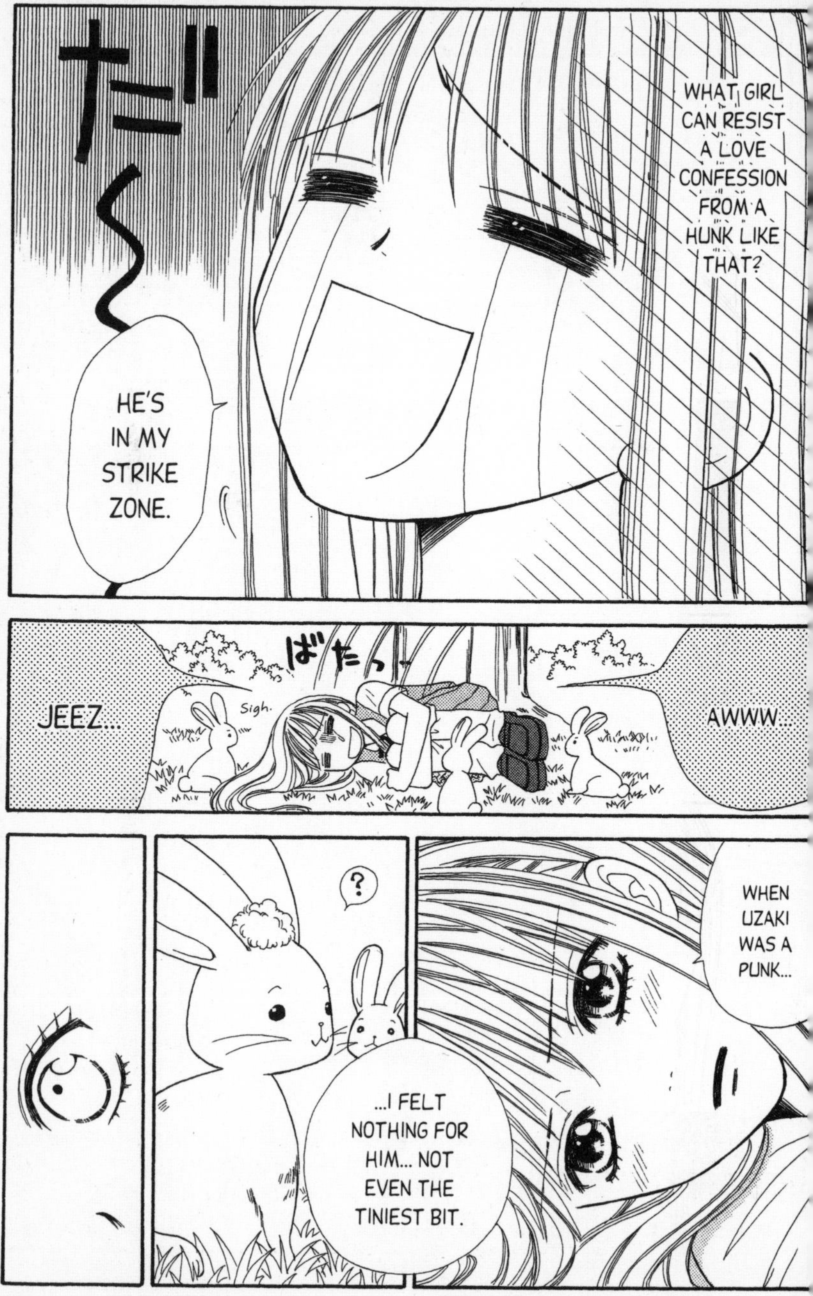
WHAT GIRL CAN RESIST A LOVE CONFESSION FROM A HUNK LIKE THAT?
HE'S IN MY STRIKE ZONE.
だく
AWWW...
ばたっ
Sigh.
JEEZ...
WHEN UZAKI WAS A PUNK...
...I FELT NOTHING FOR HIM... NOT EVEN THE TINIEST BIT.
?

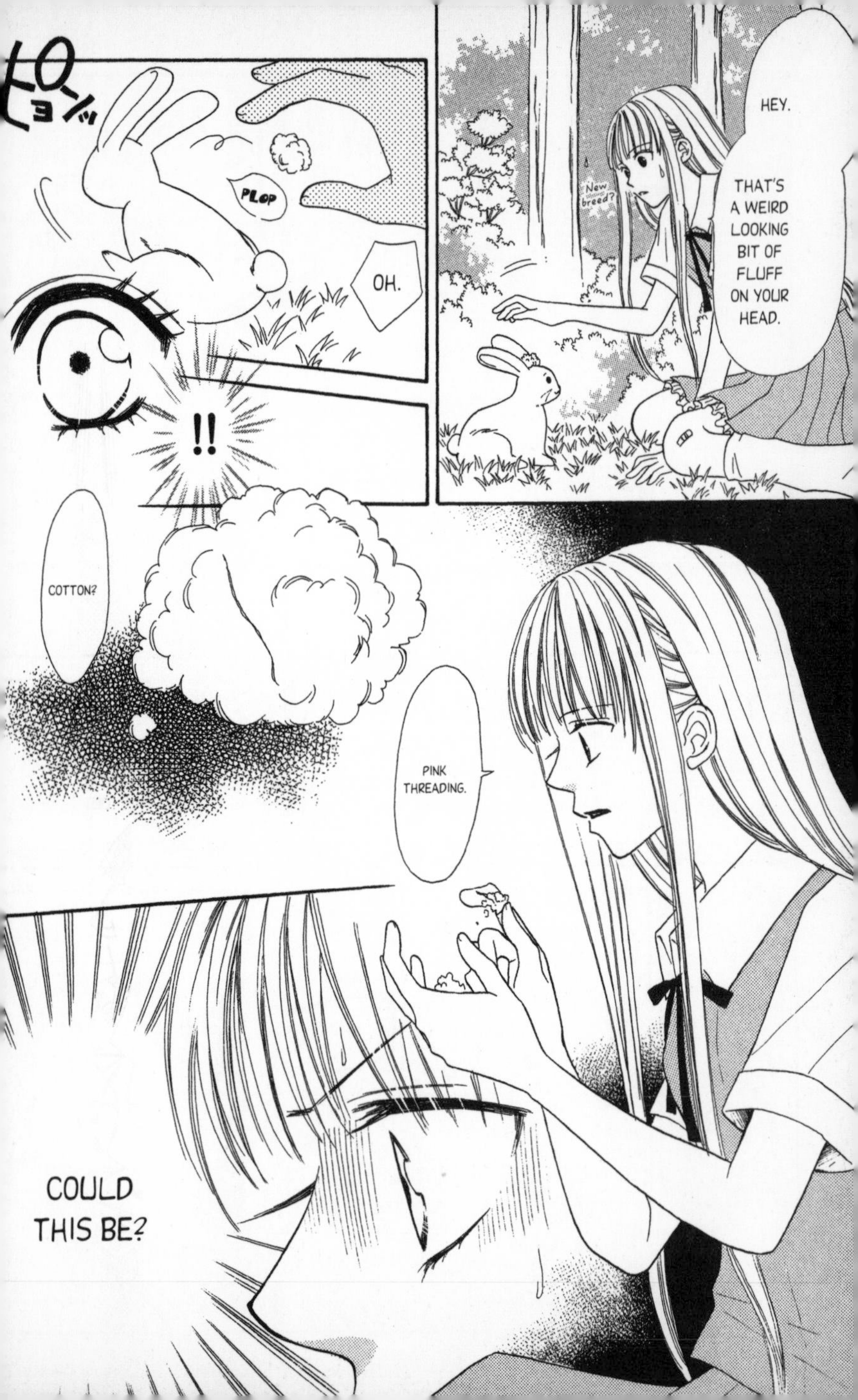
HEY.
THAT'S A WEIRD LOOKING BIT OF FLUFF ON YOUR HEAD.
New breed?
ピョンッ
PLOP
OH.
!!
COTTON?
PINK THREADING.
COULD THIS BE?

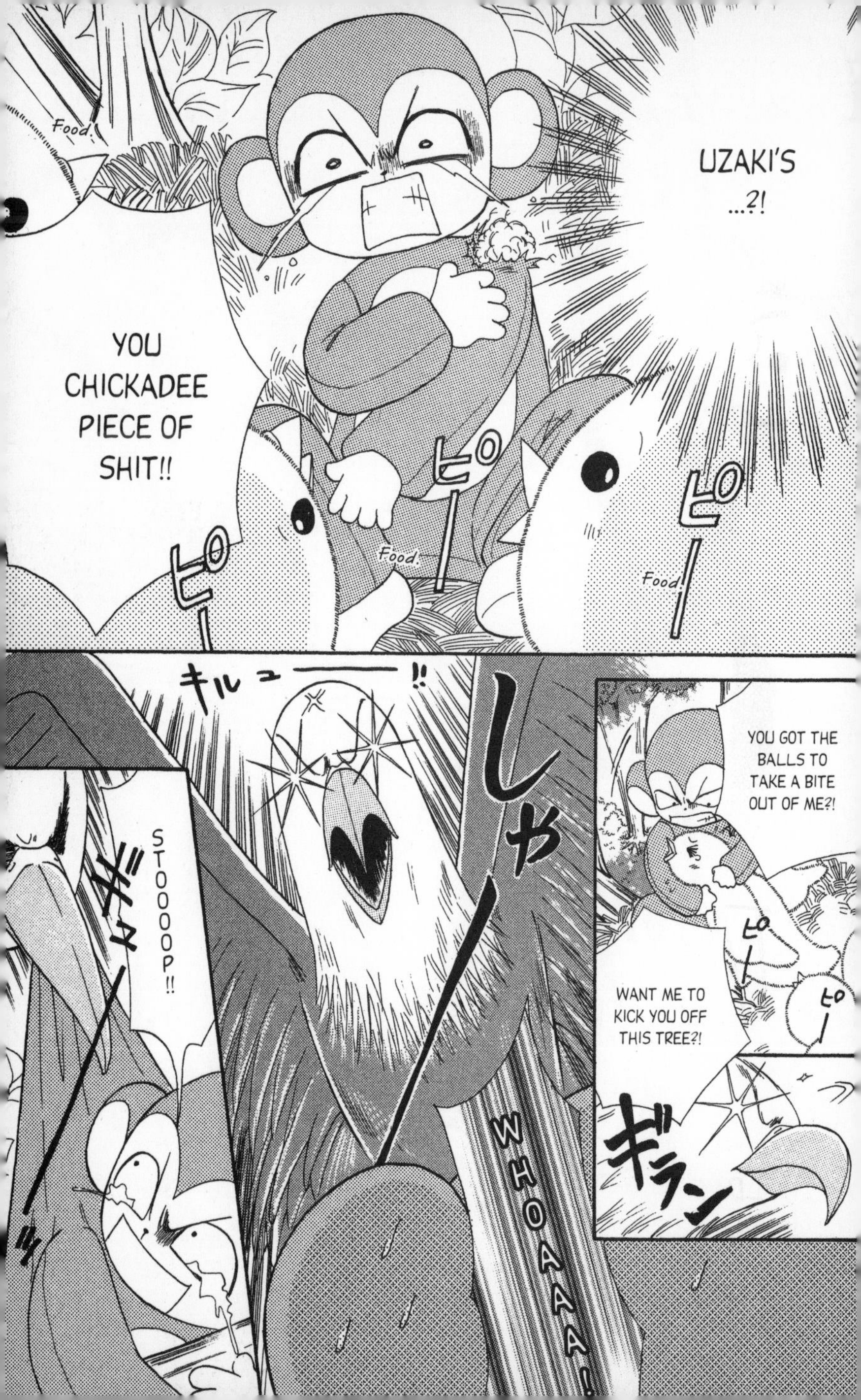
UZAKI'S ...?!
YOU CHICKADEE PIECE OF SHIT!!
ピーーー
Food!
ピーーー
Food.
ピーーー
Food!
YOU GOT THE BALLS TO TAKE A BITE OUT OF ME?!
ピーーー
ピーーー
WANT ME TO KICK YOU OFF THIS TREE?!
ギラン
キルューーーー!!
しゃ
WHOAAAA!
STOOOOP!!
ギャ

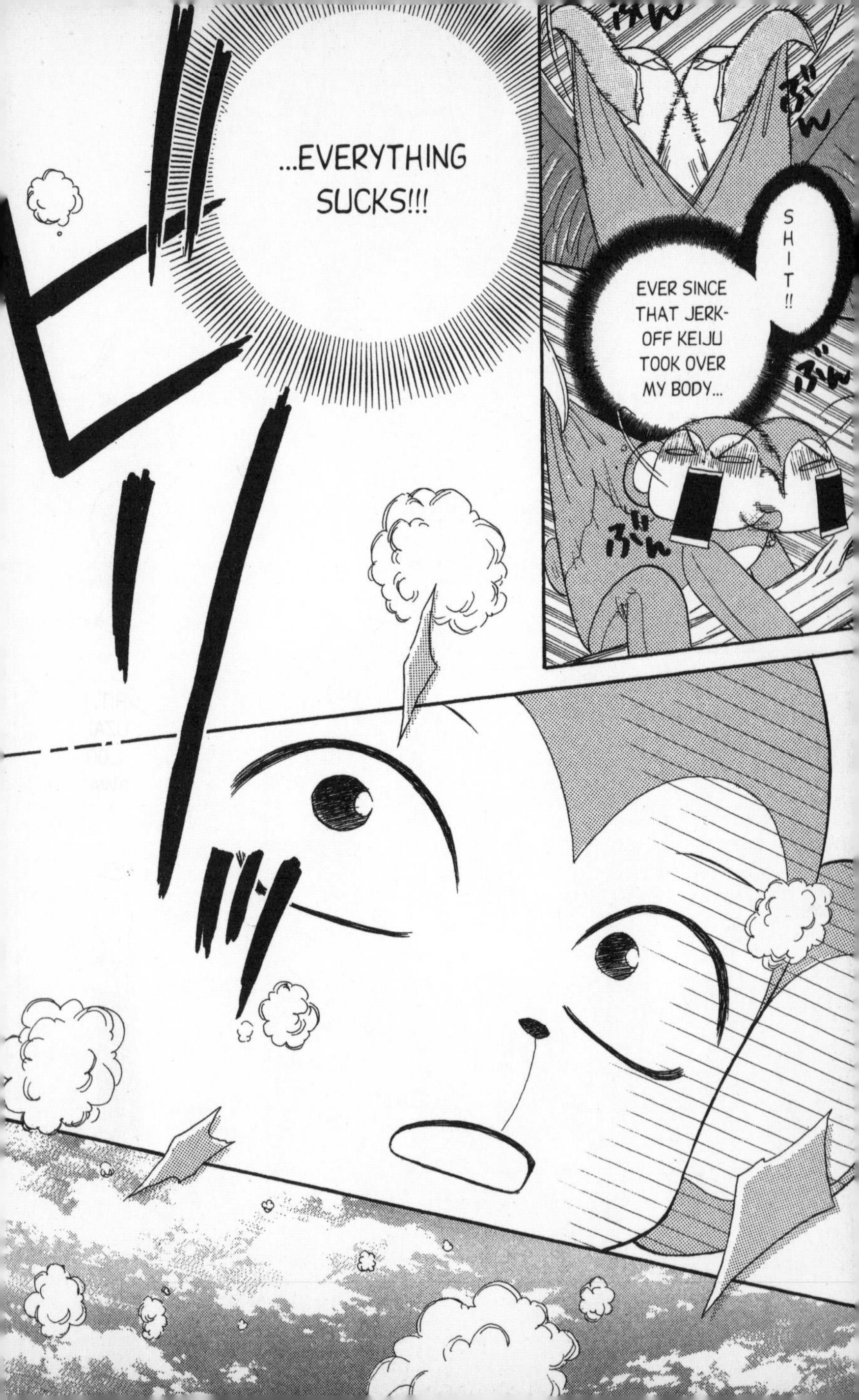
EVER SINCE THAT JERK-OFF KEIJU TOOK OVER MY BODY...
SHIT!!
ぶん
ぶん
ぶん
...EVERYTHING SUCKS!!!

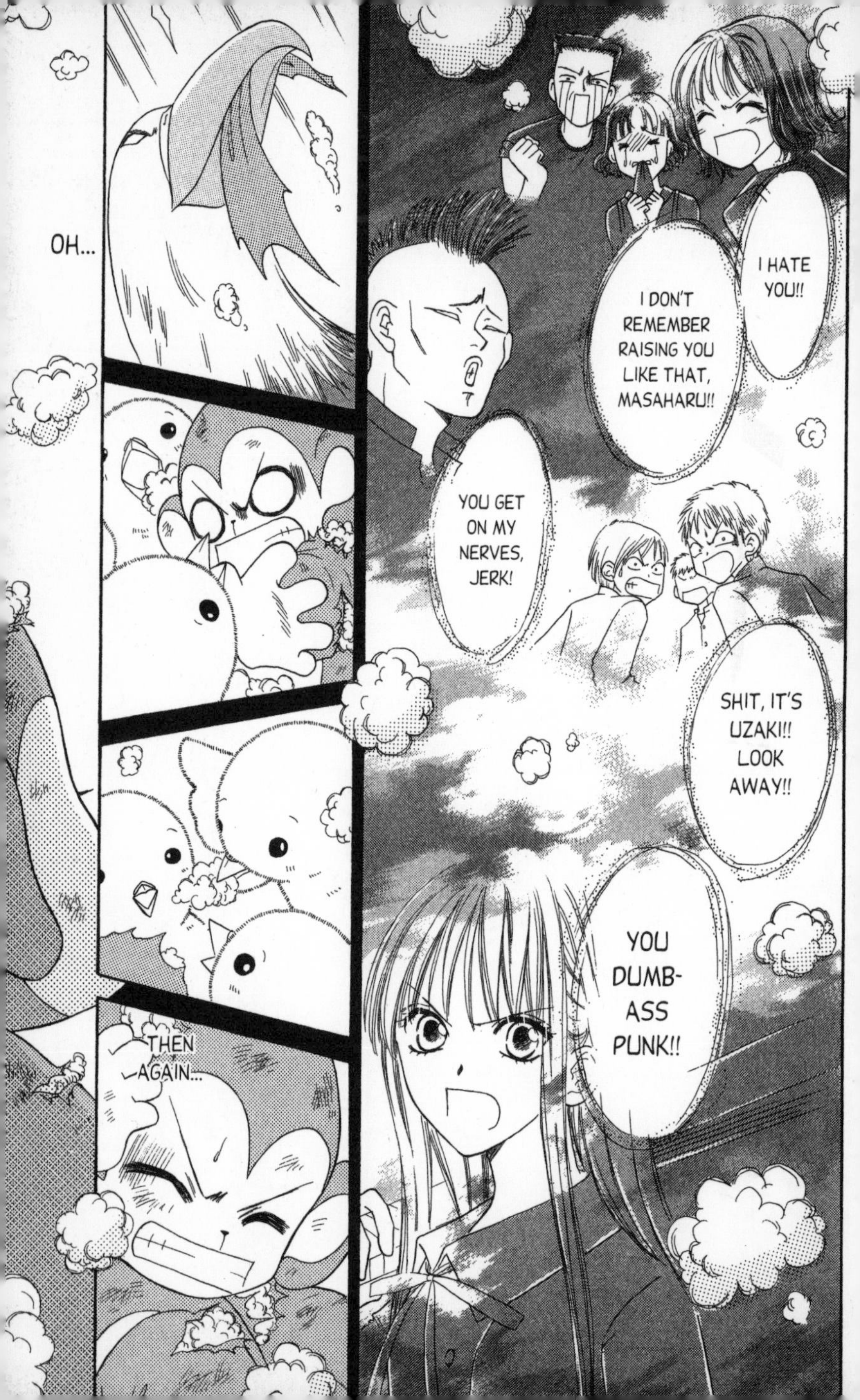
I HATE YOU!!
I DON'T REMEMBER RAISING YOU LIKE THAT, MASAHARU!!
YOU GET ON MY NERVES, JERK!
SHIT, IT'S UZAKI!! LOOK AWAY!!
YOU DUMB-ASS PUNK!!
OH...
THEN AGAIN...

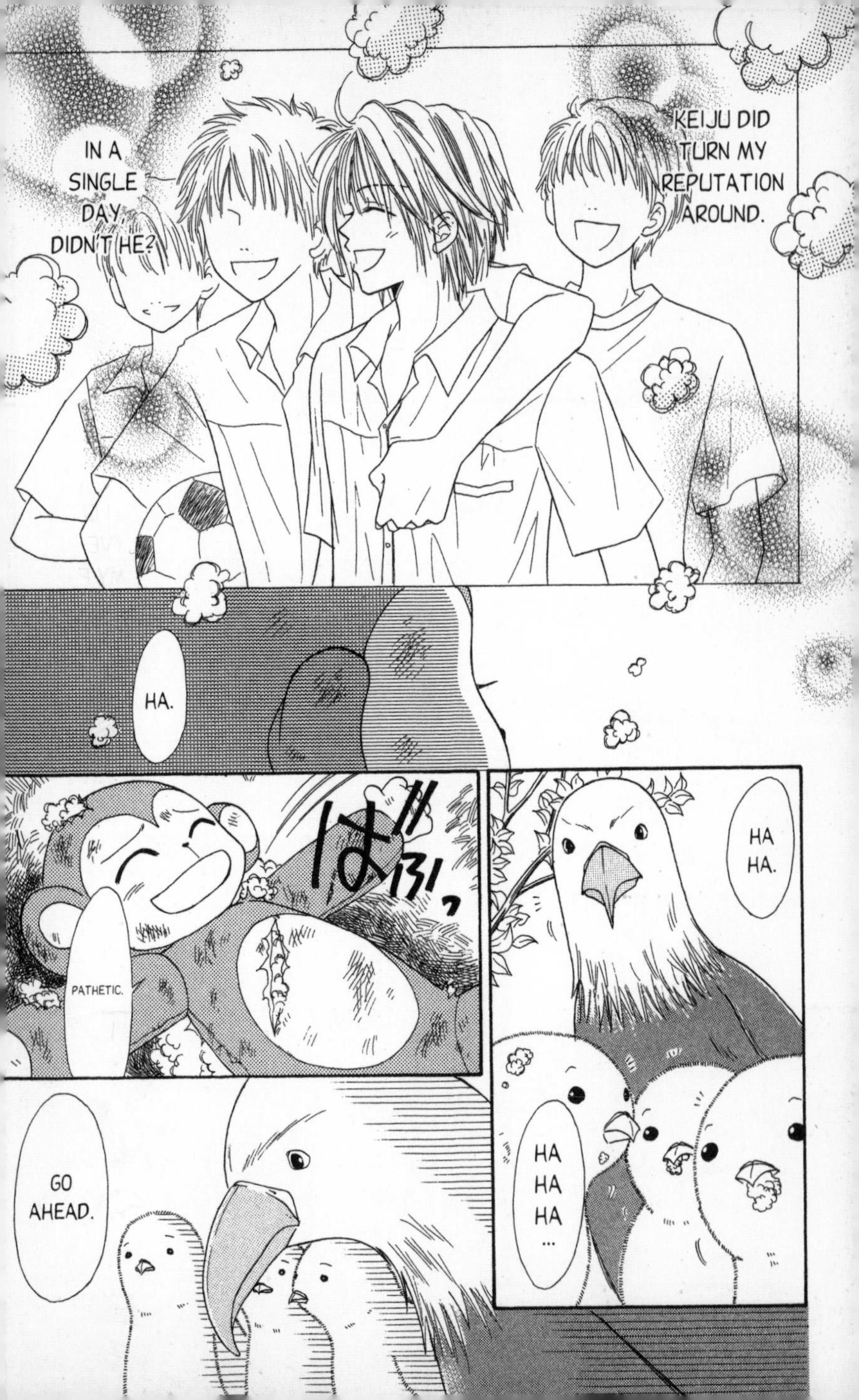
KEIJU DID TURN MY REPUTATION AROUND.
IN A SINGLE DAY, DIDN'T HE?
HA.
HA HA.
HA HA HA ...
ばぶっ
PATHETIC.
GO AHEAD.

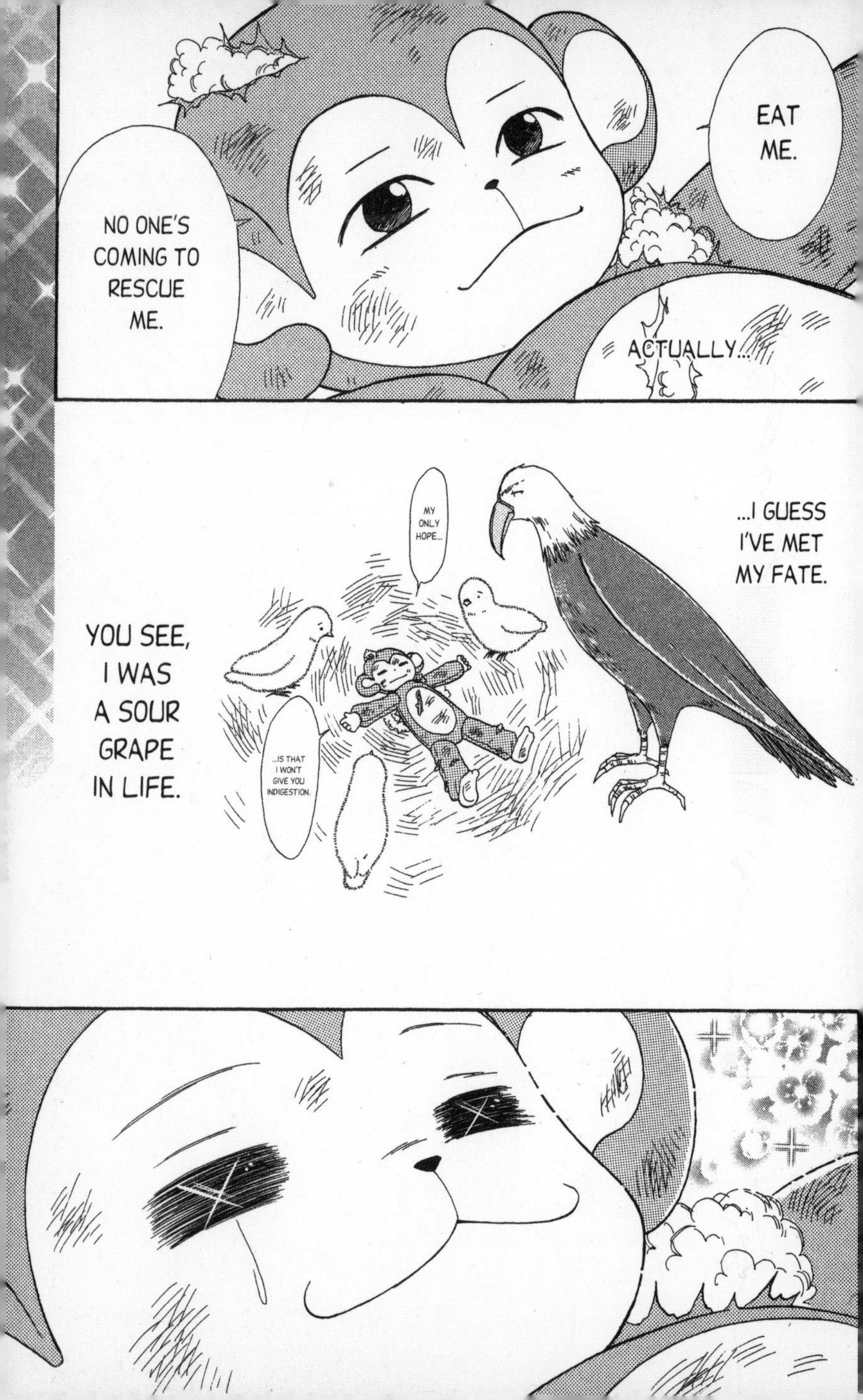
EAT ME.
ACTUALLY...
NO ONE'S COMING TO RESCUE ME.
...I GUESS I'VE MET MY FATE.
MY ONLY HOPE...
...IS THAT I WON'T GIVE YOU INDIGESTION.
YOU SEE, I WAS A SOUR GRAPE IN LIFE.

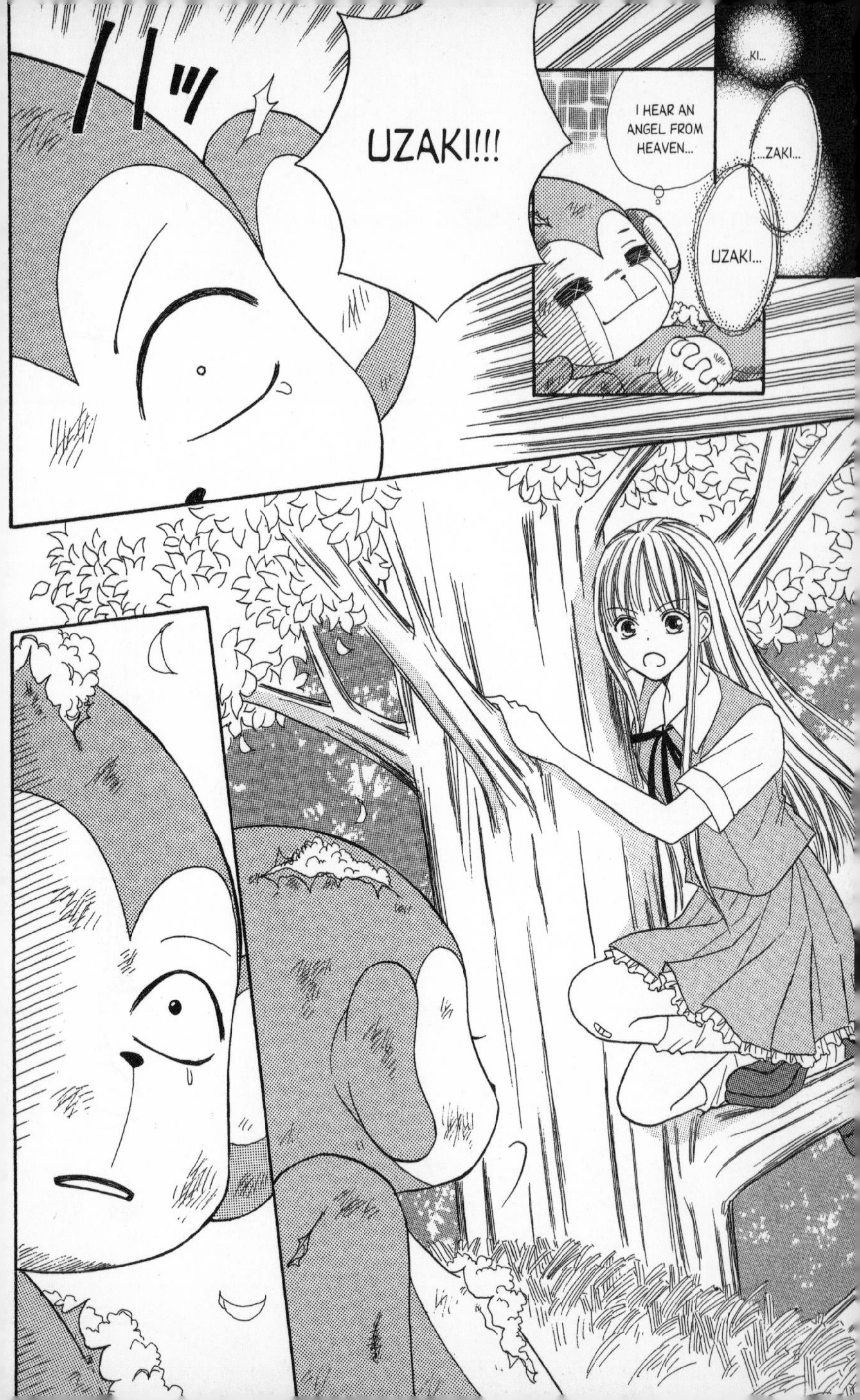
...KI...
...ZAKI...
UZAKI...
I HEAR AN ANGEL FROM HEAVEN...
UZAKI!!!
ハッ

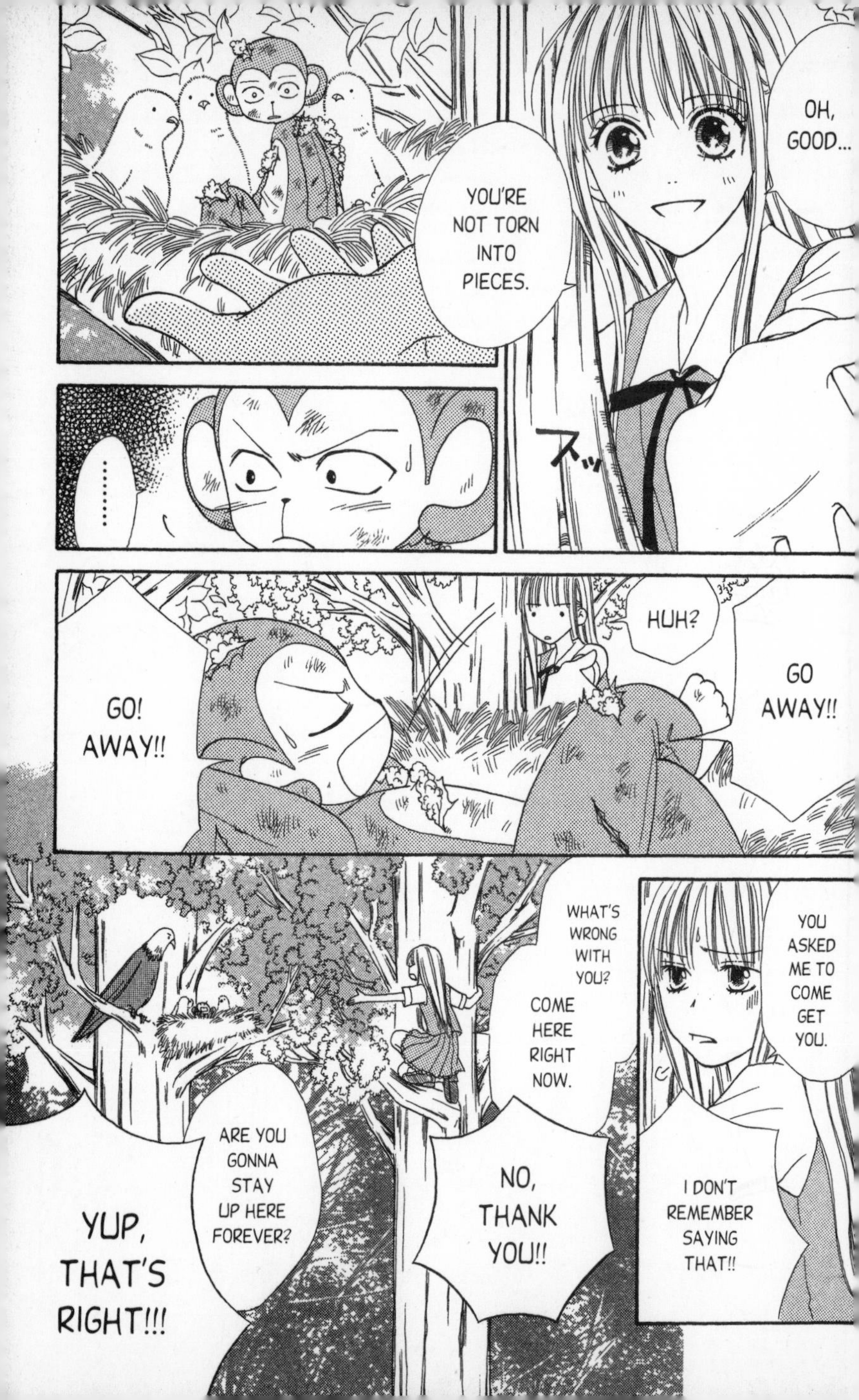
OH, GOOD...
YOU'RE NOT TORN INTO PIECES.
スッ
......
HUH?
GO AWAY!!
GO! AWAY!!
YOU ASKED ME TO COME GET YOU.
I DON'T REMEMBER SAYING THAT!!
WHAT'S WRONG WITH YOU?
COME HERE RIGHT NOW.
NO, THANK YOU!!
ARE YOU GONNA STAY UP HERE FOREVER?
YUP, THAT'S RIGHT!!!

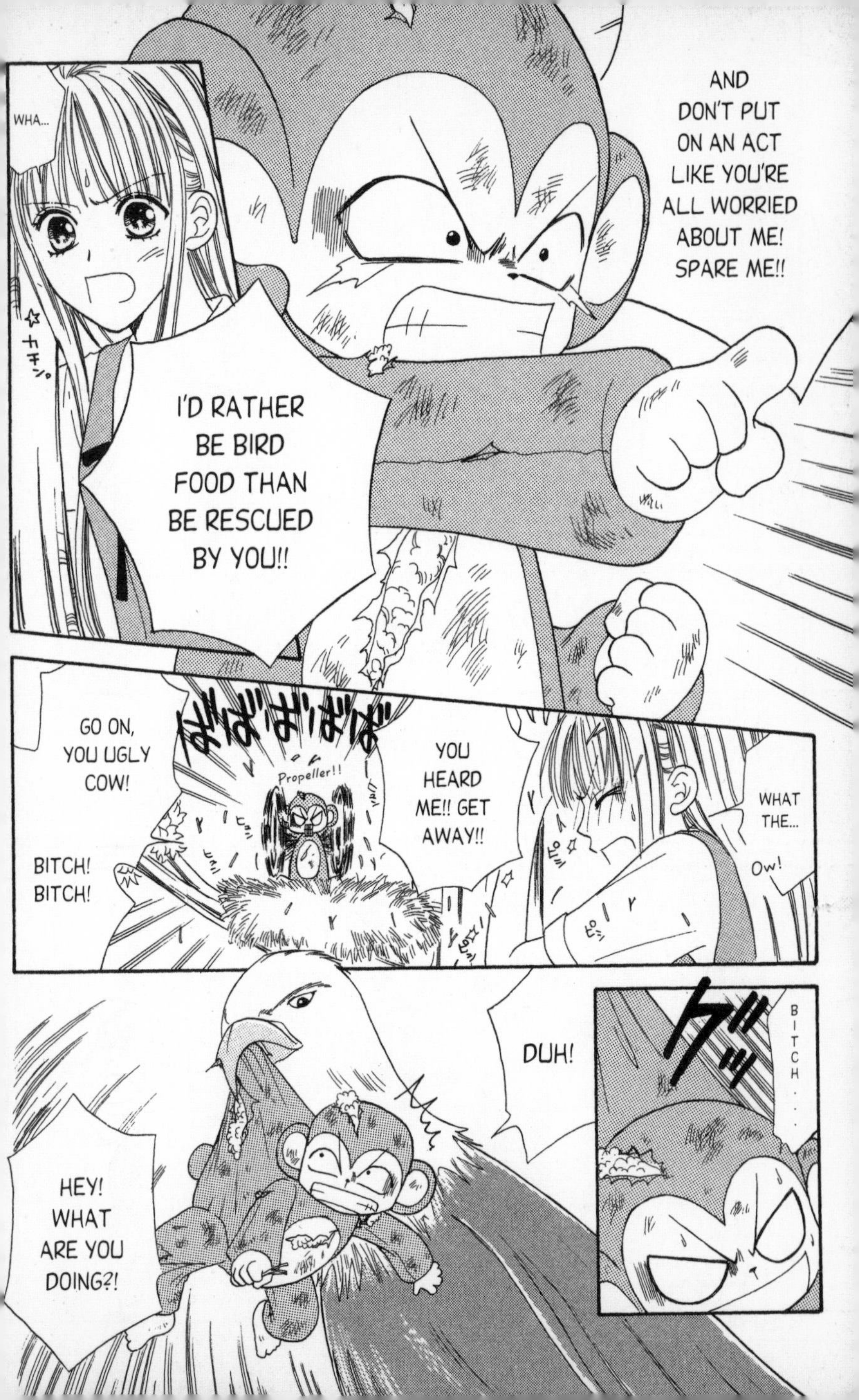
AND DON'T PUT ON AN ACT LIKE YOU'RE ALL WORRIED ABOUT ME! SPARE ME!!
I'D RATHER BE BIRD FOOD THAN BE RESCUED BY YOU!!
WHA...
WHAT THE...
OW!
YOU HEARD ME!! GET AWAY!!
Propeller!!
GO ON, YOU UGLY COW!
BITCH! BITCH!
BITCH . . .
DUH!
HEY! WHAT ARE YOU DOING?!

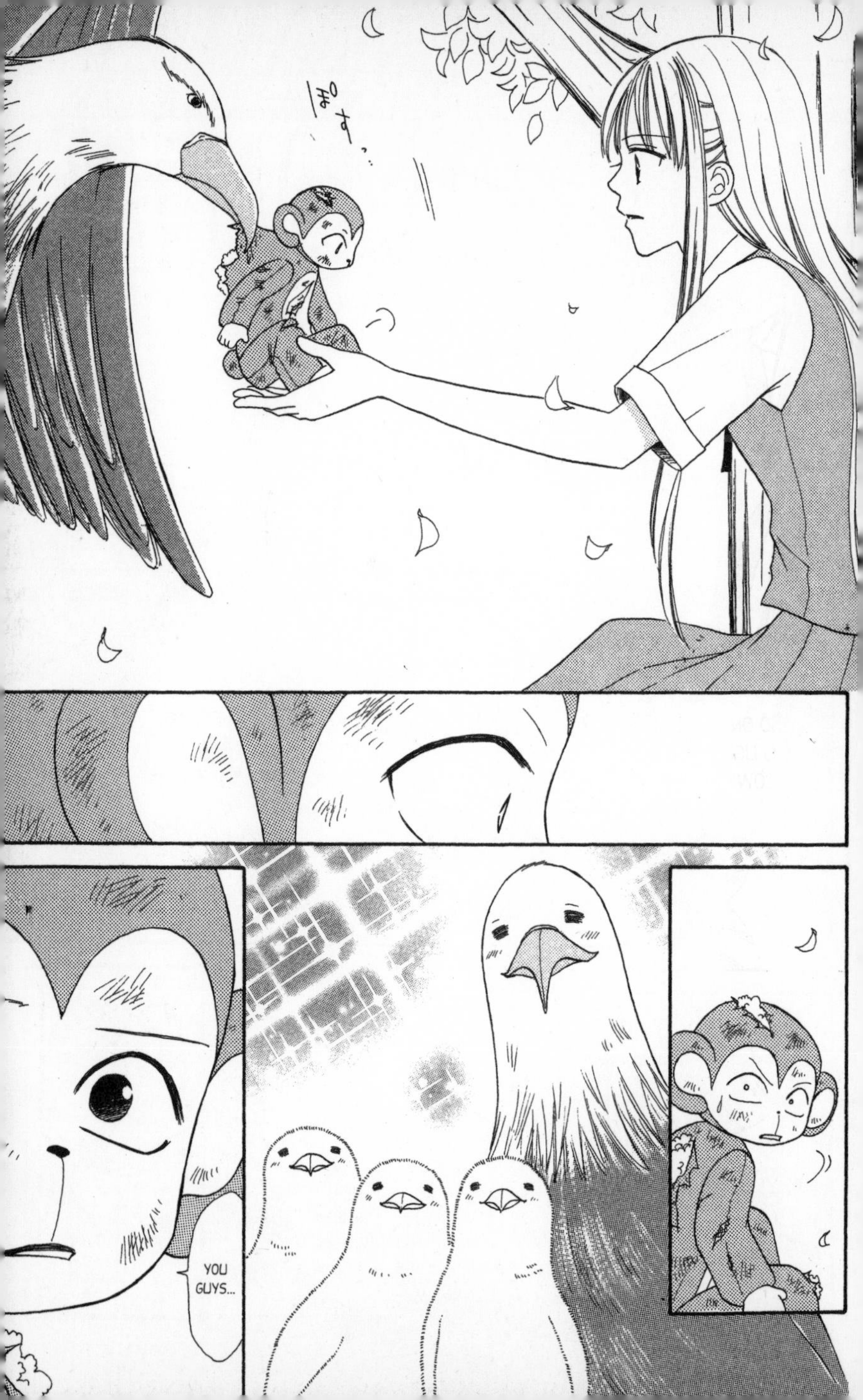
ぽす…
YOU GUYS...

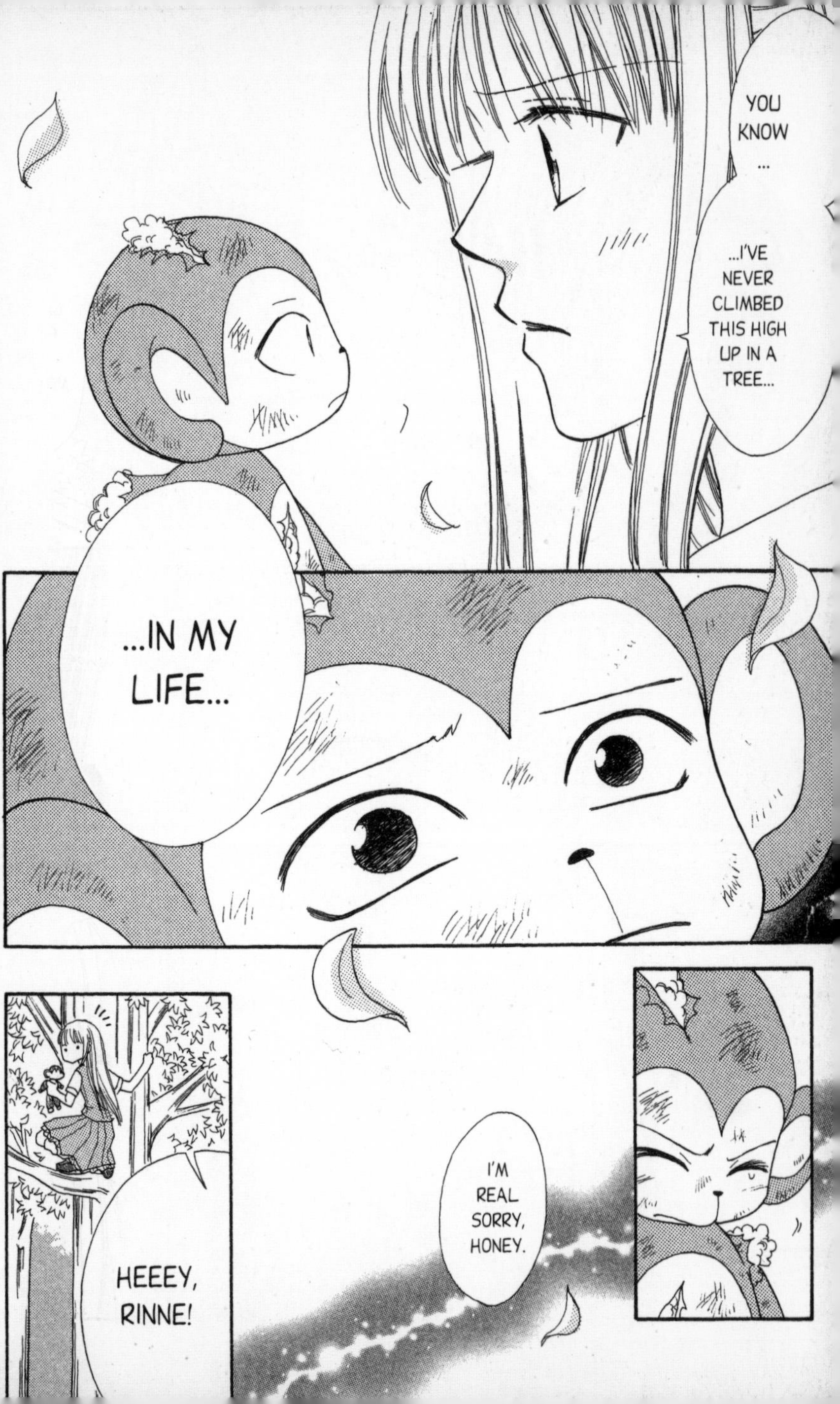
YOU KNOW ...
...I'VE NEVER CLIMBED THIS HIGH UP IN A TREE...
...IN MY LIFE...
I'M REAL SORRY, HONEY.
HEEEY, RINNE!

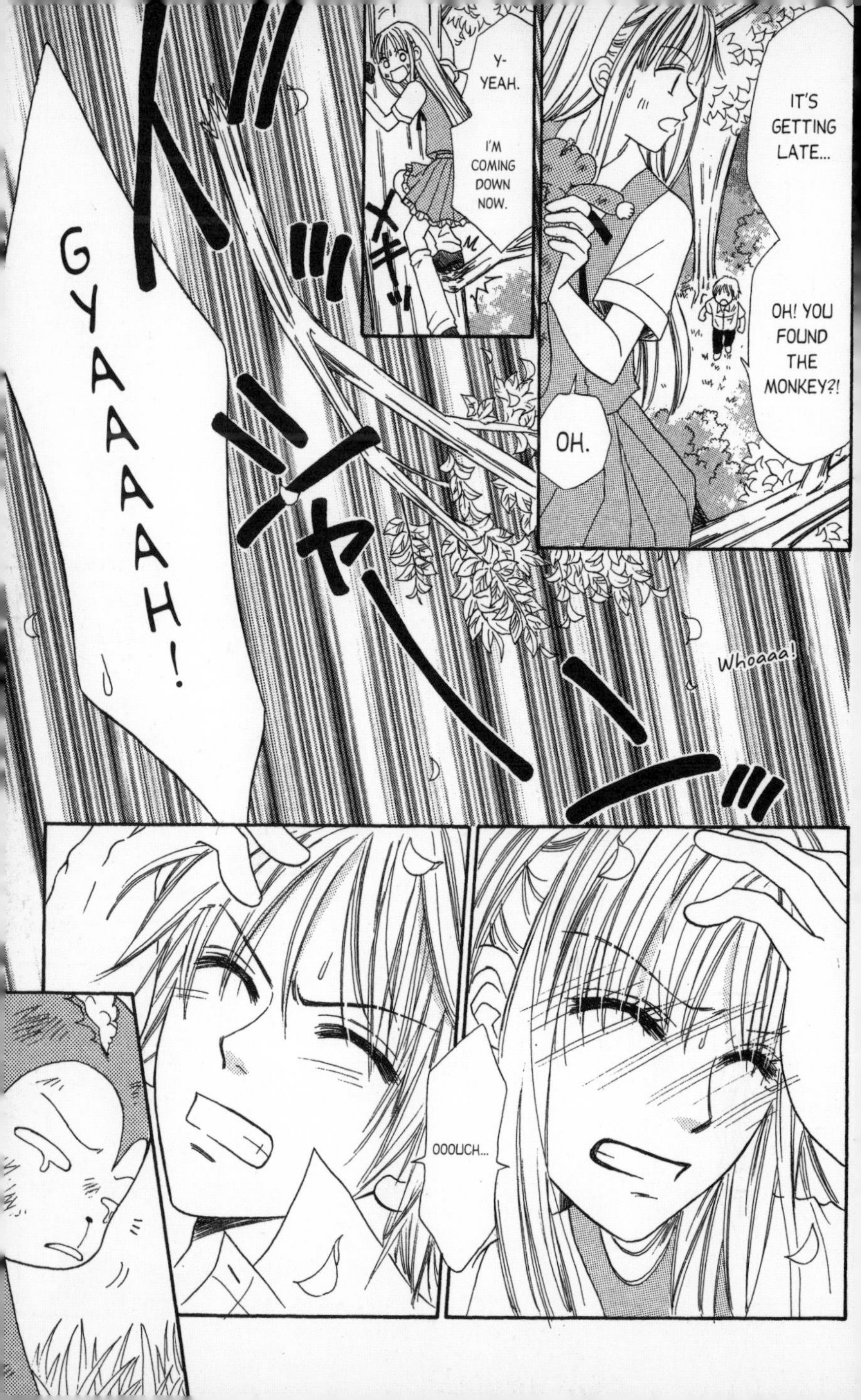
IT'S GETTING LATE...
OH! YOU FOUND THE MONKEY?!
OH.
Y-YEAH.
I'M COMING DOWN NOW.
GYAAAAH!
Whoaaa!
OOOUCH...

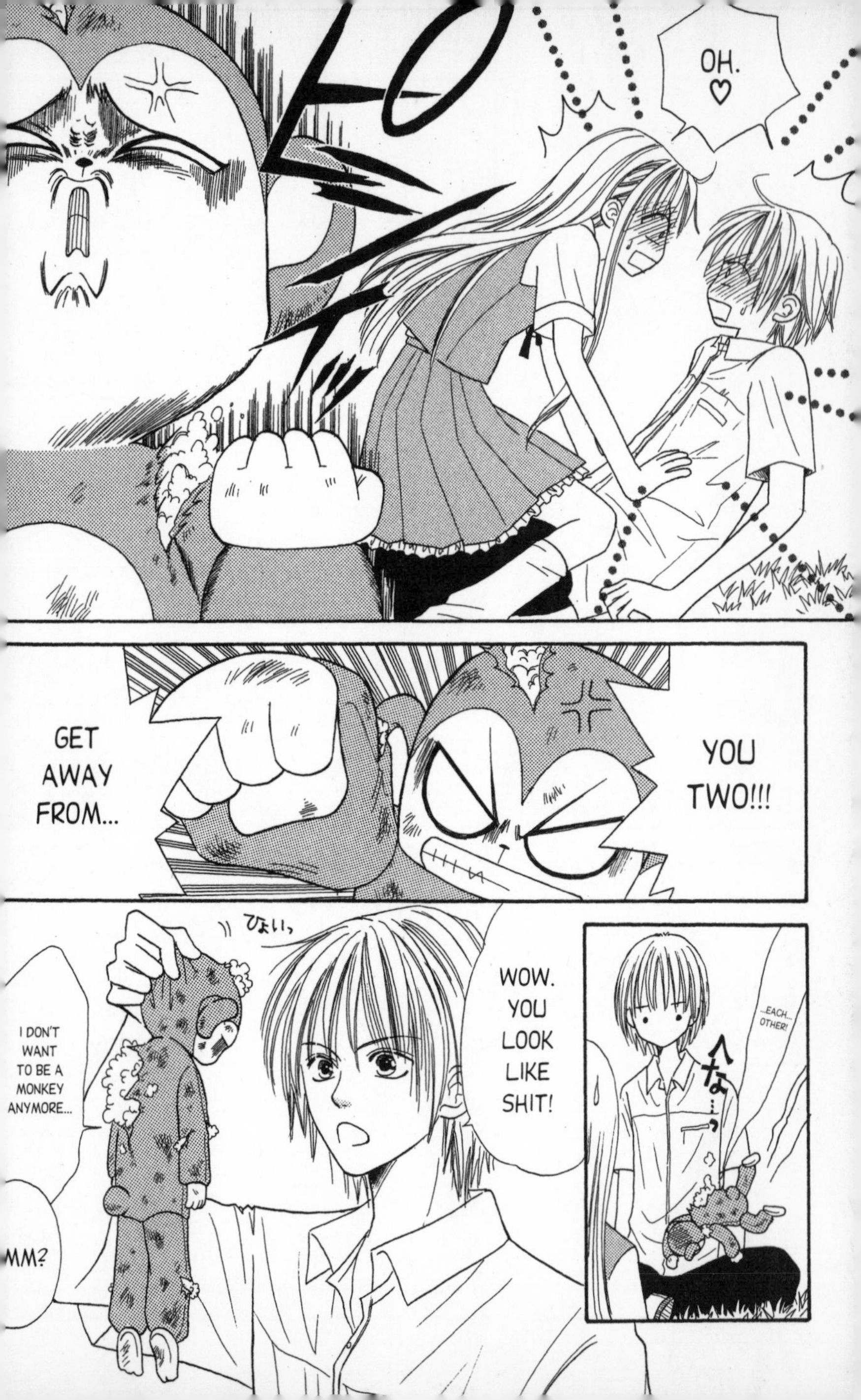
OH. ♡
YOU TWO!!!
GET AWAY FROM...
...EACH... OTHER!
へな…っ
WOW. YOU LOOK LIKE SHIT!
ひょいっ
I DON'T WANT TO BE A MONKEY ANYMORE...
MM?

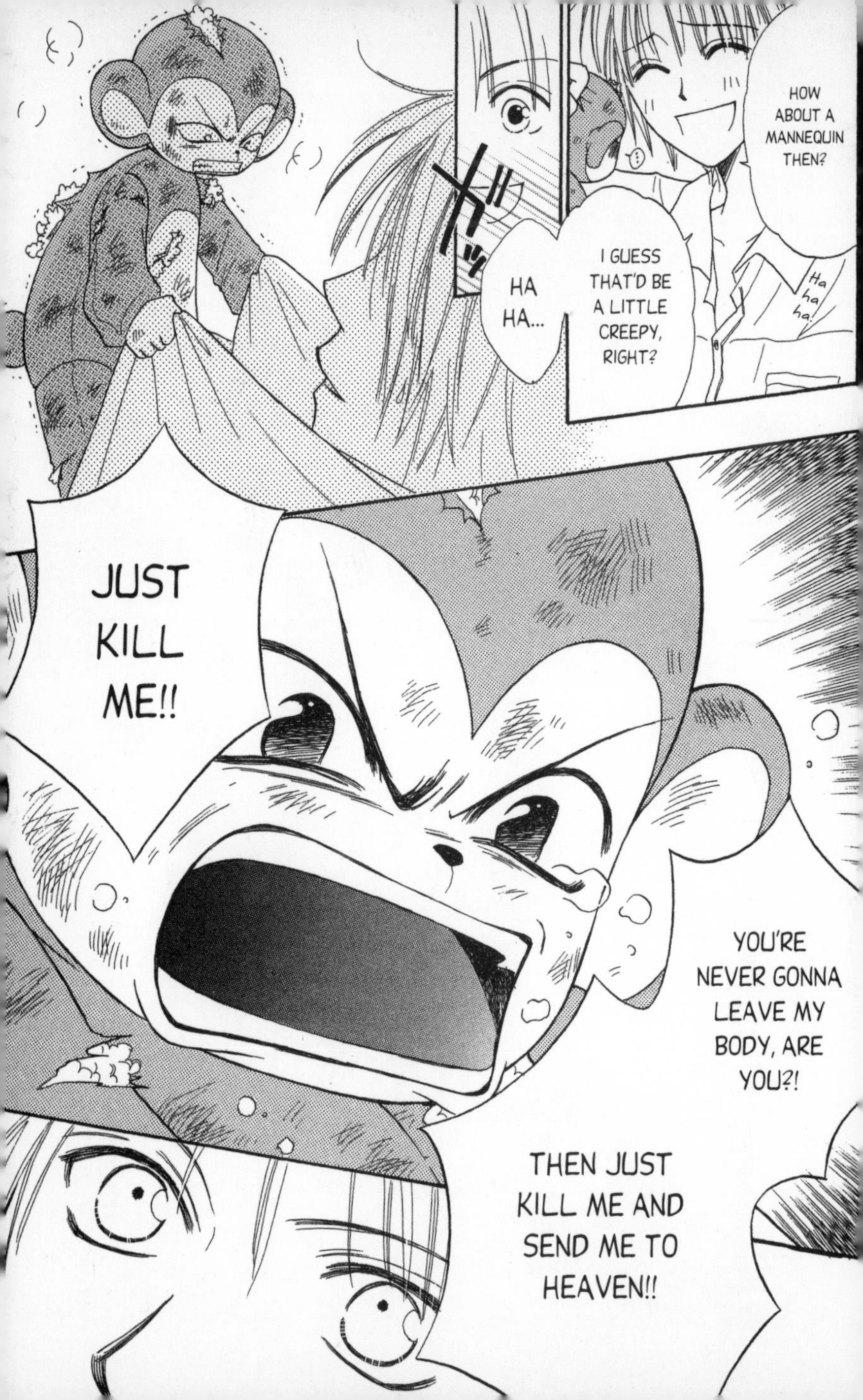
HOW ABOUT A MANNEQUIN THEN?
Ha ha ha!
I GUESS THAT'D BE A LITTLE CREEPY, RIGHT?
HA HA...
JUST KILL ME!!
YOU'RE NEVER GONNA LEAVE MY BODY, ARE YOU?!
THEN JUST KILL ME AND SEND ME TO HEAVEN!!

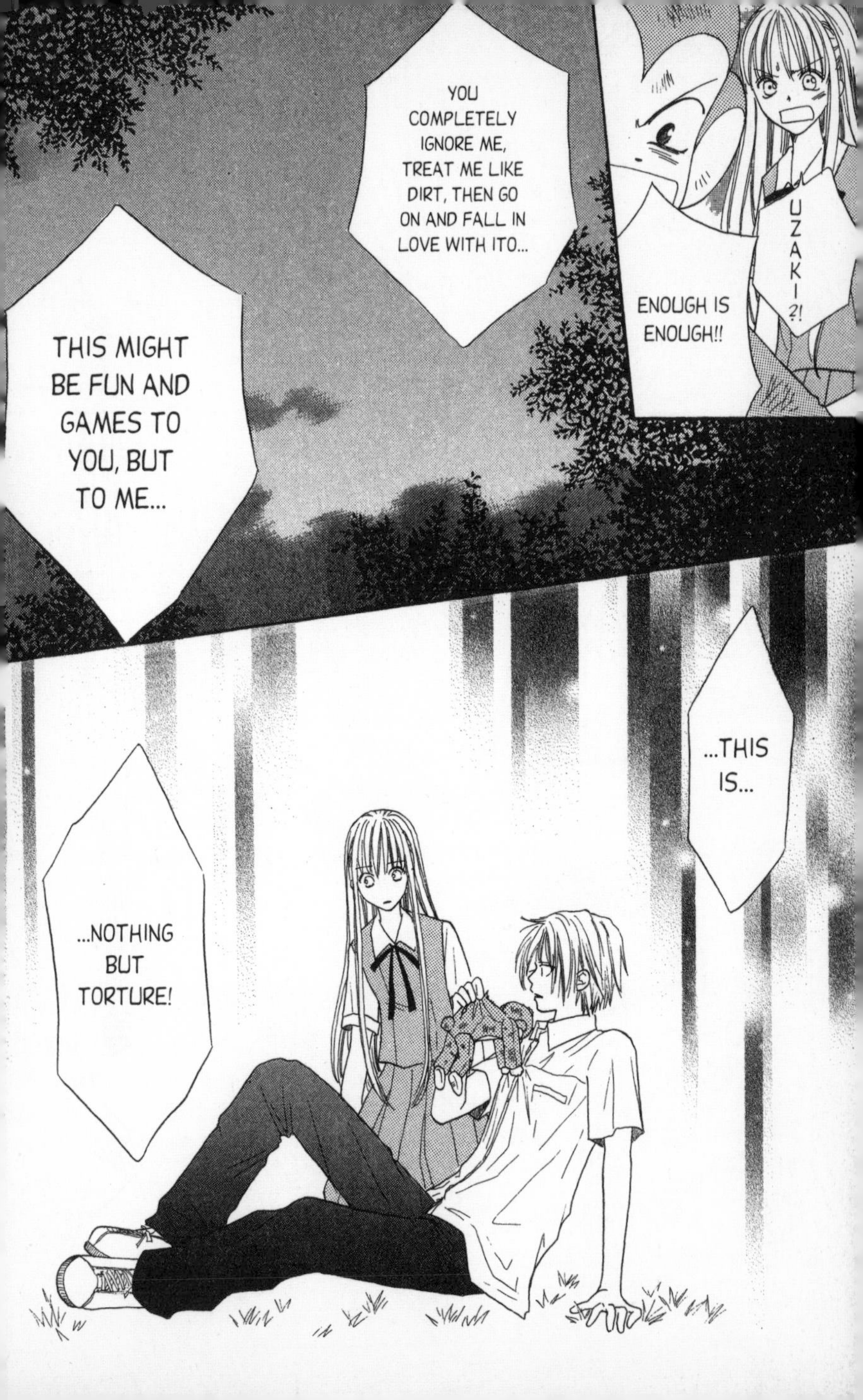
UZAKI?!
ENOUGH IS ENOUGH!!
YOU COMPLETELY IGNORE ME, TREAT ME LIKE DIRT, THEN GO ON AND FALL IN LOVE WITH ITO...
THIS MIGHT BE FUN AND GAMES TO YOU, BUT TO ME...
...THIS IS...
...NOTHING BUT TORTURE!

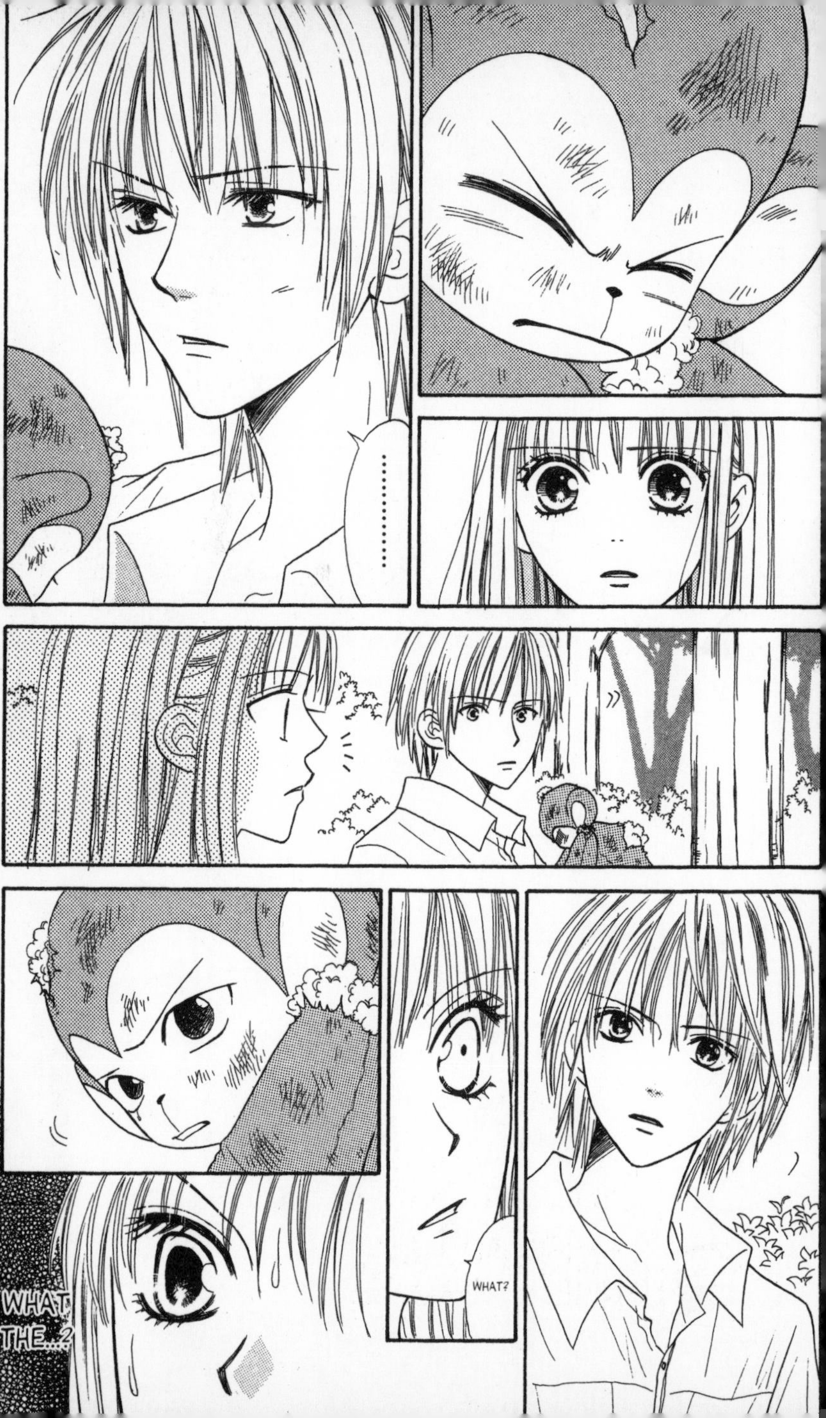
....
WHAT?
WHAT THE...?

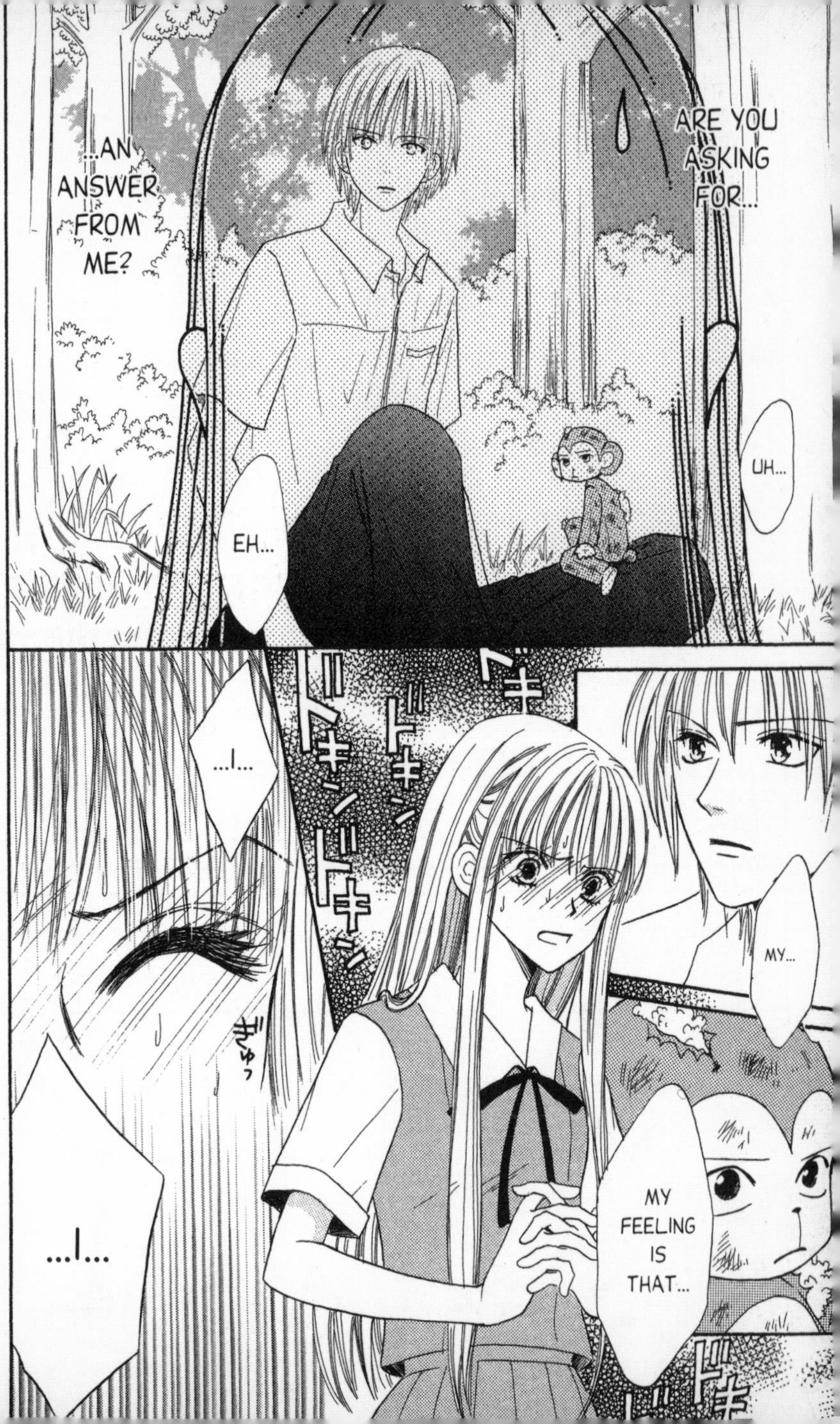
ARE YOU ASKING FOR...
UH...
...AN ANSWER FROM ME?
EH...
MY...
MY FEELING IS THAT...
...I...
...I...

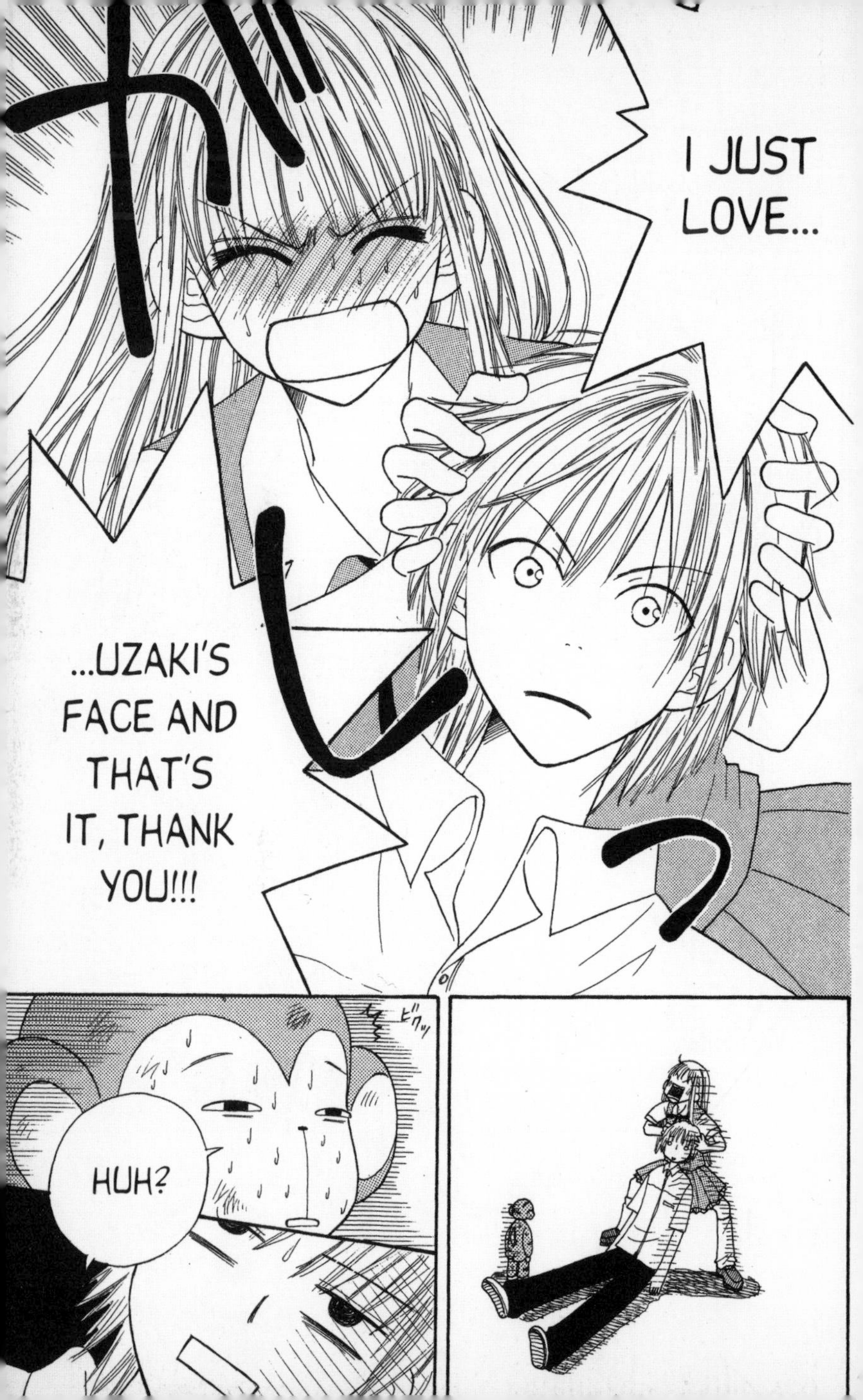
I JUST LOVE...
...UZAKI'S FACE AND THAT'S IT, THANK YOU!!!
HUH?

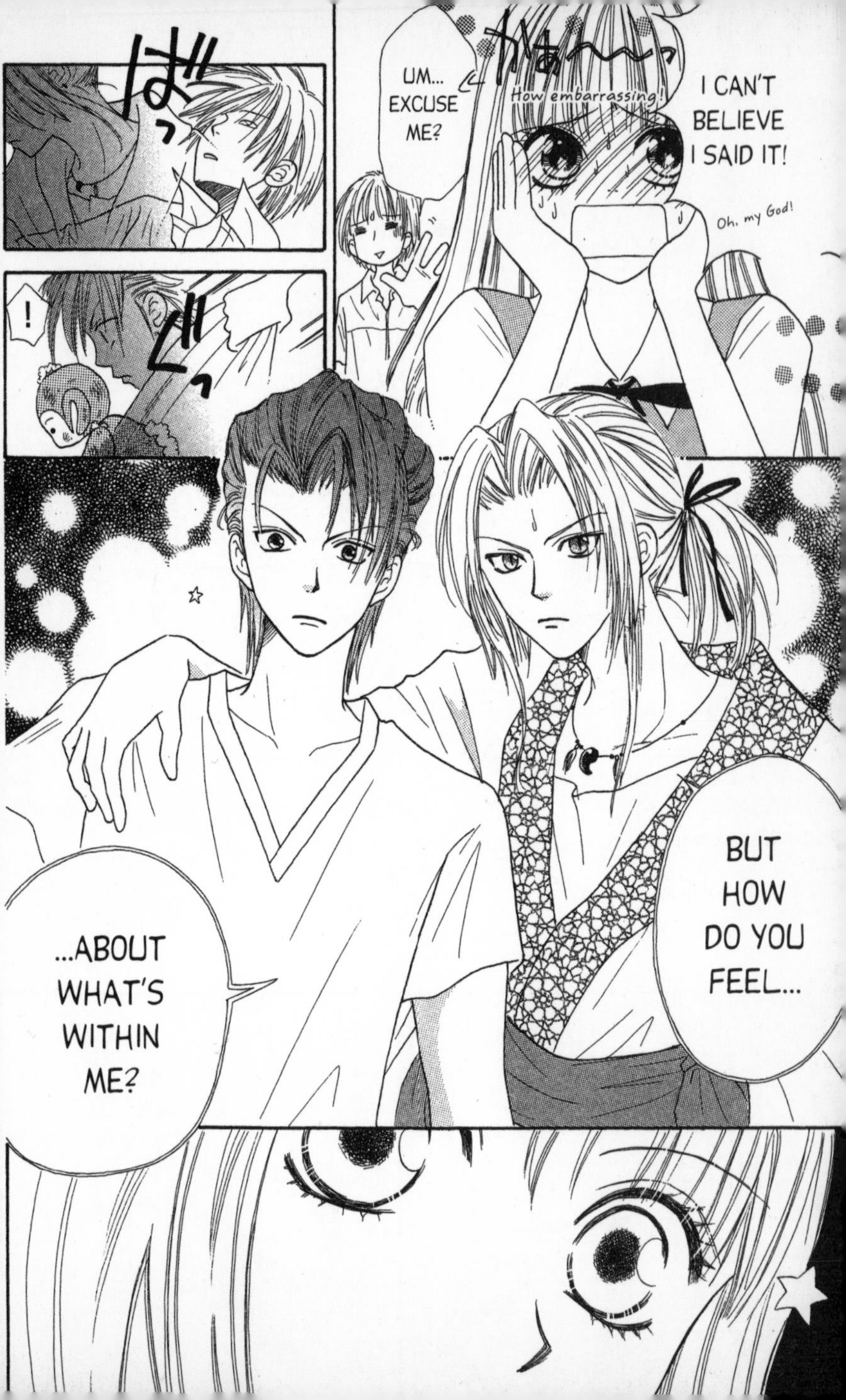
I CAN'T BELIEVE I SAID IT!
Oh, my God!
かあ〜〜っ
How embarrassing!
UM... EXCUSE ME?
ぱっ
!
ばっ
BUT HOW DO YOU FEEL...
...ABOUT WHAT'S WITHIN ME?

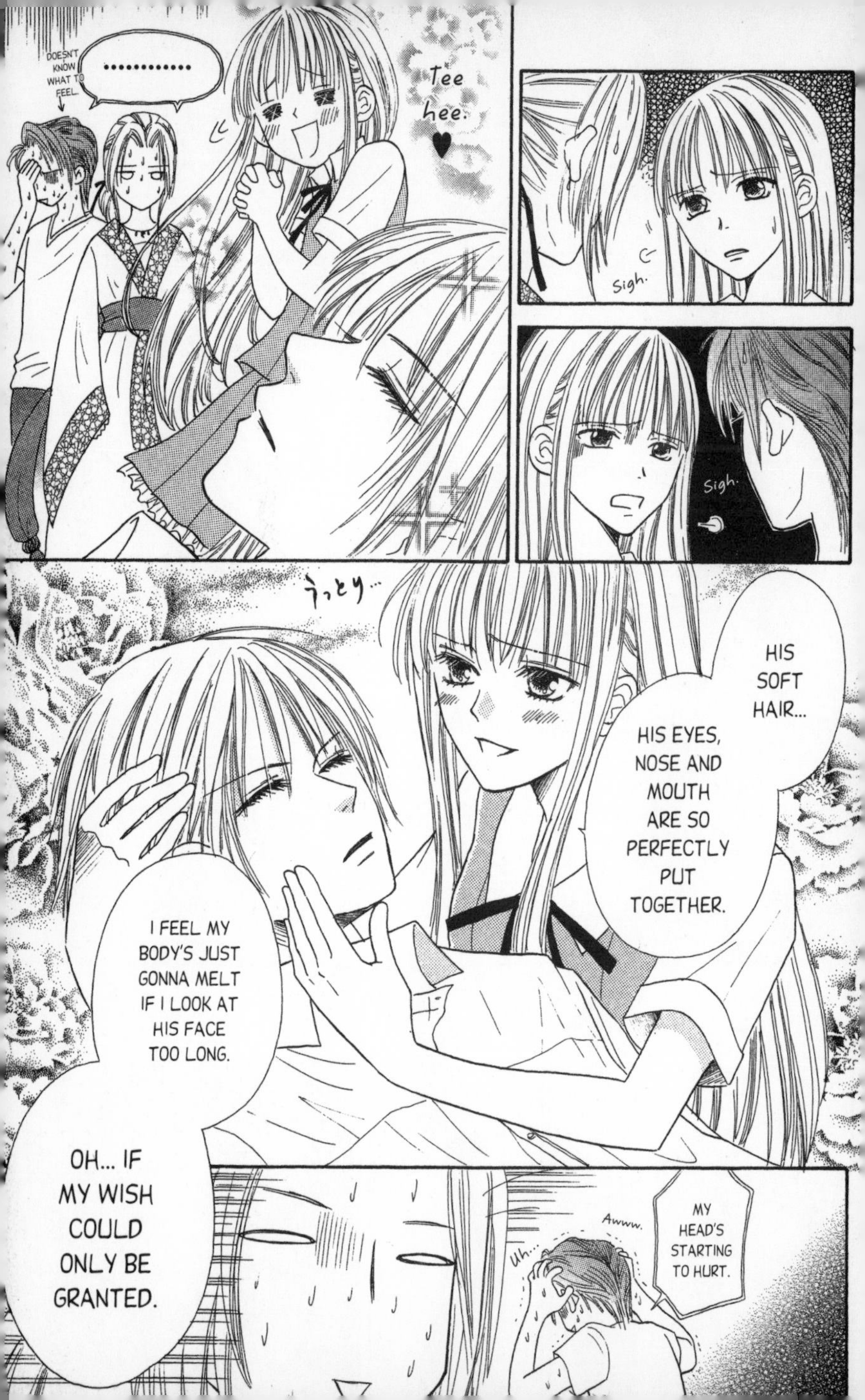
Sigh.
Sigh.
Tee hee.
....
DOESN'T KNOW WHAT TO FEEL.
うっとり...
HIS SOFT HAIR...
HIS EYES, NOSE AND MOUTH ARE SO PERFECTLY PUT TOGETHER.
I FEEL MY BODY'S JUST GONNA MELT IF I LOOK AT HIS FACE TOO LONG.
MY HEAD'S STARTING TO HURT.
Awww.
Uh...
OH... IF MY WISH COULD ONLY BE GRANTED.

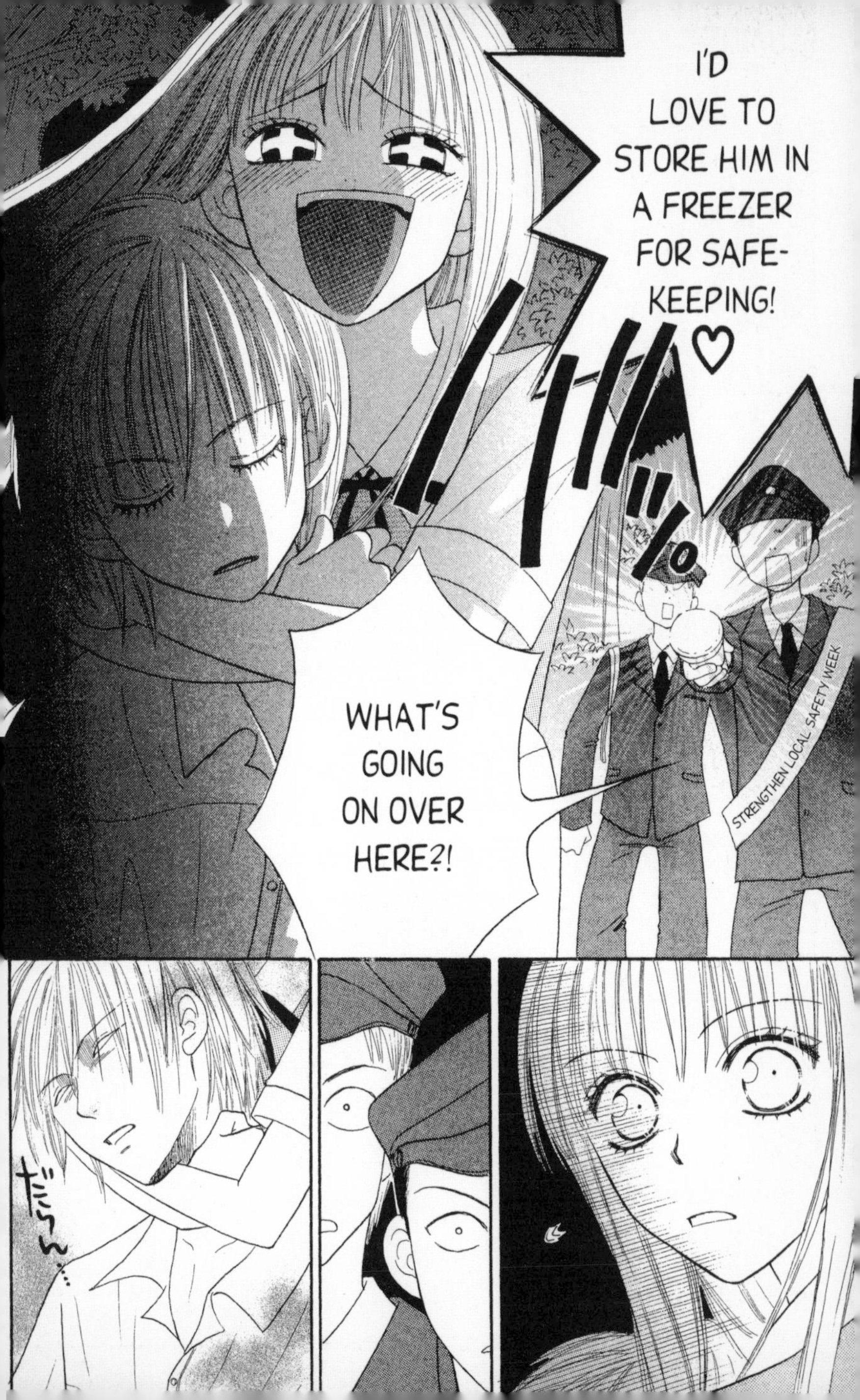
I'D LOVE TO STORE HIM IN A FREEZER FOR SAFE-KEEPING! ♡
STRENGTHEN LOCAL SAFETY WEEK
WHAT'S GOING ON OVER HERE?!
だらん…

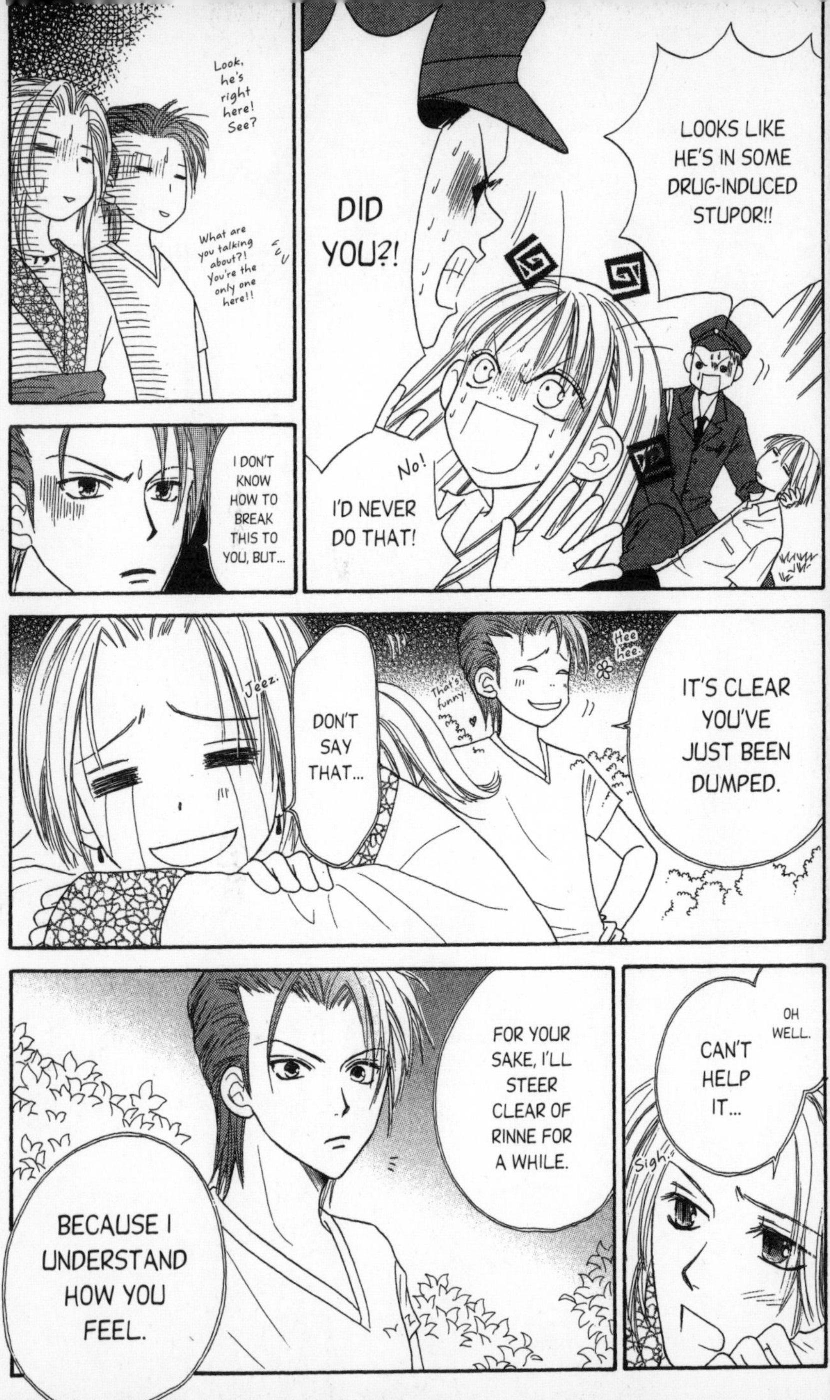
LOOKS LIKE HE'S IN SOME DRUG-INDUCED STUPOR!!
DID YOU?!
No!
I'D NEVER DO THAT!
Look, he's right here! See?
What are you talking about?! You're the only one here!!
I DON'T KNOW HOW TO BREAK THIS TO YOU, BUT...
IT'S CLEAR YOU'VE JUST BEEN DUMPED.
Hee hee.
That's funny.
Jeez.
DON'T SAY THAT...
OH WELL.
CAN'T HELP IT...
Sigh.
FOR YOUR SAKE, I'LL STEER CLEAR OF RINNE FOR A WHILE.
BECAUSE I UNDERSTAND HOW YOU FEEL.

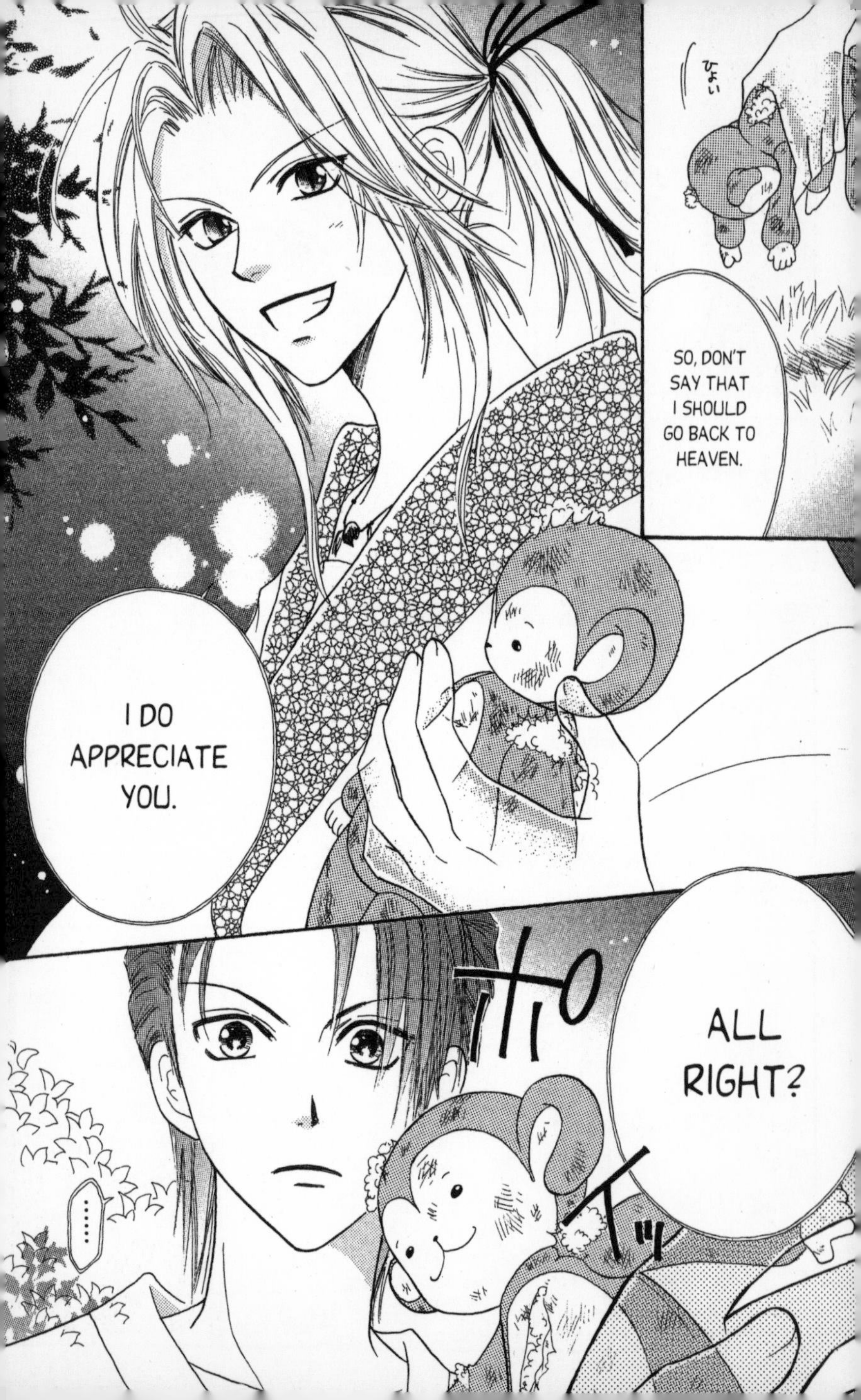
ひょい
SO, DON'T SAY THAT I SHOULD GO BACK TO HEAVEN.
I DO APPRECIATE YOU.
ALL RIGHT?
……

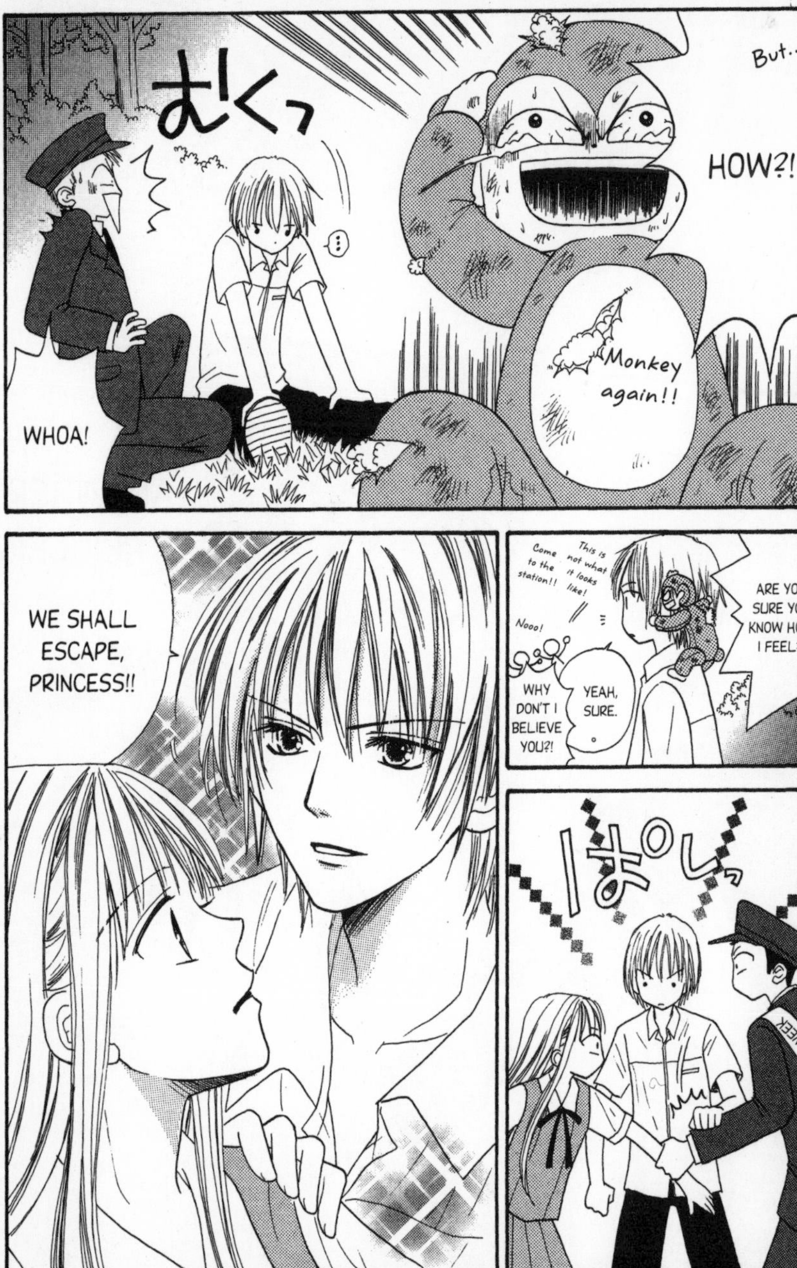
But...
HOW?!
Monkey again!!
むくっ
…
WHOA!
ARE YOU SURE YOU KNOW HOW I FEEL?!
This is not what it looks like!
Come to the station!!
Nooo!
YEAH, SURE.
WHY DON'T I BELIEVE YOU?!
ぱしっ
ETY WEEK
WE SHALL ESCAPE, PRINCESS!!

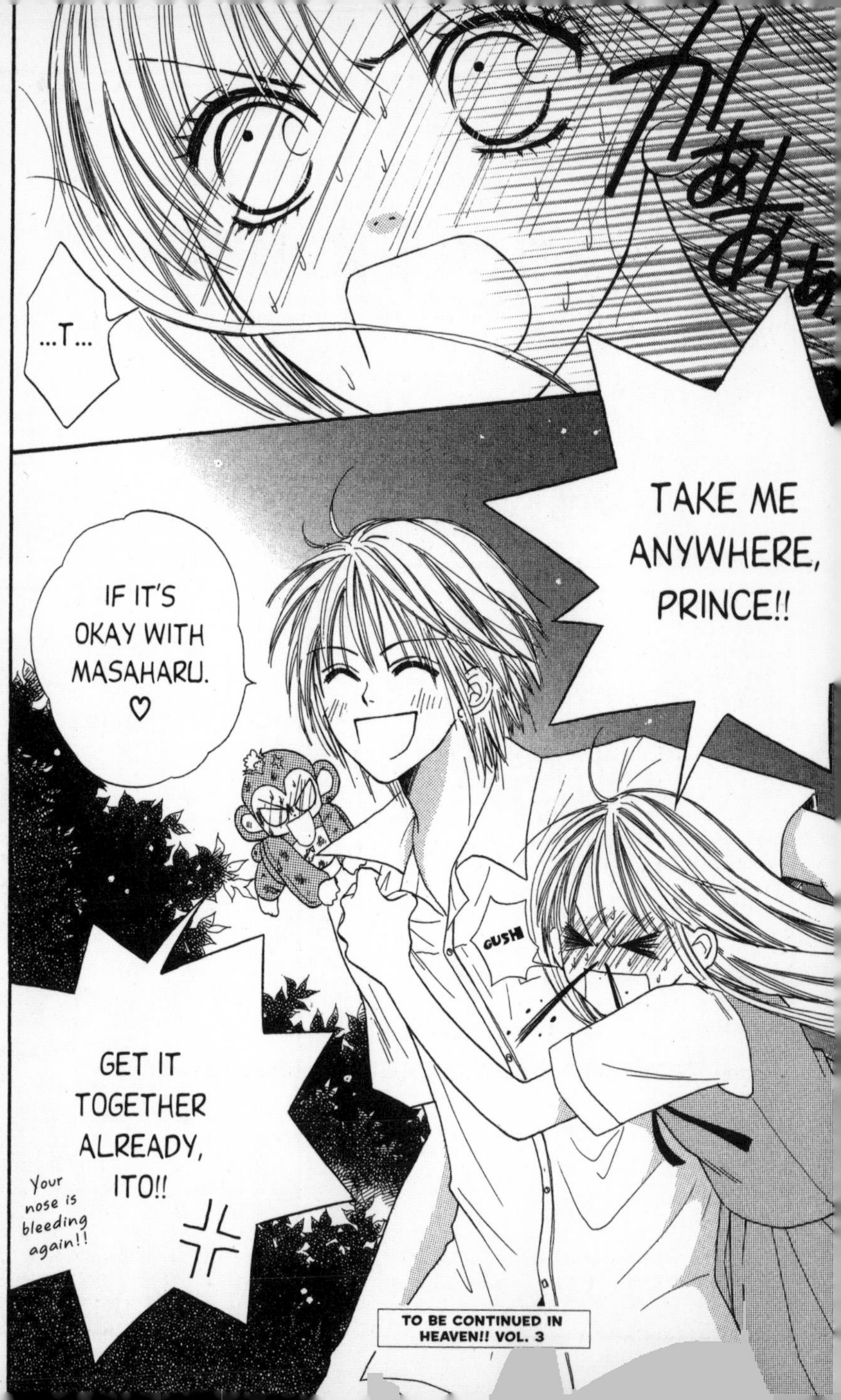
...T...
TAKE ME ANYWHERE, PRINCE!!
IF IT'S OKAY WITH MASAHARU. ♡
GUSH
GET IT TOGETHER ALREADY, ITO!!
Your nose is bleeding again!!
TO BE CONTINUED IN HEAVEN!! VOL. 3

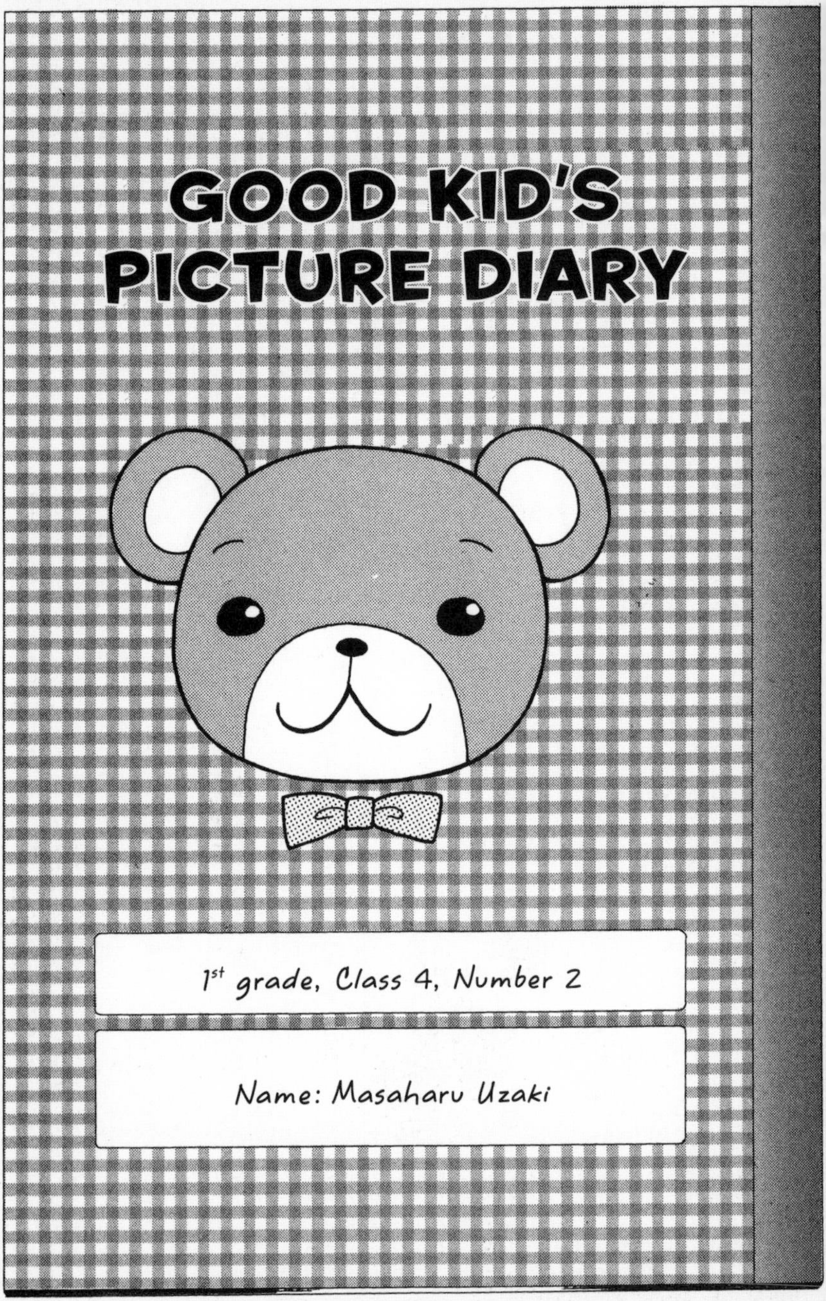
GOOD KID'S PICTURE DIARY
1st grade, Class 4, Number 2
Name: Masaharu Uzaki

DAY 1

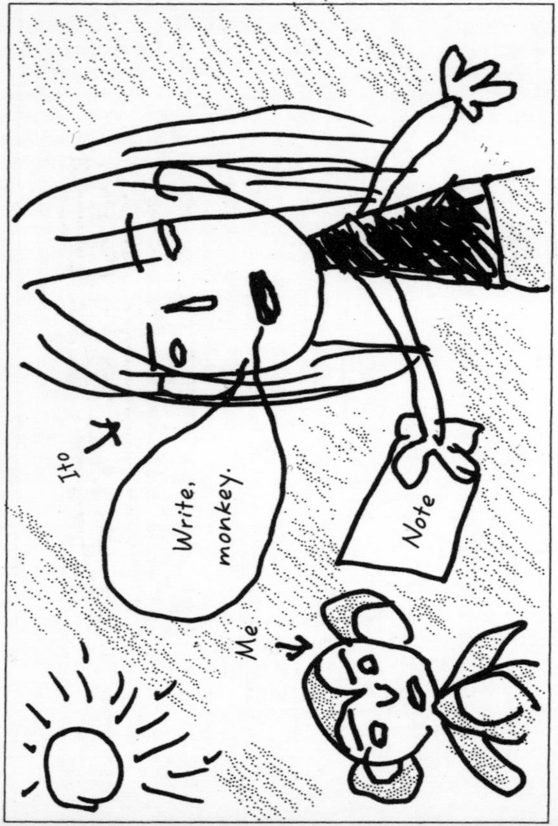
Write, monkey.
Note
Ito
Me

Sunday, June 1

Stupid Ito gave me a pen and a notebook, and said, "Why don't you write a picture diary because today is the first of June?" I had no clue what she was talking about. I was annoyed, but started to write. I don't think I'll continue though.

Monday, June 2 ☀

Day 2.

Ito made me walk VanDamme

with her. Sucks!! But VanDamme's

back is comfortable to

ride on. Made me want to

get a motorcycle license.

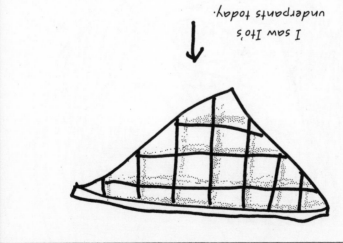

I saw Ito's
underpants today.

WALKING DOG

DAY 3

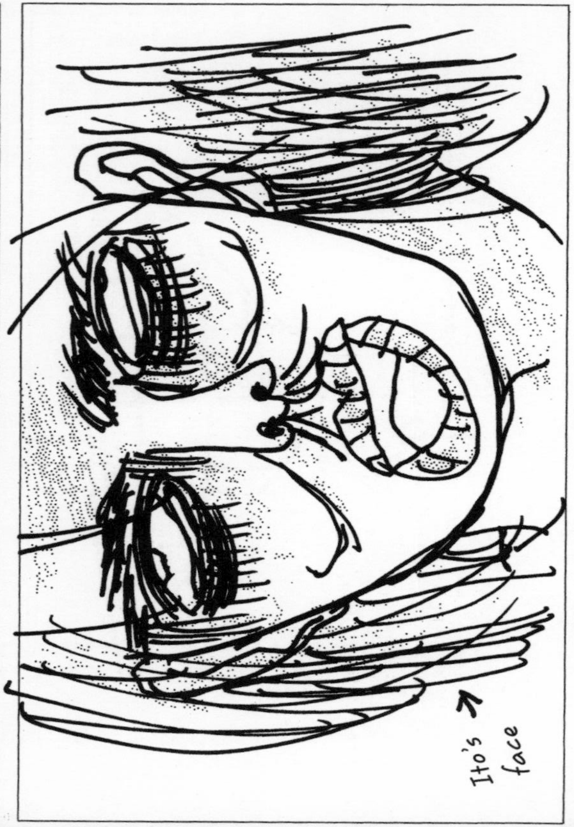
Ito's face

Tuesday, June 3

I've been writing in this diary for three days. It's amazing. Today Ito was swinging her harisen, saying, "There's a ghost." When she was swinging the harisen, her face looked more scary than a ghost. I think I'll try and write in my diary tomorrow, too.

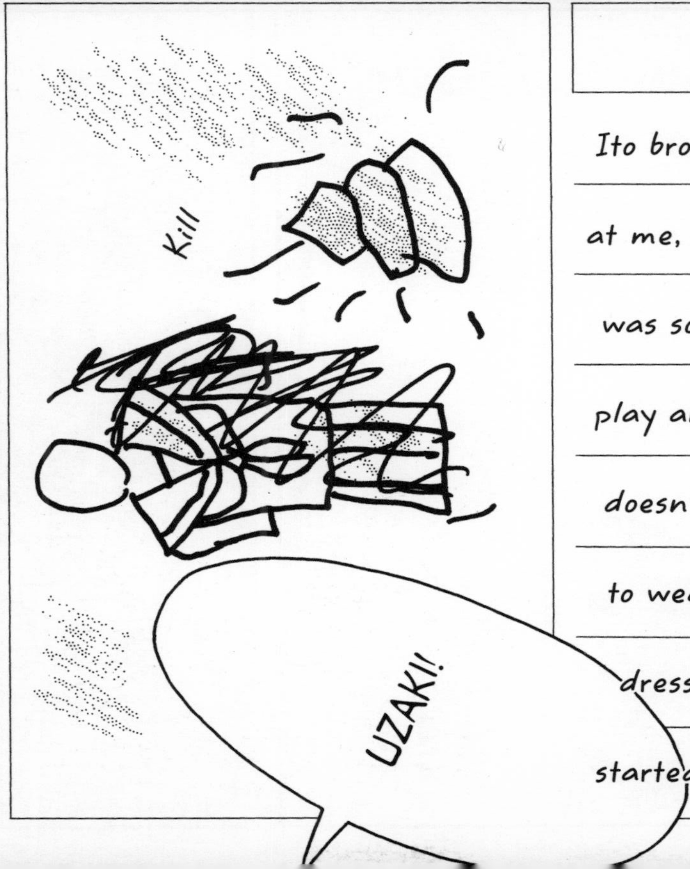

Friday, June 27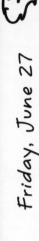

Ito brought a lot of doll clothes, looked at me, and grinned. I don't know what was so fun about it, but she started to play and dressed me up in them. Why doesn't she make real friends? I had to wear a schoolgirl's uniform, a pink dress and a ballerina's costume. Ito started laughing. I'm going to kill her.

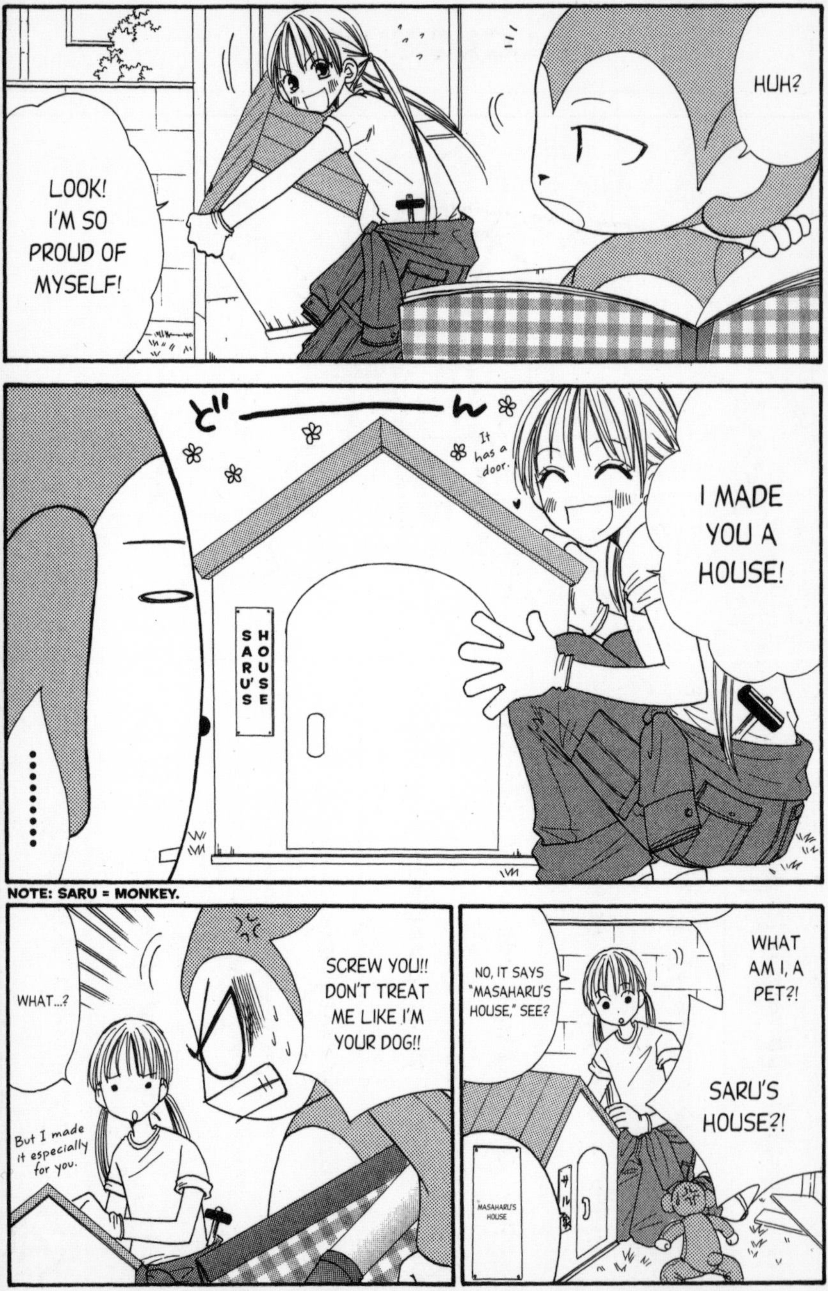
HUH?
LOOK! I'M SO PROUD OF MYSELF!
I MADE YOU A HOUSE!
It has a door.
ど————ん
SARU'S HOUSE
....
WHAT AM I, A PET?!
SARU'S HOUSE?!
NO, IT SAYS "MASAHARU'S HOUSE," SEE?
MASAHARU'S HOUSE
SCREW YOU!! DON'T TREAT ME LIKE I'M YOUR DOG!!
WHAT...?
But I made it especially for you.

NOTE: SARU = MONKEY.

POTATO CHIPS

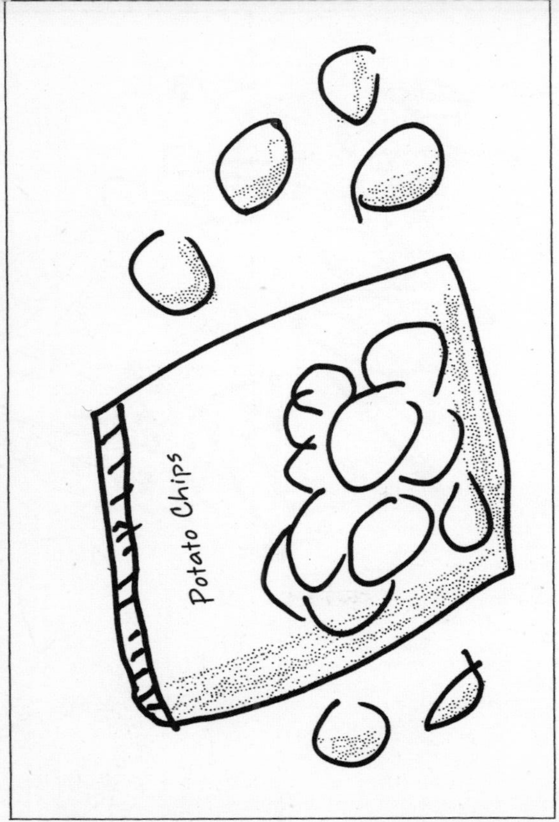
Potato Chips

Sunday, June 29

Ito was eating potato chips. She asked me, "Do you want some?" So I grabbed a few. After I ate them, I realized that there was no place to poop the chips out. I had Ito cut my stomach and take them out. It cracked her up. But I cried. I'll never eat again.

Sunday, July 8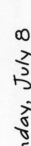

My body caught a cold. Went

to my house to rest and recover.

It was weird to see myself

suffering. I made rice porridge

with green onions. I found

out that Ito couldn't cook or

do dishes at all. I wonder

if she really is a woman.

COLD

A LOT HAPPENED

Ito's mother
VanDamme

Friday, July 18

A lot's going on with this Keiju guy, and I'm sick of it. I'm too lazy to explain all the details. My body was torn apart again, but Ito's mother sewed me back together. Ito offered to do it, but I said, "Hell no!"

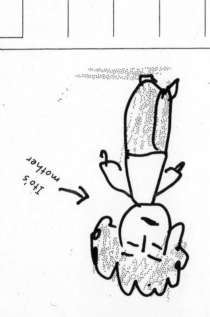

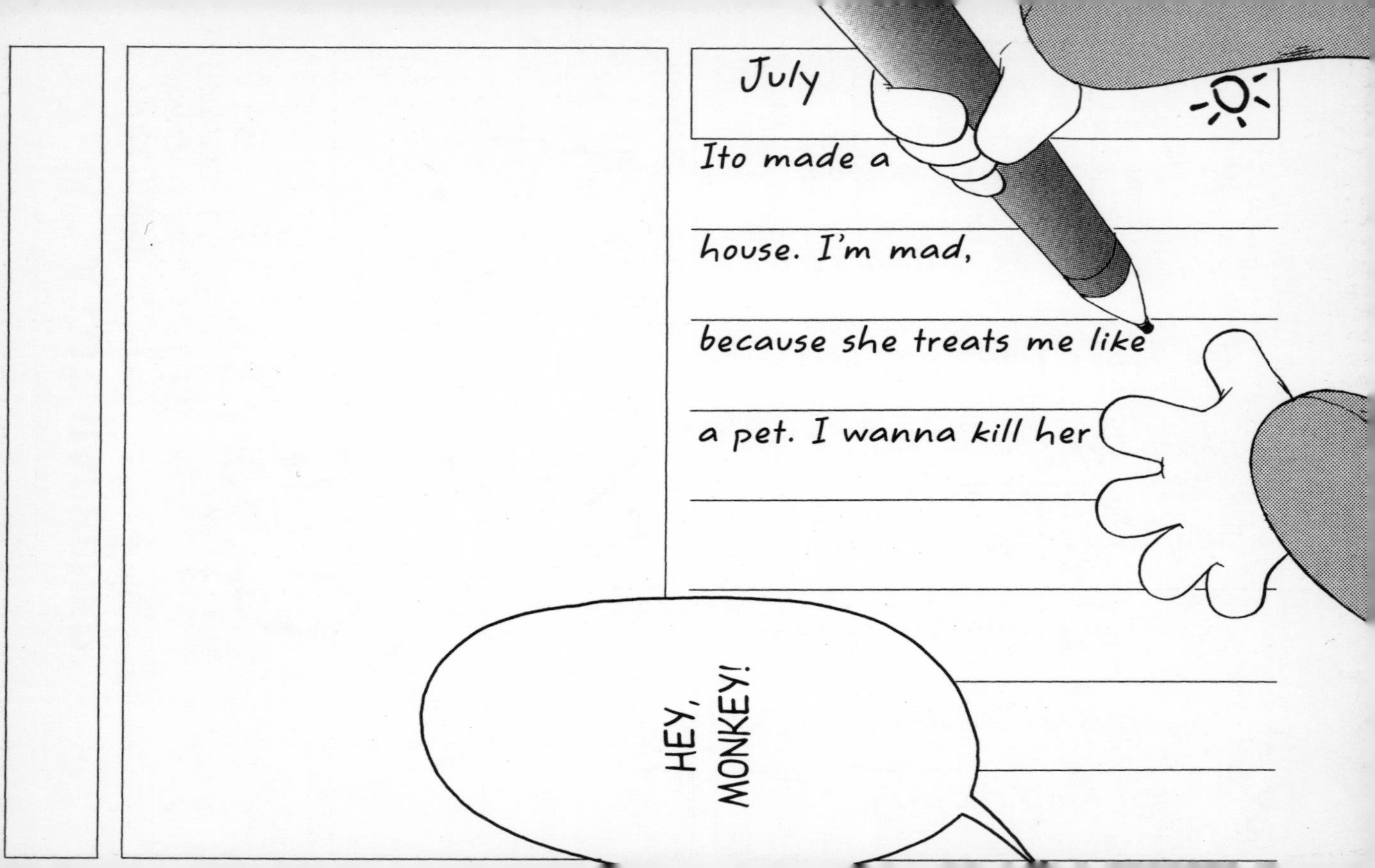
July
Ito made a
house. I'm mad,
because she treats me like
a pet. I wanna kill her
HEY, MONKEY!

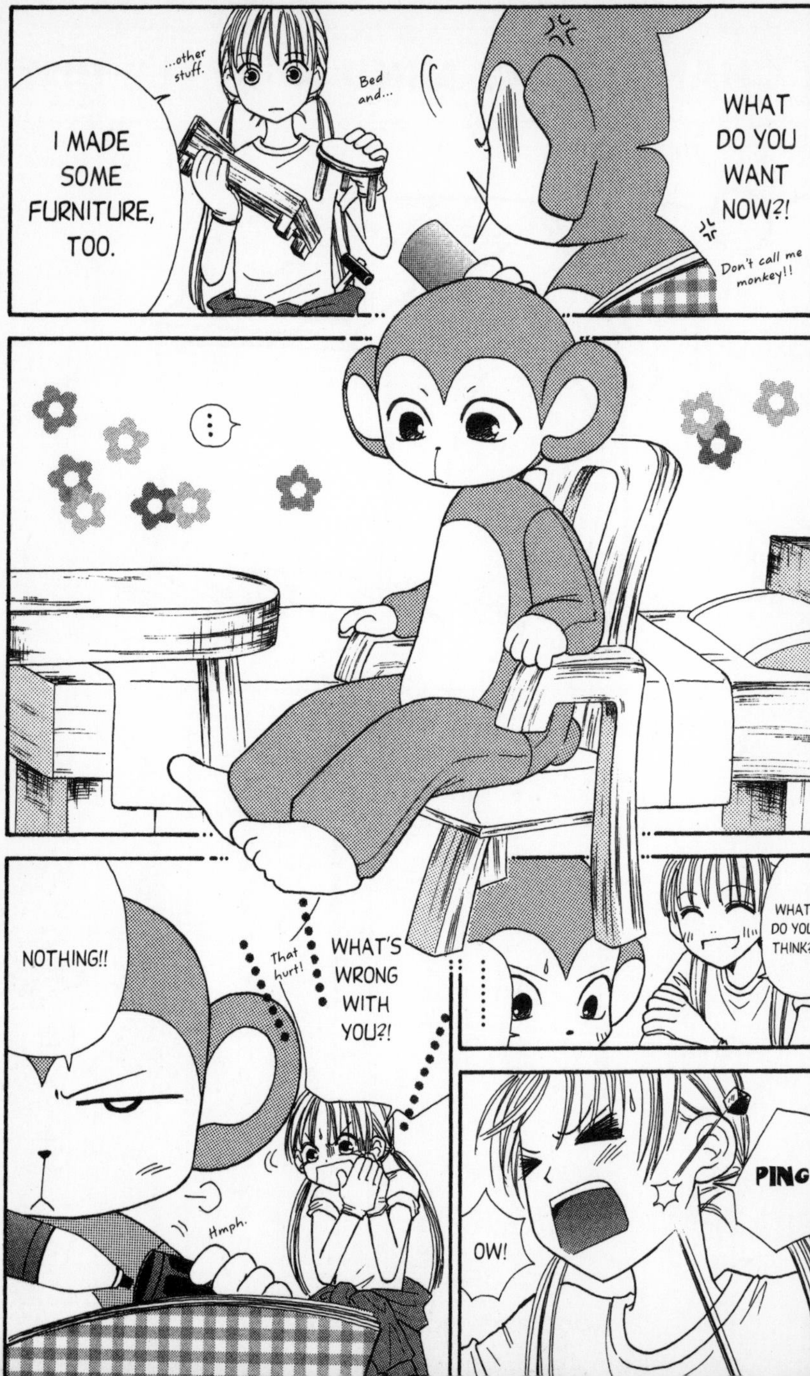
WHAT DO YOU WANT NOW?!
Don't call me monkey!!
Bed and...
...other stuff.
I MADE SOME FURNITURE, TOO.
...
WHAT DO YOU THINK?
......
PING
OW!
WHAT'S WRONG WITH YOU?!
That hurt!
NOTHING!!
Hmph.

I CHANGED MY MIND A LITTLE BIT.

Sunday, July 20

Ito made a house. I'm mad because she treated me like a pet. ~~I wanna kill her~~ But it's not a bad little house, considering Ito made it. So I guess that I should appreciate it.

SCRITCH

GOOD KID'S PICTURE DIARY END

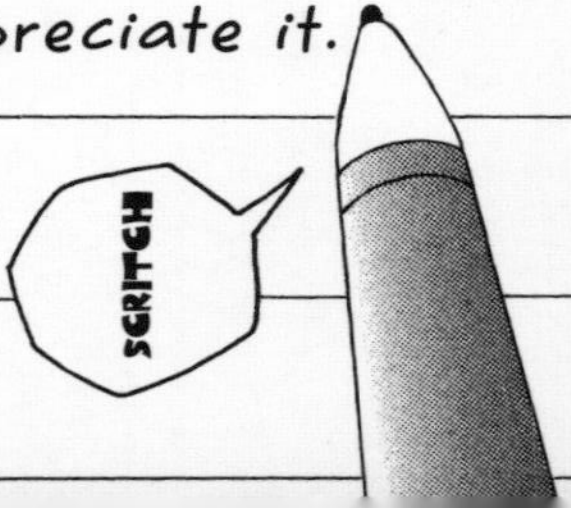

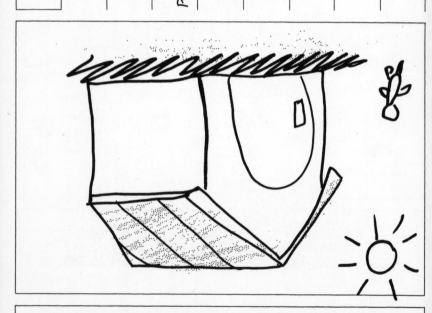

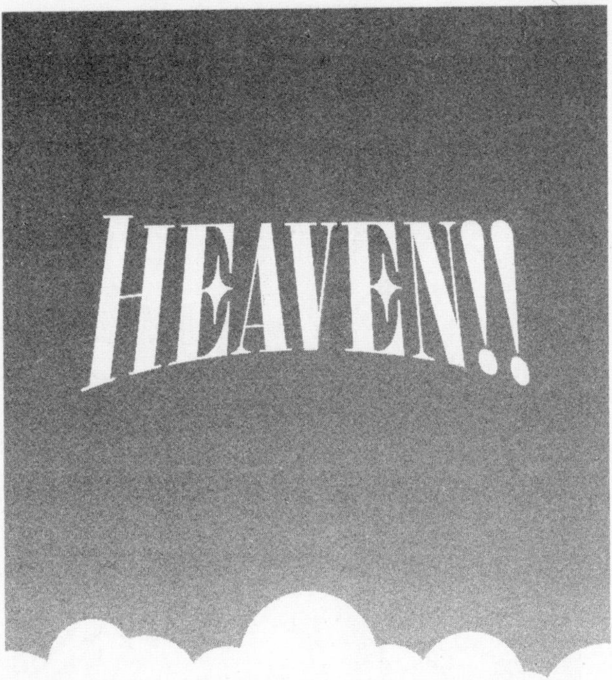
HEAVEN!!

IN THE NEXT VOLUME OF...

HEAVEN!!

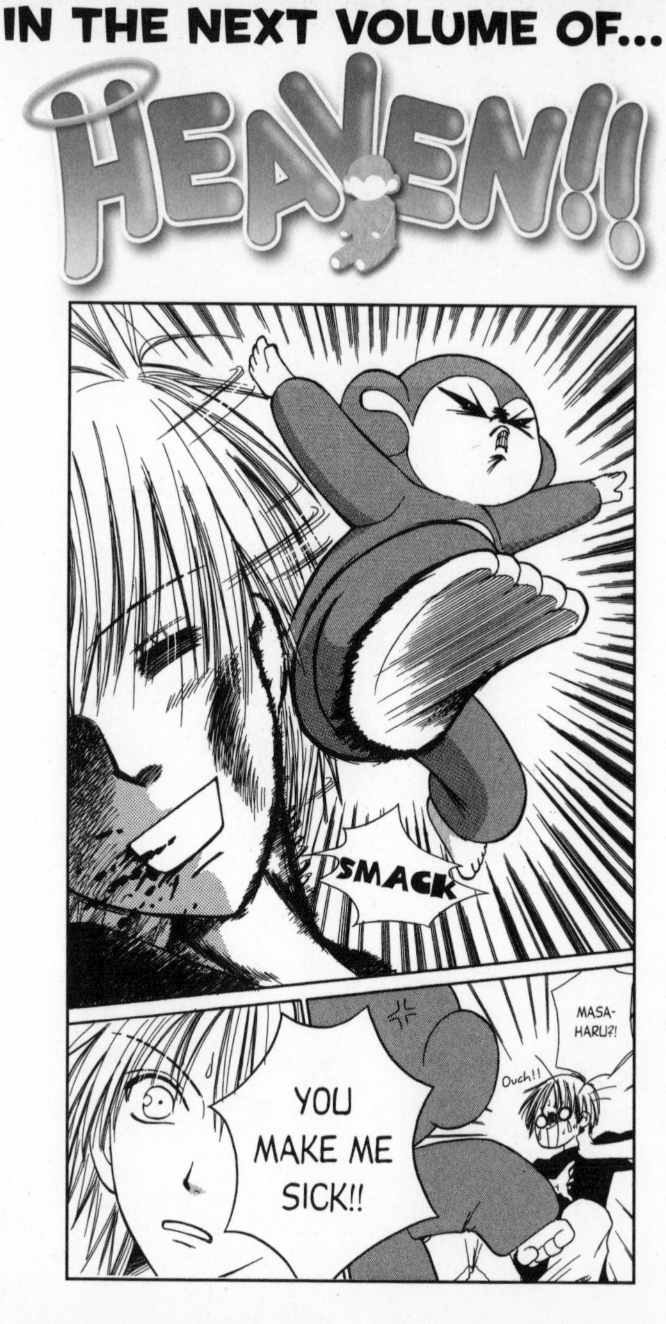
SMACK
MASA-
HARU?!
Ouch!!
YOU
MAKE ME
SICK!!

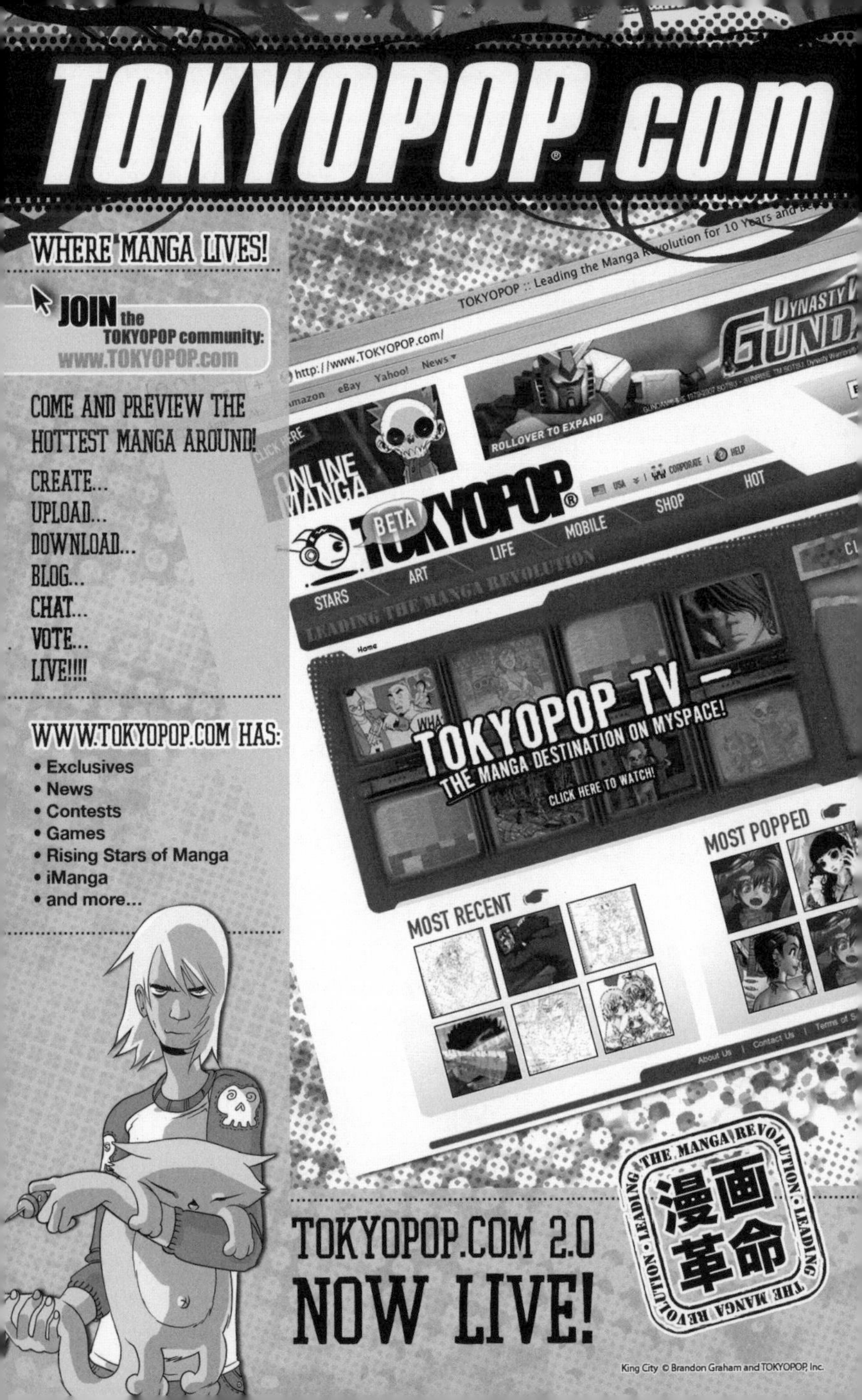
TOKYOPOP®.com
WHERE MANGA LIVES!
JOIN the TOKYOPOP community:
www.TOKYOPOP.com
COME AND PREVIEW THE HOTTEST MANGA AROUND!
CREATE...
UPLOAD...
DOWNLOAD...
BLOG...
CHAT...
VOTE...
LIVE!!!!
WWW.TOKYOPOP.COM HAS:
• Exclusives
• News
• Contests
• Games
• Rising Stars of Manga
• iManga
• and more...
TOKYOPOP :: Leading the Manga Revolution for 10 Years and Be
http://www.TOKYOPOP.com/
ROLLOVER TO EXPAND
ONLINE MANGA
BETA TOKYOPOP®
HOT
SHOP
MOBILE
LIFE
ART
STARS
LEADING THE MANGA REVOLUTION
TOKYOPOP TV —
THE MANGA DESTINATION ON MYSPACE!
CLICK HERE TO WATCH!
MOST POPPED
MOST RECENT
About Us | Contact Us | Terms of S
TOKYOPOP.COM 2.0
NOW LIVE!
漫画革命
LEADING THE MANGA REVOLUTION
King City © Brandon Graham and TOKYOPOP, Inc.

STOP!

This is the back of the book.
You wouldn't want to spoil a great ending!

This book is printed "manga-style," in the authentic Japanese right-to-left format. Since none of the artwork has been flipped or altered, readers get to experience the story just as the creator intended. You've been asking for it, so TOKYOPOP® delivered: authentic, hot-off-the-press, and far more fun!

DIRECTIONS

If this is your first time reading manga-style, here's a quick guide to help you understand how it works.

It's easy... just start in the top right panel and follow the numbers. Have fun, and look for more 100% authentic manga from TOKYOPOP®!